BOSTON

American Historical Press
Sun Valley, California

BOSTON
CITY ON A HILL

AN ILLUSTRATED HISTORY

ALAN ROGERS & LISA ROGERS

© 2007 American Historical Press
All Rights Reserved
Published 2007
Printed in South Korea

Library of Congress Catalogue Card Number: 2007932189
Bookland EAN 978-1-892724-54-0

Bibliography: p. 270
Includes Index

CONTENTS

Foreword

The history of Boston is unique because of the remarkable persistence of a theme first articulated in 1630 by its Puritan founders. The Puritans conceived of themselves as free, disciplined individuals whose pursuit of their own self-interest had to be joined by a commitment to serve the community. "See what there is to be done," urged the Reverend Richard Baxter, "and do it with all your might." The character of the city and its people has been shaped by this dynamic charge.

Boston was intended to be a "City on a Hill," a shining example of how men and women motivated by a commitment to hard work and to personal, religious, and civic reform might change the course of history. Guided by this ideal, the people of the city have, at times, acted nobly. Boston proudly boasted that it was "Freedom's Birthplace," the "Athens of America," and the "hub of the cosmos," and that its citizens were a chosen people whose special mission was to lead the way to a better America. To be sure, narrowmindedness, racism, and political corruption have sometimes dimmed the beacon light. But the ideals of reform and hard work have persisted.

These ideals were initially the preserve of a unified, homogeneous Yankee population. The Irish, Italians, Jews, and other immigrant groups challenged this claim. Beginning in the 1880s the Irish took control of the city's political life. "Honey Fitzgerald" and James Michael Curley replaced Josiah Quincy and James Jackson Storrow. At the same time the city divided into ethnic neighborhoods, each within walking distance of the other but separate nevertheless. In the 1970s and 1980s racial conflict ripped at the heart of Boston.

This divisiveness caused some to decry the death of the city. Certainly pessimists have held center stage before. In the 1840s and 1880s some prophets of doom predicted the demise of the idealistic republican dream. It was impossible, they predicted mournfully, to assimilate millions of immigrants. The city and its ancient values would be destroyed.

There have been vast and countless changes—new land, peoples, buildings, ideas, and leaders have transformed Boston. Rather than braking these developments, however, the old principles have provided a rich historical legacy that has allowed Boston not only to survive a succession of crises but also, in the words of former Mayor Kevin H. White, to stand poised for flight into the 21st century.

I
City on a Hill

Boston's history may be said to have begun at that moment in 1534 when King Henry VIII turned his back on the Pope. Henry knew, of course, that his bold act would have sharp repercussions, but it was easy for the king to be optimistic. He and his new bride, Anne Boleyn, were happy—for the moment—and thousands of Englishmen applauded Henry's decision to leave the Catholic Church. They believed it would now be possible to purify England's churches, making them truly Protestant.

But Henry VIII and his immediate successors, who after the break with Rome headed the Church of England, resisted the efforts of those militant Protestant reformers called Puritans. Still the number of Puritans increased. When Henry's daughter, Mary

Tudor, tried to return England to the Pope she was scorned publicly. Privately some Puritans called for her head. She survived, however, and the Puritans paid a heavy price for their impetuousness.

In 1558 Elizabeth I succeeded her sister Mary. The Puritans were both pleased and dismayed by the policies Elizabeth pursued. They were delighted that she defied the Pope and made England a bulwark of Protestantism against the Catholic power of Spain. She even made a few Puritans part of her inner circle of advisors. Yet Elizabeth also insisted that the Anglican Church be administered by archbishops and bishops and that all Englishmen agree to a bundle of moderate statements of faith—the Thirty-Nine Articles. For zealous Puritan reformers these measures smacked of Catholicism, but they told themselves, comfortingly, that the country was moving their way.

The Puritan way was a hard road to follow. To begin with, the Puritans adhered to the Calvinist idea that God had predestined those who were to be saved and those who were to be eternally damned before they were born. Man could do nothing. No amount of prayer and contemplation nor good behavior would alter God's plan. Puritanism required that man face this fact unblinkingly, but at the same time commit himself to a lifelong struggle to achieve salvation. Puritanism demanded that man do good, but told him he was a hopeless sinner. According to Puritan belief God commanded that the world be totally reformed, although He admitted that evil was incurable. Puritans were required to work long and hard and successfully at a job to which God had "called" them, while at the same time fixing their complete attention on God. Puritans were to live in this world but not be of it.

The anxiety caused by these contradictory commands could be overpowering. A young English tailor's apprentice, for example, made some halfhearted attempts to reform his life but fell far short of the goal of perfection demanded by Puritan preachers. He was paralyzed. "I knew not what to do, thinking God now had utterly forsaken me," he wrote years later when he was living in Boston. "And when I had cried so long that I could cry no longer, I rose up in a forlorn condition." Eventually this young man joined in the "great coming to New England," settling first in Roxbury.

The inner tension felt by those who would be Puritans might also, however, stimulate activity, a relentless drive to achieve God's grace and to fulfill His purpose. Those men and women who seemingly had been predestined by God were the "elect," saints in a sinful world struggling to make everything right. Of course no one could—or should—be certain that they were one of God's elect for God's ways were mysterious and man's reasoning weak. But doubt did not lessen the Puritan's obligation to reform religion and the world. "See what is to be done, and do it with all your might," the Reverend Richard Baxter told his congregation early in the 17th century.

The Puritans expected the Church of England and the English government to help them. The state and the churches were to work together to root out sin and corruption. Anglican churchmen believed that the Church of England provided the means to bring man to a state of grace. The Puritans disagreed. Priests and rituals interfered with a man's search for salvation, they argued. The essence of religious experience, according to the Puritans, consisted of two simple interlocking elements: a struggle by man to bring his open and willing soul into direct contact with God; and a commitment to learn as much as possible about God's plan by reading the Bible.

One other important difference divided Anglicans from Puritans. Anglicans felt that it was impossible to determine who had achieved a state of grace and who was still a sinner. Therefore orthodox clergymen argued that everyone should be a member of the church. In short the Church of England was a national church to which all Englishmen belonged by birthright. The Puritans disagreed vehemently with this position. They thought it was possible—if difficult—to determine if a person was one of God's elect by administering the proper exams and by correctly interpreting the signs of favor. This meant it was possible—and, according to zealous Puritans, desirable—to restrict church membership only to those who were thought to be saints. A Puritan congregation was an exclusive gathering of the elect, not an inclusive national church.

These differences were not mere empty theoretical squabbling—how many angels can dance on the head of a pin? Gaining entrance into a church was the central event in a 17th-century Englishman's life. When, for example, one distraught young man came to the dark conclusion that he was a hopeless sinner, he decided "it was a greater evil to live and to sin against God than to kill myself." So he slung his gun over his shoulder and walked out into the woods. Then, he tells us, "I cocked my gun, and set it on the ground, and put the muzzle under my throat, and took up my foot to let it off." Happily he had second thoughts. In fact he "thought that God's blessedness might belong to me, and it much supported my spirit." Not all Puritans were so intense, but all of them yearned to be counted among God's company of saints.

People's fears and aspirations were not allayed completely even if they were convinced that God had chosen them. Every nation, the Puritans believed, had a convenant with God. If a people abided by His laws, He would treat them well. The chief function of government, therefore, was to ensure good behavior, to stamp out sinfulness. If the government failed to do its job satisfactorily, the people were obligated to overthrow it, replacing the corrupt rulers with better ones. If they did not, God's wrath would destroy the nation.

Gradually the Puritans came to the conclusion that they were living in "evil and declining times" and that they had to act quickly to save themselves and England. Increasingly they were

John Winthrop was an English gentleman, a Puritan, and the first governor of the New World Puritan Commonwealth. (TBS)

persecuted, chased from chapel, thrown into prison, fined, and berated. Archbishop William Laud, appointed by King Charles I in the 1620s, believed the Puritans were dangerous revolutionaries. The archbishop once shouted at the Rev. Thomas Shepard that he belonged to "a company of seditious, factious, bedlams" and forbade Shepard to exercise any ministerial functions. Shepard's Puritan congregation promptly disregarded the ban.

Other Puritans were prompted to act because of their declining economic situation. Englishmen believed that they were threatened by the country's rapidly increasing population. Based on the assumption that there was a fixed and limited amount of wealth to be distributed, men worried, as one Elizabethan official put it, that "our land has not milk sufficient in the breast thereof to nourish all those children which it hath brought forth."

Puritans such as John Winthrop, a country squire forced by economic necessity to increase his law practice in order to expand his shrinking resources, were convinced that corruption and sin lay at the root of England's economic woes. Therefore their preachers called for reform. But increasingly the way to change seemed to be blocked. Lawmakers,

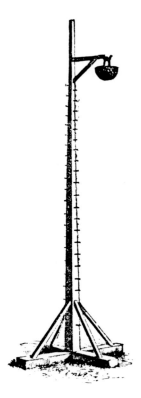

The original Beacon Hill beacon alerted the country to invasion. It was a tall mast with an iron frame projecting 65 feet from the base, holding a barrel of tar. When fired, the light could be seen for a great distance. Winds blew the beacon down in 1789. From King's Handbook of Boston, *Moses King, 1883*

members of Parliament sympathetic to the Puritans, were frustrated by King Charles II's incompetence and angered by his softness on the issue of Catholicism. When in 1629 Parliament balked at the means by which Charles II demanded money be raised for a foreign adventure, he dissolved Parliament and made it plain that he did not intend to call another.

While some Puritans began to whisper to one another about revolution, others—such as squire John Winthrop and the distraught young tailor's apprentice who once had contemplated suicide—thought about creating a "new" England. In 1628 a small group of dissenters had put together a land company and sent out an advance party to settle on Cape Ann, north of Boston. A year later the Crown granted a charter to the Massachusetts Bay Company, permitting it not only to trade and to settle in New England but also "to govern and rule all His Majesty's subjects that reside within the limits of our plantation." By chance the charter omitted any reference to the place that the company should hold its meetings.

Winthrop and 11 other Puritan leaders met in Cambridge in the summer of 1629 and decided to take advantage of the Crown's mistake. They boldly and unanimously agreed that "the government and patent should be settled in New England." Pushed by the conviction that England would soon suffer God's wrath and pulled by the prospect of establishing a prosperous Bible Commonwealth, the Puritans prepared to leave Old England for New in the spring of 1630.

John Winthrop was elected governor, the company choosing him over John Humfrey, Isaac Johnson, and Sir Richard Saltonstall. Six months of hectic preparation followed. Clergymen, of course, but also skilled workmen were especially recruited for the new colony. Not all those who won Winthrop's approval to sign on were Puritans. Not all those who were chosen were able to pay their own way. Winthrop and some other leaders, therefore, paid the fares of some

men and women in exchange for their services for a specified number of years.

Clearly the group that set sail from Southampton in April 1630 was not a homogeneous community. Some were religious dissenters—Puritans—others were not; some were wealthy, some were poor. They jammed into 17 ships, more than a thousand men and women in search of a new life. It was an exciting adventure, though tinged with sadness. "We cannot part from our native Country," they declared in a published statement, "without much sadness of heart and many tears in our eyes."

Heavy seas, a sparse diet, and the long voyage across the North Atlantic took a toll. By June of 1630, when Cape Ann was sighted, many among Winthrop's company were sick and dying. Still, Winthrop and the other leaders decided almost immediately that "Salem, where we landed, pleased us not," and they cruised up and down the coast, poking in and around the small islands and rivers that marked the shoreline, looking for a better place to settle. After some controversy and a couple of false starts, the hilly, tadpole-shaped peninsula that the Indians called Shawmut (crossing place) was the spot chosen for the colony's central community.

Boston—a name selected earlier to commemorate the English town where the Rev. John Cotton had given the farewell sermon to the settlers—was chosen primarily because it had an excellent source of clear spring water. (Dozens of settlers had sickened and died after they had come ashore at Salem, and the cause was believed to have been the water they drank.) At first glance the site seemed to have little else to recommend it. To begin with the Shawmut peninsula was almost an island. Roughly two miles long and no more than a mile wide, it was connected on the south with the Puritan settlement at Roxbury by the narrowest neck of land. To the west of the neck were large mud flats and marshes, and beyond was the Charles River that flowed into Boston Harbor and separated the peninsula from Charlestown. A deep cove carved out of the eastern side of the peninsula divided Boston into North and South ends, each dominated by a small, steep hill. Between Fort Hill in the South End and Windmill or Copp's Hill in the North End, there was a ridge, or as William Wood described it in 1634, "a high Mountain with three little rising Hills on the top of it, wherefore it is called the Tramount." The three peaks were Cotton Hill on the east, West Hill on the Charles River side,

and in the center, Beacon Hill—so-called because the government ordered in 1634 that "there shall be. . .a beacon set on the. . .hill at Boston, to give notice to the country of any danger."

By August Winthrop's group had established itself just below Cotton Hill and along a line leading to Town Cove. In the waning days of summer, children scrambled about the hills picking berries, and at low tide they jumped from rock to rock searching for mussels. The adults, meanwhile, prepared as best they could for the approaching winter. There was too little wood on the peninsula and too little time before winter to build proper houses, so the people of Boston dug in, scooping caves into the hills or digging cellars to be covered over with planks.

While the settlers were digging in, Winthrop sent a ship to England with instructions to buy provisions and return to Boston as soon as possible. At the same time the governor sent men along the coast to trade for corn with those Indians who were willing to sell. Winthrop himself sought to make contacts with local Indian tribes for the same purpose.

These efforts met with some success—one boat brought 100 bushels of corn from Cape Cod—but the winter of 1630-1631 was harsh and long and marked by death. By the time the relief ship sailed into Boston Harbor in February, 200 men and women had died. A like number decided they had had enough and returned to England.

The morale of those who survived and stayed was surprisingly good. The coming of spring boosted people's spirits and released their energies. "The winter's frost being extracted forth the earth," wrote Edward Johnson, an artisan who lived through the winter of 1630, the people "fell to tearing up the roots and bushes with their hoes; even such men as scarce ever set hand to labor before. . .readily rush through all difficulties." Gardens were planted in the fields of Boston, and on the mainland large farms were cut out of the wilderness. Winthrop, for example, set his servants to work clearing 600 acres of rich land along the Mystic River. Gradually houses began to take shape. One group of settlers clustered around Town Cove, another just to the south, where the marketplace would be built. Before long Samuel and Anne Cole opened a part of their newly built house as a tavern. Not far away a meetinghouse for both civic and religious purposes was built.

While a great deal remained to be done—there were in Winthrop's words, "All things to do as in the beginning of the world"—it was evident by 1632 that Boston would survive. By the end of the decade, farmers around Boston were producing an agricultural surplus. Dorchester was noted for its orchards, Roxbury for its cattle, and Boston's gardens and smaller fields yielded an abundance of corn, peas, barley, and oats.

The town's future, however, did not lie with agriculture. During the first 10 years of its existence Boston was sustained, and indeed prospered, because thousands of immigrants arrived in the colony each year. Between 15,000 and 20,000 newcomers swelled the population of Massachusetts Bay from 1630 to 1640. The ships on which they arrived brought a variety of manufactured goods—axes, guns and gunpowder, clothing, nails, and

pots and kettles—that were quickly sold to old settlers. At the same time the newcomers needed lumber and food, which local merchants were happy to sell. The demand for goods was so great that merchants soon adopted the practice of rowing out to meet an incoming ship as soon as it entered Boston Harbor, shouting bids, and buying goods before the ship docked at Town Cove.

The Puritan governors were embarrassed by these chaotic scenes and passed several laws designed to control Boston's burgeoning commercial life. But mere laws could not hedge the enterprising spirit. Gradually the town's economic activity was made more orderly by the merchants who came to dominate the trade. Men such as Robert Keayne, the Hutchinsons, and the Tyngs, who had family ties or friendships in London, were able to place orders for the goods they needed and so insure that their potential customers would have an adequate stock. Furthermore, these early Boston merchant families began to dominate the inland trade, acting as middlemen for merchants in the outlying towns. By the 1640s, therefore, Boston was the hub of a complex external and internal trade network, extending from England to the Caribbean and from Long Island Sound to Springfield.

"It hath pleased God," boasted a group of prosperous Bostonians in 1648, "that our Town chiefly consists of Trade .. a mart to the Country." Not everyone agreed that prosperity was a blessing. Speaking for the colony's political elite, the Massachusetts General Court expressed its shock at the social consequences of commerce. The assembly declared:
Its utter detestation and dislike, that men or women of mean condition should take upon them the garb of gentlemen, by wearing gold or silver lace, or buttons. . .or to walk in great boots, or women of the same rank to wear silk or tiffany hoods or scarves which, though allowable to persons of greater estates or more liberal education, yet we cannot but judge it

Dorchester was settled in June 1630, some weeks before Boston. An early resident, Robert Pierce, built this house in 1640. (TBS)

intolerable in persons of such like condition.

Fashion was merely the tip of the iceberg. The colony's leaders felt a pervasive sense of disorder.

The Puritans had come to Boston, after all, to build a new kind of community. It was to be a covenanted community, existing under a commission from God. Winthrop had laid out a blueprint while still on board the *Arbella*. It was God's intention, Winthrop declared, that "every man might have need of other, and from hence they might all be knit more nearly together in the bonds of brotherly affection." If the Puritans adhered to the buiding principle of "brotherly affection," if they all worked together, they would fulfill the terms of God's special commission and He would favor the community. But if the people were selfish "the Lord will surely break out in wrath against us," Winthrop warned.

The success or failure of the Bible Commonwealth would have worldwide and historic consequences. "For we must consider," Winthrop said, "that we shall be as a city on a hill, the eyes of all people are on us." The people of Boston were expected, in other words, to look forward to the final establishment of a utopian Christian community. Every individual was bound in this special compact with God and each other. The ties extended vertically, uniting classes and the society. The individual had to be concerned, therefore, not only with his own behavior but also with that of the total community. An individual's shortcomings imperiled the group. So too did attacks on authority.

Fully mindful of this danger, a group of rebels nevertheless openly and militantly challenged the spiritual and secular authorities of Boston in 1636. The dissidents were led by Ms. Anne Hutchinson, a remarkably witty, aggressive, and intelligent woman. She had come to Boston from England in 1634, as many Puritans had, in order to achieve salvation as a member of the Reverend John Cotton's church. Cotton was a brilliant theologian who articulated a position that placed him and his followers into opposition with Puritan

This gravestone for Jerome Topliff, who died in 1640, is located in the Old Burying Ground in Dorchester at the corner of Stoughton Street and Boston (now Columbia) Road. (TBS)

orthodoxy. Cotton minimized the importance of individual action, or preparation, and emphasized the belief that salvation could be demonstrated only by the individual's feeling God's grace within. He directed his Boston congregation "not to be afraid of the word Revelation."

While the majority of Puritans condemned Cotton's doctrine as smacking too much of the heresy known as Antinomianism, Anne Hutchinson and many others were attracted to his ideas. Indeed Ms. Hutchinson began to hold weekly meetings in her home in which the sermon of the previous Sunday furnished the starting point for a religious discussion. She soon went beyond Cotton's careful distinctions and argued instead for a doctrine that posited a mystic relationship between God and an individual in which a consciousness of the Holy Spirit's presence within a person was the only acceptable sign of salvation. Moreover Ms. Hutchinson declared that only those people within whom the Holy Spirit dwelt, were able to recognize others who were saints.

From the orthodox point of view,

Hutchinson's ideas were extremely dangerous, a frontal assault on the structure of Puritan society. Puritan ministers stressed the importance of the Bible, of their preaching, and of membership in a congregation. Ms. Hutchinson talked about an individual's feelings. Puritan magistrates believed that their most important job was to use their authority to hold together a stratified, hierarchical community. To the contrary Ms. Hutchinson emphasized the autonomous individual. In short Ms. Hutchinson's doctrines saw ministers and magistrates as obstacles to salvation and to equal opportunity and treatment.

Given the very limited role women were expected to play in society, Ms. Hutchinson's ideas were especially appealing to the women of Boston. A woman was supposed to be weak, submissive, and modest; she was urged to avoid books and in church to follow the apostle Paul's dictum that women were not "to teach, nor to usurp authority over the man, but to be in silence."

Ms. Hutchinson was neither silent nor submissive, and under her leadership female resistance to male authority figures and to narrowly defined social norms became more defiant. She and her followers charged that the orthodox clergymen were unfit to preach. They demonstrated their disdain by walking out of the Boston church en masse when the Rev. John Wilson rose to preach. And Ms. Hutchinson encouraged the men in her group to provoke religious debates in town meetings, within the militia, and even on the floor of the General Court.

By the winter of 1636, Boston and many of the outlying towns were divided into hostile camps. The annual elections were hotly contested. With Ms. Hutchinson's movement clearly in mind, Winthrop moaned that "All things are turned upside down among us" and asked voters to restore order by reelecting him. Because, among other reasons, women could not participate in politics, Winthrop was returned to office, and within a few months he moved to crush the opposition by attacking Ms. Hutchinson.

She was brought to trial—such as it was—in November 1636 charged with three civil offenses: that she had encouraged people to sign petitions; that she had held meetings for women and men in her home, which was not "comely" nor "fitting" for a woman to do; and that she had violated the Fifth Commandment by disobeying her "parents," the magistrates. There was no jury and no apparent procedure. Questions and accusations were flung angrily at Ms. Hutchinson and her answers brusquely pushed aside when they didn't suit the magistrates. It was obvious they were determined to get rid of her. When they were unable to best her on theological grounds, the magistrates fell back on denigrating Ms. Hutchinson as a woman. She and her female followers were accused simultaneously of usurping their husbands' authority and of encouraging "foul, gross, filthy and abominable" sexual promiscuity. Even her onetime friend, the Reverend Cotton, resorted to using the technique of guilt by sexual innuendo. "Though I have not heard, neither do I think, you have been unfaithful to your Husband in his Marriage Covenant, yet," he added disingenuously, "that will follow."

Despite this and other slurs on her character, Ms. Hutchinson was winning the debate when, in an unguarded moment, she blurted out that God would punish her accusers. Asked how she knew this, she explained, "by an immediate revelation." This was heresy. It required only the briefest deliberation for the court to agree that Ms. Hutchinson's declaration was cause for banishment from the colony.

A few months later the Boston church excommunicated Anne Hutchinson. The Reverend Wilson commanded her "as a Leper to withdraw yourself out of the congregation." Anne rose, accepted the hand of her friend, Mary Dyer, and walked out. (Twenty-two years later, Dyer returned to Boston and was hanged as a Quaker.) Together with a few others

Anne Hutchinson was tried by the magistrates in 1636 and, convicted of heresy, she was banished to Rhode Island. From Scribner's Popular History of the United States, 1897. *Courtesy, Rhode Island Historical Society*

they joined a settlement in Newport, Rhode Island, where they lived until 1642. Fearing that the Massachusetts' authorities would seize the settlement, Anne fled to Long Island. In August 1643 she and five of her children were killed by Indians.

Boston's clergymen rejoiced, claiming that the "American Jezebel" had been destroyed by God, and the magistrates heaved a sigh of relief thinking they had guaranteed their unqualified hold on power. But the freemen of the colony had their own ideas. In 1634 they had won the right to elect deputies to the General Court, which was to meet four times every year to make laws. While this process was disrupted somewhat during the dispute with Anne Hutchinson, the freemen were not willing to bow to Governor Winthrop's argument that a benevolent despotism was the best form of government. The representatives who sat in the General Court disagreed with Winthrop and did their best to enlarge their role. The House and the governor fought over the issue of whether a piece of legislation could become law over the veto of the governor and his assistants in

One spiritual threat perceived by the new Puritan Commonwealth was the "inner light" faith of the Quakers. Threatened with death twice for preaching in Boston, Mary Dyer returned a third time and was hanged. Her statue, created by Sylvia Shaw Judson, stands before the Massachusetts State House. Courtesy, Massachusetts State House

MARY DYER

QUAKER

WITNESS FOR RELIGIOUS FREEDOM

HANGED ON BOSTON COMMON 1660

"MY LIFE NOT AVAILETH ME IN COMPARISON TO THE LIBERTY OF THE TRUTH"

the upper House. When Isreal Stoughton, a freeman from Dorchester, drew up a list of arguments against Winthrop's position, the governor branded him "a troubler of Isreal" and demanded that the House burn Stoughton's article and bar him from office for three years. Winthrop still had enough prestige to force his will on the House, but his vindictiveness caused the voters to turn him out of office in 1637 and again in 1641.

With Winthrop out of the way, the members of the General Court were able to press forward with their project to articulate the general principles of government. The Body of Liberties, drafted by Nathaniel Ward of Ipswich, did not describe in detail the machinery of government in the Bible Commonwealth, but it defined and protected the people's civil rights and gave the sanction of law to the unique form of town government that had emerged in Boston and the other towns. The freemen of every town, the Body of Liberties stated, had the right to choose

each year "select persons" who would make bylaws.

Just how firmly the people were committed to the new code was illustrated in 1645. A political squabble broke out in Hingham between contending candidates for a militia command. Winthrop intervened citing one faction for contempt, but the lower house of the General Court impeached him for having exceeded the powers of his office and for having violated fundamental law. Although Winthrop was acquitted and the representatives, therefore, were forced to listen to his "victory" speech in which he defined liberty as obedience to authority, it was clear that absolute control had slipped from his hands. Social order in Boston was not destroyed by the struggle between the governor and the freemen for political power, nor by the controversy that swirled around Anne Hutchinson, nor was the Puritan world transformed. But everywhere—in all aspects of society—there were uncertainties and changes. Some were apparent to the eye. Boston had become by mid-century "the Center Town and Metropolis," with shipyards crowded in the North End and businesses of all sorts clustered around the dock and market areas. Commerce was clearly the lifeblood of Boston.

A new group of merchants had surged to the top with the town's growth spurt during the second half of the 17th century. These men had not brought wealth with them from England, but had made their fortunes in Boston. And unlike the older elite whose wealth was in farmland, the new group owned town lots and houses, invested in shipping, or owned businesses. John Mylam, for example, arrived in Boston in 1635 and bought 14 acres of land at Muddy River (Brookline) that he exchanged in a few years for several town lots in Boston, which he sold later for a considerable profit; this capital he used to launch a trading partnership with William Tyng. Thomas Leverett, another of Boston's nouveau riche, gradually put together a large commercial farm that was worked for him by laborers and tenants. In the 1650s he was one of 14 investors who built a wharf and warehouses at Town Cove. One of Leverett's partners, Thomas Clarke, was elected a constable of Boston shortly after the completion of the waterfront development.

Not everyone succeeded, of course. Some failed and some men moved on to other towns. Nor were the results of Boston's new commercial prosperity an unmixed blessing. Puritan ministers thought too many men showed "an over-eager desire after the world." Likewise, the General Court was deeply concerned in 1650 by the "many and great miscarriages. . .committed by sailors" swaggering through the streets of Boston. And one snowy evening in November 1685, Samuel Sewall, one of the new group of merchants, reported matter-of-factly that a newborn baby boy had been left at the door of Shaw's tobacco shop.

But this side of Boston's burgeoning society should not be overemphasized. The townspeople were moral, God-fearing men and women who sought salvation first and prosperity and pleasure second. A *New England* was emerging, but the changes had not yet settled into permanent new forms. A crisis—the outbreak of an Indian war in the summer of 1675—accelerated the process of change and in its aftermath a new order was plainly evident.

While New Englanders' relationship with the neighboring Indian tribes had been pockmarked by sporadic violence since 1637 when the Pequot War ended, it was the pressure of population growth and the land hunger that accompanied it that caused the long and bloody conflict known as King Philip's War. Between 1650 and 1675 the Anglo-American population in the greater Boston area doubled and both speculators and the government were eager to push westward and southward onto the lands occupied by the Naragansetts and the Wampanoags. Metacom, or King Philip as the English called him, sachem of the Wampanoags, was forced by the New England

Confederation to accept one humiliation after another. The worst came in 1671 when he was compelled to surrender a large stock of guns and to accept government control of his tribal lands. From that time on, it would seem, Metacom began building a league of Indian resistance.

The incident that ignited the league's fury was the trial of three Wampanoags for the murder of John Sassamon, a Christian and Harvard-educated Indian who had warned leaders in Plymouth that the Wampanoags were planning an all-out attack on the Anglo-American settlements. A jury of 12 Englishmen and a smaller auxiliary jury composed of Indians found the Wampanoags guilty. The three men were hanged June 8, 1675. There were immediate outbreaks of burning and looting, and before the month ended Metacom's warriors swooped down on the frontier towns of Swansea and Mattapoiset, killing nine men. Meeting in Boston, the New England Confederation created a special war committee that selected Captain Daniel Henchman to command a company of 100 men drafted from the militia companies of Boston and

The Townhouse, built in 1657, was the institutional center of colonial Boston. Residents sold products in the marketplace, received punishments at the stocks and whipping post, and met here for formal governmental sessions and informal citizen gatherings. This structure burned in 1711 and was replaced by the brick State House which still occupies the site. Courtesy, Boston Athenaeum

This weathervane of molded copper, representing the Massachusetts and Wampanoag Indians, was fashioned by Shem Drowne for the cupola of the Province House, home of the colony's royal governors. Courtesy, Massachusetts Historical Society

several surrounding towns. On the night of June 26th, drums beat for volunteers. Within hours Captain Samuel Moseley, a hard-bitten adventurer who had sailed into Boston Harbor only a few weeks earlier towing a captured pirate ship, signed up nearly 100 more men.

Boston's soldiers were soon joined by men from throughout New England. Although they were well armed and supplied and determined to fight, the troops were unable to pin down the highly mobile Indian warriors. Several sweeps of the Mount Hope peninsula, where Metacom was reported to be hiding, yielded nothing. Indeed while Captain Henchman's men slowly searched the swampy ground along the Acushnet River, Rehoboth, Taunton, and Dartmouth were attacked. The Reverend John Eliot, who had spent his life attempting to Christianize the Indians, summed up the frustration and the danger of fighting such an elusive enemy. "We were too ready to think that we could easily suppress that flea," he commented, "but now we find that all the craft is in catching of them and that in the mean while they give us many a sore nip."

Buoyed by Metacom's successful hit-and-run attacks, tribe after tribe joined the Wampanoags. By the time of the first snowfall in November 1675, the entire upper Connecticut Valley had been laid waste by Indian forays and a score of frontier towns destroyed. By March Metacom's warriors were attacking Medfield and Weymouth, less than 20 miles from Boston.

Thoughts of English superiority were gone, replaced by fear and apprehension. Resistance to the draft became a serious problem by the spring of 1676, and refugees from frontier towns poured into Boston. "Many people in these parts are souls distracted, running hither and thither for shelter, and no where at ease," wrote Samuel Gorton. The selectmen were sympathetic, but they grumbled about the cost of feeding and housing the refugees and worried about what to do with all the young unmarried people who were

footloose and fancy-free in Boston.

In the late spring of 1676, the Indian offensive began to wane. The Indians had difficulty in obtaining food and weapons; they were losing the war of attrition. First a few warriors, then groups of half-starved men, women, and children began to surrender. In July 180 Nipmucks voluntarily surrendered to Boston authorities. Among them was the sachem, Matoonas, who was identified as a leader of the first attack on a Massachusetts town. He immediately was marched to Boston Common, tied to a tree, and shot. The others were tied together by a rope around their necks, dragged through the streets, and finally imprisoned on Deer Island in Boston Harbor. Those Indians who were not executed (records indicate 14 men were either shot or hanged) or held captive (there were more than 450 prisoners on Deer Island) were sold into slavery.

Finally on August 12, 1676, Captain Benjamin Church's men launched a surprise attack on a Wampanoag village near Bridgewater. Afterwards the soldiers discovered that one of the Indians they had killed was Metacom. Church ordered the body decapitated and quartered, and he and his men proudly displayed the head on their triumphant march back to Boston. Several thousand other Indians and about as many Englishmen were killed during this bloody, bitter war. Of some 90 Puritan settlements, 52 had been attacked and 12 destroyed. Many Indian villages were devastated. For the Indians of New England it was the last gasp.

There were important and far-reaching consequences for the people of Boston as well. The war accelerated the process of change already in motion, and the result was the clear emergence of new forms and values. First of all the war legitimized the merchants' claim to elite status. Boston merchants had provided vital support to the government during the war. When the New England Confederation needed money and supplies, it turned to the merchant community, to men who had capital and connections and know-how.

And no one asked if these men were members of a Puritan church. Some were; some were not. Those merchants who were not saints were honored nevertheless by the town for their contribution to the colony's war effort. Those merchants who had been accepted as saints before the war were viewed with much less suspicion afterwards. This meant that wealthy merchants were able to break through the old social barriers. A recent immigrant to New England was astonished, for example, to discover that Boston merchants "will marry their children to those whom they will not admit to baptism, if they be rich."

Merchants thought better of themselves. Samuel Sewall, a third-generation Boston merchant who kept a diary most of his adult life, reflects the passing of rigid Puritanism. In all outward ways Sewall kept the faith. But the intensity of his spiritual life slackened as the years passed. He simply was not interested in brooding introspection; he was a genial man who succeeded in trade and lived a full, honorable life as a merchant-gentleman.

The second major change stimulated by King Philip's War was the tendency to explain events by reason, rather than by divine intervention. After the war there was a debate about the causes of the conflict and how future trouble with the Indians might be avoided. In a pamphlet published in 1676 as a part of a complete history of the war, the Reverend Increase Mather, minister of Boston's North Church, argued that the war had been punishment for the sins committed by the people of Massachusetts. The Indians were the agents of Satan. In order to avoid new calamities, Mather prescribed prayer, fasting, and a strict adherence to "the Laws which are founded upon the word of God."

William Hubbard, a member of Harvard's first graduating class and a reluctant minister, disagreed. He bluntly told the General Court in his election-day sermon that the war was not God's doing, but "can be imputed to nothing more

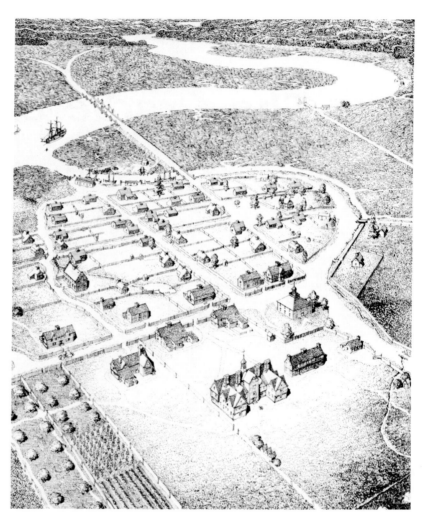

than to the contempt of our enemies, or overweening thoughts of our own skill and courage." Hubbard recommended legislation that would control the business activities of greedy land speculators, men who "easily swallow down hundreds of acres of land and are not satisfied."

Clearly the social groupings and values of the Founders were crumbling. The people of Boston had emerged from the war with a new consciousness: they were more comfortable with material success and with worldly explanations. Bostonians believed they were in control of their own destiny. When, in the next century, England threatened Boston's sense of community, there followed a series of political upheavals and ultimately a revolution.

Nathaniel Shurtleff created this conjectural view of Harvard College for Samuel Eliot Morison's Harvard College in the Seventeenth Century, *published in 1936. The large building in the foreground is probably at a right angle to the present site of Matthews Hall, while the Charles River winds through the background. Courtesy, Harvard University Archives*

II

The Cradle of Liberty

The leaders, ideas, and events that sparked
the American Revolution were Boston's before
they were America's. Eighteenth-century
Boston was a unique political community, so
intensely concentrated, homogeneous, and
self-conscious in culture that its influence
reached far beyond its borders. Boston's
political leaders did not set out to foment a
revolution. But their deep commitment to
liberty—stemming in part from the Puritan
idea that America had a special place in God's
plan—put them on a collision course with
British politicians who sought to tighten their
control over imperial trade and politics.

Before the 1750s the American colonists had
been loyal, if somewhat factious and
uncooperative subjects of the British Crown.
For more than three generations Bostonians

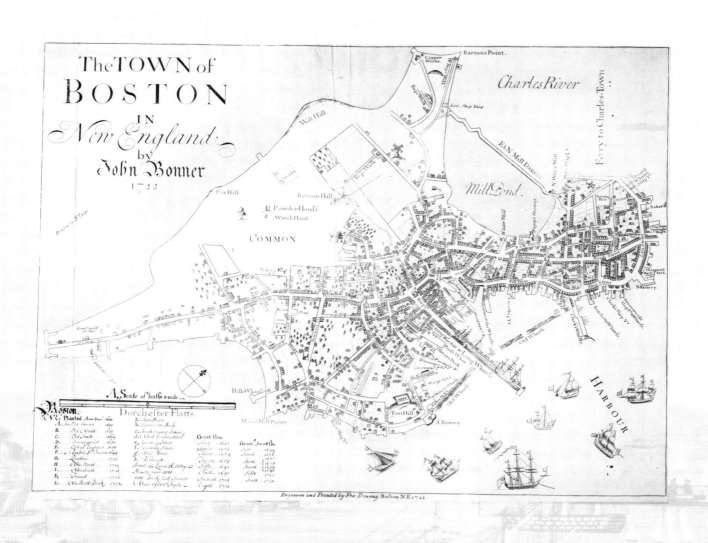

Previous page: The most well-known map of colonial Boston, Captain John Bonner's rendition of the town indicates that Boston's population was clustered about the one-half mile Long Wharf in marked contrast to the open western lands, where the rope walks and Boston Common were located. Courtesy, New York Public Library

Above: One hundred years after settlement Boston was still a walking city, only two miles long and one mile wide. Shipping and sea commerce employed the majority of workers, and the biggest trading customer was England. This photograph is part of an engraving by I. Carwitham. (TBS)

had accepted the restrictions imposed on their commercial activities by the Laws of Trade and Navigation. Based on the assumption that the colonies were in an inferior and dependent relationship to the mother country, the Navigation Acts stipulated that all American goods were to be monopolized by British merchants and shippers. England alone, it was decreed in 1660, would enjoy the profits of shipping and reexporting colonial goods. A second parliamentary act passed a few years later stated that no European goods could be shipped directly to America; all goods from Europe first had to be sent to England, unloaded there, and reshipped to the colonies.

Largely because this economic system was inefficiently and laxly administered, Boston prospered during the 17th and early 18th centuries. In fact Boston was the first American city to experience the leavening effects of trade, because it was the hub of a transatlantic trade network. Boston merchants exported molasses, rum, lumber, fish, livestock, hay, and flour to the West Indies and imported sugar from the islands. New Englanders also carried black slaves from the Ivory Coast to the West Indies. This Atlantic trade generated bills of credit drawn on English merchant houses that were used by Boston merchants to purchase manufactured goods.

While the triangle trade system was far-flung and potentially very lucrative, it was relatively flexible and easy to enter. Thomas Hancock, for example, came to Boston from Lexington at the age of 14 years as an apprentice to a bookseller. Within two decades Hancock's hard work and a "good marriage" enabled him to accumulate enough capital to finance several commercial ventures. He traded molasses from the West Indies for fish in Newfoundland and imported Dutch tea from the West Indies to Boston. By the late 1730s Hancock owned his own fleet of ships and had built a splendid mansion on Beacon Hill, complete with orchards and formal gardens. Peter Faneuil was another merchant who profited handsomely from the Caribbean trade. To show his gratitude to the city that had made possible his wealth, he gave Boston a "large brick building. . .for the use of a market" in 1742. Located near Town Dock, the building had market stalls on the ground floor and offices and a sizeable hall on the second floor. Designed by Jonathan Smibert, a portrait painter, Faneuil Hall centralized business activities, freeing other sections of the city from the noise and refuse created by unregulated commerce. Between Faneuil Hall and Long Wharf—which stretched 2,000 feet into the harbor-and along Merchants Row, other commercial structures were built during the 1730s to meet the needs of Boston's busy merchants.

About the same time, but far from the hustle and bustle of the North End, where most merchants still worked and lived, a new Congregational church was built. The Old West Church was meant to be an inducement to the development of a new residential area. Simon and Samuel Lynde subdivided their pasture land in 1737 in the hope of luring prosperous families to a life-style characterized by open space and a homogeneous neighborhood. A number of Boston's younger, wealthy merchants and professionals quickly took advantage of the opportunity. Certainly other Boston churches had members who were involved in commerce, but the Old West was noted for its "genteel congregation" and the "high dress" of the women who attended.

While it was most obvious at the Old West, conspicuous consumption, and its economic and social opposite, poverty, came increasingly to characterize Boston society. Wealth was less equitably distributed in the 1770s than it had been at the turn of the century. An assessment carried out by the town in 1774 revealed that the top 5 percent of Boston's taxpayers controlled 49 percent of the taxable assets of the community, whereas the economic elite previously had held only 30 percent. At the same time poverty scarred the lives of a growing number of Bostonians.

During the first half of the 18th century the percentage of poor people—defined as adult white males who were neither property owners nor dependents of taxpayers—more than doubled. And, most alarming to the town fathers, the lower middle class was hardest hit by the economic changes. Boston's selectmen lamented in 1757 that "besides a great Number of Poor. . .who are either wholly or in part maintained by

the Town, and so are exempt from being Taxed, there are many who are Rateable according to Law. . .who are in such poor circumstances that considering how little business there is to be done in Boston they can scarcely procure from day to day daily Bread for themselves and Families." The fact was that the average carpenter, baker, or tavern keeper who died in Boston around 1760 had less to show for a lifetime's work than his ancestor of a century before.

The difficult situation in which the growing number of poor found themselves was made worse, according to Boston's clergymen, because the wealthy had become too selfish and materialistic and too little concerned about "relieving the wants of the Indigent and Distressed." There was a lack of public-spiritedness; the interdependency of man that the Puritan founders had emphasized had fallen victim to the individualistic pursuit of wealth. Therefore there was a greater need for charity. Sermons designed to promote acts of charity appealed to self-interest. Wealthy men commonly were portrayed as the agents of an enterprising deity, making wise investments in poor relief on His behalf. The Reverend Joseph

This was Faneuil Hall as it looked during the Revolutionary War, before being enlarged by Charles Bulfinch. This print is from an engraving by C.B. Hall, first published in Massachusetts Magazine in 1789. Courtesy, Boston Public Library (BPL)

Allin, for example, told his congregation that "the Great Benefactor" would "highly recompense" the charity of liberal men. Another earthly benefit of charity, according to Cotton Mather's sermon titled *Durable Riches,* was that it helped maintain a stable, hierarchical society. Charity would affirm publicly the distinction between rich and poor. "Doing good," Mather declared, "would assert the superiority of one man above another," underscoring his claim to honor and deference. Despite repeated appeals and warnings of this sort, Boston's elite did not give enough to sustain the growing number of poor. Therefore the city's taxpayers had to shoulder a larger share of the welfare burdens. In the 1720s and 1730s, the overseers of the poor expended 25 pounds per thousand inhabitants; but per capita costs doubled in the 1740s and 1750s and doubled again in the following two decades.

While the number of those who received poor relief increased, there is no evidence of mass destitution. Poverty in Boston never approached the level that characterized England, where poverty was the most serious and most controversial social problem of the 18th century. At times one-third of the population was impoverished; in London the poor overwhelmed the charitable institutions. But even in the worst times after 1760, poor relief involved no more than 5 percent of Boston's population.

Still resentment and anxiety were endemic to mid-18th-century Boston. Although neither the poor nor the well-to-do could measure precisely their economic situations, they could easily discern the general trend. Few working men doubted that the rich merchants were amassing fortunes. At the same time the wealthy elite was deeply anxious about the social consequences of poverty.

Occasionally these hostile feelings just below the surface exploded. An incident that took place at a ferry dock along the Charles River following the Harvard commencement of 1755 reveals how potentially volatile Boston society was:

Notwithstanding the two Constables that placed themselves there, two Gentlemen's Servants were thrown over, and not less than 20 of our poor Slaves (Male and Female) were thus injuriously served that evening. The most astonishing Cursing and Swearing was continually sounding in my Ears. Women as they left the boat, were indecently talked to, and some of them most immodestly handled. That part of the Town was in the utmost Disorder and this effected by a Rabble that consisted of at least 200.

The turbulence caused by the economic tensions was moderate compared to that which developed in religion. Since American culture was still largely religious in its orientation, these tensions lay at the heart of the revival that swept through the colonies in the 1740s. The Great Awakening, as the revival was called, did not begin all at once. There were stirrings in western Massachusetts and elsewhere in the colonies in the 1730s. But when George Whitefield, the brilliant English preacher, toured the colonies in 1740 he carried the torch of evangelicalism with which he set the colonies ablaze with religious fervor for nearly four years.

Whitefield began his spectacular tour in Newport, Rhode Island, where he declared that "the word of the Lord is...sharper than a two-edged sword." In late September he moved on to Boston, where his effect was stupendous. At first he preached to hundreds who jammed into the churches. Then when the crowds overflowed the churches, Whitefield held open-air meetings. On October 12, 1740, he preached to an audience of 30,000, nearly twice the population of the city, that packed Boston Common to hear him. Sara Edwards was there. She later described Whitefield as "a born orator...with a deep-toned, yet clear and melodious voice. It is wonderful to see what a spell he casts over an audience by proclaiming the simplest truths of the Bible." "I have seen," she wrote, "thousands of people hang on his words with breathless silence,

broken only by an occasional half-suppressed sob."

Although his style was revolutionary—because he appealed primarily to his listeners' emotions—Whitefield's doctrines were not new. He stressed the need for an emotional conversion experience and downplayed the importance of reason and good works, or "preparation," in achieving salvation. In fact the evangelicals claimed to be doing nothing more than revising the standards of true Puritanism. Thomas Prince, copastor of the Old South Church, for example, insisted that Whitefield preached "the doctrines of the martyrs and other reformers, which were the same as our forefathers brought over hither." In an elaborate set of sermons published in Boston in 1743, Prince argued that the Awakening was part of God's plan for His chosen people. He insisted that no one knew who was saved, certainly not the "cold and careless" ministers who were more concerned with the "Profits, Pleasures and Preferments of the World" than with their souls. Prince's support of the revival and his attack on orthodox clergymen did not go unanswered.

Charles Chauncy, pastor of the venerable First Church of Boston, rushed into print four antirevival tracts before Prince's final sermon appeared. Chauncy was a rational man of regular habits. A friend described his daily routine: "At twelve o'clock, he took one pinch of snuff, and only one in twenty-four hours. At one o'clock, he dined on one dish of plain wholesome food, and after dinner took one glass of wine, and one pipe of tobacco, and only one in twenty-four hours." Not surprisingly Chauncy found the revival's emphasis on emotion and enthusiasm to be repugnant. He believed religion's proof and strength were derived from an orderly and optimistic world view. He appealed to reason, believing that a person's intellect controlled, or should control, his emotions. As the Boston pastor saw it, "there is the religion of the Understanding and Judgment and Will, as well as the Affections; and if little account is made of the former, while great stress is laid upon the latter. . .People should run into disorder."

Chauncy's worst fears were confirmed by James Davenport's antics. Davenport was an orthodox minister who came under Whitefield's spell. He left his own church to become an evangelist, preaching wherever and whenever he was able to find an audience. Speaking without a text, Davenport sang and prayed and encouraged those who had "seen the light" to do the same. He denounced every establishment minister as a "dead husk" and stirred crowds into a frenzy. Thrown out of Boston as a "madman," Davenport sponsored a public burning in New London, Connecticut. He called upon his audience to burn books written by those who opposed the Awakening, as well as "petticoats, silk gowns, short cloaks, red-heeled shoes, fans, necklaces, gloves and other such apparel." While hymns were sung over the pile, Davenport added his own pants, "a pair of old, wore out, plush breaches." This, commented an observer, would have obliged him "to strut about bare-arsed" had the fire not gone out.

The Reverend George Whitefield (1714-1770) was the itinerant English evangelist who led the "Great Awakening." From Dictionary of American Portraits, *Dover, 1967*

For an increasing number of Bostonians, Davenport's behavior aroused fears that all social order would be destroyed if the evangelicals had their way. But by the mid-1740s the most intense fires of the Awakening had faded. But American society would never be the same again. At least three areas of social thought were irreversibly affected by the Great Awakening.

First the authority and status of the conservative Boston clergy and those who supported the passive acceptance of the established hierarchy was permanently weakened. "It is an exceedingly difficult, gloomy time with us," wrote one Boston minister. "Such an enthusiastic, factious, censorious Spirit was never known here. . . .Every low-bred, illiterate Person can resolve Cases of Conscience and settle the most difficult Points of Divinity better than the most learned Divines." The corollary of the new anti-authoritarian attitude that the Awakening encouraged was a virulent attack on the wealthy. An anonymous Boston pamphleteer, for example, charged that the rich squeezed their money from the town's poor people. "No wonder such Men can build Ships, Houses, buy Farms, set up their Coaches, Chariots, and live very splendidly," railed the *Centinel*. "Such men," he concluded bitterly, are "Birds of prey. . .Enemies to all Communities—wherever they live." Finally the revival conditioned men to accept mass meetings as the natural and logical outcome of confrontation, name-calling, and labeling. Certainly it seemed so to thousands of Boston patriots who gathered on the Common in 1773 to hear an oration on the "Beauties of Liberty."

Like all Englishmen, before 1763 Bostonians accepted the antinomy of power and liberty as the central reality of politics. Power meant the rule of some men over others. The essential characteristic of power was its aggressiveness, its unrelenting attack on liberty. As John Adams—the Braintree lawyer who opened his office in Boston in 1768—put it, the political world was divided into two antagonistic spheres: the sphere of power and the sphere of liberty. Power was in the hands of the government and "like the ocean, not easily admitting limits to be fixed in it." Liberty, by contrast, was always weak, always "skulking about in corners. . .hunted and persecuted in all countries by cruel power." Liberty was not, therefore, as it is for us, the concern of the people and the government alike, but only of the governed.

The chief aim of a good government was to harness these contending forces for the mutual benefit of all. The British constitution—a bundle of institutions, laws, customs, and the basic principles that motivated them—accomplished this extraordinary task by balancing and checking the basic forces within society. It was commonly assumed that British society consisted of three social orders, each of which would be best served by a different form of government: royalty, whose natural form of government was monarchy; the nobility, whose natural form was aristocracy; the commons, or people, whose form was democracy. The functions of the British government were carefully distributed among these three orders so that no one dominated the others. This "mixed constitution" created a framework that insured order and the preservation of the rights and liberty of all men.

Constitutional liberty was neither license, nor the abstract liberty that existed in a state of nature. Political, or civil, liberty was the capacity to exercise "natural rights" within the boundaries of the law. The rights of all Englishmen, including the American colonists, were understood to be those maxims of reason and justice that were inalienable and God-given. But they were not explicitly written down anywhere, not codified. To assert that all rights might be articulated in a comprehensive code was, as James Otis ("the best lawyer in Boston") declared, "the pedantry of a quack, and the nonsense of a pettifogger." For free

Englishmen, rights were not constricted, but expansively expressed in the common law, acts of Parliament, and in the charters of privileges issued by the Crown.

Somehow England's constitution embodied the rights of Englishmen. John Adams argued in 1763 that the English constitution was "the most perfect combination of human powers in society which finite wisdom has yet contrived and reduced to practice for the preservation of liberty and the production of happiness." But there was always danger. The Boston Town Meeting pointed out, in 1772, that "ambition and lust of power above the law are. . .predominant passions in the breasts of most men." These are instincts that have stimulated "the worst projects of the human mind in league against the liberties of mankind," the meeting added.

Without surrendering this general belief, Boston patriots such as John Adams insisted that Americans were different, unique in their sense of virtue. Political virtue, as it was defined by Adams and other political leaders, was related to the Puritan belief that motivated Boston's settlement; namely, that God had chosen the American people to provide an example to the rest of the world of a just political order, where individuals were free to pursue the acquisition of property.

Property, however, was not a goal to be pursued singlemindedly and selfishly. A virtuous citizen eschewed "luxury and extravagance," focusing instead on what would be good for the community. "It would be the glory of this Age," Sam Adams wrote to a friend, "to find Men having no ruling Passion but the Love of their Country, and ready to render her the most arduous and important Services with the Hope of no other Reward in this Life than the Esteem of their virtuous Fellow Citizens."

Sam Adams of Boston was that man. Son of a Boston brewer, he took up a career as a professional politician soon after graduating from Harvard with the class of 1740. Initially an active participant in the Boston Town Meeting, Adams was first elected to the Massachusetts assembly in 1765. The following year he was chosen clerk of the General Court for which he received a small stipend, the greater part of his income for the 10 years prior to independence. He was simply uninterested in money or possessions. For Adams, poverty was a source of pride. He confessed to his wife, "I glory in being what the world calls a poor Man." When, in 1774, Adams was chosen a delegate to the Continental Congress, his Boston neighbors collected funds to outfit him so that he would not be an embarrassment to Massachusetts.

Although his life was politics, Sam Adams was not an ambitious, opportunistic office-seeker. He was an organizer, a committee man, whose skill was, as Charles Francis Adams observed in the 19th century, "infusing into the scattered efforts of many all the life and energy which belongs to a single will." Long unfairly accused of being the "Boston dictator" whose sly, manipulative backroom deals singlehandedly brought about the American Revolution, or the "master of the mob" whose command caused the "rabble" to initiate violence and destruction in the streets of Boston, Adams' reputation recently was rescued by Pauline Maier. She put it eloquently: Sam Adams was "the American revolutionaries' American revolutionary. . .confident that the ways of his forefathers were winning their rightful place in the history of mankind, and who died looking forward to a great liberation not from this earth but upon it."

To realize his dream Adams, knowing what all other patriots knew, argued that English tyranny—the use of arbitrary power—had to be resisted. When rulers "pervert their powers to tyrannical purposes," Andrew Eliot, minister of the New North Church of Boston, told his congregation in 1765, "submission is a crime." Jonathan Mayhew, Eliot's colleague across town at the Old West Church, was even more explicit. If public officials oppress the people it is

Above: Coffee at the Green Dragon Tavern was served in this urn, which is eighteen inches tall and six inches wide at the base. (TBS)

"warrantable and glorious to disobey the civil power." Indeed, according to Mayhew, it is the people's duty "to break the yoke of tyranny and free themselves and posterity from inglorious servitude and ruin."

The trick, of course, was to figure out at what point government policies became truly oppressive. When should the people rebel? Was English policy deliberately designed to usurp the liberties of the people? Or were the laws passed by Parliament merely the result of ignorance or incompetence? Gradually and reluctantly from 1750 onwards a majority of Bostonians came to the conclusion that English political leaders had secretly formulated a dark plan to strip Americans of all their liberties, to enslave them. The belief that a conspiracy existed—as one recent historian put it—acted as "an inner accelerator to the movement of opposition." Every law passed, every reaction, and every denial confirmed the suspicion of the patriots. Therefore people were urged to act, to rebel, before it was too late. It was from this perspective that Bostonians viewed the actions of the English government.

The first step toward the creation of a tyranny, everyone knew, was the establishment and misuse of a permanent professional army and navy. Both the royal navy and army relied upon impressment—recruitment by force—to fill their ranks. In England impressment was commonplace and accepted. But in the American colonies the practice was militantly resisted by the lower classes who were the target of recruiters and denounced by local middle-class politicians. Both groups regarded impressment as a violation of their rights as Englishmen.

On the morning of November 17, 1747, Commodore Charles Knowles sent a press gang into Boston to round up sailors for his fleet that was preparing to battle the French navy near the Gulf of St. Lawrence. The gang moved along the waterfront area collaring scores of apprentices, craftsmen, and laborers as well as merchant seamen. The operation came to a stop, however, when a crowd of angry men armed with clubs and cutlasses attacked the press gang, freeing their Boston neighbors and sending the English sailors fleeing to their warships. Later the same morning a larger crowd surged through the city looking for royal naval officers and English property upon which it could vent its anger and frustration.

Four naval officers were seized as hostages as the crowd moved toward the (Old) State House, at the corner of King (State) and Devonshire streets. Once there the now several thousand protestors hurled bricks through the windows, pounded on the doors, and loudly demanded that the governor prosecute the press gang. The governor and several councillors spoke to the crowd from the balcony, urging the men to disperse. Although Bostonians were hostile, they were not bloodthirsty; the governor was allowed to escort the naval officers inside the State House. Frustrated, the crowd returned to the waterfront "to burn a twenty gun ship now building there for His Majesty."

From the safety of Castle William in Boston Harbor, the governor called upon the town to apologize "for insults to His Majesty George II." The town meeting took a dim view of the crowd's militant behavior, but it also insisted that the press gang was at fault. The citizens of Boston, the meeting declared, had been "exposed to the ill usage of arbitrary power." The following Sunday, Governor William Shirley accepted the Boston Town Meeting's carefully worded apology and wisely considered the matter closed.

Yet this was but the beginning. During the next two decades, nearly every aspect of British policy brought to the surface of public controversy a series of conflicts linked to the very structure of imperial relations. Bostonians began to fear that the British empire and American liberty were not compatible.

Some men reached this conclusion before others. John Adams claimed the "child independence was born" in the (Old) State House in February 1761. In the council chamber on the second floor, a dramatic confrontation took place between Chief Justice Thomas Hutchinson and James Otis, Jr., over the legality and use of writs of assistance, general warrants that authorized searches for smuggled goods. Hutchinson, who had been appointed to the bench only a few months earlier, was 49 years old in 1761. His family had helped found New England, each generation adding a bit more wealth and prestige. Thomas was born in Boston; and entered Harvard at the age of 12, where, like all his ancestors, he prepared himself for a life of commerce. By his marriage to Margaret Sanford of Rhode Island in 1734, he was able to create a vast commercial network, the Hutchinsons controlling the London-Boston link, the Sanfords handling the links to the West Indies and the Wine Islands.

By 1750 Hutchinson had accumulated a fortune. While the average Bostonian's worth was declining, Hutchinson amassed 15 times more cash than his father had possessed. He owned eight houses (including a mansion in Boston and a country house in Milton), commercial lots, two wharves, and 100 acres of land. At the age of 26 Hutchinson entered politics. In 1737 he was elected a representative of Boston to the Massachusetts house. After 10 years in the lower house he was appointed a councillor and then lieutenant governor. In 1760 Governor Francis Bernard named him chief justice of the Superior Court. Although he was not trained in the law, such an appointment was not unusual, especially given Hutchinson's political experience.

Only two people were immediately critical of Hutchinson's appointment to the court. One was a 25-year-old law student and the other an unstable, if brilliant, lawyer who did not have a political following. Within a few years, however—from the time Hutchinson heard the suit brought against the writs of assistance in 1761 to his attempt to implement the Stamp Act in 1765—John Adams and James Otis, Jr., had turned their personal outrage into an all-out public assault that aroused deep political suspicions among a large number of Bostonians.

Described by a contemporary as "plump, round-faced and smoothskinned," Otis was hired by a coalition of 63 Boston merchants to block issuance of the writs of assistance. The merchants feared that the use of general search warrants was part of a plan to enforce imperial trade regulations. That was precisely the purpose. By allowing Thomas Lechmere, surveyor general of the Customs in Boston, "to enter and go into any Vaults, Cellars, Warehouses, shops or other places to search and see whether any Goods. . .shall be there hid or concealed," the Crown hoped to prevent smuggling and to increase its revenue. Boston merchants believed that they would not survive if the regulations were enforced strictly.

For example, if the duty on molasses imported to Boston from non-English sugar-producing islands was collected, the price would increase by a prohibitive 60 percent. Obviously, merchants forced to sell at this inflated price could not hope to compete with those whose molasses came from the English West Indies. Since only about 25 percent of New England's need for molasses was met by the English islands, a great many Boston merchants, including those who sold agricultural goods, fish, and lumber in the Caribbean, would be ruined if the duty was collected.

Clearly the Boston merchant community was motivated primarily by self-interest when it chose to fight the use of general search warrants. But Otis politicized their drive for economic well-being. He argued that the writs were "against the fundamental principles of law. The privilege of house." "A man who is quiet," Otis stated, "is as secure in his house as a prince in his castle." Therefore the parliamentary act that allowed the courts to issue general search warrants was unconstitutional, a violation of the rights of Englishmen.

Young John Adams sat in rapt attention as Otis spun out his powerful political argument. Otis was a "flame of fire" bombarding the five judges, including Hutchinson, "all in their new fresh robes of scarlet English cloth, in their broad bands, and immense judicial wigs," with a "rapid torrent of impetuous eloquence." Adams may have been too romantic when

he concluded: "Every man of an immense crowded audience appeared to me to go away, as I did, ready to take up arms against writs of assistance." Still Adams was essentially right. A legal squabble motivated by personal animosity and economic selfishness had been transformed into a political struggle for principle and in the process had linked the merchant community to radicals like Otis and Adams.

Hutchinson's response failed to address either the Boston merchants' anxiety or the sweeping political issues raised by Otis. He adjourned the proceedings for nine months and waited for an answer from London. The reply was "of course" the writs should be issued.

During the next few years the Boston customs collectors pried and snooped and occasionally caught a smuggler. Otis and Adams kept up their attacks, painting Hutchinson as the tool of a corrupt and oppressive English government. In April 1763, for example, Otis published an article in the Boston *Gazette* that charged Hutchinson with fomenting "animosities and civil wars" among the people. John Adams condemned him for taking "four of the most important offices in the province into his own hands" and spoke with bitterness of Hutchinson's passion for power. "The liberties of this country," Adams remarked, have more to fear from Hutchinson "than from any other man." Not surprisingly, given this barrage of criticism, Hutchinson was the chief target during the Stamp Act uprising in the summer of 1765.

The stamp tax was intended by the English prime minister, George Grenville, to raise revenue in America that would be used to underwrite the cost of running the British empire. Britain was staggering under a huge debt incurred during the Great War for Empire (1755-1763). While the rewards for Britain's military success against France were potentially enormous—India, Canada, and most of North America east of the Mississippi were seized by Britain—the costs of maintaining the vast empire were equally as large. Nevertheless Grenville hoped to raise enough money in America to pay for the expense of stationing troops there.

He assumed, as did nearly all of his colleagues in Parliament, that the tax on attorneys' licenses, cards, dice, newspapers and pamphlets, deeds for land, and the papers used in clearing ships from harbors was perfectly proper, constitutional. Grenville believed that Parliament represented all Englishmen wherever they lived and whether or not they could vote. According to this theory of government, called virtual representation, Americans were said to be virtually, if not actually, represented in Parliament. Therefore their consent to acts of Parliament could be presumed. By contrast, Americans had come to believe that they could be represented only by men for whom they had actually voted.

The most influential and powerful protests against the Stamp Act came from Boston. Otis and John Adams jumped into print, attacking the theoretical underpinning of the tax. Sam Adams and the Loyal Nine, who formed the nucleus of the Boston Sons of Liberty, militantly, and sometimes violently, resisted the act.

Otis' pamphlet, *The Rights of the British Colonists Asserted and Proved,* clearly stated the ideological dilemma: how could Americans justify their opposition to some acts of Parliament without questioning the basis for Parliament's authority over them? On the one hand Otis passionately argued that Americans were entitled to all the rights of Englishmen, including the rights not to be taxed without their consent. On the other hand Otis acknowledged that the power of Parliament was uncontrollable.

John Adams burst into print with a resolution that became *the* rationale for American resistance to England. Adams had every reason to be happy and content in the summer of 1765: he had married Abigail Smith in the fall and their first child was born in July. Yet that same summer he angrily denounced the Stamp Act and the arrogance of British colonial officials. Adams had a radical solution to

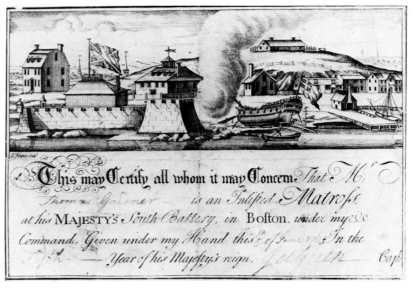

the dilemma posed by Otis. Parliament could make a mistake and when it did it need not be obeyed. The Stamp Act was a mistake, and therefore the law "was utterly void, and of no binding Force upon us, for it is against our Rights as Men and our Privileges as Englishmen."

Thomas Hutchinson flatly disagreed. His position was that American control over its own taxation was an indulgence, not a right. Therefore he publicly counseled his fellow Bostonians to "humbly pray" that as "a matter of favor" Parliament continue the old policy and repeal the new stamp tax. By shrewd, hard politicking Hutchinson won approval in the Massachusetts house for his moderate proposal.

The reaction among the people of Boston was immediate and hostile. It was charged that Hutchinson was not at all opposed to the tax, that he had written secretly to London to encourage the Stamp Act. He was at the head of a cabal, it was rumored, that sought "to advance themselves to posts of honor and profit...at the expense of the rights and liberties of the American colonies." When Andrew Oliver, Hutchinson's brother-in-law, was named stamp master for Massachusetts, the people were convinced that his secret motives had been revealed. "Vile serpent," raged John Adams.

South Battery was the fort at Boston Neck which limited land access to Boston. This document with an illustration of the fort certified the bearer as an "enlisted matross," or artillery private, assigned to the installation. Courtesy, Boston Athenaeum

Resistance to the Stamp Act boiled over into the streets of Boston on the morning of August 14, 1765. Organized by the Loyal Nine, a crowd of about 100, composed of people from a wide social and economic spectrum—laborers and artisans, apprentices and small tradesmen—hung an effigy of Andrew Oliver from a tree on Boston Common. That night a group paraded the effigy around the city, tore down a small building belonging to Oliver, and used the wood to make a bonfire on nearby Fort Hill. Oliver's effigy was ceremoniously "stamped," beheaded, and added to the fire. Then the crowd returned to Oliver's house, showered stones through the windows and demolished the garden fence before dispersing for the night.

The following day several gentlemen visited Oliver and persuaded him to resign his position as stamp distributor. One Bostonian happily boasted: "I believe people never were more Universally pleased; not so much as one could I hear say he was sorry, but a smile sat on almost every one's countenance."

Although the immediate political goal of the Boston patriots had been achieved with Oliver's resignation, another crowd action took place on the night of August 26th. This time the target was Hutchinson. Warned that an angry crowd was on its way, Hutchinson and his family fled from their house on Garden Street. The crowd attacked the house in a fury, broke through the doors, swarmed through the rooms, ripped the paneling from the walls, destroyed the furniture and paintings, and smashed the inner walls. Only the heavy brickwork construction of the outer walls prevented their razing the house completely, "though they worked at it till daylight." Hutchinson's trees and gardens were ruined and everything of value carried off. The next day the streets of Boston were littered with money, dinnerware, clothes, and books that had belonged to Hutchinson.

On November 1, 1765, when the Stamp Act was scheduled to go into effect, nothing happened. Nothing, that is, that even suggested that the stamps were going to be used. The day began with the mournful tolling of the city's church bells. Effigies of two English officials were hung on the newly-named Liberty Tree in the South End and a parade of "innumerable people from the Country as well as the Town" marched through the streets shouting "Liberty and No Stamps" and other militant slogans. Governor Bernard fled from the city.

John Adams exalted in Boston's patriotic fervor and its political importance. "The year 1765," Adams wrote, "has been the most remarkable year of my life":

That enormous engine, fabricated by the British Parliament for battering down all the rights and liberties of America, I mean the Stamp Act, has raised and spread throughout the whole continent a spirit that will be recorded to our honor with all future generations. In every colony. . .the stamp distributors and inspectors have been compelled by the unconquerable rage of the people to renounce their offices.

And Adams realized that politics would never be the same again. "The people, even to the lowest ranks," he noted proudly, "have become more attentive to their liberties. . .and more determined to defend them. . . .Our presses have groaned, our pulpits have thundered, our legislatures have resolved, our towns voted; the crown officers have everywhere trembled, and all their little tools and creatures been afraid to speak and ashamed to be seen."

The tactics used by Boston's Sons of Liberty were imitated everywhere in the colonies with the same success. "Our brethren in Boston have endeared themselves more than ever to all the colonies in America," claimed a letter in the New York *Gazette* that was widely reprinted. Parliament, under pressure from English merchants as well as an aroused American people, repealed the Stamp Act.

News of the repeal of the Stamp Act was celebrated with parades, pageants, and mass meetings. The Boston Sons of Liberty organized an annual event to be held August 14th, the anniversary of the first militant uprising. In 1769 it was held in Dorchester in a field next to Robinson's Inn (The Sign of the Liberty Tree). Under a huge sailcloth awning, 355 Bostonians heard speeches, sang two versions of the Liberty Song, and drank 45 toasts. (The figure 45 had become a symbol of resistance to England when a radical newspaper, *The North Briton,* No. 45, had been suppressed by the Crown.) Surprisingly John Adams claimed he "did not see one Person intoxicated, or near it." He did notice a growing commitment to the patriot cause. Mass meetings, Adams wrote in his diary that evening, "tinge the Minds of the People, they impregnate them with the sentiments of Liberty. They render the People fond of their Leaders in the Cause, and averse and bitter against all opposers."

After the Stamp Act crisis, American sensitivity to all forms of English taxation was highly aroused. Therefore with the enactment of the Townshend duties in 1768, which levied duties on imports such as paper, glass, and tea, a similar pattern of resistance reappeared. In Boston pamphlets and newspapers again leapt to the defense of liberty, an embargo on English goods was organized by merchants, and crowds surged through the streets threatening and harassing British customs officials.

But now there was an important difference in the patriots' tactics. When John Hancock's sloop *Liberty* was seized for allegedly engaging in smuggling, the leadership of the Sons of Liberty publicly urged Bostonians not to resort to violence. A crowd marching on the house of Benjamin Hallowell, who had ordered the *Liberty* seized, was turned back by Hancock, Adams, and Otis who called out, "No violence, or you'll hurt the cause." Later in the summer the Sons of Liberty moved one of their mass meetings from the Liberty Tree to Faneuil Hall and finally to the Old South Meeting House, so that a proper debate might be carried on. The result was a petition sent to Governor Bernard.

At about the same time the Massachusetts assembly issued a circular letter to the other colonial legislatures denouncing the Townshend duties as unconstitutional violations of the principle of no taxation without representation. The letter called for a united American front and suggested a joint petition of protest to the king. Lord Hillsborough, the first secretary of state for America, ordered the House to rescind its letter. When the House refused by a vote of 92 to 17, Governor Bernard dissolved the assembly. (Paul Revere made a silver punchbowl to commemorate "the glorious NINETY-TWO.") With the legal means for protest closed, unruly crowds once again took to the streets of Boston, intimidating merchants who were thought to be importing English goods contrary to the patriotic boycott.

A confrontation between William Jackson and Theophilus Lille, North End shopowners who insisted upon selling English goods, and a crowd of nearly 2,000 men and boys quickly turned violent. Large painted signs with the word "IMPORTER" were posted and everyone going in or out of the shops was pelted with dirt and garbage. Ebenezer Richardson, a neighbor who made a living as an informant for the customs service, threatened the demonstrators. "I'll make it too hot for you before night," shouted Richardson. Members of the crowd responded by heaving eggs and stones at Richardson's house. In a rage, Richardson stuck a musket out from a second-floor window and fired. He killed 11-year-old Christopher Seider. A group of men rushed the house and dragged Richardson into the street. Although some members of the crowd demanded a hanging then and there, William Molineaux, a leader of the Sons of Liberty, took control of the situation. He had Richardson brought to Faneuil Hall, where a hearing was conducted before four justices of the peace.

When King George repealed the Stamp Act in March 1766, a huge celebration was held throughout Boston. The Liberty Tree, planted at Essex and Washington streets in 1646, was adorned with 150 iron, tin, and glass lanterns, including this one. The tree was among those destroyed by British soldiers for firewood during the winter of 1775. (TBS)

Crispus Attucks, the first black man killed in the Revolutionary War, is featured in this work by W. Champney. The Boston Massacre scene, a lithograph printed by J.H. Bufford, was created in 1856. (TBS)

A massive funeral was held for young Seider. Just two days after a snowstorm on a cold February day, thousands of mourners walked slowly from the Liberty Tree to the Old Granary burial ground. "Young as he was, he died in his Country's Cause," solemnly stated the Boston *Gazette*. When Richardson was found guilty of manslaughter "the Court Room resounded with Expressions of Pleasure," according to Judge Oliver.

Royal officials, believing anarchy existed in Boston, dispatched two regiments of British regulars to restore order. By 1769 there were 4,000 soldiers quartered in the crowded seaport town of 15,000. Their presence confirmed Bostonians' worst fears; the redcoats were a constant reminder of the oppressive power of Great Britain.

Guards stationed on Boston Neck, the entrance to the city, checked everyone going in and out. Patrols marched through the streets day and night, stopping and sometimes harassing people. Military parades were held on Boston Common.

Women were often subjected to coarse insults and rough advances from drunken soldiers. And at a time when unemployment among Boston laborers was high, off-duty redcoats competed for scarce jobs. The atmosphere was charged for an explosion.

On March 2, 1770, workers at Gray's ropeworks brawled with some soldiers who were looking for work. Both sides regarded another clash as inevitable. Three days later on March 5, a crowd assaulted the sentries posted outside the customshouse. Hard-packed snowballs and chunks of ice were hurled at the soldiers, along with scores of insults. The bells of the Old Brick Church rang out and men shouting "Fire, Fire," poured into King Street, adding to the crowd and the confusion. Afraid, goaded beyond endurance, first one and then another soldier leveled his musket and fired into the crowd. Captain Thomas Preston shouted, "Stop firing! Do not fire!" and he rushed in front of the ragged line of soldiers pushing up their muskets with his arm.

Eight men were wounded. Five lay dead. Blood stained the snow on King Street. A massacre, "a horrid, bloody massacre," the Boston *Gazette* labeled it. Dead were: Crispus Attucks, a black man in his forties who had refused to leave the scene even when the soldiers taunted him: "You black rascal," one shouted, "what have you to do with white people's quarrels?"; Samuel Gray, who rushed into King Street because he thought there was a fire; Samuel Maverick, a 17-year-old apprentice who left his half-eaten meal to join the crowd surging through the streets; James Caldwell, a young man who spent his days learning the art of navigation and his evenings courting a young woman; and Patrick Carr, a recent immigrant from Ireland, who lived with his employer in nearby Queen (Court) Street.

The following day a mass meeting was held in the Old South. Sam Adams was instructed by the meeting to demand that the soldiers be withdrawn from the city. When he delivered his ultimatum to Lt. Governor Hutchinson, Adams later recalled, "If Fancy deceived me not, I observed his Knees to tremble. I thought I saw his face grow pale (and I enjoyed the Sight)." Hutchinson capitulated. The troops were ordered into the barracks on Castle William.

Along with six soldiers, Captain Preston was brought to trial in late October 1770. Although a few radical patriots were upset by their decision, John Adams and Josiah Quincy defended the accused men. All but two were acquitted, and those convicted were released after they were branded on the thumb. Still, Adams had the last word: "Soldiers quartered in a populous

Engrav'd Printed & Sold by PAUL REVERE BOSTON.

Paul Revere's drawing of the massacre scene has a different emphasis, with no distinguishable black victim. Revere felt that the identity of those killed was less important than the concerted fashion in which the British soldiers made the attack. (TBS)

Polly Summer purchased this doll, imported from England, a few days before the Boston Tea Party in 1773. It remained in her family for four generations, and is shown in the arms of Mary P. Langley, Polly's great-great-granddaughter. The doll become well-known in 1893 when New England Magazine published a story that described Boston through the doll's experiences. (TBS)

town," he told the jury during his summation, "will always occasion two mobs where they prevent one. They are wretched conservators of the peace."

For more than two years after the Boston Massacre, there was a superficial calm throughout the American colonies. In early November 1772, however, voters at a Boston Town Meeting established a Committee of Correspondence to publicize the Crown's decision to pay governors and judges from customs revenue rather than allowing colonial legislatures to appropriate salaries. As head of the committee, Sam Adams was charged to "state the rights of the colonists," to list the "Infringements and Violations thereof that have been made," and to send copies to other towns in Massachusetts. Boston also asked of rural towns "a free communication of their Sentiments on this Subject."

The pamphlet issued by the committee minced no words. Americans' rights were boldly stated, and the list of grievances against Great Britain unapologetically presented. It was clear that Boston had

come to the conclusion that American liberty was far more important than loyalty to Parliament. It was also clear, from the responses that poured into Adams' committee from small towns throughout Massachusetts during the spring of 1773, that Boston's views had become widely accepted. Nearly all praised Boston's courage and resolve in defense of liberty. Nearly all agreed with Boston's assessment of the current state of affairs. Nearly all stated their belief that resistance to tyranny was "the first and highest social Duty of this people." Buoyed by this show of support, Boston newspapers were talking openly about independence by the summer of 1773. At the same time the British government announced its intention to uphold the authority of Parliament at any cost. Another crisis seemed unavoidable.

The passage of the Tea Act provoked the final crisis. Parliament intended only to save the East India Company from bankruptcy by granting it the exclusive privilege of selling tea in America. Because there was already a tax on tea, Parliament's move touched every raw political nerve in Boston's body politic. Not only did the act allow Boston radicals to point out once again the unconstitutionality of taxes passed without American representation, but it angered those merchants who were excluded from the monopoly driving them into the arms of the radicals. And the Tea Act raised anew the fear that a dark conspiracy existed to destroy American liberty. Radicals called attention to the creation by the act of a "monied interest," a train of arrogant, corrupt men wholly dependent upon the British government for place and profit. Their accusation gained credence when it was learned that among the merchants consigned to sell the tea in Boston were Lt. Governor Thomas Hutchinson's two sons.

The first of three tea ships, the *Dartmouth,* entered Boston Harbor on November 28, 1773; the *Eleanor* and the brig *Beaver* were subsequently tied up to Griffin's Wharf. Warnings to the tea merchants from the Sons of Liberty not to unload the tea were followed by an order from Hutchinson not to allow the ships to leave the harbor. On December 16, more than 5,000 Bostonians crammed into Old South Church. Chaired by Sam Adams, the meeting made one last attempt to persuade Hutchinson to send the tea back to England. He refused.

When that word reached the meeting it was nearly dark. Sam Adams rose and announced, "This meeting can do nothing further to save this country." As if his statement were a signal, shouts and warwhoops rang out from the crowded hall: "Boston harbor a tea-pot tonight! The Mohawks are come!" Outside a group of about 60 men, crudely disguised as Indians, swept down Milk Street toward Griffin's Wharf, where the three tea ships were anchored. The men were well-organized and disciplined. They worked so knowledgeably and effectively that by 9:00 p.m. their work was done: 342 chests of tea were hoisted onto the deck, broken open with axes, the tea shoveled overboard, and the chests smashed. "This is the most magnificent Movement of all," wrote John Adams in his diary the next day. "This Destruction of the Tea," he exalted, "is so bold, so daring, so firm, intrepid, and inflexible, and it must have so important Consequences and so lasting, that I cannot but consider it as an Epocha in History." The Boston Committee of Correspondence, fearful that patriot leaders would be rounded up and transported to England for trial, circulated a petition pledging its signers "at the hazard of our lives and fortunes to prevent any person from being detained in custody and carry'd out of the province." Paul Revere carried a full report of the Tea Party to New York City, where the news of Boston's "bold blow at tyranny" was greeted with jubilation.

When it learned of the Boston Tea Party, the British government reacted with considerably less enthusiasm. Lord North was outraged. He insisted upon

retribution. Angry members of Parliament passed a series of laws aimed at punishing Boston and at forcing all Americans to accept Parliament's right to legislate for the colonies. Known collectively as the Coercive Acts, the punitive measures closed the port of Boston until the tea was paid for, reorganized Massachusetts government so that the royal governor had more power and the town meetings less, allowed royal officials charged with capital offenses to be tried in England, and authorized the quartering of British soldiers in private homes. One final blow: General Thomas Gage, commander in chief of the British army in America, was made governor of Massachusetts.

The Coercive Acts set in motion a chain of events that led directly to war.

In the colonies, political satirists such as Paul Revere used cartoons to garner support for the radical position. In London political cartoons were also popular. This cartoon suggests the effectiveness of the blockade of Boston Harbor. (BPL)

The British attempt to force the colonists away from Breed's Hill in Charlestown led to the misnamed Battle of Bunker Hill on June 17, 1775. This engraving depicts Charlestown ablaze, and does not show the hundreds of British soldiers who were killed and wounded, making their victory a costly one. (BPL)

Everywhere royal authority began to dissolve. The Boston Committee of Correspondence called for aid and urged all the colonies to join in a boycott of British goods. Although mass meetings were held, resolutions of support passed and implemented, and new popular political organizations created, the other provinces were not yet ready to take more drastic steps. Instead they suggested that a general congress of the colonies be convened in Philadelphia in September 1774.

Fifty-five delegates from 12 colonies (Georgia excepted) assembled in Carpenter's Hall for the first session of the Continental Congress. The part that Boston had played in the unfolding drama of the American Revolution was illustrated almost immediately. The Reverend Jacob Duche, an Episcopalian,

opened the congress by asking the delegates and the American people to pray "for America, for the Congress, for the Province of Massachusetts, and especially the town of Boston." Within two weeks this symbolic gesture was followed by a specific political gain initiated by Sam and John Adams. Carried to the congress by Paul Revere, the Suffolk Resolves (from the county in which Boston was located) denounced the Coercive Acts as unconstitutional and recommended that the people begin military training. When the congress unanimously endorsed these principles it was clear that Boston's struggle for liberty had become the nation's.

While congress debated, the British government began to prepare for military action. On April 19, 1775, General Thomas Gage sent his troops out from Boston to

BOSTON

CHARLES TOWN

Concord to destroy a cache of military supplies. Warned of Gage's move by Revere and William Dawes, the militiamen were waiting. By the end of that bloody day, 93 Americans had been killed or wounded, the redcoats had suffered 272 casualties, and the vaunted British army was trapped inside Boston by 20,000 militiamen. For nearly a year the two armies stared at each other. Only once did the redcoats attack their beseigers. On June 17, 1775, 2,500 British soldiers drove the Americans from trenches atop Breed's Hill in Charlestown. The British incurred enormous losses in that misnamed Battle of Bunker Hill: over 800 wounded and 230 killed. The Americans lost less than half that number.

Badly mauled, Gage pulled back inside Boston and settled in for a long winter. Although nearly all of the town's patriots had fled, Boston's population soared to nearly 20,000 during the winter of 1775-1776. Loyalists had swarmed into the town to be protected by 13,000 redcoats. Food and fuel were in short supply. Most of the foodstuffs brought in by the royal navy was consumed by the British troops and there was little left for civilians. Meat and milk were impossible to buy and the price of bread, cheese, and potatoes rose to staggering heights. Over 100 buildings were pulled down and used for firewood; the pulpit and pews of the Old South had been ripped up and burned, as had the steeple of the Old West.

The seige ended when Colonel Henry Knox, former Boston bookseller turned artillery officer, brought heavy cannons from Fort Ticonderoga, occupied Dorchester Heights, and forced the British to evacuate Boston. On March 17, 1776, General George Washington liberated Boston. It was a depressing sight. Trees had been cut down everywhere, including those bordering the Common, fences had been ripped up, and buildings had been razed. Public buildings had been maliciously defaced and private homes looted.

But the shock of war and deprivation did not lessen Boston's enthusiasm for independence. On July 18, 1776, the people of the city gathered at the (Old) State House. Standing on the balcony, Colonel Thomas Crafts read the Declaration of Independence. Harrison Grey Otis, who would be mayor of Boston in 1830, recalled that as a boy he had stood in that crowd. The reading of the declaration drew "the heartfelt homage and electrifying peals of men, women, and children of the whole city." And in the evening, as John Adams had suggested would be appropriate, there was a celebration with "pomp and parade ...shows, games, bells, bonfires and illuminations."

The Revolutionary vision of an independent republic, shaped in large part by Boston's sons and daughters of liberty, was now America's destiny.

This plan of a besieged Boston in 1775 depicts the North and South Batteries, the fortifications at Boston Neck, and Charlestown in ruins following the Bunker Hill battle. Photograph by Richard Merrill. (TBS)

III
Yankee Boston

The Boston ideal burned more brightly after 1783. The Revolution, it seemed, presented Americans with an opportunity to realize a new world, to put the ideals of republicanism into effect, to create an ordered society in which men were free. But something unexpected happened; the ideas that sparked and sustained the Revolution contained within themselves the seed of their own disillusionment and destruction. By 1820 the Boston ideal had been changed, turned upside down.

Before the Revolution it had been argued that Americans were especially virtuous, a people who were naturally committed to civic responsibility. This belief lay at the core of republicanism. For Bostonians in particular republicanism was a secularized version of the

Puritan's attempt to harness man's selfish and individualistic impulses and to create a political community in which men were linked to one another in harmony and benevolence. More than any other form of government, republics were dependent upon the good, selfless character of their people. "A Citizen," declared Samuel Adams, "owes everything to the Commonwealth." Or as Dr. John Warren, whose brother had died on Bunker Hill, put it in his Fourth of July oration in 1783, "when virtue fails, when luxury and corruption shall undermine the pillars of the state," it will cause "a total loss of liberty and patriotism."

Bostonians' obsession with political virtue was a radical doctrine. It flew in the face of man's natural selfishness. It caused them, therefore, to struggle with a dilemma similar to the one that had confronted their Puritan forebears. John Adams, for example, urged his countrymen to work hard, but at the same time he feared the consequences of prosperity. "Will you tell me how to prevent riches from producing luxury?" he asked Thomas Jefferson. "Will you tell me how to prevent luxury from producing effeminacy, intoxication, extravagance, vice and folly?" As Adams and a cluster of Boston's post-revolutionary leaders saw it, in other words, the development of a manufacturing economy seemed incompatible with virtue.

Unlike his cousin Sam, John did not encourage poverty. He knew that people were anxious to shake off the shackles of economic deprivation. Bostonians loved commerce "with its conveniences and pleasures" too much to put up with privation any longer than necessary. But Adams was deeply troubled by the prospect of a society divided into two competing groups—the rich and well born and the commonality, the haves and the have-nots, the aristocracy and the democracy. While Adams did not always describe the differences between the aristocratic and democratic elements in society in economic terms, he often stated flatly: "It is wealth that produces the inequality of condition." Wealth was the touchstone of social division.

Still, for several decades after the Revolution, politics moderated the distance between rich and poor in Boston. The town meeting brought together men of different economic status and praised those whose eloquence, reason, and character served the community. Boston had a board of selectmen and a variety of other municipal officers who were chosen by the town meeting, where "the meanest citizen ratable at 20 pounds beside the poll, may deliver his sentiments and give suffrage in very important matters, as freely as the greatest Lord in the Land." Dr. Thomas Young, a native of Albany who moved to Boston in the 1760s, added that positions of power were open to "everyone whose capacity, integrity, and diligence in the affairs of his country attracts the public attention." In other words respect, not simply wealth, was an important prerequisite for political power in Boston.

Although Paul Revere held only a few

Previous page: Park Street Church, built in 1809, highlights this 1812 oil painting. The artist is unknown; the original painting hangs in the Old State House. (TBS)

This painting, by F.D. Williams, provides an early look at Post Office Square, now the center of Boston's commercial district. Captain James Dalton's house was built in 1758 on the corner of Water and Dalton (later Congress) streets. (BPL)

minor offices, he was a highly regarded political activist during the Revolution whose skills as a silversmith, bell maker, and foundry master made him one of the best-known and successful artisans in Boston. Described by his neighbor, Hannah Mather, as "a man of ingenuity and exertion," Revere "accumulated a handsome property" in the years after the Revolution. Like his fellow artisans Revere worked long and hard from sunup to sundown, but without much feeling of hurry or pressure. The important thing was to do the job well. Revere was, in fact, a superb artist. Before the Revolution his silver pieces—flagons, bowls, and teapots—were ornate and embossed with scrolls, though the purity and simplicity of form that came to characterize his work in the Federal period was always evident.

Following the needs of the young republic, however, Revere made fewer decorative silver pieces after about 1790 and took up, instead, two new crafts—bell casting and the manufacture of sheet copper. His success was astounding. The bell-maker's art called for a thorough knowledge of iron casting, which Revere learned in the years after 1788 when he built his own foundry. But then his stock-in-trade was hardware, stoves, anvils, and forge hammers. To cast a large bell was quite another matter. Nevertheless in 1792 Revere successfully cast his first bell for the Second Church of Boston. Although its sound was "panny, harsh and shrill," Boston and Revere were inordinately proud of the fact that this was an American accomplishment. Indeed, by the following year, Revere justly boasted that "we know we can cast as good bells as can be cast in the world."

Late in 1800 Revere gambled again and won. Although he was 65 years old and well-to-do, he risked $25,000 of his own money to establish a mill for rolling copper into sheets. No one else in America could meet this demand. Within a few years Revere's mill had produced 6,000 feet of copper sheathing for the new State

This silver tankard was crafted by Paul Revere in the late 1700s. After achieving success as a silver craftsman, Revere risked a large part of his fortune to develop the first copper sheeting process in America. Rolled copper from the Revere mill was used to sheath the U.S.S. Constitution. (TBS)

House on Beacon Hill and enough material to copper-bottom the U.S.S. *Constitution* ("Old Ironsides"). On June 26, 1803, Captain Edward Preble wrote in the log of the *Constitution:* "The carpenters gave nine cheers, which were answered by the seamen and calkers, because they had in fourteen days completed coppering the ship with copper made in the United States."

Like Revere, Boston artisans were proud—if not quite so prosperous. They were men who had worked their way up through the craft hierarchy from apprenticeship to ownership of their own shop or business. Their goal was economic independence, defined as ownership of a moderate level of property, not unlimited "accumulation of the *Almighty Dollar.*" According to this view, artisans (or mechanics as they were sometimes called) were one of "three great classes," each representative of a sector of economic activity: the agricultural, the commercial, and the mechanic. Each class performed a special economic function, but depended on the union of all classes to achieve prosperity. "The true interest of one cannot be opposed to the real Interest of either of the others," claimed the

Massachusetts Charitable Mechanic Association, founded in 1795 by Revere and 83 other Boston artisans.

Defining class by economic function also meant that in the artisans' view classes represented vertical not horizontal unities. The commercial class included modest retailers as well as international merchants; the artisan class contained craftsmen at every level—masters, journeymen, and apprentices—and manufacturers. The logo and motto of the Charitable Mechanic Association reflected this conception of society. At the center of their membership certificate, the association placed a scale-beam with packages symbolic of commercial interests suspended from one side and the tools of various crafts hanging from the other. According to the official explanation this design signified "the truth of the maxim contained in the *motto* of the Association, that, equally balanced, the Merchant and Mechanic in being *'Just,'* may *'Fear Not.'*"

Unfortunately the artisans' idealized conception of a just and harmonious society was not a perfect reflection of reality in turn-of-the-century Boston. Many of the town's tradesmen

Elizabeth Freeman, shown here in her later years when employed as a children's nurse in Stockbridge, was the first African slave emancipated after passage of the Massachusetts Bill of Rights in 1781. Her nickname, "Mumbet," was probably the children's contraction of "Madam Bet," the name by which people respectfully addressed her. Courtesy, Massachusetts Historical Society

experienced a relative decline in their economic standing. Bakers, who were among the wealthiest of the town's artisans, had an average assessed wealth of 170 pounds in 1790; barbers were assessed at 65 pounds; and shoemakers averaged 45 pounds. By contrast Boston merchants averaged 1,707 pounds per person. In other words the average merchant was 10 times as wealthy as the average baker, 27 times richer than the barbers, and 37 times wealthier than Boston's average shoemaker. A growing awareness of the economic differences caused the committee organizing a parade honoring President George Washington in 1789 to insist that the artisans march in alphabetical order and not according to wealth or status. Government officials, professionals, and merchants led the triumphal procession through the center of town and thousands of Bostonians cheered as Washington, mounted on an elegant white charger, passed under a huge arch erected in front of the Old State House.

Washington's parade route took him through the richest area of Boston, along State and Cornhill streets. The Massachusetts Bank, the market, professional offices, and various retail shops were located there. Unlike those in the rest of the town, most of the buildings in the center were built of brick. The richest merchants and professional men and almost half the retailers lived here. Generally the further away from State Street a Bostonian lived, the lower his income tended to be.

The South End was mixed, though more than half of the people living in this section had an average assessed worth of 25 pounds or less. Large numbers of leather workers and about a third of Boston's masons, carpenters, and painters lived there. The West End was still sparsely settled in 1790. Some wealthy merchants resided in this section, but so too did most of the town's rope-workers and nearly all of Boston's black people (about 800). The poorest section of town was the North End. More than half of the people living in the two wards furthest from the center of the town owned no taxable property. Heavily populated by workers, retailers, and sailors who made their living from the sea, the North End grew much more slowly than Boston's other neighborhoods.

Those men and women who were the poorest and least successful often moved out of Boston. There was a floating population at the bottom of society, men who wandered from seaport to seaport looking for work or went to a rural town hoping to live more cheaply. Poor, often unhealthy, and without prospects, they were unwanted. The overseer of the poor in Braintree demanded in 1804 that Boston "remove Stephen Randal belonging to your town. He has been wandering about from place to place," explained the official, before he came to the point—the cost. "About four weeks ago he froze himself very bad in the feet and is at the expense of two dollars and 50 cents per week."

Despite this troubling picture the belief persisted—at least among the wealthier classes—that upward mobility was common. It was possible. A number of Boston's workers improved their relative economic standing during the decades after 1780. Nearly 20 percent of the original members of the Mechanics Association founded in 1795 and open only to master craftsmen, were not on the 1790 tax list. They had either been apprentices or had moved into Boston since that time. Likewise 71 percent of those men owning no property in 1780 who remained in Boston became property owners. Still it was not true, as a local newspaper commented, that "Men succeed or fail...not from accident or external surroundings, but from possessing or wanting the elements of success in themselves." The most obvious exception to this belief was black people.

Blacks had lived in Boston since 1638. They had come as "perpetual servants," slaves to wealthy white merchant families. Gradually slaves in Boston acquired a special status. They had the right to own property, to be tried, and to sue in the courts. Yet they were not free. The

POEMS ON VARIOUS SUBJECTS, RELIGIOUS AND MORAL. BY PHILLIS WHEATLEY, NEGRO SERVANT to Mr. JOHN WHEATLEY, of BOSTON, in NEW ENGLAND.

LONDON: Printed for A. BELL, Bookseller, Aldgate; and sold by Messrs. COX and BERRY, King-Street, BOSTON. MDCCLXXIII.

Published according to Act of Parliament, Sept.¹ 1. 1773 by Arch.ᵈ Bell, Bookseller N.º 8 near the Saracens Head Aldgate.

Revolution, however, forced Bostonians to confront the issue. The irony of owning slaves while at the same time waging a struggle for freedom from Great Britain became too obvious to ignore. James Otis identified the basic problem in 1764. If according to natural law all people were born free and equal, argued Otis, that meant *all* people, black and white. "Does it follow that 'tis right to enslave a man because he is black?" Otis asked. The same theme was voiced by Boston's black community. A petition was sent to the Massachusetts legislature in 1777, asserting that "in common with all other men," black people had "a natural and inalienable right" to freedom. The legislature responded negatively. But, led by Prince Hall, black Bostonians persisted in their campaign for freedom. Finally in 1783 the Massachusetts courts determined that the clause in the new state constitution declaring "all men are born free and equal, and have certain natural, essential, and unalienable rights" had abolished slavery in the state.

The abolition of slavery, however, did not initiate a trend toward racial equality in Boston. Laws discriminated against free blacks as they had against slaves. Therefore blacks developed their own

Phillis Wheatley was the first published black poet in America. A slave of John Wheatley, whose children taught her to read and write, Phillis began composing poetry before the age of 16 and her work was published in London before the Revolution. (TBS)

The African Meeting House, built in 1806, is the oldest church building still standing in the United States built by black laborers for a black congregation. Located on Beacon Hill, this was the site of the founding meeting of the New England Anti-Slavery Society of William Lloyd Garrison. Courtesy, Society for the Preservation of New England Antiquities (SPNEA)

separate institutions. In 1787 Prince Hall organized the first black masonic lodge in America (African Lodge No. 459); the following year Primus Hall founded a school for black children that met in his home on Beacon Hill; and in 1806 the African Meeting House was built. The successful establishment of these community institutions helped black Bostonians to survive. If they were to prosper, blacks realized they would have to rely on their own efforts rather than the good will of their white neighbors.

Women learned the same lesson. Boston's most famous 18th-century woman, Abigail Adams, prodded John to "Remember the Ladies." She wrote to him on March 31, 1776. "All men would be tyrants if they could," she instructed her husband. "If particular care and attention is not paid to the Ladies we are determined to foment a Rebelion, and will not hold ourselves bound by any Laws in which we have no voice, or Representation."

John Adams didn't take Abigail's

argument seriously. "As to your extraordinary Code of Laws, I cannot but Laugh," he replied two weeks later. But John was worried. He knew—feared—that the revolution he and his colleagues were planning could not easily be limited. "Our struggle has loosened the bonds of Government every where," he noted anxiously. John insisted, however, that women had no reason to complain. "In practice you know We are subjects. We have only the Name of Masters, and rather than give up this, which would completely subject Us to the Despotism of the Petticoat, I hope General Washington and all our brave Heroes would fight."

Abigail did not press for female suffrage, but some of the social bonds that had restricted women's freedom before 1776 were loosened somewhat after American independence was won. The traditional view of marriage, for example, had stressed the subordination of wife to husband. Like their sisters elsewhere, Boston women had expanded their responsibilities during the Revolution, single-handedly managing shops and businesses during their husbands' absences. Women also were involved in boycotts of English goods, in patriotic processions, and, according to one British army officer, "surpassed the Men for Eagerness and Spirit in the Defense of Liberty." One consequence of women's activity during the war was the emergence of a new—republican— definition of marriage. Judith Sargent Murray, who wrote a column published in a Boston magazine, emphasized mutuality as the only acceptable basis for marriage. "Mutual esteem, mutual friendship, mutual confidence, *begirt about by mutual forbearance,"* was how Ms. Murray described the ideal "matri- monial career."

Dissatisfied wives were less willing to remain in unhappy marriages than they had been previously. Divorce petitions in Massachusetts increased sharply after the Revolution. And more wives than husbands sued for divorce, though a greater percentage of men succeeded in gaining favorable action on their petitions.

The reasons for initiating divorce proceedings were varied, of course, but the bulk of the petitions filed in Boston—84 percent of the husbands' and 59 percent of the wives'—included the charge of adultery. These statistics reveal a profound change in social attitude, for only since the 1780s had the law allowed divorce for adultery by either partner.

Official acceptance of male adultery as grounds for a divorce was in part a result of women's willingness to challenge the sexual double standard. In her "Sentiments on Libertinism," published in the *Boston Magazine* in 1784, "Daphne" argued that it was unfair that a single mistake would "forever deprive women of all that renders life valuable," while at the same time "the base betrayer is suffered to triumph in the success of his unmanly arts, and to pass unpunished even by a frown." Equalizing the legal consequences of adultery did not bring about the sexual equality for which "Daphne" called. But the new law did signal to women *and* men that they were

expected to behave like virtuous citizens in both public and private life.

If the young republic was to fulfill its promises, then virtuous families must adhere to strict moral standards. This new attitude had enormous and immediate implications for the status of women. Because the home was perceived as the source of virtue and stability in government, women came to be regarded as the most influential parent. Educated in the principles of republicanism, mothers were chiefly responsible for instructing their children—especially their sons—in the joys of liberty and the benefits of order. Miss P.W. Jackson, a graduating student from Susanna Rowson's Young Ladies Academy, told the *Boston Weekly Magazine* what she had learned. "A woman who is skilled in every useful art, who practices every domestic virtue," she explained in 1803, "may, by her precept and example, inspire her brothers, her husband, or her sons, with such a love of virtue, such just ideas of the true value of civil liberty. . .that future heroes and

Aqueducts were built to Lake Cochituate when the water supply from Jamaica Plain became inadequate. A great celebration was held when the first water from the new system poured into the Frog Pond in the Boston Common. Bells rang and cannons fired, and an evening fireworks display topped the festivities. (SPNEA)

The Tontine Crescent, designed by Charles Bulfinch in 1793, was a unique building of 16 connected brick houses which curved around a courtyard. The Massachusetts Historical Society and the Boston Public Library were among the occupants before the building was razed in 1858. Courtesy, Mack Lee

statesmen, who arrive at the summit of military or political fame, shall *exaltingly declare, it is to my mother I owe this elevation.*"

Bostonians were very comfortable with the ideology of republicanism. Its demands and promises were well suited to men and women long committed to building a model city. If, however, the ideals were familiar, there was abundant evidence by the early 1800s of a new economic and cultural spirit, of a new Boston.

The town grew dramatically in size and area during the early decades of the 19th century. In 1790 the population of Boston was 18,000; by 1800 it had risen to 25,000; and by 1822 it had jumped to 49,000—an increase of 250% in just 32 years. While the center of the city was still relatively densely populated, people had been gradually moving into the West and South ends. "Where the population was thin," noted a Salem minister, "and there were fields and marshes, are now splendid houses and crowded Streets." Moreover these new neighborhoods were soon linked by bridges to Cambridge and South Boston. The Charles River Bridge (opened with great hoopla on June 17,

1786, the 11th anniversary of the Battle of Bunker Hill) was the first of four bridges built by 1810—that effectively ended Boston's isolation.

A young student traveling in Europe heard the news about the Charles River Bridge with great enthusiasm. Charles Bulfinch, son of Dr. Thomas Bulfinch and a recent Harvard graduate, hoped that when he returned to Boston from his grand tour he would have an opportunity to pursue his "taste for architecture." As it turned out Bulfinch's chosen career was suited perfectly to Boston's needs. He transformed the face of Boston. From 1787 when he submitted plans for the new State House to 1816 when he left Boston to become architect of the capitol, Bulfinch designed a score of mansions, rowhouses, and public buildings. Using a warm, red brick and local granite, his designs reflected the town's love affair with republicanism. Bulfinch pointed the way toward a distinctively American architecture, characterized by economy, symmetry, utility, and simplicity.

A committee of the Boston Town Meeting, headed by Harrison Gray Otis, chose Beacon Hill as the site for the new State House that Bulfinch was hired to design. Understated and beautifully proportioned, his design blended tall windows with inset arches, delicate wooden cornices and balustrades with classical columns. Paul Revere, whose copper sheeting lined the dome, hailed the brick Acropolis as a "safe and secure abode" for liberty.

By the time the State House was completed in 1798, Beacon Hill was well on the way to becoming a handsome residential neighborhood. A group of investors called the Mount Vernon Proprietors initiated the development by purchasing the property adjoining the capitol owned by John Singleton Copley, the self-exiled American painter. Streets were laid out and about 60 feet sheared off the top of Mount Vernon to create space for mansions and block houses. In 1800 Bulfinch designed a large, elegant house for Harrison Gray Otis on the crest of the hill, and a few years later he built a row of four-story brick houses on Park Street. The beauty of this new area was further enhanced when Bullfinch constructed his Colonnade Row, a series of 19 houses stretching along Tremont Street across from the tree-lined mall and the Common.

During this same period Bulfinch also designed a variety of public buildings. In 1799 he donated to Fr. Cheverus, the first Catholic Bishop of Boston, the plans for the Cathedral of the Holy Cross. Faneuil Hall was enlarged in 1806 by Bulfinch's skilled hand and 10 years later, on the eve of his departure for Washington, D.C., he created the superb granite building of the Massachusetts General Hospital.

In addition to the development of a residential area on Beacon Hill, a number of large, opulent houses were built in the South End during this same building boom. Several were bought by a new,

Left: "Beacon Hill" was symbolic and actual. The Puritans wanted their community to be a beacon to others, symbolizing their special relationship with God. At the same time, they built a beacon as a lookout on Boston's highest point of land. When winds blew the beacon down in 1789, Charles Bulfinch designed this brick monument in memory of those killed at the Battle of Bunker Hill. The monument still stands in a parking lot behind the State House. (TBS)

Below: This unusual house was built in 1796 by Charles Bulfinch as the summer home of the James Swan family. (TBS)

This was the original Massachusetts General Hospital designed by Charles Bulfinch. Construction began in 1816 and the hospital was the site of the first operation performed under ether in 1846. The domed operating room is incorporated into the present MGH complex. From History of Boston, *by Caleb Snow, 1825. (SPNEA)*

distinct class of merchant princes, many of whom were emigres from Essex County—the Lowells, the Higginsons, the Jacksons, the Lees, and the Cabots. This group, along with Thomas Russell, James and Thomas Handasyd Perkins, and Josiah Bradlee, formed a kind of extended family, a kinship group second to none in New England. Their wealth was linked to the development of new trade routes. By 1792 these daring, ambitious Boston merchants had established the Boston-Northwest-Canton-Boston route, trading sea otter skins for silks, chinaware, and tea to be sold either in Boston or abroad.

They sailed from Boston in the autumn, aiming to clear Cape Horn during the Antarctic summer. Still "the passage around Cape Horn," wrote one Boston ship captain, "is the most dangerous, most difficult, and attended with more hardships, than that of the same distance in any other part of the world." With luck these courageous Yankee seamen reached the Pacific Northwest by spring. Once there the Boston Nor'westmen moved along the rugged coast from one Indian village to another, bartering a myriad of goods—trinkets, chisels, molasses, tin kettles, old keys, *anything*—for the glossy, jet-black sea otter skins that the Indians had collected.

It was a dangerous business. In 1803, for example, the Indians near Nootka

Sound attacked the Amory's ship *Boston* and massacred all but two crew members. Several years later, the Winship brothers of Brighton were forced by the fierce Chinook Indians to give up their hope of establishing a permanent settlement in Oregon. If there was no major trouble, it generally took about two years to gather enough skins to set sail for Canton, the next leg of the long voyage.

China was the only market for sea otter skins and Canton was the only port in which Boston traders were permitted to do business. Here, too, negotiations had to be carefully conducted. All of the commissions, presents, and bribes had to be freely given and all the intricate diplomatic maneuvers knowledgeably followed. It was a challenge to which Yankee traders such as John Perkins Cushing (J. and T.H. Perkins' man in Canton for 30 years) responded adroitly and incredibly successfully. When the skins were sold, traders bought tea, porcelain, and silk. With hard bargaining and a bit of luck, it was not uncommon for a Boston entrepreneur to net $100,000 on a single China voyage. (By comparison the average wealth of all residents in the North End was $523 per capita.)

Many of the Boston-China merchants spent money lavishly, chasing an opulent lifestyle. At the same time some used the trade to accumulate capital and later invested it in the development of the new textile industry. One way or the other, an enormous amount of money was pumped into the New England economy by the China trade. The siren song of luxury, feared in the abstract three decades earlier by the old republicans, had become by 1820 a very real problem.

For Bostonians the issue of luxury became a hotly disputed public debate when a Tea Assembly was established. Meeting every other week at Concert Hall for dancing and card playing, this Sans Souci ("Free and Easy") Club, as it was called, was founded by a young, well-to-do group of men and women eager for some "innocent amusement." But its critics, whose attacks on the club filled the pages of the Boston *Centinel* and the *Independent Chronicle,* saw nothing funny or innocent about it. For the issue at stake seemed to the old republicans to be nothing less than the kind of society Boston was creating.

One writer, identified as "The Observer," began the debate by stating the old republican maxim: "Luxury is fatal to a free nation." To the end of his life, John Adams adhered to the same sentiment. Despite his desire to surpass Europe in the cultivation of the arts, Adams was convinced "that the more elegance, the less virtue, in all times and countries." Buildings, mansions, music, painting, and dancing, were simply "bagatelles introduced by time and luxury in change for the great qualities and hardy, manly virtues of the human heart," concluded the old patriot.

The Tea Assembly's defenders rejected the old republicans' arguments. First "A Bostonian" and the Sans Souci Club asserted that their young friends possessed "as great heroic manliness and bravery of soul at this moment as could be claimed at any period." Second the youngsters raised the specter of individualism: everyone had the right to spend some part of their earnings for amusement. Finally "One of a Number" reminded the old republicans of Boston's recent, prosperous history and its consequences. "If you wish to separate commerce from luxury," he told them, "you expect an impossibility."

In many ways the tempest over the Tea Assembly was a tepid version of the statewide and national struggles that contorted Boston politics during the period from 1780 to 1822. From the adoption of the new state constitution through the War of 1812, Boston's political leaders were curiously anxious. From most Americans' point of view, the young republic was a glorious success. But Boston's elite—the Otis's, the Lowell's, and the Cabot's—became disillusioned and increasingly despaired of the possibilities of shaping the character of the American people in the way *they* believed necessary.

Thus until the collapse of the Federalist party and the rise of a new generation of reformers in the 1820s, Boston came to symbolize the dark, provincial side of American politics rather than the bright, national side.

The Massachusetts constitution of 1780 was chiefly the work of John Adams, though James Bowdoin and Sam Adams also were named to the drafting committee by the convention. In Adams' famous phrase the constitution sought to create a government of laws, not of men. It struck a balance between the powers of the legislature and those of the governor, and between the interests of property and those of the people. This old-fashioned notion Adams blended with the radical idea that since the people were sovereign, all governmental institutions were merely different kinds of representations of the people. The governor, therefore, was not an elected monarch but, as the convention declared, "emphatically the Representative of the whole People, being chosen not by one town or country, but by the People at large."

The general frame eventually met the approval of the people of Massachusetts who assembled in town meetings in the spring of 1780 to debate and to decide if they would recommend that the convention ratify the constitution. The Boston Town Meeting—887 voters strong at its peak—met for three days. The chief obstacle to quick approval was Article III of the Declaration of Rights that proclaimed the right and duty of the state to support the teaching of "piety, religion and morality" on the grounds that these virtues were necessary for "the happiness of a people and the good order and preservation of civil government." A majority of Bostonians supported the principle forwarded by Article III, but many people wanted to "Secure the Rights of Conscience and to give the fullest Scope to religious Liberty." Someone suggested that if a citizen could not in conscience support "any of the various denominations among us they may then allot their Money to the support of

Dorothy Quincy married John Hancock and shared in the toil and privation of the Revolutionary War. Living near the State House after 1780, the couple entertained often and, when Admiral d'Estaing was invited to breakfast and requested that his 300 officers join him, Dolly Hancock sent servants to milk all the cows on the Common saying that she would personally deal with anyone who complained. No one did. (TBS)

the Poor." But that motion, as well as other proposed compromises, failed.

The key argument for the article was made by "Hieronymus" in the Boston *Gazette*. He maintained that it did not invade the right of conscience because no one was forced to believe anything. And "Hieronymus" concluded by pointing out that Article III would take effect only if a majority approved. When the question finally was put, the town meeting voted "almost unanimously" in favor of Article III.

Eight years later Bostonians were among those who met in convention to consider the new federal constitution. Heavy taxes, an unsure commercial future, and a violent uprising in western Massachusetts convinced a large majority of Bostonians from every social class that hope for prosperity and order lay with the new instrument of national government. John Hancock and Sam Adams initially were hesitant; but when a mass meeting of mechanics, chaired by Paul Revere, overwhelmingly declared themselves in favor, the old patriots joined the ranks of the constitution's supporters.

Even with their support ratification won by only a narrow margin. The divisions, however, were quickly healed. Before the convention broke up Hancock's newly adopted Federalism was being celebrated in song:

The Squire Hancock like a man
Who dearly loves the nation,
By a conciliatory plan,
Prevented much vexation.
Yankee doodle. . .

The Federalists' euphoria lasted but for 12 years. During those halcyon days Bostonians were prominent and powerful figures in the new government. But changes were taking place over which the old elite had no control. In 1800 Thomas Jefferson and his democratic supporters defeated John Adams and the Federalists. To the Boston oligarchy Jefferson was the "devil incarnate." Although younger Federalists such as Harrison Gray Otis and Josiah Quincy learned the tricks of courting the votes of the people and emphasized to the "happy and respectable classes" their responsibility to preserve order, they were fighting a rear-guard action and they knew it.

The Boston Federalists' most foolish and bitter gesture against the direction of national politics was their opposition to the War of 1812, "Mr. Madison's War." Every effort by Jefferson to prevent a conflict with Great Britain was vigorously denounced. In 1809 the Boston Town Meeting sent a petition to the Massachusetts legislature claiming that the president's policies were nothing but a "War in disguise"; in 1811 a huge meeting at Faneuil Hall decried the law stopping trade with Britain as "unjust, tyrannical and oppressive"; and late in 1814 the Boston *Gazette* declared that "on or before the 4th of July, if James Madison is not out of office, a new form of government will be in operation in the eastern section of the union."

The Republicans, meanwhile, announced their determination to win the war. They saw it as a test of the experiment in free government. Therefore although Americans

gained nothing tangible from the war, it was widely regarded as a great success. The Federalists were completely discredited and the national party passed into obscurity.

Within Boston, however, the Federalists began to campaign to change the system of government from a town to a city so that they might continue to exercise political control in their own back yard. The town meeting was a disorderly forum that was not capable of meeting the demands of a growing urban center, the elite argued. The Federalists proposed, therefore, that Boston be incorporated as a city, to be governed by a mayor and a common council elected at large.

Following an emotional and sometimes bitter series of debates, the vote in favor of incorporation passed on January 7, 1822. Shortly thereafter Governor John Brooks officially approved "an act establishing the City of Boston." The new charter called for a mayor, 8 aldermen, and 48 councillors elected by wards. A motto from the book of Kings was selected for the city's seal: *Sit Deus nobiscus sicut fuit cum patribus nostris*

("May God be with us as he was with our fathers").

When George Robert Twelves Hewes returned to Boston in 1821 after an absence of nearly 50 years, he was aghast. He had been born in the town and had been active as a young man in the stirring events leading to the Revolution. But the town he had known was gone:

The whole scenery about me seemed like the work of enchantment. Beacon Hill was leveled, and a pond on which stood three mills, was filled up with its contents; over which two spacious streets had been laid and many elegant fabrics erected. The whole street, from Boston Neck to the Long Wharf, had been built up. It was to me almost a new town, a strange city; I could hardly realize that I was in the place of my nativity.

Although the physical appearance of the city had changed, Hewes was pleased to observe that its ideals had not. Bostonians still were committed to the struggle to create a free, humane, and disciplined City on a Hill.

IV
Hub of the Universe

"The demon of reform" is loose in the land, Ralph Waldo Emerson excitedly announced in 1841. Bostonians were indeed busy reforming their society. Dozens of volunteer groups sprang up during the first half of the 19th century to reform the city's religious, political, and economic institutions and to perfect the individual. "Matters have come to such a pass," one observer grumbled, "that a peaceable man can hardly venture to eat or drink, or to go to bed or to get up, to correct his children or to kiss his wife, without obtaining the permission and direction of some. . .society."

As they had been in 1630, Boston's reformers were concerned both with building an integrated, harmonious community and with goading individuals to recognize their moral

responsibilities. They sought to influence the public mind in the interest of some large social transformation. "The reformer," argued one of Boston's most outspoken abolitionists, Wendell Phillips, "is careless of numbers, disregards popularity and deals only with ideas, conscience and common sense." Reformers also shared an unconquerable faith in moral progress.

Most of the men and women who wanted to change Boston during this period were optimistic, motivated by an "adoration of goodness" and a belief in the nobility of man. "We are in an age of improvement," gushed Edward Everett, a Boston-born, Harvard-educated reformer whose speeches sped thousands along the road toward a new society. A few reformers, however, insisted that the road to change should be straighter and narrower. They tended to support only those changes that would help to control the "dangerous classes of society."

Josiah Quincy, the second mayor of Boston, seemed an unlikely reformer however defined. His political career, before his election as mayor in 1823, was characterized by fruitless, vitriolic attacks on Jeffersonianism. By his own admission Quincy was thought of as "a raving Federalist," an "embarrassment" to his colleagues in the United States Congress. Yet during his six terms as mayor, Quincy initiated a series of reforms that substantially improved the quality of life in Boston for decades.

Quincy wanted nothing else from life than to be a politician. His family background, education, and wealth seemed to ensure him of a long and distinguished career in public service. But when he resigned his congressional seat in protest to the War of 1812 and returned to Boston, it looked as though his political life was over. He was bitter. Passed over by his own party for positions he wanted, Quincy adamantly and publicly refused to join in the "era of good feelings." He dabbled. At the Brighton Cattle Show of 1819 he sang the praises of farming and at the same time made money speculating

in urban real estate. Most of all Quincy brooded. "Time, now a days," he wrote a friend in 1820, "spins along without noise or apparent motion. . .Nothing to find fault with, and yet nothing to make [me] happy."

Finally at the age of 48, Quincy narrowly won election to the Massachusetts lower House, one of 15 representatives from Boston. The 1820 session of the legislature was the first in Massachusetts history to begin to cope with the problems of urbanization. In particular Governor John Brooks urged the house to address the growing problems of crime, poverty, and overcrowding at the Charlestown Prison and public welfare.

Quincy responded enthusiastically. He conducted an investigation of the pauper laws, and in 1821 he issued a report that clearly demonstrated the scope and consequences of the problem. He called for an end to direct relief to the poor. Of all methods for aiding the needy, Quincy declared, "the most wasteful, the most expensive, and most injurious to their morals, and destructive of their industrious habits, is that of supply in their own families." He advocated instead institutionalizing the poor, removing them from the temptations in their communities, and rehabilitating them by insisting that anyone who received public funds be taught the lesson of hard labor.

Quincy's report broke with the past. He began by asserting that the civic ties that had transcended class lines and bound communities together in the past were no longer as powerful. Therefore another more realistic approach was needed. While the Quincy report flirted with the idea of abolishing all poor laws and either casting individuals on their own, or throwing them to the mercy of private charitable organizations, it finally was decided that such a strategy would be "inconsistent with a humane, liberal and enlightened policy." The poor, in other words, were acknowledged to be a social problem and therefore a proper object of community reform.

Order and regularity, together with hard work within the institution, would bring the "hope of amendment to the vicious and assistance to the poor." Such a regimen, Quincy claimed, would correct rather than confirm habits of idleness. Inmates of a workhouse would learn "constancy and diligence" and "to obey and respect" in a setting that gave the highest priority to "reformation." The lives of the poor would then be "more comfortable and happy," Quincy predicted.

The report established Quincy as the state's leading authority on poverty and welfare. Not surprisingly, therefore, in May 1821 the Boston selectmen asked Quincy to study the feasibility of establishing an almshouse, where the "honest poor" would be put to work. Early in 1822 the city accepted Quincy's recommendation and a House of Industry was built in South Boston. The design reflected the new philosophy toward the poor. Rather than resembling a large house as had its predecessor, Boston's House of Industry had a rigid, massive,

institutional appearance. At its center was an administrative building, where the keeper and his family lived, with two long wings radiating out from each side—one for men, the other for women.

Before construction of Boston's newest poorhouse was completed, Quincy had become a municipal judge. His interest in poverty, it seems, had led him to study crime. It was not a prestigious position, but he had "the most honorable intentions . . .and the ability to be useful," according to one of his friends, William Sullivan. The same flattering assessment was made subsequently by many others during Boston's first mayoral campaign.

Harrison Gray Otis thought he was going to be the city's first mayor. His friends in the Federalist party told him that he had the backing of "Webster, Lowell, Tudor, all the judges and those whom I know you feel a high respect for." To their astonishment, however, Quincy entered the race, the candidate of the so-called "Middling Interest," shopkeepers and artisans. "A man of forty is a fool to wonder at anything," snorted Daniel

This Staffordshire platter by Ralph Stevenson displays the almshouse on Leverett Street. When it was built in 1800, the almshouse was considered to be the most modern method of housing and caring for the poor. Mayor Josiah Quincy later criticized it by saying it did "not comport with the honor and interest of the town." In 1822 the city built a new House of Industry in South Boston and the almshouse was closed. Photograph by Richard Merrill. (TBS)

Scrimshaw is the art of carving on whalebone and whale ivory. It was popular in 19th century Boston as a result of the large whaling industry in Boston and Salem. This six-inch tooth features a familiar household scene. Photograph by Richard Merrill. (TBS)

Webster, "and yet one is in danger of committing this folly when he sees Mr. Quincy the very darling of the Boston Democracy!"

Webster's elitism caused him to exaggerate. Boston's working-class voters refused to embrace Quincy. "His whole political life has rendered him obnoxious," one North End resident explained. The result was that neither Quincy nor Otis won a majority and both men withdrew before the run off. The voters, therefore, settled on John Phillips, described by contemporaries as "disinterested, considerate and candid." His administration was brief. Halfway through the year he fell ill and announced he would not stand for reelection. Quincy won the nomination and easily defeated his Republican opponent.

Quincy's enthusiasm and energy suddenly seemed boundless. One hour after his inauguration on May 1, 1823, he called the city council into session and presented a plan for cleaning the city's streets. A couple of weeks later he appointed Benjamin Pollard, a young lawyer, to the newly created office of "marshal of the city." In addition to his duties as police officer, Pollard also was charged with maintaining public health.

Cleaning up Boston required a herculean effort. There was no effective system for cleaning the streets and "house dirt" and "street dirt" went uncollected for long periods of time; the city's sewage emptied out into Town Dock right behind the market; and the odor of "noxious effluvia," as Quincy delicately termed it, permeated the center of the city. Within a remarkably short time, however, the mayor and his marshal accomplished what the old town Board of Health had failed for generations to do. The streets were cleaned by teams of sweepers, the refuse collected on a regular basis, and the sewers brought under public control. By the end of his first year in office, 6,000 tons of street dirt had been collected. Boston had become, under Quincy's guidance, one of the healthiest and cleanest cities in America.

The crowded, old market district was the next object of Quincy's vigorous urban reformation project. Since its construction in 1742, Faneuil Hall had been used as a meeting place and a public market. Although it was expanded in 1804 by Charles Bullfinch, by 1820 it was again hopelessly inadequate. On market days the streets around the hall were jammed with carts and there were not nearly enough stalls available for vendors. Quincy proposed that a new market be built, along with a docking facility and several new access streets. Although he

This map of Quincy Market shows changes that were made for this early landfill and urban renewal project. Several streets and buildings were removed and the shoreline was changed to create a broad expanse of land for the new complex (indicated by the shaded area). (TBS)

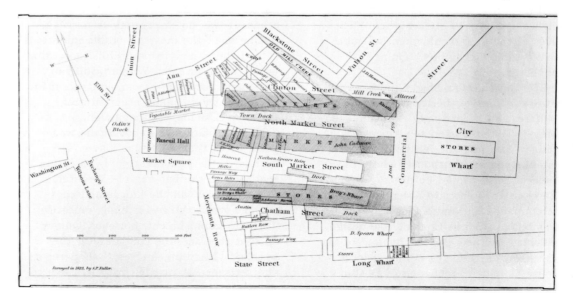

ran into opposition from some members of the council who were alarmed that the city's taxpayers were to assume the cost of his "mammoth project," the mayor won a public referendum approving the expansion.

The cornerstone for Quincy's new market was laid on April 22, 1825, a little over two years after he had become mayor. "Quincy Market," as it immediately came to be called, was a two-story, classically styled granite building, more than 500 feet long with a copper-sheathed dome in the center. In addition to the market building, six new approach streets and a new wharf were constructed. Completed in 1826, the new market complex transformed the city's center. Bostonians swelled with pride. "Boston has long enjoyed the reputation of a neat city," boasted the Boston *News-Letter,* "it bids fair indeed to gain the additional reputation of being a handsome one."

Mayor Quincy was eager to do far more than change the face of Boston. He wanted to restore the community's organic unity, to make the people of Boston "happy, secure and contented" and aware of "the advantage of a vigorous and faithful administration." One important step toward achieving these goals, according to Quincy, was to reduce crime in the city. His principal concern was protecting society. He had little sympathy for the "vicious poor" or the "hardened criminal," nor was he interested in the debate over how best to rehabilitate criminals. Quincy believed that crime was an inevitable feature of a modern, urban society. The Boston Prison Discipline Society, founded in 1825 by Louis Dwight and Samuel Gridley Howe, tried in vain to convince the mayor that with the proper prison system criminals would be reformed. Howe advocated isolation: "left in total solitude, separated from evil society. . .the progress of corruption is arrested," he argued. The mayor remained unconvinced, but he did agree that the

From the moment Faneuil Hall Market opened in 1826, people called it Quincy Market, in honor of "The Great Mayor," Josiah Quincy, who built the project to serve as Boston's central marketplace. Quincy Market today is the focus of major waterfront restoration efforts, and its specialty shops host thousands of visitors annually. (TBS)

Joy's Building was an early shopping center located on Washington near State Street. Built on the site of Boston's First Church, the building had a circular staircase surrounded by over 40 stores and offices. This lithograph suggests the variety of businesses located in the building and the ways in which they advertised. (BPL)

old Leverett Street jail was grossly inadequate and, therefore, pushed through major improvements.

Howe did succeed in demonstrating to the mayor the need for a separate facility for juvenile offenders. Rather than commit youngsters to the state prisons ("those well-endowed seminaries of crime"), Quincy came to believe that they ought to be segregated from adult criminals and given special attention aimed at making them useful citizens. Completed in 1828, the House of Reformation for Juvenile Offenders in South Boston operated on the basis of a strict regime designed to instill order and method into the boys' lives. For example the youngsters were forbidden to talk to one another as they went about their assigned work; periodically all of the boys were brought together in the gymnasium, where, standing at rigid attention, they were required to shout in unison answers to questions from the superintendent; and they were required to attend chapel each day to listen to a sermon about the benefits of "habits of submission, self-denial and benevolence."

The quasi-military doctrine of the House of Reformation did not guarantee success in the long run. By the 1850s the

city's well-intentioned attempt to rehabilitate delinquent children had lost its special purpose. Moral reform gave way to custodial care, the work ethic to enforced idleness, and young immigrants—Irish Catholics for the most part—accounted for a disproportionate share of the residents compared to their numbers in the general population of Boston.

Mayor Quincy's conservative approach to reform, manifested by his skepticism about the possibilities of rehabilitating criminals, also was demonstrated by his handling of the controversy over education for girls. Compared with other American cities in the 1820s, Boston had an outstanding public school system. More than 7,000 students were enrolled in the city's 72 schools, including a high school for girls. Quincy's commitment to public education in general was not very deep, and by 1826 he was on record as opposing the girls' high school. Although the school was popular and, according to an investigation carried out by the school committee, successful, Quincy charged that the school was "undemocratic" because it admitted girls only by exam (as did the boys' high schools) and was too costly. Resistance by some school committeemen collapsed and in June 1828 the Girls' High School closed its doors. It would be 33 years before the city reconsidered Quincy's judgment that Boston could not "provide fit wives for well-educated men" at public expense.

Well before that time, however, Quincy had been turned out of office. The headmaster of the girls' school publicly attacked Quincy charging him with bias and dishonesty. Others objected to the mayor's autocratic manner and his elitism. On the eve of the election in December 1828 the Jacksonians issued a circular quoting the mayor as stating that if the Girls' High School were allowed to continue "the education of our servant girls will be equal to that of our daughters, and perhaps enable them to force connections with our sons!" Quincy said nothing in his defense and Harrison

Gray Otis became Boston's third mayor.

The democratic upsurge among Boston voters that helped defeat Quincy was part of a national Jacksonian movement. But there were local roots as well. The old Puritan view of the depravity of man and the struggle for salvation that had dominated the Boston mind for nearly two centuries gave way in the early 19th century to a new, optimistic spirit. Without questioning either the existence of God or the authority of the Bible, Unitarians emphasized the goodness of God and the perfectibility of man. They argued that reason was able to clarify Christianity. Unitarianism easily captured the middle and upper classes of Boston. Nearly all the important Congregational pulpits were taken over by Unitarian preachers: Nathaniel Frothingham was at the First Church; Henry Ware Hollis, Professor of Divinity at Harvard, was called to the Second Church; Francis Parkman led the congregation at the New North; and William Ellery Channing, the founder of Unitarianism, spread his gospel of the "adoration of goodness" at the Federal Street Church.

Unitarianism relied on character—defined as the process of understanding, accepting, and acting on moral truths—to bring about social harmony. Creating a moral society was as important to Unitarians as achieving personal salvation. Therefore although Unitarians did not zealously seek converts they did actively engage in various reform programs. Joseph Tuckerman, for example, left his comfortable church in Chelsea in 1826 to become the first Unitarian minister at large to the poor of Boston. He used books, sermons, home visits, and voluntary associations to adapt religion to a society in which life no longer centered on the church. The primary objective of Tuckerman's efforts was the moral improvement of the working class by personal contact with exemplary Christians. Training sessions for middle-class volunteers were held each week at Channing's Federal Street Church. Self-improvement, an "awakening of a deeper concern" for the poor, also was crucial to Unitarianism's campaign for social justice.

Orestes Brownson, a member of Boston's Transcendental Club, rejected Channing's easy solution to the problem of class conflict. In 1836 Brownson organized a free church for workers called the Society for Christian Union and Progress and preached a doctrine that made Christianity a weapon of class struggle. Most of the men and women who participated in the small circle of Transcendentalism, were neither as Christian nor as radical as Brownson.

Ralph Waldo Emerson, the son of a Boston minister and the descendant of five generations of New England clergymen, began his career as a Unitarian but left the church a few years after he graduated from Harvard Divinity School. He rejected both rationalism and ritualism. In a series of brilliant essays, Emerson articulated the basis for Transcendentalism by emphasizing the virtues of individualism, self-reliance, and self-improvement. "Who so would be a man," he told his audience, "must be a non-conformist." To the youth of America he delivered the reassuring thought: "Trust thyself; every heart vibrates to that iron string." He castigated Bostonians for their single-minded pursuit of wealth and fame, for their obsession with material things. He called upon American scholars to look for ideas and inspiration in the familiar and natural sources of beauty right around them. "We walked this afternoon to...Walden Pond," Emerson recorded in his journal on April 9, 1842. "The world is so beautiful," he wrote half in pain, "that I can hardly believe it exists." Emerson and the Transcendentalists made the unity of nature and man their god.

As Emerson saw it the great peril that threatened the American people was not injustice but a fragmentation of the soul. "The reason why the world lacks unity and lies broken and in heaps," he told a Boston audience in 1837, "is because man is disunited with himself." We must

Brook Farm was a Transcendentalist community, established in 1841 in West Roxbury, near the present West Roxbury High School. Residents and supporters established an innovative school and participated in cooperative work ventures. Financial problems and a major fire in 1846 led to the closing of the farm. (SPNEA)

recover a sense of the whole. Still Emerson welcomed social heterogeneity, Boston as a melting pot. "The energy of Irish, Germans, Swedes, Poles, and Cossaks, and all the European tribes—and of the Africans, and of the Polynesians—will construct a new race, a new religion, a new state, a new literature, which will be as vigorous as the new Europe which came out of the smelting-pot of the Dark Ages," he predicted. It was this robust optimism born of a faith in the common person that made Emerson America's most popular philosopher in the 19th century. He offered something for everyone and thus nourished the ideal of an integrated, harmonious community to which Boston still aspired.

Emerson's critique of materialism and his call to idealistic unity awakened other reformers in the City on a Hill. Women entered a variety of reform movements, to pursue their self-interest as well as to improve their society. Mothers formed groups to discuss how best to raise children. Other women focused on

reforming formal education outside of the home. Moral reformers attacked the double standard of sexual morality and the victimization of prostitutes, exposed the state's dreadful treatment of the mentally ill, and joined in the abolition movement.

Women were entrusted with the morals and faith of the next generation. Local maternal associations and the child-rearing literature of the time were responses to the contemporary cultural and religious elevation of the mother's role. Ministers declared repeatedly that women's pious influence was not only appropriate to them but also important for society. "We look to you ladies," the Reverend Joseph Buckminister told a group of Boston women, "to raise the standard of character in our own sex; we look to you to guard and fortify those barriers, which still exist in society, against the encroachments of impudence and licentiousness."

The women who formed the Dorchester Maternal Association did so because they were "aware of our highly responsible

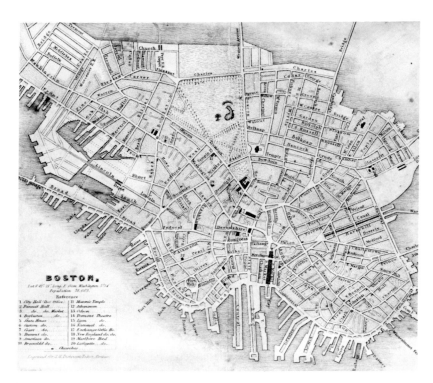

situation as Mothers and as professing Christians." The women considered it each member's duty to pray with her children and to read the appropriate, helpful books on child-rearing. One of the most widely read of the advice-to-parents books was Lydia Maria Child's *The Mother's Book*. Born in nearby Medford, Child settled in Boston in the 1820s, where her novels and advice books quickly established her in the city's intellectual and literary circles. She told mothers to train their children to respect authority. A combination of firmness and gentleness, she wrote, would cause children to obey without argument. Should a mother fail in this task, the most dire consequences would result. Another author of an advice book told the Mount Vernon Maternal Association of Boston that the mother of George Washington had said: "A good boy generally makes a good man. George was always a good boy."

Women who joined maternal associations were anxious to shape their children's lives while they were at home. Other Boston women and men joined together during the 1830s to see to it that children were educated properly while in school. But what constituted "proper" education was a matter of controversy that divided Boston's educational reformers.

Infant schools, for example, were hailed enthusiastically in 1829 by the Boston *Recorder*. If the children of the poor were placed in infant schools from the age of two years until age five years when the public school system would accept them, the *Recorder* predicted they would learn "at least a hundred times as much, a hundred times as well, and [would be] a hundred times as happy." A year earlier, prompted by William Russell, an educational reformer who came to Boston from Scotland, 90 women founded the Boston Infant School Society. They were committed to the idea that urban problems—crime, vice, and poverty—could be ameliorated by taking the children of the poor from their families and

inculcating them with the values of discipline and morality.

The Boston school establishment came out in opposition to the society's infant schools and its philosophy. Public school teachers reported that they found children from infant schools "intractable and troublesome." And school administrators publicly doubted the efficacy of the infant school's social mission. "Such is the power of a bad example—especially that of parents," one headmaster declared, "that it will probably do much to counteract the good influence of the infant school."

The final blow to the infant school movement in Boston was struck by Amariah Brigham. In 1833 he published a book called *Remarks on the Influence of Mental Cultivation and Mental Excitement upon Health* that was aimed directly at the theory underlying the infant school movement. Brigham's thesis was explicit: "Too early cultivating the mind and exciting the feelings of children" was one of the most important causes of insanity. The danger of the "hothouse effect" was publicized widely by the very journals that just three or four years earlier had embraced the social benefits of infant schools. Within months after the appearance of Brigham's book all of the infant schools had closed, reformers recoiling from the thought that their benevolence might be contributing to the

With Beacon Hill a residential district and the shoreline filled in, the Shawmut peninsula was getting crowded in 1837. Wharves covered the waterfront, and the only remaining large open space was the Common. (TBS)

mental instability of future generations.

Bronson Alcott was one of a number of young teachers who had been drawn to Boston by the infant school movement. Although the idea failed Alcott acquired a reputation among Boston's avant-garde as an educational Messiah, and in September 1834 he and Elizabeth Peabody launched the Temple School. Thirty boys and girls from some of Boston's leading families became participants in Alcott's revolutionary "love-oriented" educational experiment. By giving praise and affection as rewards, Alcott believed children would learn to behave conscientiously. He held lengthy conversations with his students, probing "the consciousness of the children" and encouraging them to tell the truth about their own feelings. This practice led him to conclude that children were a source of divine revelation, he explained in the preface of his book, *Conversations with Children on the Gospels.* Published in 1836, the book enraged influential Bostonians and resulted in the closing of the experimental school.

Alcott left Boston as he had come—a penniless idealist. Still, from the safety of Concord, Massachusetts, he rejoiced that he had been "saved" by his association with, and study of, children. Years later Alcott's daughter, Louisa May, used her family's trials and joys as the backdrop for her stunningly successful novel, *Little Women.* Within the confines of their home the fictional March family conducted a pilgrimage, defining as they went the solid values of Boston's middle class.

Most of Boston's reformers, however, doubted the competence of the city's poor and immigrant families to accomplish the goal of transferring society's all-important values of hard work, discipline, and morality to their children. Horace Mann was the most influential spokesman for a generation of school reformers who believed that the solution lay in the establishment of common schools, where rich and poor were educated side by side. Mann had come to Boston to practice law, but he soon found himself drawn to several reform groups. After a decade of work as an all-purpose reformer, however, Mann came to the uncomfortable conclusion that he had been wasting his time trying to reform men and women too far corrupted to be rehabilitated. Therefore in the mid-1830s he shifted his focus from the already-corrupted parents to their children, because, as he put it, "men are cast-iron; but children are wax."

In 1837 Mann was given the opportunity to put his ideas into effect. He became the first secretary to the Massachusetts Board of Education, a position from which he exercised personal leadership over the public schools for 12 years. And over the next generation scores of reformers emulated Mann, hailing him as the "Father of the American Public School."

Mann's initial success in Massachusetts was due in no small part to his connections with the wealthy and powerful. He appealed directly to their self-interest as businessmen whose profit margin depended on a stable, productive work force. After sending out questionnaires to prominent manufacturers, Mann published their conclusions on the "difference in the productive ability. . .between the educated and the uneducated." Not surprisingly the employers agreed with Mann that schooled workers were worth more than

Bronson Alcott, a Transcendentalist and an educator, opened an innovative school in Boston in 1834. Although recitation was the common teaching method of the day, Alcott's students wrote in journals and practiced "conversations" which gave them an opportunity to think about their reading and develop their own ideas. (TBS)

QUARTER CARD OF DISCIPLINE AND STUDIES IN MR. ALCOTT'S SCHOOL FOR THE WINTER TERM CURRENT 1837.

unschooled. The advantages, spelled out by Mann in his *Fifth Annual Report,* were manifested in the worker's character and habits. Workers who had been educated in a common school showed "docility and quickness in applying themselves to work"; "personal cleanliness"; "standing and respectability among co-laborers, neighbors and fellow citizens generally"; and "punctuality and fidelity in the performance of duties."

These characteristics also were applauded by Bostonians who professed to find an exact correlation between an increase in immigration and social instability. Samuel Bates, chairman of the Boston public school Visiting Committees, explained that "our Public School System is a branch of Government itself; as much so as are our courts, our police, criminal and charitable regulations for the poor." The chief aim of city government in establishing and maintaining schools, therefore, "is its own preservation."

In 1849 the Boston School Committee, composed almost entirely of supporters of Mann, proposed to make schooling compulsory for all children. The committeemen were alarmed about the number of Irish children who were loose in the streets, a condition the schoolmen took as positive proof that the parents were not exercising proper control. And the reformers claimed that when parents failed to do their job, the city had no choice but to intervene. "The parent is not the absolute owner of the child," the Boston School Committee declared in 1853. "The child is a member of the community [therefore] Government has the same right of control over the child, that it has over the parent. . .Those children should be brought within the jurisdiction of the Public Schools," the committee concluded, "from whom, through their vagrant habits, our property is most in danger."

Boston's Irish community knew why a mandatory school attendance law had been passed. The law was designed, stated an Irish newspaper, to destroy the "work of the Church, and of the Family," to

cause children to lose respect for their parents, their church, and their traditions as Irish. Although school reformers denied such a motivation, they were forced to admit by the 1850s that the city's overcrowded common schools had not broken the chains of poverty.

One supposed Irish tradition that Boston Protestants in particular attributed as the cause of poverty was drink. Ironically the Irish arrived in Boston at a time when the campaign against the evils of alcohol had achieved some success. Per capita consumption of liquor had climbed during the 1820s when the average adult American consumed about 37 gallons of spirits each year, then suddenly leveled off, and by 1840 began to plummet toward an unprecedented low.

Reformers, such as Dr. John Warren who founded the Massachusetts Society for the Suppression of Intemperance, saw themselves as carrying on the work of the Founding Fathers. Anti-liquor reformers asked Bostonians to sign pledges and celebrate their dry oaths on the 4th of July. The symbolism was explicit, as shown by the frequent references in the temperance literature to the struggle for independence. On one occasion a speaker declared that when future generations assembled to honor the Founding Fathers, they would be able to say, "On this day, also did our fathers, of a later generation,

The Quincy School opened in 1848 as an example of the best of modern schools. Its four stories housed 12 rooms (each seating 56 students) plus a 700-seat hall. There were separate rooms for each class and an individual desk for each scholar. (TBS)

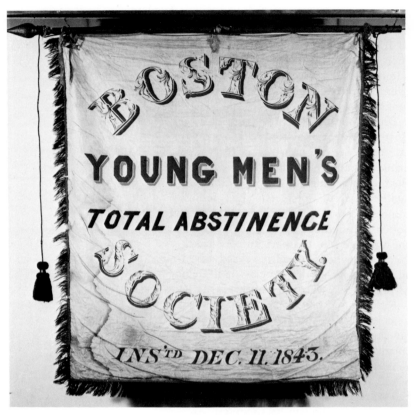

Like other temperance groups, the Young Men's Total Abstinence Society was active in local politics. They educated young men about the dangers of drink in an effort to persuade them to take the pledge of abstinence. Temperance reformers often went on to support other reform groups, many of which optimistically set about improving conditions for Bostonians in the 1840s. (TBS)

declare and maintain a SECOND INDEPENDENCE. . .from Prince Alcohol."

Even though consumption of alcohol was declining, opposition to the temperance movement spurred by the presence of an increasing number of Irish, did not weaken. In order to make liquor less readily available, Massachusetts outlawed the retail sale of distilled spirits in 1838. The law had two unintended effects: first, it clearly demonstrated the Yankee's lack of understanding or sympathy for the cultural alienation and impoverishment that often led the Irish to drink excessively; second, because the new law made mere possession of small quantities of liquor a crime rather than punishing public drunkenness as had the old laws, there were far more clashes between the police and the poor, including the Irish, after 1838.

In addition to a cultural bias, temperance advocates were driven by a belief that alcoholism led to the destruction of the family or to the degradation of young men and women, especially those who lived in the city. For this reason women's moral reform societies saw an explicit link between alcoholism and male licentiousness and prostitution. Therefore there was a considerable overlap of membership among temperance societies and those groups aimed at eliminating the sin of licentiousness and upholding chastity.

The Boston Female Moral Reform Society had two immediate goals: to reform "fallen" women and to publicize and ostracize men who visited prostitutes. The society's literature expressed the women's rage. "Our mothers, our sisters, our daughters are sacrificed by the thousands every year on the altar of sin," declared the *Advocate of Moral Reform* in 1835, "and who are the agents of this destruction? Why, our fathers, our brothers, and our sons." These Boston women were not accepting the double standard; they urged virtuous men and women to "esteem the licentious man as little as they do the licentious woman." The Moral Reform Society also raised the specter of revenge. Women who had become prostitutes were described as "abandoned girls, who having been ruined themselves by the treachery and depravity of man, have sworn to glut their vengeance by dragging to their own depths in guilt and infamy such young men as might otherwise have been the flower and stamina of our country."

Never a popular position, this assertion of destructive power by women turned out not only to be illusionary but also self-destructive to women's drive for equal treatment. This was demonstrated by a sensational murder trial that took place in Boston in the fall of 1845. In a significant way the question of the guilt or innocence of Albert Terrill, accused of murdering his mistress Maria Bickford, hinged on how women in Boston society were perceived.

Early on the morning of October 27, 1845, a fireman summoned to a house on Charles Street, charged up the stairs through thick smoke to a bedroom that seemed to be the source of the fire and stumbled over the body of a woman. An investigation conducted by the Boston police revealed that the woman's throat had been slashed. There was blood on the mattress, suggesting that the body had been dragged from the bed. The water in the wash basin was thick with blood.

The woman was identified by Joel Lawrence, owner of the house, as Ms. Maria Bickford. Lawrence also told the police that Albert Terrill had been with Ms. Bickford on the evening of October 26th. Several articles of clothing identified as belonging to Terrill were discovered; they were bloodstained and partially burned. In December Terrill was arrested in New Orleans, returned to Boston, and charged with the murder of Maria Bickford. The trial took place in March 1846.

Before the trial even began Bostonians had been treated by the local press to the sordid details of the adulterous relationship between Bickford and Terrill. Readers of the *Daily Mail* and *Daily Times* were told that Terrill was from a solid, successful manufacturing family in Weymouth, Massachusetts. At the time of the trial Terrill was 22 years old; he was married and had two children. Young Terrill deserted his wife and children in the summer of 1844 when he met Ms. Bickford. Like Terrill, she was in her early twenties and had married young. Born and raised in Bangor, Maine, she had married James Bickford, a shoemaker, when she was 16 years old. After three years Marie left Bickford and came to Boston with another man. Once in the city, he abandoned her. Alone, without friends or means of support, Bickford turned to prostitution.

From the time they met in a New Bedford tavern, Bickford and Terrill were together constantly. They traveled together as man and wife, moving from hotel to boardinghouse to house of assignation. At least one landlord, however, refused to tolerate their blatant disregard for the law and morality. The owner of the Hanover House in Boston

brought charges and Terrill was arrested and indicted late in September for adultery. He was bailed out by his brother-in-law and with the help of letters to the court from his wife, mother, father-in-law, and a Weymouth selectman, the judge suspended proceedings for six months on good behavior. On October 21st Terrill was released; he went looking for his lover, Maria Bickford.

While no one witnessed Bickford's murder, all of the circumstantial evidence pointed to Terrill. He had been with her in a room at the Lawrence House on Charles Street on the night of the murder. Between 4:00 a.m. and 5:00 a.m. Terrill had gone to a stable near the Lawrence's and asked to be taken to Weymouth. He talked about a fight with a woman and said something to the carriage driver about a fire. In addition Samuel Parker, the prosecutor, described Terrill as a rogue without moral principles.

Terrill's defense attorney was one of the best in the business. Rufus Choate was a brilliant trial lawyer with years of experience and a flamboyant style. He launched a two-pronged attack that undermined the commonwealth's case. First, Choate attacked the credibility of Lawrence and the other witnesses who had testified against Terrill by pointing out that they worked at a house of ill-repute. Second, Choate worked hard to convince the all-male jury that Ms. Bickford was a depraved woman, a common prostitute without promise or hope of reformation.

Two hypotheses followed from Choate's second argument: Ms. Bickford had committed suicide (somehow managing to throw herself off the bed after she slit her throat from ear to ear). This theory was based on a syllogism: Bickford was a "fallen" woman; women of bad character always commit suicide; therefore Ms. Bickford had committed suicide. Then Choate maintained that even if Ms. Bickford had not killed herself, she was the destructive force. Because she was intent on dragging down Terrill, punishing him, he had to kill to free himself. Terrill was the victim.

The jury acquitted Terrill. Choate's defense, it would seem, played into the prejudices of the nine men who sat in judgment. In fact most New Englanders probably would have reacted similarly, though perhaps they would have shown a bit more sympathy for Maria Bickford. It was a common belief, after all, that young women from rural areas were corrupted by the sin and licentiousness of city life.

Francis Lowell, Nathan Appleton, and Patrick T. Jackson were well aware of this prejudice. For this reason among others, therefore, these wealthy financiers determined to build their new, modern textile factory in the countryside away from the existing urban centers. Lowell, the spot chosen by the Boston Associates, was located 15 miles north of Boston on the Merrimack River. It was a place of great natural beauty with rolling hills on either side of the river. The mill buildings were laid out to take advantage of the setting; there were grassy open spaces between the buildings so that the river could be seen and shrubs and trees separated the factory from the boarding houses. The whole effect was peaceful and inviting.

The rural character of Lowell was not mere aesthetics. The guiding idea was that the moral values of country life could be maintained while simultaneously promoting industrialization. Material advance through technology, in other words, would not sacrifice morality. This was especially important to the Boston Associates because the workers were "the daughters of respectable farmers." Workers in the manufacturing cities of Europe were notoriously men and women of low character and intelligence. But here in America Appleton, Jackson, and Lowell hoped to prove that industrial employment would not inevitably result in physical and moral deterioration. "Ours is a great novel experiment," declared Appleton. "Whatever the result, it is our destiny to make it. It is our mission—our care should be to understand it and make it succeed."

Succeed it did—for a time. Every European visitor sang the praises of the "celestial city." The young women who worked in the mill invariably were described as "clean," "fresh," "moral," and "healthy." Cautious and normally critical, Charles Dickens was surprised to find that the young women workers produced a literary magazine. *The Lowell Offering* "will compare advantageously with a great many English Annuals," Dickens happily concluded. And in the evenings the lecture hall often was crowded.

The Lowell workers themselves did not regard their work and their living arrangement in the same light as the visiting dignitaries. The actual working conditions were not utopian. Women operatives worked a six-day week, averaging 12 hours per day. Bells dictated every activity: beginning at 6:00 a.m. bells awakened the women; they rang again to call the women to and from meals; and bells marked curfew and the end of the day. All the while company officials stipulated that the women "must devote themselves assiduously to their duty during working hours" and "on all occasions, both in their words and in their actions, show they are penetrated by a laudable love of temperance and virtue animated by a sense of their moral and social obligations." If they worked steadily and their behavior was good, the workers earned an average weekly wage of $1.00 to $2.00, exclusive of room and board.

This policy of strict social control was reinforced by the hierarchical arrangement of the Lowell factory system. The directors and officers did not live in Lowell but in Boston. The first chief executive for the corporation was Kirk Boott who lived in an imposing Georgian mansion just below the original factory. Under Boott were the overseers who lived in simple yet substantial houses at the ends of the boardinghouses where the women operatives resided. These quarters were intended to serve as dormitories, six to eight women to each bedroom. Similar arrangements were provided for male mechanics. At the bottom of the hierarchy were the Irish day laborers who built the canals and mill buildings. No housing was planned for this group, and they lived in shacks crowded into an area near a Catholic church called "New Dublin" or the "Acre."

Despite this corporate insensitivity to the needs of immigrant workers and a few brief work stoppages led by women, the Boston Associates' new industrial plan was imitated widely throughout the 19th century. Visitors continued to admire Lowell, praising it as a productive, cohesive, and harmonious community, a reflection of the ideals of republicanism.

Not everyone agreed. A minority of dissident workers and their spokesmen protested their oppressive working conditions and the hierarchical conception of society that sustained them. Among the earliest and most articulate critics of industrialism were Edward Everett and Seth Luther. Everett was a liberal Unitarian who joined with a group of striking East Boston ship carpenters in 1825, taking up their demand for a 10-hour work day. Although the strike failed, Boston workers formed a Workingmen's party committed to electing candidates favorable to the needs of laborers. Everett conceived of more sweeping goals. He told a Charlestown audience that the aim of the party was not simply to "elevate this or that candidate for office, but to promote the prosperity and welfare of working men and. . .to produce *happiness*."

Everett and the Boston Workingmen's party looked backward to the era when workers necessarily became artisans and independent producers. But by 1832 when the ship carpenters struck again, Seth Luther, a self-educated labor reformer, had no such illusions. Speaking for the striking carpenters, Luther denounced the employers as hypocrites for refusing to allow workers to form unions when the shipyard owners had formed a "detestable combination" in order to drive Boston's workers "into starvation or submission."

During the summer of 1832 Luther

published an *Address to the Working Men of New England* in which he attempted to speak to all workers, including those men and women in Lowell. The motives of *all* employers, he argued, sprang from "Avarice," which always "destroyed the happiness of the MANY, that the FEW may roll and riot in splendid luxury." The wretched Irish laborer living in a hovel in Lowell—the so-called industrial utopia—represented, in Luther's view, the vanguard of "hundreds of thousands of the miserable and degraded Population of Europe" who would be enticed to America and thus be degraded by the factory system.

So long as gross inequities existed, he contended, the American Revolution would be unfinished. The imperative of the Declaration of Independence, that "all men are created equal," Luther perceived of as a radical injunction against all social distinctions and he urged workers to unite and demand a fair share for their labor.

In 1834 workers from 16 craft unions heeded Luther's call. They formed the Boston Trades Union (BTU), one of the first organizations of its kind. At its peak, the BTU enrolled nearly 4,000 workers who helped carry the struggle for a shorter work day to the outlying mill towns, including Lowell, where women

This lithograph depicts the interior of the Glendon Rolling Mill and Forge Works which made sheet metal and machinery parts. Boston didn't have a large factory district but there were numerous small factories and mills, and Boston money financed the large mills in Merrimack Valley communities such as Lawrence and Lowell. (BPL)

operatives struck against wage cuts in 1834 and 1836.

Beginning in the 1830s many Boston reformers shifted their attention from moral reform, education, temperance, and factory legislation to the campaign against slavery in the South. Like the other reforms Bostonians had embraced, abolitionism was motivated by moral frenzy, not economic discontent. "Our enterprise," declared Wendell Phillips, the most socially prominent Bostonian opposed to slavery, "is eminently a religious one, dependent for success entirely on the religious sentiment of the people."

Phillips was an unlikely agitator. He had everything—family, wealth, an education at Boston Latin School and Harvard. In 1835 he opened a law office on Court Street; his success seemed assured. But one afternoon not long after he began his law practice, Phillips came upon a mob that had seized and threatened to lynch William Lloyd Garrison, publisher of the *Liberator* and founder of the Massachusetts Anti-Slavery Society. Such a blatant violation of civil liberty revolted Phillips. He drew closer to the abolition movement. When he married Anne Terry Greene, daughter of a wealthy Boston shipper and a militant abolitionist, he became an outcast in upper-class society. "My wife made me an out and out abolitionist," he declared lovingly years later.

Phillips' assaults on slavery continued to be tolerated by many Bostonians as long as his targets were southern aristocrats. In March 1839, however, he burned the last of his bridges to polite society when he gave a speech to a massive meeting condemning the Massachusetts legislature for refusing to heed antislavery petitions. Phillips was especially critical of the legislators for rejecting a plea from a group of Lynn women, many of whom were black. According to Anne Weston, a cousin of Phillips, he tore the legislators to bits, "then ground them to atoms, then strewed them on the waters." The result, according to another friend, was that Boston was "convulsed with rage."

Phillips' acceptance of William Lloyd Garrison's leadership was the last straw. Garrison's strategy and style were anathema to everyone outside the movement. His famous declaration, published in the *Liberator* in January 1831, permitted no ambivalence: "I will be as harsh as truth, and as uncompromising as justice. On this subject, I do not wish to think, to speak, or write, with moderation. . . .I am in earnest—I will not equivocate—I will not excuse—I will not retreat a single inch—AND I WILL BE HEARD." For Garrisonians there was no neutral ground regarding slavery: a person was for immediate emancipation or for slavery.

The *Liberator* was not read widely, nor did Garrison's position win many supporters in Boston or anywhere in the North. In its first year the paper had only 50 white subscribers and two years later barely 400. In the black community, however, Garrison and his program was enthusiastically supported. Of course black leaders such as William C. Nell and Benjamin Roberts had been actively opposed to slavery and involved in improving racial relations before Garrison arrived in Boston. In 1826, for example, a group of blacks dedicated to abolition formed the Massachusetts General Colored Association and two years later helped publish and distribute David Walker's incendiary *Appeal* for freedom. Although Walker's approach was rejected by Garrison, he was loved by the black community. He was often a guest in the homes of blacks living on Beacon Hill and in 1833 he was given an inscribed silver cup in appreciation for his commitment to the welfare of black people.

With Garrison's prompting the Boston Female Anti-Slavery Society resolved in 1838 that white abolitionists should make a greater effort to socialize with blacks. The fact that the resolution caused a furor, even among those who were opposed to slavery, made it clear how deep racial prejudice was in the "cradle of liberty." One of the most obvious examples of racial discrimination was Boston's public school system. Barred from attending the white public schools, blacks organized a private school that met in the African Meeting House beginning in 1806. As a result of a legacy from Abiel Smith, a white merchant, the city accepted financial responsibility for the education of black children after 1820.

But separate was not equal. In 1844, therefore, a group of black leaders organized to integrate public education in Boston. They petitioned, investigated,

THOMPSON, THE ABOLITIONIST.

That infamous foreign scoundrel THOMPSON, will hold forth *this afternoon*, at the Liberator Office, No. 48, Washington Street. The present is a fair opportunity for the friends of the Union to *snake Thompson out!* It will be a contest between the Abolitionists and the friends of the Union. A purse of $100 has been raised by a number of patriotic citizens to reward the individual who shall first lay violent hands on Thompson, so that he may be brought to the tar kettle before dark. Friends of the Union, be vigilant!

Boston, Wednesday, 12 *o'clock.* Oct 21. 1835

publicized, demonstrated, and finally in 1849 brought suit against the city. Benjamin Roberts, a black printer, asked the School Committee to allow his five-year-old daughter, Sarah, to attend the white school closest to her home. (She passed five white schools on her daily trip to the black school.) Roberts' request was denied. The case was argued before the supreme judicial court by Charles Sumner, an abolitionist and later United States Senator from Massachusetts. Sumner asserted that segregated schools were not only unconstitutional but also damaging socially and emotionally to both black and white children. Segregation of children according to race, he maintained, would create a sense of caste distinction that would make social interaction among blacks and whites difficult or impossible later in life. Such a situation, Sumner concluded, would prevent "those relations of equality which our constitution and laws promised to all."

The court rejected Sumner's plea and ruled in favor of the Boston School Committee's right to set educational policy. Finally in 1855 the Massachusetts legislature passed a law abolishing separate schools. Other racial bars quickly fell; most public theaters were opened to blacks and railroad travel was integrated.

While Boston's optimistic reformers did not achieve their utopian goals, their ideals still burned brightly. Against all odds Bostonians clung to the idea that they could establish a new order, a harmonious community. This ideal would be severely tested, but never forgotten, during Boston's next two centuries of growth and change.

Left: Boston eventually gained a reputation as the center of abolitionist activity. There was also strong anti-abolitionist sentiment as indicated by this broadside that was circulated before the visit of George Thompson, a British anti-slavery lecturer and organizer. (TBS)

Left: After escaping from slavery in Kentucky, Lewis Hayden moved to Boston and became a leader in the abolitionist movement. Hayden and his wife, Harriet, used their home as a station on the Underground Railroad and assisted numerous fugitive slaves. Hayden was elected to the state legislature in 1873, and served as messenger to the secretary of state from 1859 until his death in 1889. (TBS)

V

The Coming of the Irish

They came to Boston on "coffin ships." Driven from Ireland by hunger and unbearable hardship, nearly one hundred thousand Irish immigrants were spewn upon Boston's shores between 1846-1849; 15,500 in 1846, 25,250 in 1847, 25,000 in 1848, and 34,000 before the "Black Forties" ended. Not until 1864 did the tide abate; by then 2.5 million Irish had abandoned their homeland.

The causes of this demographic disaster were woven into the web of Irish economic life decades before 1846. A sharp increase in population at the turn of the 18th century accompanied by the collapse of agricultural prices, revealed a serious problem that English landlords sought to exploit by raising rents and by converting farmland into grazing land. By the mid-1840's, therefore, the potato—a

Previous page: This was
the official photograph
of Boston's first
Irish-Catholic mayor,
Hugh O'Brien. O'Brien
made no effort to
challenge conservative
Yankee financial or
political practices, yet
his election represented
the beginning of the
steady push of Irish
leaders into the political
institutions of Boston.
(BPL)

cheap source of food that could be grown easily on the tiny plots of land still held by the Irish peasantry—was the only food of about one-third of the Irish people. In the autumn of 1845 a potato disease destroyed all but a fraction of the crop. After a wet spring and a humid summer, the crop of 1846 was a total failure. The two following years were no better. This crisis was aggravated further by a very poor grain harvest.

Starvation stalked Ireland. The death toll rose sharply. And, as if the horrors of starvation were not tragic enough, the Irish people were forced to endure the most severe winter in memory during 1846-1847. With snow blanketing the fields and roads, with icy winds making outdoor work nearly impossible, thousands died of hunger and from exposure. Malnutrition, poverty, and an inadequate relief program (the British government was reluctant to interfere with the "natural laws of supply and demand"), led to the outbreak of virulent diseases. Typhus, dysentery, scurvy and relapsing fever, reached epidemic levels. Finally, early in 1849 a serious outbreak of cholera added more victims to the grim toll.

Laborers, cottagers and small farmers in the southwestern counties suffered the worst. Corpses were left unburied for days, because people feared the contagion of fever. Dead bodies were discovered lying in the streets of villages and in ditches along country roads. A magistrate from Cork visited Skibbereen in late December 1846 and filed a chilling report:

I entered some of the hovels. . .and the scenes that presented themselves were such as no tongue or pen can convey the slightest idea of. In the first, six famished and ghastly skeletons, to all appearance dead, were huddled in a corner on some filthy straw, their sole covering what seemed a ragged horse-cloth, and their wretched legs hanging about naked above the knees. I approached in horror, and found by a low moaning they were alive; they were in fever—four children, a woman and what had once been a man. . . .

Small wonder that these calamitous years burnt themselves deep into the imagination of the Irish and haunted their descendants for generations. An American relief drive, including a massive effort by Boston's Irish Catholic population as well as a number of the city's prominent Protestants, certainly helped end the terrible crisis. More encouraging, by 1848 the potato blight had run its course. New crops showed no sign of the disease. But for thousands of the survivors there seemed to be no hope for a better future for themselves or their country. The land was ruined; there was no work, only the prospect of eviction.

In desperation they fled from Ireland. Somehow they scraped together the cost of a ticket—about 3 pounds—crossed the Atlantic and for no very good reason many settled in Boston. The city was innundated. In the single year 1847, 35,000 Irish immigrants landed in the city. Most were weak, sick, and half-starved. Few of the "famine Irish" had any occupational skills except for a rudimentary knowledge of farming.

Boston offered little. There were relatively few jobs for unskilled workers. In contrast to other eastern American cities, Boston was not a growing, labor-poor industrial center. This meant Irishmen were forced to take jobs doing back-breaking pick and shovel work for the railroads or the huge Back Bay landfill project of the 1850's and 1860's. To supplement the meager wages men were able to earn at such menial jobs, Irish women sought work as domestic servants. In 1850 nearly two-thirds of the adult Irish work force in Boston consisted of unskilled laborers or domestics.

The sick and destitute were forced to turn to the city's charitable institutions, which were large and newly built but soon overwhelmed. Those men and women who were in need of medical care were sent to a hospital on Deer Island, while the poor and insane were housed in an asylum in South Boston. Despite these modern facilities, there were, according to the *Boston Transcript*, groups of "poor wretches" in every part of the city "resting their weary and emaciated limbs at the corner of the streets and in the doorways of both private and public houses." Between 1845 and 1851 the number of foreign-born paupers supported by public funds increased from 4,000 to 12,000. Alarmed by this threat to the "orderly and peaceful city of the Pilgrims," a Massachusetts Senate Committee asserted that Boston was being turned into another Botany Bay, a dumping ground for Europe's poor and criminal population.

Although the legislators' accusation was widely regarded as nonsense, Boston officials did implement a policy of sending back those people who were discovered to have been "paupers in another country," "lunatics" or "infirm persons." In 1855 more than 600 emigrants were refused admission to Boston and were sent back to Great Britain. The Boston *Daily Advertiser* sympathized with two of those who were evicted, Mary Williams and her infant child, Bridget. "The offense of this poor woman, for which she was thus violently and ignominiously expelled from Massachusetts, was the fact that she was born in Ireland and called a pauper....a crime which Massachusetts punishes as no other crime is punished in America, by banishment...."

Those Irish immigrants who stayed in Boston found living conditions wretched. Because Boston was a city surrounded by water, most of the poor crowded into the already overcrowded sections of the old city. They packed into the North End and around the Fort Hill district so that they could avoid paying tolls to cross over to Cambridge, Charlestown, or South Boston. At mid-century, the average number of people living in a house in the North End was eighteen, as compared to the city's average of ten.

Living conditions were miserable. Old houses, once fashionable, were divided and re-divided to make tenements; deserted warehouses near the docks were filled with immigrant families. Those who were unable to pay the exorbitant rents

charged by slumlords, were forced into make-shift shanties, or worse, cellars and basements. Without light or fresh air, these underground caverns bred disease and pushed the death rate far above the norm. During the cholera epidemic of 1849, for example, 460 or 60% of the 707 cholera victims in Boston were Irish immigrants.

The deplorable conditions under which the Irish people in Boston were forced to live often led to crime—drunkenness and brawling. Whiskey was cheap (28¢ a gallon) and plentiful. In 1851, City Marshall Francis Tukey, reported that of the fifteen hundred shops selling liquor, nearly nine hundred were owned by Irishmen and almost half were located in the North End and Fort Hill. Tukey and

Boston was known as a walking city, yet horses and carriages were very much a part of the street scene in the mid-1800s. This advertisement for Samuel K. Bayley's Carriage and Horse Bazar suggests the wide variety of carriages available. (BPL)

Mayor John Bigelow pleaded with the Board of Aldermen to drop the "noble experiment" of using "moral suasion" to prevent drunkenness and to substitute strict licensing and tough police enforcement of the law. Within a few years, the Aldermen came around to Tukey's position and the number of arrests for drunkenness soared. In 1856, for example, the Boston police arrested 17,538—14,067 of whom were foreigners, chiefly Irish. Nearly 7,000 of the arrests were for drunkenness and another 3,500 for the related crimes of disorderly conduct and assault and battery.

As well as making more arrests, the police began the practice of raiding notorious areas of the city. In the spring of 1851, Marshall Tukey's men raided Ann Street in the North End. Sixty men and ninety women were swept up in the police net. Thirty-five men were sentenced as "keepers of brothels" and the women as prostitutes. For many Yankee Bostonians, the rowdies on Ann Street were typical of all Irish.

Natural history was a new area of study in the 1800s, as increased travel and literacy brought more people in touch with animal and plant wonders of the world. Entrepreneurs created animal shows with a variety of interesting and little-known creatures. This is an advertisement for one such business. (BPL)

The Aquarial Gardens

THE LEARNED SEALS.

This intensely interesting Exhibition has lately received very important additions, namely,

A LIVING PELICAN, from the Gulf of Mexico.
That rare and interesting animal, the AGOUTI, from Para.
A pair of live OPOSSUMS, from Georgia.
A Magnificent living specimen of the AMERICAN GOLDEN EAGLE.
A pair of splendid AMERICAN HORNED OWLS, &c. &c.

The MARBLED SEALS astonish and delight every one by their wonderful intelligence; they readily shake hands and bow to their friends, take a bath at the suggestion of their keeper, go through the manual exercise as seen in the cut above, and one is now taking lessons on the hand organ and exhibits remarkable proficiency.
The LIVING ALLIGATOR and all the great variety of Fish in the Glass Tanks entrance the lover of Natural History.
Also to be seen, the DEN OF SERPENTS, which contains within its transparent walls a large family of Serpents, some of which are over twelve feet in length.

Aquarial Gardens, 21 Bromfield Street.
CUTTING & BUTLER, Proprietors.

ADMITTANCE 25 CTS. CHILDREN UNDER 10 YEARS, 15 CTS.

The Pilot, voice of the Boston Catholic community, pointed out that most Irish were good citizens, "quite invisible to the vigilant night police." Others observed that the Irish constituted only about 18 percent of the state prison population. Critics were quick to add, however, that almost two-thirds of the petty criminals—men and women convicted of drunkenness, assault and other related offenses—were Irish.

Bishop John Fitzpatrick's leadership of the Boston Catholic archdiocese during these hard times was characterized by his sensitivity to the problem of assimilation faced by Irish immigrants and his firm belief in taking a diplomatic approach to the Yankee community. Fitzpatrick was a Bostonian. He was born in Boston in 1812, graduated from the Boston Public Latin School, and after he completed his studies for the priesthood in Montreal and Paris Fitzpatrick returned to Boston in 1830. He was welcomed into an intellectual circle that included Dr. John Warren, Francis Gray, Oliver Wendell Holmes, and Abbot Lawrence.

Fitzpatrick shared the chief political and social values of the dominant Yankee community. He regarded as dangerous and subversive any radical or liberal political movements. Indeed he used the pages of *The Pilot* to urge immigrant voters to elect conservative Whigs rather than Democrats. And, perhaps most important to the hardworking Yankees, Fitzpatrick, as Professor Thomas O'Connor argues in his biography, worked hard to impress upon his parishioners the importance of hard work, self-reliance and temperance. Finally, Fitzpatrick firmly believed in assimilation. "We should make ourselves American as much as we can," *The Pilot* urged. "This is our country now. Ireland is only a recollection."

Of course, Fitzpatrick's social and political beliefs were not necessarily those of his parishioners. Still, it seemed likely, in 1846 when Fitzpatrick was named the third Bishop of Boston that he would enjoy a peaceful, if administratively challenging, tenure. But Fitzpatrick's cordial relations with the Brahmin elite did not prevent the growth of a virulent anti-Catholicism.

Immigrants had not been especially welcome in Boston before 1852 when the American Party, a national political organization, was formed to protect the United States from the "insidious wiles of foreigners." There had been two major outbreaks of anti-Catholicism. Following the publication in 1834 of a sensationalistic novel that purported to reveal in lurid detail what *really* went on inside a Catholic convent, and a series of violent anti-Catholic sermons delivered by the Rev. Lyman Beecher, an enraged mob smashed its way into the Ursuline convent in Charlestown. After allowing the nuns and children to escape, the men set fire to the convent. A crowd of several hundred, including a fire company, watched as the building burned to the ground. Three years later, in June 1837, violence surfaced once again. On a hot afternoon a company of Yankee firemen clashed with a Catholic funeral procession along Broad Street. Mayor Samuel Eliot ended the battle only by calling out the state militia.

The wave of Irish immigrants in the 1840's and 1850's and the birth of the American or Know-Nothing Party, as it commonly was called because its members were pledged to secrecy, escalated and legitimized hatred and bigotry. Many native Bostonians were convinced that the poor, illiterate, hard-drinking, brawling Irish were a threat to their beloved city. As the cost of poor relief soared and the older sections of the city were transformed into slums, native Bostonians grew angry and embraced Know-Nothingism.

Although there are good reasons for doubting the validity of the analysis commonly made about the election of 1853, militant nativists were right when they predicted that the Irish-Catholic vote would be an important factor in all subsequent elections. "For the first time in the history of the state," wrote the *Daily Commonwealth* "the Catholic Church [has] taken the field as a power."

K. N.

SIX HOURS IN A CONVENT:

— OR —

THE STOLEN NUNS!

A TALE OF CHARLESTOWN IN 1834.

RUINS OF THE URSULINE CONVENT AS THEY APPEARED AFTER THE FIRE IN 1834.

BY CHARLES W. FROTHINGHAM.

SIXTH EDITION.

GRAVES & WESTON:
OFFICE "AMERICAN UNION," 36 WASHINGTON ST., BOSTON.
1855.

In 1834 the Ursuline Convent was attacked and burned by an anti-Catholic mob, responding, in part, to unproven tales such as Six Months in a Convent, *the story of a young woman forced to remain in a nunnery. The "K.N." refers to the Know-Nothing political party which experienced brief but strong popularity in the 1850s by appealing to anti-Catholic sentiment. (TBS)*

This realization stimulated bitterness among those voters fearful of the power of recent immigrants and led to a Know-Nothing landslide in the state elections of 1854. Know-Nothings captured every one of the senate seats and all but three places in the House. Henry J. Gardner, a former president of the Boston Common Council, was elected governor. Jerome V.C. Smith, a surgeon, an amateur sculptor and a member of the Know-Nothing movement, became Boston's fourteenth mayor.

In his inaugural address Gardner painted a dark picture of the "horde of foreign barbarians" who endangered the republic. The dominant race, he stated, meaning his own, must regulate the incoming class, meaning Irish emigrants. One means of "regulation" was an amendment to the constitution requiring a twenty-one year residence for citizenship. Another was an investigation of Catholic schools, including one in Roxbury.

"Boston and Its Environs," an engraving by J. Poppel, was published in Munich, Bavaria, in 1858. The East Boston Shipyard and the peninsula are featured in the center, bordered by important buildings and scenes of the period. (TBS)

Bishop Fitzpatrick and *The Pilot* did what they could in a quiet way to undercut the nativist movement. Fitzpatrick urged his parishioners to vote as a means of demonstrating their loyalty and commitment as an American citizen. And, he steadfastly refused to develop a separate parochial school system—although many Boston Irish believed that Protestant teachers used "every cunning" to cause Catholic students in the public schools to abandon their faith. Fitzpatrick did write to the Boston School Committee to explain the official teachings of the Roman Catholic church and to emphasize the seriousness with which Catholic students and parents regarded the doctrines of their religion.

Although polite, the school committee was deaf to Fitzpatrick's argument. As they perceived it, the King James version of the Bible, which was required reading every day in Boston public schools, was "nonsectarian" because it was acceptable to all Protestants. Likewise, schoolmasters saw nothing wrong with textbooks which

presented a Protestant world view and mentioned Catholicism only as an example of the corruption and venality against which Protestant reformers rebelled. Boston Catholic parents were so enraged by this situation that many kept their children out of school. In 1854 Barnas Sears, secretary of the Massachusetts Board of Education, stated that the single most important cause for the decline in school population was the opposition of Catholics to the use of the Protestant Bible in the public school system.

While the controversy over education continued until Fitzpatrick's successor, Bishop John Williams began a parochial school system in 1880, the most militant aspects of the nativist movement in Boston collapsed by 1856. Bigotry—especially a prejudice as contrived as the "Catholic Menace"—was simply not enough to hold together a national political organization. Moreover, the issue of slavery had become a consuming passion for men and women in all sections of the nation.

Boston, and the liberal part of the Brahmin community in particular, was the center for the campaign to abolish slavery. William Ellery Channing, Wendell Phillips, Samuel and Julia Ward Howe, and Theodore Parker took the position that slavery was a moral offense that should be purged from the body politic. William Lloyd Garrison, outspoken and uncompromising editor of the *Liberator,* agreed with this analysis, but differed from the polite Brahmins in that he argued for immediate abolition and attacked the United States Constitution for protecting slavery, calling it a "covenant with death."

Most Irish Catholics in Boston reacted negatively to both Garrison and the upper class abolitionists. To begin with, Catholics believed that a number of anti-slavery advocates had been active in the Know Nothing party, that "secret order" of bigots and hypocrites which sought to deny white immigrants their civil rights. The hearts of the abolitionists, charged *The Pilot,* are as "soft as butter" toward the oppressed black laborer in the south, but "hard as flint" toward the white laborer in the north. *The Pilot* also condemned Garrison and his followers because the newspaper was convinced that the kind of militant tactics used by radicals would promote civil disorder and public violence. Fr. John Roddan, editor of *The Pilot,* reminded Boston Catholics that the famed Irish patriot, Daniel O'Connell, had said that "the greatest political advantages are not worth one drop of human blood." Therefore, Fr. Roddan concluded, it would be better if black people remained in "nominal bondage" rather than attempting to win their freedom by force.

The Boston Catholic weekly's conservative views about slavery seemed to be in harmony with the United States Supreme Court's decision in the Dred Scott case. Speaking for the majority, Chief Justice Roger B. Taney, a prominent Catholic from Maryland, argued that Scott had not become a free man as a result of his residing in free territory. Black people, Taney wrote in 1857, were "beings of an inferior order" who possessed "no rights which the white man was bound to respect" and had never been included under the term "citizens" in the Constitution.

Based on these shaky propositions about slavery and black people, *The Pilot* advocated that its readers support Stephen A. Douglas, the presidential candidate of the Democrats in 1860, rather than Abraham Lincoln, candidate of the "Black Republican party" which was supported by the "scattered and broken forces of the know-nothing party." In short, Boston's Irish Catholic community came to almost the same position as did conservative, upper class Bostonians. Both groups feared a black uprising and loathed the social upheaval they believed was caused by abolitionists. Both shared the common prejudices about blacks. Both were opposed to any threat to the textile industry—the "Lords of the Loom" (in Thomas O'Connor's phrase)—because southern secession would endanger profits and the Irish working class because free blacks would compete with poor whites for scarce jobs.

Still, like most northerners, Boston's Irish Catholic community was shocked by the Confederate attack on Fort Sumter in April 1861. Their earlier hostility toward abolitionists and self-interested concern for the economic viability of the cotton textile industry, was forgotten in an outpouring of patriotism, of support for the preservation of the Union. Thomas Cass, an Irishman and former commander of a Massachusetts unit called the Columbian Artillery (disbanded by the Know-Nothings) immediately volunteered to raise a regiment of Irishmen. Governor John A. Andrew enthusiastically accepted Cass' offer and within months the 9th Regiment, Massachusetts Volunteer Infantry, was organized. On June 24, 1861 the 9th marched through the streets of Boston to the State House, where to the cheers of thousands the governor thanked Colonel Cass for having raised "this splendid regiment" and, in a rare gesture of unity and city pride, Mrs. Harrison Gray Otis presented Cass with an American flag and an Irish flag of green silk.

The "Fighting 9th" distinguished itself, fighting courageously in every major campaign waged by the Army of the Potomac. In the bloody battles in the Virginia wilderness the Irish Ninth—led by General Thomas F. Meagher, one of the few prominent Irish Republicans in the commonwealth—never faltered. From this point forward, the patriotism of Boston's Irish Catholics was never again questioned. Indeed, the more favorable climate of toleration even withstood the storminess created by a draft riot in the summer of 1863.

The conscription law that Congress passed in March 1863 was particularly unfair to poor people and immigrants because it permitted wealthy young men either to hire a substitute or to buy exemption for $300. And the quotas established for each Boston ward were weighted in favor of the rich. A Catholic priest confided in his diary a sentiment believed by many working class Bostonians: the government was "drafting poor people, our Irish people."

On July 14, the anger that had been bubbling just beneath the surface exploded. When provost marshalls sought to distribute conscription notices on Prince Street in the North End, a group of women assaulted the marshalls. They soon were joined by hundreds of Irishmen. The police, who had come to the assistance of the marshalls, were forced to retreat to their station house. Mayor Frederick Lincoln called out three militia companies whose first order was to save the armory on Cooper Street. When the crowd tried to break through the doors of the armory, the militiamen opened fire, killing six people. After an unsuccessful foray into Dock Square where there were a couple of gun shops, the crowd melted away into the night.

Although there was considerable anxiety among state and city officials for the next few days, no further rioting occurred. The Catholic Church played an active role in restoring peace in the city. Fr. James Healy, who was acting head of the archdiocese while Bishop Fitzpatrick was in Europe, instructed the Boston clergy to persuade their parishioners to avoid "all fractious assemblies." Following a plan outlined by Fitzpatrick during the tumultuous 1850's, the priests left their churches and patrolled the neighborhood streets, dispersing crowds and calming angry people. As a sign of the new attitude of toleration, Mayor Lincoln distinguished between rioters and Irish Catholics. He publicly thanked those Catholic priests "who labored to preserve quiet among their congregations."

The war greatly increased the degree of understanding between Yankees and Irish. The Irish were no longer treated as unwanted immigrants. Thousands of young men—those in the "Fighting Ninth" and other units—had fought and died to save the Union. While the boys were at war, other changes that signalled a new era were made. In July 1861, Bishop Fitzpatrick was awarded an honorary degree by Harvard University, the first time a Catholic ecclesiastic was so honored. The Boston School Board repealed the law making it compulsory to read the King James version of the Bible in the public schools. And upon the recommendation of Governor Andrew, the legislature repealed the amendment requiring the foreign born to reside in Massachusetts at least two years before they were eligible to vote.

Irish continued to come to Boston after 1865. They were not driven from Ireland as they had been in the "Hungry Forties", but rather they were attracted to the city by relatives and friends, persuaded that Boston was a good place to live. By 1865, too, more than three-quarters of all immigrants came by steamship. The steamers were in every way better—faster, more comfortable, safer—than the "coffin ships" on which the earlier immigrants had come. Those of the "famine Irish" who survived the crossing, had worked hard and begun to

Below: The Macullar Parker Company employed over 600 workers in its ready-made menswear business. The company housed all functions of the business in one building. This photograph was taken in the 1880s when operatives earned between $2.50 and $4.00 a week. From Boston, Massachusetts, by George W. Engelhardt, 1897. (TBS)

establish themselves in Boston. Each year more of the Irish increased their modest incomes and moved a rung higher on the social ladder.

Still, as late as 1880, over 30% of Boston's Irish remained unskilled workers. More than 10,000 men were common laborers, working irregularly on the docks or a construction project. Over 7,000 Irishwomen were servants for middle and upper class Yankee families. Many of them hated the work. One Irish domestic informed a journalist that she told "every girl I know, 'whatever you do, don't go into service. You'll always be prisoners and always looked down on.'"

A handful of Irish achieved middle class status by the end of the 19th century. In 1880, for example, there were only 18 Irish lawyers out of a total Celtic population of 35,000. Only about 1400 Irish had become businessmen—mostly saloon keepers, morticians, grocers and real estate salesmen. Only 6% of the Irish between 1860 and 1880 made it into the

business and professional classes, as compared to 31% of the native-born Bostonians. According to Geoffrey Blodgett's brilliant study of Massachusetts politics, however, the lowly economic position of the Irish "did not breed automatic resentment among Irish spokesmen toward Yankee domination of

business and the professions. It remained as much an incentive to greater efforts toward mobility as it did a cause of class hostility." In fact, by the 1870's and 1880's some Irish were able to gain acceptance from Brahmin society without surrendering their ethnic pride.

The foremost example of this phenomena was John Boyle O'Reilly. Born in County Meath, Ireland in 1844, O'Reilly was exiled to Australia for participating in the Irish revolutionary movement. In 1869 he escaped and eventually settled in Boston, where through luck and pluck he landed a job as a reporter for *The Pilot,* then edited by Patrick Donahoe. O'Reilly prospered, becoming owner and editor of the paper in 1876. His advice to a young friend in Ireland, reflected O'Reilly's new status. "Go into business as soon as you can," he told John Devoy, adding, "keep out of these Irish or American political 'rings'."

O'Reilly's drive to succeed in Boston also included a commitment to his writing. In addition to his editorial work at *The Pilot,* he wrote several romantic novels and dozens of poems and essays. His reputation as a writer won O'Reilly entry into the exclusive Boston literary circle. O'Reilly certainly helped his cause by writing commemorative poems honoring the Yankee heroes of Boston's glorious past and by criticizing his fellow Irishmen's lack of intellectual achievement. "No people," he wrote in July 1877, have been "more neglectful of its poor than the rich and educated Irish in America. What schools and colleges have they endowed?. . .What reading rooms have they established to keep men from liquor stores and for their mental improvement? None whatever."

O'Reilly's blast overlooked at least one important sign of the Boston Irish Catholic community's commitment to intellectual achievement. In March 1863, Bishop Fitzpatrick's dream of a "college in the city" came to fruition. The Massachusetts legislature approved a charter incorporating Boston College. Although it had taken more than a decade, the hard work and dedication of Fr. John McElroy, S.J., finally resulted in the founding of a college that soon claimed the loyalty of the Boston Irish and whose graduates eventually would break Harvard's grip on the city's financial and legal institutions.

Although he was forced by poverty to leave school at the age of twelve, Hugh O'Brien rose above his humble origins. Born in Ireland, O'Brien worked in publishing before he entered politics in 1875. Ten years later he was elected Mayor of Boston, the first not of native birth. O'Brien proved such a popular and efficient administrator that he was re-elected for four consecutive terms. Despite an occasional gesture to the Irish—the creation of public parks and ordering the Boston Public Library closed on St. Patrick's Day—his commitment to decreasing the tax rate and expanding the powers of the mayor's office—made him appear to be very much the same as his Yankee predecessors.

In 1890, O'Brien and O'Reilly and a few dozen other Boston Irish were celebrated in James Cullen's *History of the Irish in Boston*. Published ten years after Justin Windsor's *Memorial History of Boston,* Cullen's history emphasized that it was "brains not brawn" that distinguished the Irish. Among other signs of accomplishment, Cullen listed all the Irish people who owned homes or businesses in Boston. By contrast, Windsor's four volume *History* all but omitted the Irish and focused on the colonial, revolutionary and early federal periods of Boston's proud—Yankee—history.

Recounting the glories of the Yankee past did not, however, assuage the anxieties of those Brahmins who formed the governing elite. They could now see that their hope of assimilating the Irish into the Boston way of life was hopeless. Some gave up and left the "city on a hill" their ancestors had founded two hundred

READY FOR THE BATTLE!

and fifty years earlier. Others of this elite believed it was their responsibility to maintain the high standards of leadership and the cultural benefits for which Boston was famous. Still others struck back, by working to cut off new immigration, hoping, therefore, to cling to a piece of national political power.

Clearly, Boston's passage from the past to the 20th century was not going to be easy.

John L. Sullivan, an Irish immigrant living in the South End, became one of the best prize-fighters in the country at a time when fights were bare-fisted and lasted as many rounds as the contenders could stand. Sullivan won this bout with Ryan and collected the $5,000 prize. (TBS)

VI

The Athens of America

Boston's old elite had great affection for their town—for its historical and religious traditions, for its town meeting form of government, for its compact size, and especially for its small, homogeneous population. Slow to admit to growth and change, Bostonians had been reluctant to become a city in 1822. As if to deny the break with the past, the new city had not built a city hall. The mayor and city council met first in the Old State House, then for a time in Fanueil Hall, and in the 1850s in the old courthouse on School Street.

Finally, in 1862, Mayor Joseph Wightman pushed through a bill providing funds to build a city hall. Gridley Bryant, Boston's most distinguished architect, was chosen to design the building. Bryant understood the need for a monumental public building that

*Previous page: By 1880
most of the Back Bay
was filled in and
devoted to upper class
homes and institutions
with a valuation
exceeding $100 million.
(TBS)*

*The class picture was
serious business for
these third-graders at
the Winchell School in
the West End circa
1890. The class reflects
the ethnic composition
of the area which was
changing from
predominantly Irish to
Italian and Eastern
European. The class size
and lack of decoration
and visual aids were
standard for public
schools of the period.
(BPL)*

would affirm the new Boston. He chose to use the new French Second Empire style which was popular in Europe, but relatively unknown in America. The result was a stately building of white Concord granite, topped with a great dome and flanked by graceful pavilions. To reaffirm the relationship of the city's past and present, a small plaza in front of the new city hall was decorated with the statues of two of Boston's great men, Benjamin Franklin, who had done so much to create a new nation, and Josiah Quincy, who had done so much to modernize an old city.

Although explicitly linked with the past, the new city hall signalled the beginning of a sweeping transformation. From 1862 to 1900 Boston grew more rapidly and expanded further from its original center than it had during its previous 230-year history. The population of the city jumped from 140,000 in 1865, to 341,000 in 1875, to 560,890 in 1900. Before the Civil War Boston had been a town confined to a small tract of 780 acres, but by filling in the marshes and bogs on either side of Roxbury neck and by annexing the

neighboring towns, Boston became, by 1900, a city of nearly 24,000 acres—almost thirty times its original size.

A new cultural tone was present as well, manifested in the rows of elegant brownstone houses, broad tree-lined boulevards and parks, and by the number and quality of the city's newest public institutions. During the last quarter of the 19th century, Boston became the cultural capital of the United States, the "Athens of America."

At the same time, the Brahmin elite that created this new, fashionable, vibrant city feared that its considerable cultural and social accomplishments were endangered by the new immigration from southern and eastern Europe. The 1890 census showed 10,000 Italians and Jews living in the city; by 1910 there were 30,000 Italians jammed into the old North End, and more than 40,000 Jews packed into the West End. The Irish at least spoke English and had a smattering of knowledge about Anglo-Saxon culture. These new people—Italians, Jews, a growing number of Poles, Lithuanians, and Greeks,—spoke a babel of tongues and cultivated their own quite different social customs. The percentage of foreign-born rose to 64% in 1880, to 74% in 1900.

The eastern and southern European Jews and southern Italians who poured into Boston after 1880 settled in the North End. Once solidly Irish, by 1895 there were more Italians and nearly as many Jews as Irish in the North End. By 1920, the Jews had moved into the West End, and the Italians accounted for more than 90% of the population in "Boston's first neighborhood," as historian Paul Tedesco so aptly called the North End.

The Jews were driven from Russia, Poland, and other eastern European countries to Boston to escape the pogroms that threatened their lives, and they came to Boston with the hope of economic success. Jewish immigrants settled primarily in a triangular area roughly bounded by Hanover Street, Endicott Street, and Prince Street. There were some families who lived between the North End and the newer Jewish neighborhood of the West End.

A strong family life was important to members of the Jewish community, but like other immigrant groups, it was often the case that a man came alone in order to earn enough money to bring his family. When the family did arrive, the demands of hard work and long hours sometimes created crises that pulled the family apart. Charitable groups assumed responsibility for the maintenance of families who had been deserted by the husband and father. Although Jews in the North End had a lower rate of desertion than other immigrant groups, desertion was one of the major problems confronting the benevolent associations.

Most of the Jews who came to the North End came from villages or small towns, and many turned to peddling or operating a small store to make a living. An elderly Jewish woman recalled that "everybody who came to Boston would take a basket." The immigrant would fill his basket with merchandise from a store

that extended credit and then set out to sell in a neighborhood which was not yet visited by many peddlers. Those newcomers unable to speak English were taught to say "Look in the basket." Good merchandise, fair prices, credit, and a desire to please bridged the gap between a Jewish peddler and his Yankee or Irish customers.

Jews who owned retail stores formed a financial and social elite in the North End community. Some especially successful businessmen supplied other peddlers, as did Harris Garfinkle and Company and Freedman Brothers. Others sold clothing, such as Michael Slutsky and Richmond, Cohen and Reinherz, who specialized in men's clothing. Yente Rabinowitz owned a small grocery that the family eventually built into Stop & Shop, a food store chain. I.B. Reinherz began as a peddler, then became a steamship ticket agent, and finally a banker.

Not all Jews who lived in the North End were in trade. A majority worked at whatever job they could get. Some used the streetcar to travel to Boston's suburbs where they found work as shoemakers or garment workers. A number of North End Jews drove horse-drawn cabs. Others bounced from one job to another; a man

In 1905 peddlers traveled the streets of Boston and its suburbs bringing a variety of products to residents. Many of the peddlers were recent Jewish immigrants from Eastern Europe, who began business with a horse and cart, and later opened shops throughout the city. (BPL)

who grew up in the North End recalled that "father worked in an iron foundry at Charlestown. Later, he became a street-car conductor and finally he became a *shames* at a Lithuanian synagogue."

Like other immigrant groups, Jews attempted to retain the patterns of European life. Russian Jews were devoutly orthodox and especially determined to maintain religious discipline. There were two main synagogues in the North End: Congregation Beth Abraham, founded in 1873, and Congregation Beth Israel, on Baldwin Place, established in 1890. Synagogue services followed the Eastern European pattern; congregants prayed in Hebrew, although prayerbooks usually had a Yiddish translation. Because they were perceived as more American, reform ideas had a wider appeal among younger Jews in the North End. The children's religious liberalism gradually affected the older generation. For example, the son of one of the pious and learned leaders of the Chevra Shas (Talmudical Society) noted: "While father observed all religious rites in every possible way, he would make certain statements that indicated to me that his ideas were entirely liberal. But living in a community as he was he naturally followed the dictates of the community."

Although there was some tension between younger and older Jews, both groups slowly became more acculturated to American life. As the second generation prospered, they moved out of the North End and were assimilated into the larger Boston community. "By 1910," Paul Tedesco tells us, "the last North End Jews were moving on into the mainstream of society, leaving the North End and its memories of poverty behind them."

The southern Italians who arrived in the North End about the same time as the Jews were not as quick to make the transition to a new American way of life. In part, this was due to the fact that 79 percent of the Italian immigrants who came to Boston did not intend to stay. These "birds of passage," as they were called, came to work, to make money, and then to return to Italy. The number of men who fled the grinding poverty of southern Italy for Boston was staggering: from 1895 to 1920 the number of foreign-born in Boston increased by 76 percent. The Italians of the North End accounted for much of this increase. In 1895, 26.6 percent of the people crowded into the North End were Italian; in 1920, 90 percent. The North End was home to 23,000 people in 1895 and 40,000 by 1920. Only in Calcutta were there more people

The age of these students and the apparent ethnic mix suggests that this was an "Americanization" class. Local settlement houses sponsored such classes in the late 1800s for those seeking American citizenship. The woman in the photograph probably was the teacher. (BPL)

per square mile.

The results of this severe overcrowding were predictable: the infant mortality rate was appalling; sanitation was almost non-existent; and more than a hundred families were living in one room per family. The North End at the turn of the century was Boston's "classic land of poverty." Still, they came. Poor, and illiterate, they depended on *paesani* (Italians from the same village) or a *padrone* (labor contractor) for survival. Because almost two-thirds of the men were unskilled laborers the jobs available to them were limited. They worked on the docks, in the granite and stone quarries, and on the railways, or left the city each day to build a sewer system in Brockton or Beverly or even as far as Northampton. A few sold fruit and vegetables in the market and a tiny number became clerks or professionals. Almost all single women worked and nearly a quarter of all Italian married women worked at least part time in a local garment or confectionery factory. Women's wages were lower than men's.

Because work was scarce, there was fierce competition between the Italians and the Irish, who resented the intrusion of the Italians. Irish gangs controlled the waterfront. During the day anyone could walk through the area unmolested, but after dark the Irish gathered on the street-corners and it became dangerous for an Italian to try to pass through their territory. Often, during the early years, if a Sicilian fishing boat came in after dark the men chose to sleep on board rather than run the gauntlet to their homes.

When the Italians established a numerical majority, the streets and institutions of the North End were more under their control. Although both Irish and Italians were Catholics, the Italians soon formed separate churches. St. Leonard's was founded in 1873, the Sacred Heart Church in 1888. A variety of community benevolent societies, schools, and social clubs sprang from these churches. One of the customary duties of these societies was to honor their patron saint with a yearly festival. The Feast of Our Lady of Grace, sponsored by former villagers from San Sossio Baronia, began in 1903. Sicilian fishermen honored the Madonna each year for her help in protecting the men while they were at sea. A procession during which a statue of the saint was carried around the North End was always a part of the festival.

These children gathered in the North End in 1890 when area residents were predominantly Italian and Jewish. The house with the awning belonged to Paul Revere during the 18th century and was a commercial and residential building until 1908 when it was restored and opened to visitors. The Revere house became a national landmark in 1961. (TBS)

Boston Latin School, the first high school in America, was established in 1635 to prepare young men for Harvard. In the 1890s the growing immigrant population and Irish political advances forced the school to diversify the student body. (TBS)

Societies honoring patron saints were usually carried over from the particular village from which people had come. Although the North End was made up of people from southern Italy, it was divided into separate enclaves of Avilanese, Calibrese, Neopolitians, Sicilians, and a handful of Genoese from northern Italy. Each group had their own dialect, their own *campanelisme,* their own way to maintain "la via veccia," the old way of life and their own section of the North End. People who identified themselves as living on "North Street," near St. Mary's," "lower Prince Street," or "down on Salem Street" also identified the part of Italy from which their family came, where they went to church, the societies to which they belonged, and often what occupation they pursued.

William DeMarco, a historian of the North End who has carefully charted the numerous and distinct enclaves, drives home his analysis with an anecdote about an "impostor,"

I went to Naples from Siracusa, Sicily, in 1905, in search of work. I went to Avellino during the grape harvest season and met my wife. Because I was Sicilian, I was not accepted by her family, so we decided to run away, and get married. Of course, we couldn't go back, so we came to Boston, where we found more Avellinese. Since I picked up my wife's dialect quickly, I decided to pass as Avellinese. This worked well. I opened a barber shop which attracted Neopolitians and Avellinese. With a wife who cooked Avellinese-style and my speaking the dialect at my shop, everyone thought I was from Avellino. I passed as Avellinese for almost thirty years, until a paesano from Siracusa told everyone I was Sicilian as part of a bet. By that time I was accepted by the Avellinese, so it did not hurt my business. Twenty-five or thirty years earlier, who knows what would have happened.

These subcultures, or "urban villages," were very much a part of the vitality of Italian immigrant life, but contained two disadvantages. First, Italians in the North End were so divided among themselves they did not participate in city politics. In part, too, this was because of a general distrust of government shared by all southern Italians. The North End was therefore merged with the West and South End wards, and ward boss Martin Lomasney was able to maintain his hold on Boston's political life until the 1930s. Second, the existence of distinct enclaves led Robert Woods and other Yankee urban reformers to despair of ever Americanizing the Italians. They concluded that the Italians lacked two essential Yankee characteristics: a commitment to active citizenship and to the work ethic. Without these qualities, Woods predicted, Boston would remain an urban wilderness.

Although they were anxious about what effect foreigners would have on their city, most Brahmins were still social creatures. As had their Puritan forefathers, they believed in community. While deploring aspects of society, Brahmins never rejected the idea of society. For this reason, they held fast to a belief in stewardship, that it was their special responsibility to see to the well-being of Boston.

The magnitude of that responsibility increased as the city grew. In 1850 the area of dense settlement barely exceeded a two-mile radius from the Old State House. Horse-drawn carriages were a common sight on Boston's downtown streets. Because enormous marshes and tidal basins were the dominant geographical feature, men cramped for space began damming and filling the marshes and flats. Hills were leveled and sea walls built. By the 1850s developers had reclaimed the area around Charles Street and much of the South End, had cut down a big chunk of Beacon Hill, and had completely leveled Fort Hill (the area around Pearl, Milk, and Broad streets) to create a new waterfront area along Atlantic Avenue.

In 1857 a special commission composed of representatives of the commonwealth, the city, and several private developers was formed by the legislature to fill the Back Bay and sell the lands. The project was breathtaking in scope. It called for filling hundreds of acres of tidal flats and

a shallow bay to create land west of Arlington Street to Kenmore Square along Commonwealth Avenue and from Beacon Street to the tracks of the Boston and Providence Railroad in the south, and to create a new shore line for the Charles River to the north. Norman Munson and George Gross, two railroad builders, were contracted by the commission in 1858 to carry out this enormous job, in return for four blocks of the newly created land.

The railroad and the steam shovel, two products of new technology, were utilized by Munson and Gross to fill the Back Bay and make the city an integral part of the mainland. The gravel was brought from Needham, about ten miles from Boston, by a specially designed train consisting of 35 cars to which two locomotives were attached. There were three such trains on the road day and night; one arrived at the Back Bay every 45 minutes, dumped its contents and returned to Needham to be re-filled by two giant steam shovels, an operation that took only about 10 minutes. In the first year, 300,000 yards of gravel were taken out of the hills of Needham and 1,400 acres of land were made in the Back Bay.

By 1861 the shore line of the bay was just west of Clarendon Street. Ten years later, Boylston and Newbury streets and the south side of Commonwealth Avenue were filled as far as Exeter Street and the northside reached Gloucester and Hereford streets. The entire area extending to Kenmore Square had been filled by 1882.

Ten years before the Back Bay project was completed, Boston suffered from a devastating fire. The fire burned out of control on November 9 and 10, 1872, causing many deaths and immense property damage. By the time the fire had been brought under control nearly sixty acres of downtown Boston had been reduced to ashes and rubble. This included most of the wholesale and warehouse district in the oldest part of the city, where houses were wedged together and streets were crooked and narrow. Although most of the buildings

were constructed of granite and iron, their owners had in recent years bowed to fashion and the demand for cheap space and had added mansard roofs, wooden frame superstructures covered with tarpaper. The fire easily jumped from one mansard roof to another.

Still, the conflagration could have been controlled but for two circumstances. First, there was an inadequate supply of water. Because Boston had not modernized its water system, commented a reporter, "there were more engines than water; the water pipes were too small to supply the draught of more than two engines." The second handicap was the complete absence of horses. All that year, horses in New England had suffered from a contagion of distemper, known as epizootic, or "horse disease," which incapacitated the animals and sometimes killed them. When the fire began, therefore, fire-fighters from Boston and neighboring towns were forced to pull their engines themselves, often for miles.

When the fire burned itself out, and while the extent of the damage was being assessed, two reforms were called for: the widening of the streets and the

prohibition of mansard roofs. No such ordinances were passed. "Building brokers," indifferent to safety and architectural beauty, jammed a greater number of plainer, taller buildings into the area than had been there before the fire. In this process, small shopkeepers and tradesmen, many of whom periodically came into Boston from the country to sell a wagonload of goods, were forced out, victims of big business's, demand for efficiency. The lasting effect of the Great Fire of 1872 was to speed the transformation of Boston into a collection of distinct sections, each with its own social and economic characteristics.

The attractions of the newly made Back Bay, for example, were obvious: it was detached but not remote from the business section; its neighbors were Beacon Hill and the Public Garden; and it was new and expensive. Boston's wealthiest families were able to create an unusually homogeneous upper class environment. They flocked to the Back Bay, building large five-story houses of brown sandstone inspired by the Second French Empire style of the 1860s, a considerable number of chaste but elegant brick houses, a number of homes whose vigorous Romanesque style was developed by Henry Hobson Richardson in the 1870s, and a rich profusion of homes in other styles, including those homes built during the classical revival in the 1880s.

A few mansions in the Back Bay were designed to look like medieval castles or 16th century chateaux with the lavish sculptural decoration of the Renaissance. The Albert Burrage mansion at 314 Commonwealth Avenue, for example, was built in the same magnificent style as W.K. Vanderbilt's Fifth Avenue mansion in New York. Charles Francis Adams' home at 20 Gloucester Street was not as ostentatious, but its heavy masonry towers and arched entrances affected a medieval style that was quite grand.

The Back Bay quickly became the center of Boston's intellectual and cultural life. The public buildings in and around Copley Square, in particular, symbolized

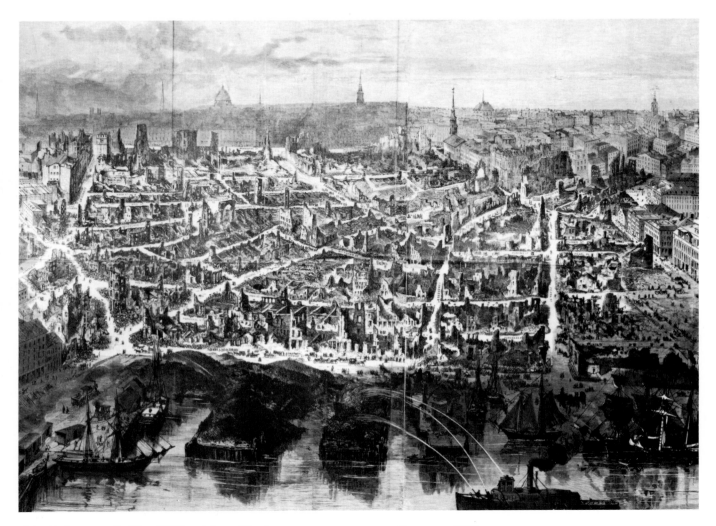

the city's new vitality. Without benefit of a plan—it began as an awkward space caused by the odd angle at which Huntington Avenue started off—a handsome square gradually took shape.

Located on the south side of the square, the first permanent home of the Museum of Fine Arts was completed in 1876. Designed by Sturgis and Brigham, it was a curious-looking striped red brick and terra cotta Victorian Gothic structure that housed the museum's growing collection of paintings and sculpture. The museum featured frequent exhibits from its permanent collection of old masters, as well as shows focusing on modern French paintings that had been purchased for the museum by Boston artists who traveled abroad.

Above: The 50th anniversary of Quincy Market was celebrated with a parade of stallholders representing businesses that had been located in the market since it opened in 1826. (SPNEA)

Facing page, top: This was a women's ward at Boston City Hospital before 1900. The hospital treated the poorer classes and people avoided being admitted to the hospital if they could since the recovery rate was not high. The plain walls and floors and tightly wrapped bedridden patients suggests the unpleasantness of a hospital stay. Courtesy, Boston University Library

Facing page, bottom: The Bigelow Operating Room at Massachusetts General Hospital was used to teach Harvard medical students in 1893. (SPNEA)

On the east side of Copley Square H.H. Richardson designed the masterpiece of his short career. Trinity Church, the Episcopal Church of the South End, led by the most distinguished clergyman of his day, the Reverend Phillips Brooks, was begun in 1873. A massive Romanesque structure with a single tall tower similar to those built in the 12th century, Trinity posed several engineering problems because it was built on "made land." First, Richardson had to figure a way to support the tower weighing more than 9,500 tons. He accomplished this by sinking four huge truncated pyramids of solid granite deep into the ground. Second, Richardson poured a mass of gravel more than thirty feet deep, through which 4,500 piles were driven into the bedrock. Finally, he decided at the last moment to omit the top fifty feet of the central tower and to reduce the height of the walls by several feet.

Trinity Church was consecrated on February 9, 1877. Alexander Rice, the governor of the commonwealth, Frederick O. Prince, the mayor of Boston, more than one hundred clergymen, and the warden and vestrymen of the church walked in procession to their seats, reciting Psalm 24. Reverend Brooks and several of his old friends shared the

service, speaking from small platforms projected over the five full-width steps leading to the spacious apse. The bishop of Massachusetts celebrated Holy Communion, bringing the memorable service to a close.

Several of Boston's major cultural and educational institutions were located near Trinity Church. Just one block east of Copley Square, the Boston Society of Natural History built a three-story brick museum (now Bonwit Teller's), and one block west, at Boylston and Exeter streets, the Harvard Medical School moved into a large facility chosen for its proximity to both Massachusetts General and City Hospital in the South End. Nearby, the Massachusetts Institute of Technology—known commonly as "Boston Tech"—was established in 1872. Presided over by the distinguished scientist William Barton Rogers, MIT pioneered in the effort to link high-quality scientific education and industrial research.

The Boston Public Library, opened in 1895, completed Copley Square. Built on land granted by the commonwealth, across the Square from Trinity Church, the library's splendid Renaissance building not only housed a vast collection of books, but manuscripts and original materials given to it by Brahmins who spent a

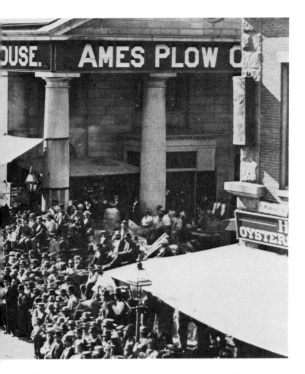

Higginson, by contrast, was committed to using his vast personal fortune to hire an orchestra of "sixty selected musicians and a conductor and paying them all year" so that he had the "right to all their time needed for rehearsals and concerts." Indignant critics of professionalism attacked Higginson's restrictive contractual arrangement with his musicians as "deluded wealth with arrant charlatanism." Most Bostonians, however, supported Higginson, pointing out that the quality of the Boston Symphony Orchestra depended upon the dedication of the players.

After eight months of preparation under

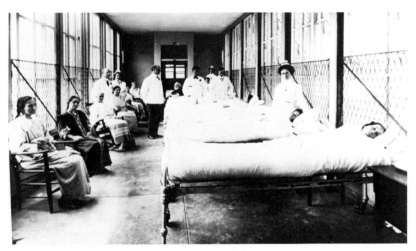

lifetime traveling and collecting. Heir to a fortune derived from textile mills, Thomas Gold Appelton bought a collection of valuable 17th century engravings in Rome which he donated to the library. Many other acts of civic generosity followed.

Founded in 1881 by Col. Henry Lee Higginson, the Boston Symphony Orchestra owed its origins to the city's long and deep interest in music and to Higginson's personal desire "to have a part in some good work which would leave a lasting mark." In the decades prior to Higginson's publicly announced intention to form the Boston Symphony Orchestra, Boston had supported an opera company—though a division over the relative merits of Italian versus German opera created what a critic labeled "the battle of the Operas"—as well as the Handel and Hayden Society (founded in 1815), four magazines devoted to music, and a professional music school. After the Civil War two symphonic groups were added to this early medley: the Harvard Musical Association, which devoted itself to classical programs; and the Boston Philharmonic Orchestra, formed in 1872 in response to the demand for more modern music. Neither group had solid financial backing or permanently employed professional musicians.

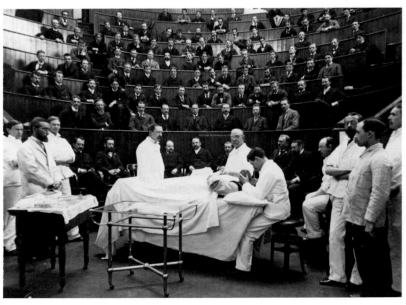

the direction of Georg Henschel, a German-born singer-pianist-composer-conductor, the Boston Symphony Orchestra gave its first concert on October 22, 1881, in the Boston Music Hall. The orchestra gave 20 Saturday evening concerts and an equal number of public rehearsals during its first season. Bostonians were delighted. A total of 83,359 people flocked to hear the orchestra. Indeed, the Boston Symphony Orchestra was so popular ticket speculators did a brisk business, spoiling Higginson's plan to make available inexpensive seats for "impecunious students and lovers of music."

In subsequent years the Boston Symphony Orchestra became a more disciplined and widely known orchestra. There was some grumbling among the musicians about the music director's penchant for long, grueling rehearsals, but Higginson cleverly undercut their complaints by offering those who stayed summer employment playing popular concerts, or "Pops." He also arranged a post-season tour in 1886, to help achieve visibility. Higginson's strategy paid off: critics in the cities on the tour praised the orchestra for the quality and precision of its playing.

Although they were proud of their orchestra, Bostonians were not as quick as outsiders to praise it. They seemed to prefer to indulge in what Philip Hale, long-time music critic for the *Boston Home Journal* and the *Herald,* called "A Boston Habit," the tendency "to be of a critical spirit concerning everything that pertains to art..." Any new piece of art, Hale observed, causes "many of the unemployed an unrest that only finds relief in spoken opinion and in long letters to the newspapers." But for every self-appointed critic, Hale found—and applauded—an equal number of amateur choral singers, "men and women (who) quietly attend the necessary rehearsals and go through the inevitable drudgery attending the preparation for a concert..." such as the performance of the *Messiah* given each year by the Handel and Hayden Society. Such

dedication to music, Hale concluded, "is a surer sign of true musical interest than the buying of seats for Symphony concerts at an exorbitant price."

Mrs. Isabella Stewart Gardner was a wealthy, flamboyant, not-all-together-proper Bostonian who belied Hale's characterization that the rich knew nothing about the arts but were willing to pay a high price to sustain the illusion that they did. Mrs. Gardner was the city's most famous and knowledgeable private collector of art. Born in New York, the daughter of David Steward, a wealthy department store owner, Isabella married a proper Bostonian, John Lowell Gardner in 1860. From that time until her death in 1924 at the age of 85, "Mrs. Jack," as she was popularly known, did "everything that Proper Boston women do not do, and then some." Among other outrageous acts that set Bostonians' tongues wagging, she drank beer rather than tea, walked down Tremont Street with a lion on a leash, became a Buddhist, and spent thousands of dollars on clothes and jewels. Her portrait, painted by John Singer Sargent in 1888, pictured her in a lowneck, tight-fitting black evening dress. After a brief public exhibit caused a rash of risque comments, Mr. Gardner demanded that the portrait never be shown again.

Despite her eccentric behavior, Mrs. Jack was an intelligent, careful collector of fine paintings by Titian, Vermeer, Rembrandt, Raphael, Whistler, and Degas. To house her collection she bought a Florentine palace and had it shipped piece by piece to Boston where it was rebuilt in the Fenway. On New Year's night 1903, Mrs. Gardner staged a grand opening of her palace for Boston society. While the Boston Symphony Orchestra played, Mrs. Jack allowed her guests to pay homage to her, to recognize—however grudgingly—that she was the queen of Boston society. When the concert concluded, she signaled for a large mirror to be moved so that the magnificent palace courtyard, filled with flowers, was visible to all the guests. There was at first, one man wrote, "an intense silence broken only by the water trickling in the fountains; then came a growing murmur of delight and one by one the guests pressed forward to make sure it was not all a dream."

Proper Boston society was even more impressed when it was learned that according to Mrs. Gardner's will, the palace and its magnificent art collection were to become the property of the people of Boston. It was an act of civic responsibility worthy of the most proper Bostonian. Henry Lee Higginson recognized Mrs. Jack as a Brahmin: "You and I have held the same view of life and its duties," the benefactor of the Boston Symphony Orchestra told her.

Other outsiders who made a contribution to the city's development also eventually won accolades from Boston's elite. Three businessmen, Isaac Rich, Lee Claflin, and Jacob Sleeper, active Methodists, founded Boston University, which was chartered officially in 1869. The University began with a school of theology, later linked to a college of liberal arts and ultimately to professional schools of law, medicine, and music. At his death, Rich, son of a Wellfleet fisherman, left Boston University a gift of several million dollars. The bequest turned to ashes, however, when the Great Fire of 1872 consumed all of the downtown property Rich had left to the university. His vision was intact, and although Boston University was forced to struggle in cramped quarters on Beacon Hill for several decades, it established itself as a great university long before it moved in 1939 to its present Commonwealth Avenue campus.

John Simmons was another Boston businessman who dreamed of founding a college to serve his adopted city. He was a farm boy from Rhode Island who made a fortune in the clothing business and real estate during the last half of the 19th century. In his time the clothing business was organized as a "putting-out system," a method which used the labor of poor, immigrant women working in their homes. Simmons made money, but he was haunted by the vision of those working women who were degraded because they had not been able to develop their intellect. When he made his will, Simmons endowed a college whose primary purpose would be to offer professional education for women. Simmons College opened the doors of its Fenway campus in 1901.

Just a few years later, Boston College left its original home in the South End and moved to Chestnut Hill. According to Rev. Charles Donovan, a historian of Boston College, the move was probably precipitated by an article that appeared in a Jesuit magazine in 1898, critical of the mingling of high school and college students, as was the case at Boston College. The author argued that American Jesuit colleges had lost a good bit of their prestige because good college students were "ashamed to be seen in the company of so many 'kids.'" Father Thomas Gasson apparently agreed. When he became president of Boston College in 1907, he moved the college to the spacious rural location in Chestnut Hill.

The new, open site implied nothing; the curriculum at Boston College remained a fixed classical course of study. Students were required to master Greek and Latin, "as they are languages with a structure and idiom remote from the language of the student, the study of them lays bare before him the laws of thought and logic." This rationale, which first appeared in the academic catalogue in 1894, was articulated by Fr. Timothy Brosnahan, president of Boston College from 1894 to 1898.

Fr. Brosnahan's statement emerged from a controversy with Charles Eliot, then president of Harvard. In his inaugural address in 1869, Eliot had vowed to turn Harvard into a great world university. He subsequently opened up the curriculum, introducing more scientific courses, and giving students a wide choice among subjects. This so-called elective system was necessary, Eliot maintained, in order to equip Harvard men with the ability to solve complex modern problems.

During his campaign to encourage

secondary schools to adopt the elective system, Eliot chose as a whipping boy the fixed Jesuit curriculum, which he said had "remained unchanged for 400 years." Fr. Brosnahan took up the defense of the classical curriculum, pointing out first that many Protestant college administrators were opposed to the open system. Finally, Brosnahan attacked Eliot as "pathetically naive" for denying that some graduates of Boston College were as well, or better, educated than some graduates of Harvard. Eliot was unmoved.

While the quality of university education was the chief concern of the Protestant and Catholic elite, most Bostonians were enmeshed in the process of creating a new life for themselves and their children. From among the city's earliest immigrant groups a middle class was emerging. Second, and third-generation Irish and Germans were eager to leave their original ethnic centers and take their place in the general life of the American middle class.

In the 1870s and 1880s thousands of Bostonians, ranging from those in the upper middle class—lawyers, brokers, large storeowners, manufacturers—to those in the central middle class—teachers, salesmen, contractors—to the artisans, office workers, and sales personnel who constituted the lower middle class, moved to the suburbs. Specifically, these groups left the crowded inner city for the spaciousness of the three formerly independent towns of Roxbury, West Roxbury, and Dorchester. Before 1870 these towns were mere villages; in 1870, when the suburbanization process was well underway, the towns had a population of 60,000; by 1900 they had boomed to 227,000.

Both real estate speculators and individual families wanted the modern services—schools, libraries, water, gas and sewer—offered by the city of Boston. The main water and sewer lines, therefore, were run as rapidly as possible out to the principal suburban streets, connecting the fast-growing towns with the central city system. Roxbury residents voted to give up their independent identity and become part of Boston in 1868; Dorchester made a similar decision in 1870, and West Roxbury in 1874.

Although there was a tendency for

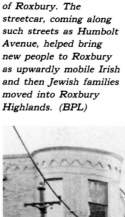

In 1868 Boston annexed the predominantly Yankee, Protestant town of Roxbury. The streetcar, coming along such streets as Humbolt Avenue, helped bring new people to Roxbury as upwardly mobile Irish and then Jewish families moved into Roxbury Highlands. (BPL)

particular ethnic groups to settle in distinct areas, the general economic mobility of second- and third-generation immigrants meant that the ethnic composition of Boston's new suburbs reflected the city's population proportions of about 30 years earlier. In 1880, for example, the foreign-born and their children made up about 46 percent of Dorchester's population; by 1905, the percentage had risen to 57%. Not surprisingly, the dominant ethnic group in 1880 was Irish, but by the turn of the century, Canadians, Russians, Germans, and Jews left the working class districts of the inner city and moved to Dorchester in significant numbers. This steady flow of ethnic groups to the suburbs demonstrated the continued openness of metropolitan society in general and of Boston's ability in particular to provide a middle class environment for the children of its immigrants.

Boston's suburban growth was made possible by the development of the street railway. Not coincidentally, Sam Bass Warner tells us in his book *Streetcar Suburbs,* "many of the founders and investors in street railways were real estate speculators who wanted to attract

new customers for their land." Henry Whitney, for example, established the West End line to Brookline in 1887, where he owned a large tract of land. A short time later, Whitney bought enough stock in several competing companies to effect a merger and create the first urban transit system in the nation. In 1888, Whitney began replacing the horse-drawn cars with electric streetcars and expanded further into the suburbs. He defended his monopoly by arguing that street railways had a positive "moral influence" on city development; street railways made it possible for workingmen to own homes and to escape the debilitating effects of living in crowded tenements.

Indeed, according to their promotors, street railways added significantly to the quality of all Bostonians' lives. By offering cheap transportation to parks and cemeteries outside the city, family togetherness was bolstered. On Sundays, thousands of Bostonians traveled out from town to spend the day at Castle Garden Amusement Park, or Norumbega Park in nearby Newton, or Forest Hills Cemetery, or Arnold Arboretum.

Within the city, the elevated railway and the subway—the nation's first, in

Center Street, in Jamaica Plain, was a typical business area in a streetcar suburb with its variety of stores and services, a thriving real estate company, and a new apartment building. There were similar scenes in Dorchester, West Roxbury, and Brighton. (SPNEA)

Frederick Law Olmsted
designed Boston's park
system in the 1880s.
Olmsted also created
Central Park in New York
City, Mount Royal in
Montreal, Golden Gate
Park in San Francisco,
and hundreds of smaller
parks and residential
gardens and estates.
Courtesy, National Park
Service, Frederick Law
Olmsted National Historic
Site

1893—made travel easier for both workers and shoppers. After 1901 people were
able to speed across town from Sullivan
Square in Charlestown to Dudley Station
in Roxbury in just twenty minutes on the
el. And, according to a brochure distributed by the Boston Elevated Railway,
such a trip would be not only fast, but an
aesthetic experience as well. The stations
used building materials "with finesse and
ingenuity, from large sheets of copper
molded into classical details to heavy
steel beams forming complex composi-
tions, some of delicacy, others of power."
And the elevated platforms, the company
boasted, "provide travellers with unusual
panoramas of Boston as well as views of
the tracks which seem to float inplausibly
between houses, commercial buildings,
and distant tree tops."

For some Bostonians, fast, efficient
transportation, however aesthetically
pleasing, was a sign of the "devouring
eagerness and intellectual strife" of city
life. In an attempt to do something about
curbing the excesses of city life, Charles
Eliot Norton of Harvard invited his friend
Frederick Law Olmsted to Boston.
Olmsted was the most famous landscape
architect in the nation. Among scores of
other projects he had designed Central

Park in New York City and the park
system linking Buffalo and Niagara
Falls, and played a major role in the
planning of the capitol grounds in
Washington, D.C. In Boston for a conference sponsored by the Lowell Institute,
Olmsted read a paper, "Public Parks and
the Enlargement of Towns," that was a
detailed explanation of his views on the
planning of cities.

He believed that cities symbolized
mankind's historic social progress. At the
same time, he acknowledged the rising
rate of social problems caused by the
closer proximity of people. Therefore,
Olmsted concluded, one of his principal
goals was to create an environment that
would make possible calm recreation and
be conducive to a healthy state of mind.
In other words, he believed parks were
civilizing forces. They were also great
democratizing experiences, bringing
people of all classes together.

The Boston City Council had a much
more mundane goal in mind: to do something about the danger and stench from
the polluted, stagnant Muddy River, a
tidal swamp and creek left over from the
time when all the Back Bay was a shallow
body of salt water. Olmsted offered to
remedy the problem, but only if the
Muddy River were made a part of a whole
new park system for Boston. In 1877 his
elaborate plan to form a green belt of
pleasure drives, parks, and ponds around
the city was accepted. His proposed
Arborway and Fenway would give access
to the western suburbs and link Franklin
Park and the Arnold Arboretum to the
Charles River and to tree-lined Commonwealth Avenue which ran downtown to the
Public Garden and the Common.

Muddy River was the first segment of
Olmsted's "Emerald Necklace." Although
it appears to be the fortunate preservation
of a piece of natural wilderness, the Fens
was created entirely by Olmsted from
rotting tidal flats on a barren river edge.
He made a charming fen-like wooded area
around the Muddy River while separating
the sewage from the stream by way of a
hidden conduit. The Fens was linked with

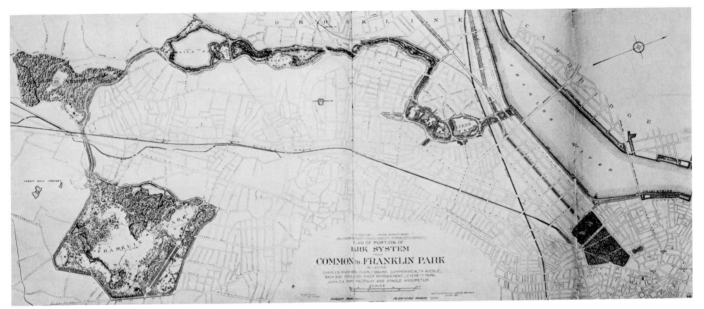

Commonwealth Avenue in Back Bay, then on to the Riverway to Jamaica Pond and the Arnold Arboretum, an experimental horticultural area managed by Harvard College. In what was called the West Roxbury Highlands, he created Franklin Park, then carried the concept through Columbia Road in Dorchester to the South Boston beaches and Castle Island.

The work of almost two decades, it was a magnificent accomplishment. Olmsted took great pride in having completed the first metropolitan system of parks in the United States. In 1893, he urged his colleagues to concentrate their best efforts on other projects in Boston. In their historical and educational impact they were, he declared, "the most important work of our profession now in hand anywhere in the world."

Not all landscape architecture conformed to Olmsted's ideals. His parks were designed to encourage contact between Boston's rich and well-born and the city's immigrants. However, many of the wealthy abandoned the dream of cultural integration, opting instead for protection and isolation. For example, in 1882 the nation's first exclusive, private country club was established in Brookline by J. Murray Forbes, a member of one of Boston's oldest families. Proudly consuming immense acreage for the benefit of a few golfers, The Country Club was touted as "a rendezvous for a colony of congenial spirits." Or, in more blunt language, no immigrant need apply.

The establishment of private preserves for the wealthy and public parks for the poor epitomized the ambiguous character of Boston society at the end of the 19th century. For Samuel Eliot Morison, a young Boston Brahmin who later became a Harvard professor, the new century "was a high moment of hope and glory— (with) vistas of progress looming ahead. . .This opening year of the new century for me, marked the transition from childhood to youth. . . .Those last years of the nineteenth century were a great time for a boy to grow up in Boston." Morison's youthful observation was correct; Boston did have much of which to be proud. But what young Morison didn't notice amidst the self-congratulatory celebration was the tendency of members of his class to look anxiously for islands of security in a Boston society that had become so diverse that culture, education, and government seemed to be threatened. The "proof" that their fears were real came in 1905 when John F. Fitzgerald, an Irish Catholic ward boss, became mayor of Boston.

Boston's park system is called the "Emerald Necklace" because it is a string of green jewels, beginning with the Charles River Basin and ending at Franklin Park. Courtesy, National Park Service, Frederick Law Olmsted National Historic Site

VII
Ward Bossism and James Michael Curley

Barney McGinneskin wanted to be a cop, one of Boston's finest. But he was Irish. And, in 1850, that was enough to disqualify him. Although more than one-third of Boston's population at this time was Irish, they had almost no political influence, no access to jobs on the city's payroll.

Power was in the hands of a wealthy, Yankee elite. Nearly two-thirds of the city's Aldermen between 1838-1850 were either merchants or lawyers; more than 90% of the men who were elected mayor during that same period were well-to-do attorneys or businessmen. All were Protestants. Nearly all were descended from one of New England's founding families. Like the priestly Brahmin class of ancient Hindus who performed the sacred rites and set moral standards, Boston's

Above: A common sight in the West End, the hurdy-gurdy man attracted the attention of children of all ages. (TBS)

Previous page: Mayor Curley threw the first ball of the season at Fenway Park in 1924. (BPL)

leaders perched on top of a modern caste system in which they were recognized as the superior group. The Lorings, Grays, Lowells, Everetts, Cabots, Shaws, Forbes, Winthrops, Peabodys, Cushings and Saltonstalls proudly and naturally assumed responsibility for the city's political life.

A shakeup in state politics in 1850 led the Boston wing of the Whig party to which the Brahmin's belonged to look—however reluctantly—to conservative Irish Democrats in order to counter an ascendant liberal coalition. One part of the deal was a promise by the Whigs that an Irishman would be added to the Boston police force. Barney McGinneskin was that Irishman. He was 42 years old, a cabby, and had been a taxpayer for 22 years when he was interviewed by the police board. McGinneskin wanted the job for very practical reasons: a policeman earned $2.00 a day—nearly twice what a common laborer was paid—and it was guaranteed work all year.

Following a careful investigation and a lengthy interview, the police board recommended McGinneskin to the Board of Aldermen. Initially only John Bigelow publicly objected, stating "that it is a

dangerous precedent to appoint a foreigner to stations of such trust." Other critics, including the City Marshall Francis Tukey soon joined Bigelow. Opposition grew until the entire night shift of the Boston police department marched to the polls to elect Benjamin Seaver mayor in the hope that he would bar McGinneskin from joining the force.

The policemen miscalculated badly. Mayor Seaver was unwilling to acknowledge publicly his anti-Irish bias. Rather, he re-instated McGinneskin and fired the entire night shift. By this point, however, McGinneskin was exhausted and embarrassed and he resigned.

While Irishmen joked—"there goes the force"—McGinneskin's struggle, together with the development of Irish political power in the last quarter of the 19th century, eventually opened the police force to Irishmen. By 1871 there were 45 Irish policemen; in 1900 an even 100. This dramatic change was brought about by a handful of shrewd, ambitious and energetic Irishmen who seized control of their neighborhood by providing help to their own people when they were unable to get what they needed from any other source. "The earliest leaders," William Shannon writes, "organized the Irish voters as a battering ram to break the power of a hostile majority."

The political machines built by Irish ward bosses in Boston developed out of family and neighborhood loyalties, from old country ties; and, most importantly, from the idea that politics was a struggle for power among competing groups. Yankee political leaders, to the contrary, took the position that a good citizen was called to "service", motivated by the ideal of civic responsibility, and committed to the goal of a stable, moral community. Because of their working class backgrounds, Irish politicians were far more practical minded. They entered politics as a career because, if successful, politics made possible rapid upward mobility for the ward boss and his Irish neighbors.

Beginning in the late 1880s, Boston's

political life began to be transformed by the new Irish ward bosses. John F. Ftizgerald—"Honey Fitz"—controlled the densely populated North End, "Smiling Jim" Donovan's sartorial elegance and flashing spending habits endeared him to Irishmen in the South End, Joe O'Connell used his power to dominate Ward Twenty in Dorchester, and Pat Kennedy directed East Boston. The most powerful and successful ward boss was Martin Lomasney. Known as the "Mahatma," Lomasney ran Ward Eight in the West End for more than fifty years. He knew what politicians wanted—votes—and he knew what the people needed—"food, clothing and shelter." There has to be someone in every ward to turn to for help, he once told a friend. "Help, you understand, none of your Yankee law and justice, but help." In exchange for the votes "his people" delivered to an office-seeker, Lomasney demanded and got access to jobs which he distributed to his loyal supporters. It was simple: power and patronage went hand in hand in the Irish neighborhoods.

In 1895, in the midst of a severe economic depression, a number of Irish ward bosses united to elect Josiah Quincy IV, the last of the Yankee Democrats, mayor of Boston. Quincy responded to the demands of working people by ordering

The "visiting nurse" served people who could not get to a doctor. Here a nurse, in striped dress, is visiting these women and teaching them about haircare. Courtesy, Visiting Nurse Association, Boston University

city departments to hire organized labor for specific projects and by establishing a city owned printing plant staffed by workers whose benefits included paid holidays and the 8-hour day, still regarded as a rare and bold innovation. Indeed, Quincy's experiment in municipal socialism caused him to lose the support of at least one Irish ward boss, Patrick "Peajacket" Maguire. He told his followers that they would "forfeit public confidence and come to grief" if they

Sleigh rides were popular in Boston around the turn of the century. This view of Beacon Street was taken following a 1901 snowstorm. (BPL)

The Boston subway, which began operation in 1897, was the first underground railroad in the country. This group of dignitaries and conductors made one of the first official trips under Park Street. (BPL)

listened to the siren song of radicalism.

Elected mayor in 1902 and again in 1905, Patrick Collins was more to the liking of those ward bosses who wanted city government to be less socialistic and more Irish. Collins came to Boston at age four, fleeing famine-stricken Ireland. Forced to leave school before he was twelve, as well as an apprenticeship as a machinist a few years later, because of militant anti-Catholic bias, Collins flirted with radicalism. He joined the Fenian Brotherhood—the political culture developed by Irish nationalists battling British imperialism—and helped form an upholsters union. Still, he threw himself into his work, winning promotions and achieving prosperity. In 1867 Collins was elected to the Massachusetts House and three years later he became the first Irish Catholic elected to the state senate. He studied law, served three terms in the United States Congress, and became a wealthy man, director of the International Trust Company.

By the time Collins became mayor (the second Irish Catholic) his youthful flirtation with radicalism was long forgotten. His conservative fiscal policies earned him the support of a great many Republicans, and his conservative demeanor, the admiration of the Brahmin elite in general. Collins was hailed as an

example of how an illiterate Irish immigrant could be transformed by residence in Boston into a sober, responsible citizen.

Mayor Collins' sudden death in 1905 cleared the way for Fitzgerald, the North End ward boss, to run for the city's highest office. "Honey Fitz" won easily, becoming the first American-born son of Irish parentage ever to be elected mayor of Boston. Municipal reformers despaired. Fitzgerald was not only regarded as a brash opportunist, but a representative of the corrupt ward system of patronage politics that spelled doom to the old Brahmin ideal of disinterested political service.

To counter the frightening prospect of a complete Irish-Democratic takeover, Yankee "progressives" formed the Good Government Association. Calling for reform, the institutionalization of professional and efficient processes to improve city government, and commited to supporting candidates who were qualified by education, breeding, and experience, the GGA threw its weight behind James Jackson Storrow in 1910.

The GGA firmly believed that Storrow, an able, civic-minded banker, could beat Fitzgerald. In part the Yankees' optimism stemmed from a series of changes that had been made in the city's charter between 1907 and 1909. First, in an obvious move to cripple the Democratic ward bosses, city elections were to be non-partisan. Second, a special Finance Commission, composed of prominent, independent citizens, was formed to oversee "all matters pertaining to the finances of the city." Third, the mayor's term of office was extended from two to four years, but his patronage powers were reduced considerably.

These reforms, together with the candidacy of Storrow, led the Brahmins to believe they had found a short cut through the Yankee-Irish conflict. But the reformers had ignored a democratic imperative—majority rule.

"Honey Fitz" launched a vigorous campaign that exploited the economic and social differences between Celtic and Yankee. Specifically, Fitzgerald charged that Storrow was trying to buy the election. The aggressive Irishman called upon Storrow to make public his total assets as well as the amount of money he was spending on the campaign. Storrow refused. He angrily maintained that he was doing nothing wrong; and he insisted, in typical Yankee fashion, that his word was his bond.

Fitzgerald seized upon Storrow's wealth and arrogance and made it the key issue in the campaign. "Honey Fitz" criss-crossed the city's wards, on some evenings visiting as many as eight clubs, meeting halls, and taverns, enjoying food and drink with the crowds, giving a rousing speech and then singing a chorus or two of his theme song "Sweet Adeline" before moving on. Stiff, awkward and shy, Storrow was no match for Fitzgerald.

Although the business community regarded Fitzgerald with loathing, "Honey Fitz" did not attack basic Yankee values. His campaign slogan was "A Bigger, Better and Busier Boston," and he was an untiring promoter of the port of Boston. In short, Fitzgerald was colorful, but respectable enough for the Catholic clergy and the emerging "lace curtain" Irish. He defeated Storrow by 1,402 votes.

Fitzgerald's narrow victory marked a

turning point in Boston political history. It signaled the end of Yankee control and the emergence of a new Irish-style of politics. Using the personal networks created by ward bosses to stage rallies and meetings of all sorts, an Irish candidate for city office made scores of appearances in order to convince voters that he was one of them.

Fitzgerald's energetic campaign style was matched by his drive once in the mayor's office. He built schools and playgrounds, founded a hospital, and extended the subway to Cambridge. He also increased the pay of city laborers and gave all city employees a half-day off on Saturdays. His solid record and charismatic personality seemed to insure Fitzgerald of a second four-year term.

It came as a complete surprise, therefore, when a young, aggressive Congressman named James Michael Curley announced that he was going to oppose Mayor Fitzgerald. After a good deal of hesitation, "Honey Fitz" withdrew. In his place the panicky Democratic City Committee chose a scholarly lawyer from South Boston, Thomas Kenny. The Good Government Association quickly endorsed him, and both Fitzgerald and Storrow backed him against Curley. Not a single ward boss sided with Curley. Not one newspaper endorsed him.

The latest addition to Boston Consolidated Gas Company's fleet of vehicles for transporting workers to the job is seen in this circa 1905 photograph. Courtesy, Boston Gas

This fit perfectly with Curley's two-fisted style. He loudly and crudely assaulted everyone who opposed him and appealed directly to the people by tapping into the deep-seated anger and envy of the Irish working class. Curley ridiculed the Democratic City Committee as "a collection of chowderheads"; branded the GGA as simple-minded "goo goos"; and denounced Yankee business leaders as "the State Street wrecking crew." At the same time, Curley assured the voters that he would be independent and accessible to everyone. He would be the people's mayor, fighting the people's enemies.

Curley wound up his 1914 campaign in his opponent's home district. "I'll be elected mayor of Boston, and you don't like it," he boasted to a hostile audience. And then he threw out a challenge: "Here I am. Does any one of you bums want to step up here and make anything of it?" Curley won by more than 6,000 votes, carrying sixteen of the twenty-six wards, including all the working class sections of the city.

The style and substance of Curley's politics came from his experiences as an Irish "slum brat" in Roxbury. Growing up in the "waterfront slum of ward seventeen," he wrote in his autobiography

I'd Do It Again, the mansions in the Back Bay "seemed like castles." His father's death in 1884, when James Michael was ten, meant that he and his brother and his mother all had to work to maintain the family. Sarah Curley sometimes found work as a maid in one of the wealthy homes on Beacon Hill, or as a scrubwoman in an office building along State Street. James Michael sold newspapers after school until he graduated from grammar school. After that he took a job delivering groceries in a horse-drawn cart and then, briefly, as a machine operator at the New England Piano Company. Hard work and long hours taught young Curley that "barons. . .exploited Irish labor." He learned that he "belonged to an Irish Catholic minority. . .despised socially and discriminated against politically." It was this sense of rage and the possibility of rapid upward mobility that brought Curley into politics. "Curley," the Boston *Transcript* observed sarcastically in 1933, "was born not with a silver spoon, but with a wooden ladder in his mouth, which he proceeded forthwith to climb."

Curley began his audacious climb as soon as he reached voting age in 1895. As always his approach was a frontal assault. He challenged "Pea Jacket" Maguire, long time boss of Ward 17: first Curley won Maguire's seat on the Common Council; next young Curley seized control of the ward's Democratic Committee. Now he was boss.

But Curley's ambition, his flamboyant style, and his egotism made him unsuited for the stale game of petty politics played by the old-style ward boss. He was not the least bit interested in being a cog in someone else's machine. He sought to be the most powerful figure in Boston politics, the one person to whom thousands would look for jobs, of course, but also for inspiration and revenge. His poor Irish followers were thrilled to learn, for example, that Curley had told the Harvard Board of Overseers: "The Massachusetts of the Puritans is as dead as Caesar, but there is no need to mourn the fact. Their successors—the Irish—had letters and learning, culture and civilization when the ancestors of the Puritans were savages running half-naked through the forests of Britain. It took the Irish to make Massachusetts a fit place to live in."

Curley's aggressive—and to the Irish, funny—attacks on wealthy Yankees, were matched by his showy appearance, oratory, and life-style to create an image that delighted his constituents. Strikingly handsome, Curley usually wore a black coat, white vest, gray-striped trousers, a gray soft hat, and a velvet-collared Chesterfield coat. He affected a Harvard accent and developed a mellifluous speaking voice that was his greatest political asset. Shortly after he was elected mayor in 1915, Curley left Ward 17 for a magnificent house he had built in Jamaica Plain. A huge dining room, mahogany paneling and a winding staircase were only a few of the house's expensive features. Although his detractors gossiped and an inconclusive public investigation was launched, Curley's working-class supporters didn't begrudge his life-style, nor did they doubt that he was still "one of us."

Curley's political strength also had a practical basis. During his first term on the Common Council in 1900 he sponsored a bill that ended the practice of laying off city laborers without pay during inclement weather while clerks and foremen remained on the job and drew a full salary. Likewise, in his first term as Mayor of Boston, Curley helped working people by firing nearly 600 city employees who had been appointed by Fitzgerald or had worked for Thomas Kenny's election. "Mr. Fitzgerald has left in office a number of people who are hostile to me," Curley announced, "and as I have no desire to be ambushed in my own camp, I am removing them."

Soon the corridors of city hall were crowded with voters who came looking for jobs and favors of every description. Curley saw every one of them, rewarding those who had been his loyal supporters and friends. More than personal demagoguery or mere showmanship, this process—the beginning of Curleyism—realigned political power in Boston. Curley's move to take into his own hands the distribution of all city jobs, cut the political legs out from under the ward bosses. From now on, Curley alone would dispense patronage.

In a city plagued with chronic unemployment, jobs were the chief means of patronage. Therefore, Curley began a series of building projects. (He "rivaled Caesar Augustus as a monumental builder," a recent historian has quipped.) He greatly enlarged Boston City Hospital, created a number of smaller health units in the neighborhoods, and developed the mudflats along the South Boston ocean front into a recreational mecca that included miles of beaches, several bathhouses, and a solarium. Elsewhere in the city Curley built playgrounds, stadiums, and parks. He expanded the subway system, extended the tunnel to East Boston, and undertook to widen and pave thousands of miles of streets. In short, Curley set in motion an energetic government that provided tangible and enduring benefits for Boston voters.

Curley's construction projects were expensive and soon conservative businessmen and bankers were howling. They contended that "Curleyism" was irresponsible, that his reckless spending would bankrupt the city or at least send the tax rate soaring. Curley brushed aside these criticisms; tax money was meant to be used to help the people. Besides, he pointed out, the tax rate had inched up slowly—from $1.15 to $1.80—during his tenure in office, while it had skyrocketed during the terms of his immediate predecessors.

Curley did admit—with his political tongue in cheek—that he may have been too compassionate toward those in desperate need. "I have known what it is to be hungry," he wrote in 1929, "and I have known what it is to be cold, and if I have sometimes erred in response to the dictates of the heart rather than the head, perhaps I am not altogether to blame. . . .My sympathies and purse have been ever freely given to those who stood shivering in the shadow of adversity." His critics called this kind of rhetoric pure demogoguery, but thousands of Bostonians believed he was sincere.

His actor's skill for personalizing issues and his commitment to using government to resolve those issues, made it possible for Curley to dominate Boston politics for more than thirty years. His triumph wasn't easy; he made enemies as well as friends. First, the ward bosses fought him. They wanted their patronage powers restored. To accomplish that, the bosses entered three Democratic candidates in the race for the mayor's office in 1917, two of whom had Irish names. The winner was Andrew Peters, a conservative Yankee.

The bosses victory over Curley was short-lived, however. He waged a spectacular campaign in 1921, defeating John R. Murphy, a respected veteran Boston politician. Curley derided Murphy's experience: he was "an old mustard plaster that has been stuck on the back of the people for fifty years."

Curley won by fewer than 2,500 votes. Once again he began knocking down old buildings to make way for new construction projects. Within two months after he was sworn in, Curley had reduced unemployment from 75,000 to 45,000. While his enemies charged that he produced an "administrative wilderness," even they had to concede that he did get things done.

Because a provision of the city charter prohibited a mayor from serving successive terms, Curley made a bid to become governor of Massachusetts in 1924 but he was defeated by Alvan T. Fuller, a Republican. Curley's constant appeals to emotionalism and to the prejudices of the Irish working class made it difficult for his candidacy to transcend Boston's city limits.

Curley's formal announcement that he intended to run for mayor again in 1929, therefore, surprised no one. The GGA

backed Frederick Mansfield, a conservative Irish Democrat who had previously served as state treasurer and president of the Massachusetts Bar Association. Mansfield made Curley the issue; Curley wisely made "work and wages" the focus of his campaign. He proposed a fifty year program for public work in Boston. With new construction at a standstill and unemployment increasing daily, Curley easily won the endorsement of the Boston Central Labor Union and of his old foes, the ward bosses. Curley's margin of victory was smaller than he (and other experts) had predicted, but as a floral tribute, placed in front of city hall on the day after the election proclaimed — Curley was *still* "Champion of Them All."

But Curley's old formula of personal patronage was hopelessly inadequate as the recession of 1928-1929 became the Great Depression. As the lines of unemployed men and women grew, the search for a quick remedy caused the rift between Curley and the Council to grow.

Of course the mayor loved it. He encouraged confrontation. Labeling his old Yankee enemies "tools of Wall Street," Curley chastized them for not using their "vast wealth" to help "those in need."

Curley's tough rhetoric and his early alliance with President Franklin Roosevelt propelled him into the governor's office in 1934, his only state-wide victory. His two years on Beacon Hill were at once tumultuous and disappointing. Curleyism was wearing thin, especially among the "lace curtain" Irish who lived in Boston's suburbs, and even among the younger generation who remained in the city but whose emotional attachment to an ethnic neighborhood was much less intense than their parents.

In 1936 Curley suffered a major defeat. He was beaten in a race for the United States Senate by the young, inexperienced Yankee, Henry Cabot Lodge, Jr. The following year Curley lost on his home turf. Maurice Tobin defeated Curley by more than 25,000 votes. Although Curley became mayor of Boston once more when

he won a fourth term in 1945, the days of "Curley's Boston"—of Yankee baiting and personal power—were gone. All that remained was the legend.

Curley's notoriety began in 1903 when he took a civil service exam for one of his constituents. His ruse was discovered, however, and Curley was sentenced to sixty days in the Charles Street jail. Showing not the smallest hint of embarrassment, let alone repentance, Curley boldly explained, "I did it for a friend." To his supporters, Curley's action was not a crime but a heroic gesture.

Thousands of Bostonians claimed to have been the recipient of James Michael's personal generosity and concern. "He really cared about us and took care of his own," an Irishman from Brighton recalled. Another added, "If you were in trouble or needed help, you could always count on Curley."

Because he used power to help the poor, Curley was characterized as a Robin Hood by those who felt oppressed by Yankee Boston. When he was convicted of misappropriating city funds and sentenced to prison (after serving five months, his sentence was commuted by President Harry Truman) the man-on-the-street asked, "How can you call it stealing, if you take the money and give it away to people who need it?" Or, as one South Boston Irishwoman put it: "He never kept a cent of it for himself. He was always giving money away to people who needed it."

Curley's final, hapless bids to be mayor (1951 and 1955) did nothing to tarnish his legend. When he died in November 1958, Boston wept. Countless stories of his largesse and his larceny were retold. He was loved for his sentimentality and cursed for his divisive use of power.

Both characterizations are correct. Why else would there need to be two statues of James Michael Curley—one seated on a park bench seemingly listening attentively to someone in need of help, the other stuck in a speaking pose, pausing perhaps to enjoy one of his slashing rhetorical attacks on an opponent.

Facing page and left: When Bostonians erected a statue of longtime mayor, James Michael Curley, they decided to build two to represent both the public and private qualities of Curley's tenure—the official leader of the city and the friend of hundreds of individual citizens. Courtesy, Boston Art Commission

VIII
Turmoil and Triumph

For many Bostonians the first half of the 20th century is memorable only for two thrilling victories by the Red Sox: in 1918, behind the pitching and hitting of Babe Ruth, the Sox won the World Series; and in 1946, when "The Kid," Ted Williams, batted the Bosox to their second American League pennant. The years between these two triumphs were one long string of inexplicable, heartbreaking failures for Red Sox fans. ("Some Bostonians criticize art, some music, some Harvard," noted a local pundit, "but most just criticize the Red Sox.") Bostonians' unconquerable faith in mankind was tested in more serious ways as well. These were tumultuous years, characterized by a wave of protest by blacks and women demanding equal rights, a devastating epidemic, a rash of bitter strikes often

Above: In the late 1800s, when blacks began moving from the West End to the South End and Roxbury, the African Meeting House was sold to a Jewish congregation. The Museum of Afro-American History purchased the structure in 1970 and is renovating it in collaboration with the National Park Service. (SPNEA)

Previous page: Mayor Curley adjusts the microphone for Franklin D. Roosevelt during the 1932 presidential campaign. Curley supported Roosevelt despite pressure from the state Democratic leadership to back Al Smith. (BPL)

Soon after 1890, Boston's black population increased rapidly, though it remained small in proportion to the city's growing white population—never more than 2 percent before 1940. In 1890 there were 8,590 black people living in Boston, nearly 12,000 in 1900, and 16,350 by 1920. As a result blacks burst out of the West End, where they had been congregated, on the northwestern slope of Beacon Hill, and began moving into the South End, and by the 1920s into lower Roxbury. They moved into the old brownstone apartments that dotted the area between Washington Street and Columbus Avenue; then, in the early 1900s, along Columbus Avenue and Tremont Street into the upper portion of the South End. When, by the 1930s, the black community numbered more than 20,000, it extended into Roxbury by way of Dudley Street and Massachusetts Avenue.

Within the South End-Roxbury ghetto Boston's black people built a viable and proud community, although they were subjected to a virulent racism. Job discrimination, for example, systematically deprived black artisans of their trades. This meant that many men were forced to seek low-paying, unskilled jobs in the railroad yards and station of the South End. Job discrimination also accounts for the fact that married black women worked in much greater proportions than their counterparts in other immigrant groups. While only 5 percent of all white married women worked, nearly 30 percent of all black married women worked outside the home. It was also quite common for black families to take boarders into their homes so that they might cut living expenses and boost their income, which was the lowest in the city. By utilizing these various survival strategies, the black family held together.

The black churches of Boston helped provide stability for the family. They were agencies of social control, centers for adult education and an arena for political action. Indeed, Robert Hayden claims in his study of *The Black Church in Boston* that churches "represent pillars of

aggravated by a fear of Bolshevism, the trials and execution of radicals Sacco and Vanzetti, the Great Depression, and the rapid and disruptive effects of the transformation of Boston's economy.

Because it had been the intellectual center of the abolitionist movement, Boston was popularly known as "Freedom's Birthplace," a label that paid homage to the myth of racial equality. The central conception of the myth was the notion that Boston was the ideal place for black people to live during the early decades of the 20th century. Like all powerful myths, that of Boston's special commitment to racial equality did influence Bostonian's perception of reality and also therefore, their behavior. But it also masked reality, the ugly marks of social and economic injustice and discrimination. Before he left North Carolina in 1928, Edward Cooper was told, "When you get to Boston the only way you'll know you're colored is to look in the mirror." "I had been here just three weeks," Cooper recalled, "and I was called a nigger for the first time in my life."

strength, the foundations on which black life in Boston have been built and survived." It is not surprising, therefore, that the church was often the first institution established when the black community expanded into the South End and Roxbury. By 1915 the Fourth Methodist, Twelfth Baptist, the People's Baptist and the Columbus Avenue A.M.E. Zion church all had moved from the West End into the South End of Roxbury. The Charles Street A.M.E. church remained in the West End until 1939, when it too moved to Roxbury.

The Reverend Reverdy Ransom was pastor of the Charles Street church while the population shift from Beacon Hill to Roxbury was occurring. Because he had such a towering reputation as a speaker, however, many black people chose to attend Charles Street rather than a more conveniently located church. In 1905 the Reverend Ransom spoke in Faneuil Hall commemorating the one hundredth birthday of Wendell Phillips and William Lloyd Garrison. The *Boston Transcript* reported that Ransom's speech "stirred a crowded audience of Negro men and women. . .as no white speaker has been able to stir them throughout the whole series of Garrison addresses at previous meetings. . . . They cheered, they shouted. . .they threw their handkerchiefs and hats in the air."

Like other black clergymen, Reverend Ransom also was an important political leader within the black community. He spoke out forcefully against racial prejudice. Although he conceded that discrimination in Boston was not as brutal as it was in the South, he argued that "where it appears it is nonetheless deadly and humiliating. The aloofness of manner, a politeness of speech and the kid glove handling of social and economic contacts," Ransom told his audience, "are under the surface, just as hard and unyielding as one finds in the solid South." In fact, he added, "one feels it more on the soil that was dedicated to freedom than on the Southern soil that fell on deaf ears. To outsiders, Boston

William Monroe Trotter, publisher of the Guardian *from 1901 until his death in 1934, was an equal rights activist. With W.E.B. DuBois, Trotter founded the Niagara Movement, which led to the founding of the NAACP. An elementary school in Roxbury bears his name. Courtesy, Museum of Afro-American History In Boston*

continued to be perceived as a marvelous example of racial harmony. And because white Bostonians rarely had contact with black people living in the South End-Roxbury ghetto, that myth was perpetuated. In fact, as we have seen, blacks in Boston were victims of racial injustice. But they continued to struggle for complete equality.

Black protest in Boston was led by William Monroe Trotter, editor of the *Guardian* and a militant activist in the campaign for civil rights. Trotter devoted his life to protesting anything that drew a color line. He demanded full and immediate equality. Therefore, he adamantly rejected the conciliatory, gradual strategy espoused by Booker T. Washington, who had laid claim to national leadership in a speech he made at the Atlanta Exposition in 1895.

Washington assured his audience that "the wisest among my race understand that agitation of questions of social equality is the extremest folly." Progress and prosperity for black people, Washington argued, will come "in

Residents gathered at the Swift River Hotel in 1916 for the centennial celebration of Enfield's incorporation. By 1940 the town had been dismantled, the hotel removed, and the river valley flooded to create the Quabbin Reservoir. (SPNEA)

proportion as we learn to dignify and glorify common labor. . . ." If blacks had economic opportunity, Washington believed, whites would eventually "blot out" race prejudice and establish absolute justice. To Washington it seemed that he was not giving up much in such a compromise.

Trotter believed otherwise. Angrily, he pointed to the disfranchisement of blacks, to lynch mobs, and to the doctrine of "separate but equal" as proof that white America was building a caste system which relegated black people to a status of inferiority. He filled the pages of the *Guardian* with invective, lashing out at Washington as a traitor to his race.

The criticism of Trotter and his group mounted to such an extent that Washington decided to come to Boston to challenge his opponents on their home ground. More than two thousand black people packed into the Columbus Avenue A.M.E. Zion Church on a hot July night in 1902 to hear Washington. Trotter had organized a group of hecklers who began to hiss Washington when he came onto the platform. Refusing to let him begin his prepared speech, they shouted questions about his attitude on civil and political rights. Trotter jumped onto a chair and demanded the right to speak. People pushed and shoved, shouted, fights

broke out. The police rushed into the church, ousted the hecklers and hauled Trotter and his sister off to jail.

Trotter's tactics were condemned and he was branded an extremist by newspapers across the nation. But he had a disregard for popularity. As he saw it, his function was not to maintain polite debate, but to stimulate people to action. To be sure, sometimes his passion caused him to be unwise and unfair in his attacks. But his cause was just and he staid the course.

On Patriot's Day, April 19, 1915, Trotter led nearly two thousand singing, chanting, black Bostonians up Beacon Street toward the State House. They marched to protest the showing of a new film, *The Birth of a Nation,* by D.W. Griffith. Trotter charged that the film provoked racial antipathies and hatred and was damaging to the image of black people. The film was not art at all, but propaganda designed to appeal to the idea of white supremacy.

The Birth of a Nation cost nearly $60,000 to produce, ran for two and one-half hours, and cost patrons a minimum of $2.00 per ticket. The focus of the film was the Cameron family of South Carolina, a tragic victim of black rapine. After losing two sons in the war, the Cameron's home is looted by vicious black soldiers and their daughter Flora leaps to her death rather than succumb to the advances of a black man. Still other travails follow until the Klan, a band of hooded, armed riders, came to the rescue. White audiences cheered.

Before the film opened in Boston, Trotter and several activist clergymen met with Mayor James Michael Curley and Police Commissioner Stephen O'Meara. They demanded that the film not be shown, or, if shown, that two especially objectionable scenes be cut. Curley's answer was evasive, causing Trotter to organize a protest at the Tremont Theatre where *Birth of a Nation* was playing to packed houses.

A large crowd of blacks gathered outside the theatre on the night of April

17. They first tried to buy tickets, but were refused. A melee occurred during which several blacks forced their way into the theatre. Once inside they shouted epithets and hurled rotten eggs and tomatoes at the screen before they were arrested. Outside, angry blacks and whites scuffled until the police intervened shortly before midnight.

Trotter's protest march, designed to pressure Governor David Walsh into banning the film in the interest of public safety, temporarily united the black community. Supporters of Washington's cautious approach to change joined with members of the recently formed Boston branch of the National Association for the Advancement of Colored People and with Trotter's militant group. Still nothing happened.

Because he believed that the civil rights of black Americans were being ignored, Trotter was not very enthusiastic about President Woodrow Wilson's call "to make the world safe for democracy." He was a loyal American, but he refused to participate in a meeting called by the Secretary of War to undercut "unrest among the colored people." Rather, in June 1918, Trotter brought together in Washington, D.C., under the banner of the National Liberty Congress, a group of militant blacks who petitioned the Congress to make Wilsonian idealism a reality at home while black soldiers fought and died in Europe. Essentially, the NLC demanded an end to racial segregation and the integration of the armed forces.

Nothing happened. Trotter called for black representatives at the approaching peace conference so that the American racial crisis would be brought to the attention of the world. The State Department refused to issue passports to Trotter or the other delegates. Crushed, he returned home to Boston in the summer of 1918 and sat by helplessly as his wife died.

By the late summer of 1918, Bostonians began to believe that the rumors of a German collapse and of an impending armistice were true. Perhaps now the sickening parade of black-bordered newspaper stories about death—"Gassed Dorchester Soldier's Funeral Today," "Boston Flyer Downed"—would stop. But rumor was not yet reality and at Fort Devens, thirty miles west of Boston, and at other camps thousands of soldiers still were being trained for combat in France.

Recruiters for World War I urged men to enlist, assuring them it would help to protect American womanhood. Photograph by Leslie Jones/Boston Herald. (BPL)

Boston residents converted the open space of the Common into a "victory garden" during World War I. The service buildings were temporary. (TBS)

Major General Henry McCain, who commanded the new Twelfth Infantry Division at Camp Devens, announced on August 20, 1918, his firm intention to have the division ready for embarkation to France in fourteen weeks. Less than three weeks later, thousands of General McCain's soldiers were hospitalized, stricken with influenza or pneumonia. Both were killers.

The Camp Devens hospital normally accommodated two thousand; by mid-September there were 8,000 men who needed treatment. The death rate was accelerating at an alarming pace. During a single 24-hour period the *Boston Globe* reported 66 men had died.

A navy ship tied up at Commonwealth Pier in Boston reported eight cases of influenza on August 28, 58 the following day, and 119 on the third of September. On September 11—the day the Red Sox won the World Championship—the navy announced that 26 sailors stationed in Boston had died from influenza or pneumonia.

Boston's public health officials initially were skeptical and poorly informed about the dangers of the epidemic. Although army and navy doctors had concluded by early September that "air and sunshine and an avoidance of crowds" were the best preventative measures that could be taken, Bostonians insisted upon holding mass rallies for the Liberty Loan campaign and jamming into Fenway Park.

Influenza raced through the city. The hospitals were inundated. Doctors and nurses worked nonstop. From September 1918 to March 1919 the Massachusetts Department of Health recorded more than 85,000 cases of influenza. Each day the death toll mounted. On September 14, 21 Boston residents died; on September 24, the *Globe* reported 109 deaths; and on October 1, the grim number reached 202. By spring more than 6,000 had died, about 1.5 percent of the population of Boston.

Everyone knew death. There was no end to the tragic stories told by the survivors. Visiting nurses often walked into scenes of horror, like those of the Black Death in the 14th century. They drew crowds of supplicants, or people ran from them fearing that their white dresses and gauze masks carried the disease. One nurse found an eight year old in his pajamas lying on the sidewalk. She took him into his home and found his father

In the months following the end of World War I, hundreds of residents died during a worldwide influenza epidemic. Tents were set up on the grounds of City Hospital to accommodate the numbers of ill Bostonians. Courtesy, Boston University Library

sick and exhausted. Three other children and their mother seemed on the edge of death. When a Catholic sister was asked by a reporter for the *Boston Evening Transcript* to describe her most recent case, she replied, "Well, the mother just had died, and there were four sick children in two rooms, and the man was fighting with his mother-in-law and throwing a pitcher at her head."

Although the epidemic continued through the fall of 1918 and the summer of 1919, the ban on public gatherings was lifted on October 21, 1918. "Boston is wide open once more," trumpeted the *Globe.* "Everything will be done today to make folks forget the epidemic and its awful price," added the newspaper.

But bright lights, a movie, and a soda were not enough to dispel completely thoughts of the dark days through which people had just passed. Many were forever changed by the influenza epidemic. Francis Russell was seven years old in 1918 and lived on top of Dorchester Hill from where he could see Boston and the ships moving silently in and out of the harbor. He bought thrift stamps at 25¢ each as his part in the Liberty Bond drive, and had a birthday cake without

frosting so that the Belgians wouldn't starve, and ate peaches and saved the stones and baked them dry so that they could be used in gas masks. He watched the funeral processions pass by on Walk Hill Street and saw the coffins pile up and noticed that "Pig-eye" Mulvey set up a circus tent that billowed in the wind to hold the coffins that came faster than the grave diggers could dig. One day he and his friend sneaked into the cemetery and watched a funeral. A man with white hair chased them away.

When Francis walked home that

Newsboys from the Boston Globe *pause for a group photograph before fanning out across the city to sell their newspapers. Photograph by Lewis Hines. (BPL)*

On January 15, 1919, a truck carrying a reported 2,300,000 gallons of molasses exploded and sent a huge wave of syrup down the streets of the North End. Twenty-one people were killed and 150 were injured. Photograph by Leslie Jones/Boston Herald. (BPL)

evening he became conscious for the first time of the irreversible rush of time. "And I knew then," he recalled years later, "that life was not a perpetual present, and that even tomorrow would be part of the past, and that for all my days and years to come I too must one day die."

Clearly World War I and the influenza epidemic were traumatic experiences for Bostonians. The postwar period was not much better. Protest, strikes, and paranoia often characterized the period from 1919 to 1929.

A number of Boston women were deeply involved in the struggle for and against the right to vote and to earn a decent living. Maud Wood Park, for example, was an activist who was born in Boston in 1871. Park's brilliance won her a scholarship to Radcliffe College from which she graduated in 1898. Her commitment to reform was already evident: she was one of two members of a class of seventy-two to favor votes for women, a decision which led her to join the Massachusetts Women Suffrage Association. During the next few years she helped two other Boston women, Vida Scudder and Emily Balch, found a settlement house in the South End, organized the College Equal Suffrage

League, and established the Boston Parent-Teachers Association.

In 1915 Park threw herself into the effort to pass a referendum favoring votes for women in Massachusetts. The MWSA sought to dramatize its cause with street meetings and a variety of publicity stunts. The strategy failed, however, due in large part to the opposition by the Catholic Church and a group called the Massachusetts Association Opposed to the Further Extension of Suffrage to Women. Many women who belonged to this group were themselves active in the reform movement; they held positions on the State Board of Charity, the Massachusetts Prison Commission, and the Boston Overseers of the Poor among others. They argued that voting would not help advance those reform interests which women held in common. Mary M'Intire echoed the sentiments of the Boston archdiocese. Women's participation in politics, M'Intire wrote in the *Boston Sunday Herald*, would necessarily take them outside the home and, therefore, endanger the family.

Although the referendum lost decisively, Park gained a great deal of valuable experience, especially in dealing with politicians. In 1917 she became head of the National American Womens Suffrage Association's lobby in Washington, D.C. Here, at last, her persistence was rewarded: the House and Senate approved the 19th Amendment in 1919 and the necessary ratification by the states was completed on August 26, 1920.

That same year Park became the first president of the League of Women Voters, an organization that sought to use the lobbying skills honed during the suffrage campaign to win approval for various other reform measures. Most working class women in Boston tended to be more concerned with immediate problems—a living wage and decent working conditions.

In April 1919, for example, Julia O'Connor led the Boston Telephone Operators out on strike. The International Brotherhood of Electrical Workers supported the women's union, nearly six thousand strong. Telephone service was tied up throughout New England, which so alarmed the business community that the women's demands for an increase in wages (from $16.00 per week to $19.00), better hours, and cafeterias in some of the exchanges, were agreed to after only a week of negotiations.

Although their grievances were just, the women who belonged to the International Ladies Garment Workers Union did not have as much success as the telephone operators. Florence Luscomb, an organizer for the ILG and an activist in the women's suffrage movement, denounced the conditions under which women had to work in Boston garment shops. "Safety and sanitary conditions required by Massachusetts laws were not enforced," Luscomb charged in 1921. The lighting was poor, there was trash on the floors, the toilets were filthy, but neither the owners, who had organized the Boston Clothing Manufacturers' Association to fight the ILG, nor the Commonwealth would take any action. A long, bitter strike resolved nothing: the garment union was weakened and the Boston clothing industry began to move to the South where there were no unions and an abundance of cheap labor.

Breaking the garment workers union did not end labor strife in Boston. On July 4, 1918, five thousand New England fishermen began a strike that lasted thirty-eight days; the maritime workers followed. Nine days later the elevated railroad workers stopped working. For four days during a summer heat wave, Bostonians were forced to walk. An editorial in the Boston *Herald* expressed the anger shared by many: "Every self-respecting person must have a feeling of disgust over the thought that an army of public service employees can get their wages raised by so despicable a performance as quitting their jobs while an adjustment is pending. . . ."

Still, the workers won their demands and other workers who also were suffering from the effects of low wages and postwar inflation began to consider a similar course of action. In February 1919 more than a thousand policemen, meeting in the Intercolonial Hall in Roxbury, voted by a large majority to empower their executive committee to open negotiations with the American Federation of Labor for a union charter. On August 1, 940 policemen voted to join the AFL. Not one man voted no.

While the petitions favoring affiliation with the AFL had been circulating in each of the 19 police districts, a new Boston police commissioner was appointed by Governor Samuel McCall. Edwin Upton Curtis was a 57-year old Republican who had no previous police experience and was an uncompromising martinet. William Allen White characterized Curtis in *A Puritan in Babylon* as a man who "embodied the spirit of traditional wealth, traditional inherited Republicanism, traditional inherited skepticism about the capacity of democracy for self-government and a profound faith in the propertied classes' ultimate right to rule."

The policemen were predominantly Irish Catholics. They worked seven days a week, with one day off in fifteen. Day patrolmen, in addition, had to spend one night a week in the station house on reserve. Even during their free time the patrolmen could not leave the city without express permission. James Long of the LaGrange Street station grumbled: "We had no freedom, no home life at all. We couldn't even go to Revere Beach without the captain's permission." The police also complained about the condition of the station houses. Most of the stations were old, bug-infested and overcrowded. In the Court Street station, just behind City Hall, there were four toilets and one bathtub for 135 men.

When Commissioner Curtis learned that the Boston police had been chartered by the AFL, he issued an official addition to the rules of the department. "No member of the force," he stated, "shall belong to any organization, club or body composed of present and past members of the force which is affiliated with. . .any organization, club or body outside of the department. . . ." Veterans' groups were exempted. Moreover, Curtis added that policemen were not employees, but state officers.

The patrolmen were angry and determined for a showdown, which they were confident of winning. On August 19 the men elected John F. McInnes, a veteran officer with a distinguished war record, president of their local. His first public statement was polite and mild. "I decry strike talk," he said, but added that the men firmly believed they had a right to organize a union.

Commissioner Curtis bolted into action. He ordered Superintendent Crowley to call in all policemen's night sticks, cancelled all vacations for "division commanders, lieutenants and sergeants" and set in motion a plan to recruit a volunteer police force. And following a brief, perfunctory hearing, Curtis dismissed 19 men, including McInnes, whom he held responsible for organizing the union. "WAR ON POLICE UNION IS ON," the *Herald's* headline shouted!

Monday, September 8, 1919, was a sweltering, humid day when the policemen jammed into Fay Hall to take a strike vote. First they were encouraged by a shouting, red-faced, James Moriarity from the Boston Central Labor Union which represented 100,000 workers. He told the men that the BCLU had resolved "to bring victory to the police or quit." Individual locals—the plumbers, mechanics, and typographers—also vowed to support the police. Second, the 19 suspended patrolmen pushed their way into the hall and were greeted by loud, long cheers and prolonged applause. The excitement was so intense that President McInnes actually held the men back from taking a strike vote then and there. McInnes wanted to be sure Commissioner Curtis would carry through his verdict.

At the afternoon roll call in station houses across the city, Curtis' order formally suspending the 19 men was read. The men were told to clear out their lockers and turn in their badges,

revolvers, and signal box keys. Outside several stations crowds had gathered. When the suspended men emerged carrying their uniforms, the crowds applauded.

Now that Curtis' action was official, McInnes proceeded to a vote. The strike sentiment was overwhelming: 1,134 men voted to strike; only two were opposed. In South Boston a huge crowd assembled outside the station house waiting for those patrolmen who did not strike. When they appeared, first youngsters and then others pelted them with ripe tomatoes, mud, and rocks.

Governor Calvin Coolidge, tight-lipped as usual, called together in his office Commissioner Curtis, who arrived with a revolver strapped to his waist, and Mayor Andrew Peters, who was extremely nervous. Peters wanted the state guard mobilized, but Curtis insisted, "I am ready for anything." Coolidge knew that if he called out the guard prematurely it would be political suicide. He sided with Curtis.

Meanwhile, Jordan Marsh and other large, downtown businesses, fearful of vandalism, organized their male employees into a security force, arming some of them. Curtis approved the swearing in of 100 volunteer police. Scores of young Harvard men, middle-aged lawyers and

Co. A. 1st Motor Corps. "Police Strike Duty" Boston, Mass. September, 1919.

bankers, and a retired admiral were issued badges and a night stick and instructed in the rudiments of police work by those few patrolmen who had stayed on the job.

There was some trouble that first night. Crapshooters gathered in boisterous knots on Boston Common, an angry crowd set out toward one of the station houses intent upon teaching the "scabs" a lesson, and teenagers snake-danced their way through city streets in complete disregard for people hurrying home from work. On Washington Street someone lobbed a brick through the window of a shop and within minutes it had been looted, stripped bare. Again the sound of glass shattering; again the crowd surged through a store.

"A night of disgrace," the *Herald* called it. "Somebody blundered. Boston should not have been left defenseless last night." In fact, while there were scattered incidents, most Bostonians had been able to go on with their life as usual. But Coolidge had seen enough. He called out the state guard. His terse statement, "There is no right to strike against the public safety anywhere, anytime," swung public opinion against the strikers and vaulted Coolidge into national prominence.

At the same time both the AFL and the BCLU weakened and back-pedaled away from their earlier support for the striking policemen. Curtis cleverly

recruited an entire new police force largely from among unemployed war veterans. The strike was over. The men scattered, defeated, alone now.

The police strike erupted in the midst of the worst red scare in the nation's history. Some hysterical newspaper accounts even claimed that Boston's striking policemen were Bolsheviks. People were on edge. Everyone feared a violent outbreak. In 1919 a May Day parade composed of a lusty band of radicals was set upon by an angry mob, and later the headquarters of the Socialist Party in Boston were destroyed.

Cardinal O'Connell, Archbishop of Boston from 1908 to 1944, abhorred violence. In an address celebrating the centenary of the Archdiocese in 1908, O'Connell briefly reviewed the history of Puritan-Catholic antagonism. At the same time he saluted those Bostonians who had worked to create a good, moral community. Those "good men whose ashes have mingled with New England soil. . .did their duty well," he said. Now, O'Connell continued, it is time for Catholics to shoulder the responsibility for fraternal charity and civic duty. And, like those "good men" who built the "city on a hill," O'Connell reminded his listeners that the cement that held together a republic was education, public morality

The National Guard Motor Corps was mobilized during the Boston police strike in September 1919. Governor Calvin Coolidge was catapulted to national prominence by his harsh treatment of strikers. Over two-thirds of the striking policemen lost their jobs. (TBS)

127

and the protection of the rights of property.

These themes characterized O'Connell's tenure. He revitalized the Boston parochial school system, established three Catholic women's colleges—Emmanuel in 1915, the College of the Sacred Heart in 1924, and Regis in 1927—and encouraged and aided his alma mater, Boston College. He was an outspoken opponent of "modernism," whether it manifested itself in women's fashions or pseudoscientific theories of human behavior. O'Connell also believed that the basic political institutions of American life were under attack in the 1920s. He recognized the inequities of industrial society, but he was quick to denounce those whom he suspected of being socialists or communists. As O'Connell perceived it, there was good cause to be on guard against reds.

Many Bostonians—Catholic and Protestant alike—shared O'Connell's political perspective. The city's anxious, belligerent mood was a result, in part, of a national campaign against radicalism launched by the Attorney General of the

United States, A. Mitchell Palmer. On January 2, 1920 Palmer and local police launched a series of sweeping raids. More than four thousand "radicals" were arrested nationwide, about eight hundred in greater Boston. Half of those arrested—nearly all of whom were recent immigrants—were chained and marched through the streets of Boston to be transported to Deer Island.

Two Italians who were members of an East Boston anarchist group who were not swept up in Palmer's raid, but feared they soon would be, hid their literature and armed themselves. On May 5, 1920, Nicola Sacco and Bartolomeo Vanzetti were arrested in Bridgewater, charged with armed robbery and the killing of a paymaster and his guard.

Believing they were being arrested for anarchist activities, Sacco and Vanzetti lied about their politics and friends when they were interrogated. Because witnesses at the South Braintree holdup gave conflicting testimony about whether either Sacco or Vanzetti had been present, they were found guilty largely on the basis of their behavior when arrested. According to Judge Webster Thayer—who had boasted he would get those "anarchist bastards"—Sacco and Vanzetti's conduct before and after their arrest showed a "consciousness of guilt."

After a few hours of deliberation, the jury found the two men guilty. "They kill an innocent man!" Sacco shouted in a shaken voice as the judge and jury were leaving the courtroom. Years of appeals proved fruitless. The death sentence set by Judge Thayer in 1921 was carried out on August 22, 1927. Shortly after midnight, in the Charlestown jail, Sacco and Vanzetti were electrocuted.

As in life, so in death, various political groups squabbled over who should assume responsibility for the bodies of the two men. Finally a committee decided to use Joseph Langone's funeral parlor in the North End. For three days, from August 25 through Saturday, August 27, the bodies lay in state. 100,000 people filed by the two coffins.

In 1937 Harvard University presented an honorary degree to William Cardinal O'Connell. Here the archbishop stands with retired Harvard president, A. Lawrence Lowell. Courtesy, Archives of the Archdiocese of Boston

Left: The Boston archdiocese received a large financial gift from the Keith family, whose fortune was made in the RKO theater chain, early in the 20th century. Cardinal O'Connell endowed Keith Academy and Keith Hall in Lowell; here students from these schools meet their benefactor before his residence in Brighton. Courtesy, Archives of the Archdiocese of Boston

On Sunday morning crowds lined Hanover Street silently awaiting the funeral procession. At 1:30 in the afternoon, a column of mounted police forced their way along the narrow street forming a barrier between the people and the path the hearse would take. Behind the two hearses came open cars heaped with flowers and two limousines carrying family members. 5,000 marchers followed in close-packed ranks. It was a gray day. A heavy drizzle soaked those marchers who made it all the way to Forest Hills cemetery. Inside the small chapel Mary Donovan, who had volunteered to help the Defense Committee six years before, spoke a few, bitter last words: "You, Sacco and Vanzetti are the victims....Massachusetts and America have killed you."

While Sacco and Vanzetti still were struggling to prove their innocence, Congress, in 1924, passed the National Origins Quota Act which limited immigration from Europe to 150,000 a year and allocated most of the places to Great Britain, Ireland, Germany and Scandinavia. Members of the Immigration Restriction League of Boston were delighted. Founded by three young Brahmins in 1894, the League enrolled dozens of Boston's oldest families, including the Lees, the Paines, the Saltonstalls and the Warrens. Congressman Henry Cabot Lodge also added his voice to the cause of immigration restriction. He argued that those races "most alien to the body of the American people" should be excluded.

Immigration restriction cut the flow of unskilled labor to Boston, but by the 1920s the demand for blue-collar workers was less than it had been. Boston's economy was diversified, characterized by light industry and periodic building

Sacco and Vanzetti were convicted of murder and executed in 1927, despite protests by thousands who felt that the men did not receive a fair trial. Courtesy, Boston Globe

These women were demonstrating machines that by 1932 revolutionized commercial communications and record-keeping and opened thousands of clerical jobs for women in Boston. (BPL)

booms. The impact of the Great Depression was, therefore, somewhat less severe in Boston than in cities dominated by large industries. More than half of the labor force in Boston never lost a day's pay. Still, between 1933 and 1940 about 100,000 workers (25 per cent of the labor force) were unemployed. Everyone knew of someone engaged in a desperate struggle.

A barely literate Charlestown woman who was receiving relief wrote to President Franklin Roosevelt that it was "terriably huiating to Mother and Father to feed three children, say nothing about keeping a roof over there head and trying to give them nurishment to strengthen them for school." However difficult some people's lives became, pride still was important. A black worker wrote to the WPA in 1936: "I do not want to be taken care of. I want to work and support my family."

Generally those Bostonians who suffered the most were men and women who lived in areas of the city which had

been the most depressed at the time of the crash. The bulk of the unemployed came from "the Boston where acres of ugly wood tenement houses line the drab streets; where ten dollars a month rented a three-room flat in a wooden fire trap without heat, lighting, running water, or indoor toilet." Specifically, the groups that were most likely to be unemployed or dependent on some relief program were the Italians of East Boston and the North End, the Irish of Charlestown and South Boston, blacks from the South End-Roxbury ghetto, and the most recent immigrants from Eastern Europe. Unemployment in the Italian North End was 50 percent higher than the city as a whole, and three times as high as the Back Bay. More than one-third of all employable workers in the oldest neighborhoods of the city still held no jobs in the private sector as late as 1939.

Elected to his third term as mayor in 1929, James Michael Curley used every trick in his patronage grab bag to help the jobless. As a stopgap, he immediately hired workers to clean up the city for its tercentenary celebration. And in February 1930 he hired 1,000 men to shovel snow at $5.00 a day. More drastic measures were needed. Unemployment worsened.

Unable to get an increase in state and federal funds and faced with skyrocketing municipal relief rolls (from 1929 to 1932 the number of families aided by the city increased six times), Curley reluctantly endorsed a private philanthropic campaign. Hoopla became the order of the day. A wrestling match at the Boston Garden raised $5,000; football teams from Boston College and Holy Cross played a benefit game on Thanksgiving day; and a "carnival for the unemployed" was held at Braves Field featuring, among others, the current world heavy-weight champion, Boston-born Jack Sharkey, the Red Sox, the Braves and aviator Amelia Earhart. These events created some excitement but failed miserably to stir the public into aiding the unemployed.

Likewise, Boston's jobless workers did

not benefit as much from the various New Deal programs as they had hoped. A feud between Mayor Curley and President Roosevelt and a lack of cooperation between New Deal administrators and Boston's ward bosses badly undermined the effectiveness of federal relief programs. According to Martha Gelhorn, an employee of the Federal Relief Agency in 1934, Boston's management of federal emergency relief was so "blatantly bad" that the government's efforts had become "an object of disapproval (if not disgust) for the unemployed classes."

By the late 1930s the New Deal had gained a better reputation among Boston's workers. Legislation such as social security, unemployment insurance, workmen's compensation, and housing loans, together with more federal jobs, made it possible for Bostonians to regain some measure of prosperity and stability.

The Great Depression had a dampening effect on many aspects of Boston's life, but not its enthusiasm for sports. As far back as the turn of the century, Yankee

reformers had argued that physical activity would help overcome the debilitating impact of city life. Social workers like Robert Woods, who were concerned about "inferior amusements degrading the people," advocated the physical and moral benefits of organized sports, especially for the immigrant working class.

Proper Bostonians were less keen, however, about the behavior of the city's sports fans (short for fanatics). In 1914 when the Boston Braves swept four straight games from Connie Mack's powerful Philadelphia Athletics, 25,000 baseball fans unable to get tickets swarmed onto the Common opposite the *Herald* building so that they could see the score posted on a giant billboard. When the Red Sox won the World Series four years later the celebration was much more subdued—Boston boys were dying in France and the deadly influenza had begun to take its toll—but when the following year the Knights of Columbus and the City Council designated

Above: Here Ted Williams hits one of his two world record-breaking homeruns in the 1946 All Star game at Fenway Park. Williams played for the Red Sox from 1939 until 1960 and set many records. He was fifth in all-time homerun percentage, second in walks. (BPL)

Above, right: Babe Ruth began his career with the Red Sox in 1914, and was traded to New York after six years. There he amassed one of the best records in baseball: first in homerun percentage and walks, and second in homeruns, runs, and runs batted in. Babe Ruth returned to Boston to play with the Braves his final year in the game. (BPL)

September 20 "Babe Ruth Day," Fenway Park rattled and shook as it never had before. Fans shouted, clapped, whistled, roared, and jumped up and down when Ruth broke a ninth inning tie by driving a home run over the left field fence.

After 1920, when Ruth was sold to the New York Yankees, the glory days of Boston baseball were mere memory for twenty-eight long years. In the interim college football eased the pain for some sports fans. For Brahmins the Harvard-Yale game—THE GAME—was the highlight of each fall season. For the city's Catholic ethnic groups, the Boston College Eagles were the team to cheer. Its roster in 1939 read like an ode to the melting pot—Charley O'Rourke, Chet Gladchuck, Henry Toczylowski, Gene Goodreault, and the first black player at Boston College, Lou Montgomery. The team was coached by 30-year-old Frank Leahy, whose arrogance belied the fact that he was beginning his first season as a head coach.

Leahy was immediately popular with Boston's fans and sports writers. Following a reverent reference to his old coach, Knute Rockne, the *Boston Globe* raved, "Rockne lives again in Frank Leahy." Leahy's Eagles began with an easy romp, rolled to victories over Temple, Auburn, and Detroit, and then, in a game played in a raging snowstorm before 41,000 people at Fenway Park, Boston College beat Holy Cross 14-0.

In December 1939 Boston College accepted a bid to play Clemson in the Cotton Bowl. Thousands of alumni, students, and Boston fans cheered lustily when the team's special train pulled out of South Station for Dallas. Star running back Lou Montgomery was not on board. Black players were not allowed to play in the segregated South. "Sure I hate not being there," Montgomery said, "but I know there isn't a man on the team that doesn't hate the fact that I can't be there." After losing 6-3, Leahy told Montgomery, "Lou, if they had let us bring you along we wouldn't have lost." "I'm always going to believe that, coach," Montgomery replied.

The Eagles were an even better team in 1940. Along with most of the starters from the previous year, Leahy had recruited a hard-running Polish kid named

Mike Holovak. Once again, Boston College ended its regular season by beating Holy Cross (a last minute, heart-stopping 7-0 victory) and accepted an invitation to play in a post-season bowl game. This time the Eagles would meet the Tennessee Volunteers in the Sugar Bowl. Tennessee was a slight favorite, but with less than three minutes left to play, O'Rourke sprinted 24 yards for the winning touchdown.

Boston was delirious. A crowd estimated to be 100,000 stood in the snow at South Station to welcome its heroes home. Later, at a testimonial to the team, Leahy spoke emotionally about his attachment to Boston College. "I told these lads at halftime they were upholding the honor of dear, old New England," Leahy said. "I told them. ..I would always be with them. I love Boston College and will never leave it." A month later he became the head coach at Notre Dame.

Boston College had some good years after Leahy's departure, but as Jack Falla, historian of Boston College sports, put it, "the flood tide of success slowly, almost imperceptibly, began to recede." The Sugar Bowl victory in 1941 climaxed one of the last "normal" sports seasons. By the end of the year the United States was at war and strapping young men from colleges and professional teams were playing more serious games.

Ted Williams, who enlisted in the Marine Air Corps shortly after hitting .406 in 1941, returned to the Red Sox after the war along with Dave (Boo) Ferris, Dom DiMaggio, Bobby Doerr and Johnny Pesky. With good pitching and plenty of power, the Red Sox were the pre-season favorite to win the American League pennant. But manager Joe Cronin had come close too many times to be overconfident.

Williams, on the other hand, boasted publicly that he was betting all takers $100 that he would be the American League batting champion in 1946. His arrogance sprang from the phenomenal physical skills that everyone agreed he

Eleanor Roosevelt visited Simmons College in 1944 to talk with students about the problems faced by returning servicemen. Photograph by Leslie Jones/Boston Herald. (BPL)

possessed. His insistence on perfection, however, often caused Williams to be angry, usually with himself, but sometimes with fans and always with sports writers. His moody behavior earned him the label "baseball's foremost problem child." He refused to chase an obvious foul ball, stood with arms folded over his chest while playing left field, and announced, "They'll never get me out of the game running into a wall after a fly ball." Still, at mid-season Williams had fifteen homeruns and was hitting .351. Boston fans either loved him or hated him with a passion.

The Red Sox won 41 of their first 50 games in 1946, largely on the strength of Williams' and DiMaggio's hitting and Pesky's and Doerr's brilliant play in the infield. The team easily raced to the American League championship. When the Sox clinched the pennant after winning the first game of a double-header, Boston fans could wait no longer. They poured onto the field with gifts for every player. Later they danced and laughed and cheered their way through the streets of Boston until well into the night. How sweet it was!

Now, at last, Boston was ready for a new beginning.

IX
New Boston

One hundred years had passed since Boston's first city hall had been built. The glory of old Boston represented by the city hall on School Street had receded well into the past by 1962. "Boston was a hopeless backwater, a tumbled down has-been among cities," the *Globe* sadly concluded. It was a huddle of old, low-rise buildings—the tallest of which was the Customs House Tower built in 1914—clustered around a somnolent waterfront. When the Rev. Seavey Joyce flew into the city in 1946 to join the faculty at Boston College, he wondered as he looked out of the airplane to the city below, "where is Boston?"

When the plan to build a new civic center was launched in 1962, therefore, it was perceived as one part of a strategy to recapture Boston's glory days, to rekindle civic

pride. Much more than bricks and mortar were needed. Not even a decade of sports thrills provided by the Celtics and the Bruins could lift the spirits of old Boston. Post-war Boston was divided still between Protestant and Catholic, confused and angry about the impact of a growing, militant, black population, anxious about its economic future and in need of new political leadership.

In 1945, James Michael Curley was re-elected mayor for the fourth time. Curley was 71 years old. His career had begun at the beginning of the century and by design had always symbolized polarization and stasis. Curley's re-election half a century after he began his career served to emphasize the hold that the past had on Boston. To make the links even clearer, Curley spent part of his term in the federal penitentiary in Danbury, Connecticut, for mail fraud, an odd parallel to his jail sentence in 1903 for civil service fraud.

During the five months that Curley spent in jail, his place in city hall (the old city hall) was taken by city clerk John B. Hynes. The son of Irish immigrants, Hynes was born in Boston in

1897. Forced to leave school at an early age to help support his family, he worked first for the telephone company then, after service in World War I, he was able to get a job with the city while studying law evenings at Suffolk University. He passed the bar in 1928, but remained a civil servant. Moving from department to department, Hynes earned a reputation as a serious worker and a good bureaucrat. After 23 years in city service, he reached the pinnacle of the bureaucracy when he was named city clerk in 1945.

As was his style, he worked quietly and efficiently during his acting mayoralty, winning him the nickname "Whispering Johnny." Pardoned by President Truman after five months in jail, Mayor Curley triumphantly returned to the city and dismissed Hynes' efforts with the words "I accomplished more in one day than Johnny Hynes did in five months." Underestimating the appeal of Hynes' style, Curley had set the stage for his own defeat.

No one gave Hynes a chance when he announced that he was going to run for mayor in 1949. Quiet, a career bureaucrat who had never held an elective office, and

Previous page: Copley Place, which occupies 3.5 million square feet between Copley Square and the South End, features two major hotels, four office buildings, a shopping center with restaurants, a 15-cinema complex, 100 units of housing, and parking for 1,400 cars. Courtesy, The Architects Collaborative, Inc.

Right: The 1956/57 World Champion Boston Celtics. Standing left to right, Walter Brown, Dick Hemric, Jack Nichols, Bill Russell, Arnie Risen, Tom Heinsohn, Harvey Conn, Lou Pieri. Sitting, left to right, Lou Tsioropoulos, Andy Phillip, Frank Ramsey, Red Auerbach, Bob Cousy, Bill Sharman, Jim Loscutoff. Courtesy, Boston Celtics

without a political base in the neighborhoods, Hynes seemed destined to fall back into obscurity. But he ran an effective, hard-hitting campaign that appealed to the growing number of middle class Irish-Americans who were tired of the old ethnic rivalries and the old-fashioned style of the ward bosses. "Curley's day has passed," announced Hynes. "And I respectfully remind this tired and battle-scarred political war-horse that the majority of his votes are now in the cemeteries of an era long past."

In fact, a new political coalition composed of younger, more affluent Irish, Italians, Yankees, and Jews was formed to support Hynes. In striking contrast to Curley's bombast, Hynes conducted an impersonal, dignified campaign, and shockingly upset Curley, beating him by 11,000 votes. Curley had had his last hurrah.

The desire for a more conciliatory "new Boston" that manifested itself in Hynes' election, was stimulated in other ways as well. The long and fruitful relationship between town and gown that had served Boston so well in the past once more played an important role in the development of the post-war city. Specifically, many of the scientists who had been brought to MIT during the war to develop military projects stayed in the Boston area after the war in order to put what they had learned to commercial use. Over 100 new "high tech" companies were begun by scientists from MIT in the immediate post-war years. Both private and public institutions helped launch this new industry. Boston banks provided venture capital and the federal government appropriated funds to build a highway around Boston that opened up easily accessible space.

From Gloucester in the north to Braintree in the south, Route 128 had been planned to relieve urban traffic congestion, not to be a focal point for scientific enterprise. But just at the time of its opening in 1951 the new high tech companies were beginning to outgrow their early, informal, start-up quarters and

were looking for space. The land adjacent to Route 128 was ideal for the new style of industrial park required by this industry, and it was within easy distance of the intellectual community in Cambridge and the financial community in Boston. And, according to an urban development expert interviewed in the 1950s, the high tech companies were enormously distrustful of the city. Still, the development of high tech along Route 128 offered the city a growth industry and the prospect of economic revitalization, because the bankers, lawyers, accountants, and other service companies connected to high tech suddenly needed more downtown office space.

Another hopeful sign for Boston in the early 1950s was the beginning of a consensus between Yankee businessmen and Irish politicians. These groups had distrusted one another for decades, and that hostility had done much to cause the city's stagnation. Ephron Catlin, who was a senior official of the First National Bank of Boston, recalled that in the minds of those in the business community "there was a feeling that Boston was in

Boston is a city of neighborhoods that once were separate towns. Annexation increased the city's size and resources, and expanded city services including gas, electricity, and public transportation. Brookline alone remained independent. Courtesy, Boston Redevelopment Authority

Political notables joined Archbishop Richard J. Cushing on the reviewing stand of the Holy Name Society parade in 1947. From left are Senator Leverett Saltonstall, Senator Henry Cabot Lodge, Governor Robert F. Bradford, the Archbishop, and Mayor John B. Hynes at far right. Courtesy, Archives of the Archdiocese of Boston

the hands of supercrooks. Nobody had ever seen an honest Irishman." The leadership to break this impasse came from Rev. Seavey Joyce, then dean of the School of Management at Boston College. Bringing together leaders from banking, the utilities, industry, and politics to discuss the common problems of the city sounds obvious in retrospect, but it was a precedent-shattering move in 1954. The Boston Citizens Seminars, as Joyce called the meetings, began in a mood of nervous uncertainty, but soon moved to a spirit of accommodation that surprised and pleased the participants. These seminars provided the format for several decades of shared efforts to develop a civic consensus.

That a Roman Catholic priest took the lead in this civic effort reflected the new religious rapprochement that was beginning to emerge. Catholics had been a majority of the city for over half a century but still maintained a posture of defensiveness that had roots in their earlier status as an unwanted, maligned immigrant minority. Under the leadership of the austere William Cardinal O'Connell the Catholic Church had concentrated on its own affairs while maintaining a position of detachment from the city's affairs. O'Connell's long episcopate came

to an end in 1945, and his successor, Archbishop Richard J. Cushing, was animated by a fresh new spirit. Cushing, a native of South Boston was an earthy, charismatic figure, as approachable as O'Connell had been remote. Cushing was fully as ambitious for his church as O'Connell had been, and set in motion an ambitious building program of parishes, schools, and hospitals. But he also had a concern for Boston that was quite different from that of his predecessor. "I'm for everything that will promote Boston's welfare," he announced at his installation as sixth bishop of Boston. He began to reach out to establish better relations with Protestants and Jews. Delighted at his openness, these other Bostonians responded, and for this reason the national ecumenical movement had a special meaning for Boston.

The third hopeful sign that contributed to the development of a "new Boston" came from the federal government in the form of an urban renewal program. Realizing the stagnant conditions in many cities in the aftermath of the long Depression and World War II, Congress had instituted a program to revitalize the downtown sections of cities such as Boston. The late 1950s and the early

1960s were the golden age of federal largess. But it was a new and complex program that required sensitive handling. Many problems stemmed from the failure of planners to understand that often the so-called "blighted areas" that appeared to need massive change and/or demolition were also neighborhoods of people who could not be disregarded. The conflict in interests between downtown revitalization and neighborhood preservation was not easy to reconcile, and it is not surprising that Boston officials were not always able to determine how federal funds should be used to the city's best advantage during these years.

One of the first large urban renewal projects, begun during the Hynes Administration, was the Prudential Center complex in Back Bay. It was initiated by an out-of-state corporation because no Boston firms were yet willing to build on so large a scale. A pioneering project, built on abandoned railroad yards in the Back Bay, the "Pru" did not conflict with a neighborhood, but nonetheless was inordinately difficult to start. The project involved a tangle of decisions including legal rulings about blighted land, legislative permission for air rights, city guarantees on financing, and design problems. Building the Pru gave a tremendous psychological boost to the city. A *Globe* columnist optimistically wrote in 1958, "All the daring and imagination in this country today is not being spent on launching space missiles. Boston and Prudential are shooting for their own moon."

The West End project was launched in the same year as the Pru. Under the control of the Boston Redevelopment Authority, it was asserted that the West End—the area between the back side of Beacon Hill and the Charles River—was "so clearly substandard that sweeping clearance of buildings is the only way the area can be restored." Once home to 23,000 people mostly Italians and Jews, the West End's population had declined to about 7,000 in 1957. Poor, old, and inward-looking, they were dubbed "urban villagers" by Herbert Gans, a sociologist who made a critical study of the process of urban renewal.

Although the Boston Redevelopment Authority began planning the redevelopment of the West End in 1953, public hearings were not held until 1957. There were a few protesters, but the inhabitants were too disorganized and too powerless to stop the juggernaut of renewal. In January 1958, the federal government and the city signed the final agreement, and a month later the demolition began, and went on inexorably for the next 18 months.

The stupidity of this approach was soon appreciated. There was widespread national recognition that it was ridiculous to destroy a neighborhood to save it. This negative reaction did not prevent another of Boston's early urban renewal projects from getting underway. The "New York Streets" neighborhood in the South End was also marked for destruction without regard for the people who lived there. This was also justified by the rationale of "slum clearance." Black political leader Mel King later reminisced about that justification. "There was a series of articles (about the demolition) that called the area Boston's 'Skid Row.' I was surprised," King wrote, "because I had always called it home." The city cleared the area to attract light industry, but 30 years later there are still large amounts of vacant land in this part of the South End, another testimony to the fallibility of the planning process as well as its insensitivity to neighborhoods.

Yet another neighborhood fell victim, although only partially, to government improvement projects. To alleviate traffic congestion in the center of the city, the Central Artery was built. A massive "green monster" of elevated highway snaking through the middle of the city, from South Station across the Mystic River to Charlestown, the Central Artery caused the demolition of part of the North End.

The bitterness aroused by the wrecking ball approach to redevelopment paralyzed urban renewal in Boston. Poor people in other parts of the city, who were organized politically, were fearful that their neighborhood was next. "TO HELL WITH URBAN RENEWAL," angrily proclaimed a huge sign posted in Allston. South End activist Kay Gibbs complained that the process was manipulative. People didn't know—or weren't told—recalls Gibbs, "that they could hold out for relocation to the place of their choice." She and others now were determined not to allow bureaucrats and bankers to push them around.

By the time Mayor Hynes' term ended in 1959, it was clear that any new plans for urban renewal would have to be much more sensitive to the needs of the people in the neighborhoods. It was also apparent that Hynes's initiatives had not yet restored confidence among potential investors or revitalized the city's sagging economy. John Hynes had been a conciliatory mayor in a hopeful time, but the old Boston still seemed the same. The mayor's race in 1959 seemed to offer Bostonians more old politics. It was generally believed that John E. Powers of South Boston would succeed Hynes. Powers was deeply involved in city politics; he was undisputed boss of Ward Six and he had run a close second to Hynes in 1955. Then president of the Massachusetts Senate, Powers also had solid labor backing and endorsements for the mayorality from local newspapers. His close identity with the political world, his links to all the traditional bases of power, and his high visibility as a politician made Powers the solid favorite.

Powers' opponent in the run-off election was John Collins, former city councilor and then registrar of probate for Suffolk County. Collins was less well-known than Powers, but shared the same background: he was a native-born Bostonian of Irish heritage who grew up in Roxbury, attended local schools, and graduated from Suffolk University Law School in 1941. Immediately after graduation, Collins enlisted in the army and rose to the rank of captain before he was

discharged in 1945. Collins also had considerable local political experience. However, Powers had much more the image of the "pol," the old-style political operator. Collins, appearing to be more the disinterested public servant, sought to distance himself from Powers by linking him to old-style politics and to underworld figures with the slogan, "Stop Power Politics."

Collins had other advantages. His courageous comeback from a crippling bout with polio in 1955, which left him confined to a wheelchair and crutches, conjured up an image in the voters' minds of Franklin Roosevelt. A handsome, clean-cut man, Collins was able also to enhance his wholesome political image by appearing on television and contrasting himself with Powers, a short, tough, arrogant "little Napoleon."

Collins' campaign touched a nerve in the electorate that the experts had not identified. Boston voters rejected the old-style politics represented by Powers and embraced the politics of civic improvement, what Collins called the campaign for a "new Boston." Collins was swept into office by 24,000 votes. He saw his victory as a mandate to change the face and spirit of Boston, a formidable job. "After I took office in 1960," he recalled years later, "I remember going into (old) city hall. The place smelled, the toilets were overflowing, the front of the building was covered with pigeon droppings. The linoleum floor was so dirty that you couldn't tell what color it was. There was a kind of malaise of the spirit—we were all kind of ashamed. People had given up on Boston."

Not Collins. He immediately reactivated the coalition of bankers, politicians, and academics put together by Hynes and began a search for a strong administrator from outside Boston to lead the Boston Redevelopment Authority. In 1960 he persuaded Edward J. Logue, an experienced city planner from New Haven and an Irish Catholic, to become development administrator in order to give urban renewal a more professional

Urban renewal was made possible in the early 1960s through an influx of federal money to the city. Here Mayor John Collins receives a $1.2 million check from Bernard L. Boutin (left). Looking on are U.S. Senators Edward M. Kennedy and Leverett Saltonstall; behind the mayor is Msgr. Francis J. Lally. Photograph by Richard Brelinski/Boston Herald. (BPL)

and more forceful direction. At once, Logue made it clear to Bostonians that he too rejected the wholesale demolition that had characterized earlier urban renewal programs. "It is the function of distinguished architecture and imaginative city design," he said, "to see that beauty is the hallmark of the renewed city. Beauty once flourished in Boston. It must again."

Collins next involved the two most powerful segments of the private sector, the financial establishment and the Catholic Church, neither of which had been enthusiastic about his election. He appointed Msgr. Francis Lally, a public spirited priest who was editor of *The Pilot* as chairman of the Boston Redevelopment Authority. He coordinated all planning initiatives with the sensitive neighborhoods and the financial community. "The Vault" as the financiers' planning committee was popularly known, was headed by Ralph Lowell, president of the Boston Safe Deposit and Trust Company and director of the Lowell Institute.

Under Collins, Logue, and Lally, urban renewal went full speed ahead—carefully.

Collins announced a "90 Million Dollar Development Program for Boston" which included renewal of both the downtown and the neighborhoods. Indeed, 25 percent of the land area of the city came under this plan. The Government Center projects alone, in the view of Walter Muir Whitehill, were "almost as dramatic in their effect upon the topography of Boston as the filling of the Back Bay."

The new city hall, set in a broad open space covering some 60 acres previously occupied by Scollay Square, Haymarket Square, and Bowdoin Square, was the focal point of downtown development. The design characteristics of the entire Government Center area had been established by I.M. Pei, an internationally known architect who had studied Boston since his student days at MIT. The city hall itself was designed by Kallman, McKinnel and Knowles, a New York firm chosen from a national competition. Their design, richly modern and iconoclastic, was hailed by Whitehill "as fine a building for its time and place as Boston has ever produced." Surrounded by the refurbished Sears Crescent building and the John F. Kennedy Federal Building,

Above: The curved street in the foreground is Cornhill, a crescent of attached buildings that was the bookselling center of the city circa 1900. The corner building in the foreground is the Sears Block and in the distance is Faneuil Hall with a flag flying from its cupola. Quincy Market is visible behind Faneuil Hall. (TBS)

Right: The Old Howard was the most popular vaudeville theater in Boston. Its closing in 1953 marked the end of Scollay Square's heyday. The area was totally redesigned during the urban renewal of the 1960s. Photograph by Leslie Jones/Boston Herald. (BPL)

the completion of Government Center demonstrated a spirit of cooperation and innovation rare among government agencies. Almost two-thirds of the money for this development came from the federal government which was motivated, in part, by a desire to stimulate private investment in new office skyscrapers.

But it took awhile for Logue to convince local bankers to take the risk. For example, in 1961, the only bidder to develop a downtown site near Government Center was a British firm. "Every bank advised them not to build," recalled one Boston banker. The success of their venture was assured, however, when the State Street Bank agreed to move into the $22 million office tower. From that hesitant beginning, private development came gradually, then with a rush that remains unabated. The "Boston Boom" was on.

By contrast, the neighborhoods continued to feel threatened by urban renewal. Because Collins and Logue were committed to upgrading existing housing whenever possible rather than wholesale demolition, their plan gained some community support. Middle-class blacks in Roxbury welcomed the Washington Park project; the new gentry in the South End

were delighted to be provided with parks, streets, and loans for refurbishing their town houses; and Charlestown residents were generally pleased with Boston Redevelopment Authority plans. But for many poor people the results of urban renewal seemed to be the same as they were in the West End: disregard, destruction, and dispersal.

Before he left office in 1967, at the expiration of his second term, Mayor Collins moved into the unfinished new city hall, to dramatize his special relationship to the new Boston. Certainly, no one challenged his claim. He had set in motion far-reaching plans that drastically changed the appearance of Boston. At the same time, other changes became visible during Collins' administration over which he had no control. Boston underwent a demographic revolution.

The population of Boston changed in two significant ways in the years after 1960. First, the number of people declined from the 1950 high of 800,000 to 575,000 in 1980. The Boston metropolitan area remained one of the 10 largest in the nation, but the city itself dropped to 20th.

Second, the composition of Boston's population was very different after 1960. The old white ethnic balance in the city that had come about in the wake of European immigration half a century earlier was destroyed by the influx of blacks and other minorities. Boston became a racially diverse city. As with the great ethnic immigration of the 1840s, Boston experienced significant racial immigration later than most large cities. Again in parallel with the 1840s, the changes that came with this influx were sharply resisted. The spirit of religious and ethnic accommodation that had come to mark the new Boston of the 1950s was supplanted by the bitterness of racial strife.

There was movement within greater Boston that stimulated profound changes, as well. Many of the children of immigrants, newly prosperous after World War II, moved to the suburbs. At the same time a small but significant number of students and professionals were attracted by the city's vibrant economy. These new "gentry" tended to be more liberal than whites in Boston traditionally had been, and were less concerned with the old issues of the city. Taken together, this new gentry and the older traditional ethnic white population totaled 390,000 in 1980 and accounted for 70 percent of the city's population. The differences in their politics, however, meant that they did not form a cohesive bloc.

The influx of the gentry gave a fillip to the old elite residential areas of the inner city that had been neglected for decades. Back Bay and Beacon Hill had their Federalist and Victorian facades burnished and became prestigious addresses again. Other inner city neighborhoods experienced gentrification for the first time. In the South End, for example, long-time residents were amazed when brownstone homes that their immigrant owners could not sell for $5,000 in 1950 were being sold for more than 10 times that amount a decade later. Gentrification was a process that for better or worse inexorably spilled over into other parts of

the city, including the North End, the waterfront, and Charlestown, delighting some residents while angering many others.

The older ethnic neighborhoods were threatened by population shifts among non-gentry too. Some of the shifts came from a loss of their own population as neighborhood people moved to the suburbs. South Boston, for example, lost more than half of its 1950 population of 50,000 in the three decades that followed. Other demographic shifts came from expansion of new neighborhoods which caused destabilization of traditional ethnic "turf" in a way reminiscent of the 19th century. Newer Bostonians—Blacks, Hispanics, Asians,—were pressing on older established neighborhoods of Jews in Mattapan and North Dorchester, of Irish in Roxbury and Jamaica Plain, and what had seemed permanent homes became bitterly contested turf.

The shifts that threatened old white neighborhoods reflected the expansion of racial neighborhoods. The established black neighborhoods in Roxbury had been created about 1900 by black Bostonians displaced from the West End by Eastern European immigrants, as well as by newcomers from the South. Together they

This view shows the City Hall Plaza created during the 1960s. Cornhill Street no longer exists, although the Sears buildings were restored. City Hall faces the plaza, and behind it are Faneuil Hall and Quincy Market. Photograph by Peter Vanderwarker.

The Robert Gould Shaw Memorial, erected in 1807, honors the first black regiment from Massachusetts to fight in the Civil War. The sculpture, located across from the State House, was restored and the names of the soldiers in the regiment were carved into the granite. Photograph by James Higgins. Courtesy, Ann Beha Architects

created a community of more than 25,000 people in the area around Massachusetts and Columbus avenues in the South End. In the post-war years black migration to Boston increased steadily. Although blacks accounted for only 2 percent of the total population in 1950, that percentage jumped to 9 percent in 1960, 16 percent in 1970 and to 22 percent in 1980. After 1960, therefore, the South End-lower Roxbury ghetto became too small to house all the newcomers, and blacks began to expand into the remainder of Roxbury, past Dudley Station and to Mission Hill and Fort Hill, along Blue Hill Avenue through Dorchester beyond the G & G Deli, past Franklin Field and by 1968 were approaching Mattapan, and Jamaica Plain near the Bromley Heath public housing project. Suddenly there was a new neighborhood configuration and a large black community in the city.

As a result of this increase, the black community became more dynamic, more complex, and more assertive. Before 1960 Shag and Balcolm Taylor ran black politics in the South End-Roxbury area. From their Tremont Street pharmacy, the

Taylors organized meetings and rallied black voters to support white politicians such as Curley, in return for which they were given a few city and state jobs to distribute, were chosen delegates to the Democratic National Convention, and were allowed to run an after-hours social club. They were ward bosses. But as Mel King points out in his book *Chain of Change,* the Taylors' power "was more illusory than real;" it was dependent upon the "white power structure's handouts rather than organizing the community to demand satisfaction of Black needs."

Royal Bolling, Sr., was the first black politician to ignore the Taylors and to organize people in the Franklin Park area around specific community issues. Something of a black political renaissance followed Bolling's successful campaign for state representative in 1960. In 1962 Edward Brooke was elected attorney general, the first black to hold a state office in Massachusetts; four years later he became the first black United States senator since Reconstruction. In 1967, Tom Atkins, executive director of the Boston branch of the NAACP, was elected to the City Council.

During these same years Melnea Cass, long-time activist and president of the Boston NAACP from 1960-1962, and Otto and Muriel Snowden began Freedom House, and Elma Lewis created the cultural center that bore her name. Other black activists, including Mel King, created organizations that challenged the Boston Redevelopment Authority and the School Committee, sponsored rehabilitated housing and agitated successfully for jobs through the United Community Construction Workers, the New Urban League, and the Boston Job Coalition.

With new leaders and specific goals, the black community was ready by the mid-1960s to tackle school desegregation in Boston. Specifically, Citizens for Boston Public Schools decided to run a slate of candidates for School Committee in 1965. Although the Citizens group had some success—all five Citizens' candidates made the final election and for the first time in the city's history a greater percentage of black voters than whites cast ballots in a primary election—the campaign also made heroes of John Kerrigan and Louise Day Hicks, two incumbents. Hicks won almost 90 percent of the votes cast for School Committee by appealing to the alienation of white voters.

In the summer of 1967, Hicks announced she intended to run for mayor. "You know where I stand," she said simply and frequently. It was a code for anger, alienation, and racism. She was against busing and for law and order. At least one of her supporters had no trouble reading between the lines: "I'd like to see the next mayor take a gun and shoot every goddamn nigger in the city," a man from Jamaica Plain told Alan Lupo, a reporter for the Boston *Phoenix*.

There were other candidates who wanted to succeed Collins. Ed Logue, who had resigned from the Boston Redevelopment Authority in order to run, told Boston voters he was a progressive. He promised "planning with people" would save the city. John Sears, a Beacon Hill Republican, likewise spoke politely about remedying the troubles in the neighborhoods. He too was a progressive.

The final candidate was Kevin Hagan White. Once dismissed as "Joe White's boy" or as a "lightweight," by 1967 Kevin White had served three terms as secretary of state, the youngest person in the history of Massachusetts to hold that office, and won a reputation as an articulate reformer who was a tireless campaigner. White inherited political ambition and the connections to realize his passion for public office from his father Joseph, the most prominent "pol" in Boston before 1950, and from his father-in-law, William "Mother" Galvin. Born in Boston in 1929, White was educated at Tabor Academy, Williams College, Boston College Law School, and, most importantly, in the parlor of his West Roxbury home.

White's strategy in the race for the mayor's office in 1967 was to set himself

apart from his opponents. By championing neighborhood reforms, White easily distinguished himself from Ed Logue, who could not shake the charge that he was interested only in downtown development. White out-maneuvered Hicks by stressing his reasonableness and his grace under pressure. "The thing most voters don't consider," White said to a reporter casually, "but which is vitally important, is emotional stability. You've got to remember that's power you're giving a man." It was a thinly disguised, brilliant attack on Hicks' inability to cope with the emotional uproar that her anti-busing rhetoric stimulated.

The second part of White's strategy was to put together a new coalition that included liberals, the new gentry, a variety of older ethnic groups, especially Italians who had felt left out of city government because it was dominated by Irish, and the newly invigorated black voters. At the same time, though, White was careful to retain his connections with the traditional Irish bloc with whom he shared his roots.

On election day, White's coalition

Martin Luther King led hundreds of Bostonians in a march against racism and discrimination in 1965. King is seen in front of the first poster as the march moves along Columbus Avenue, near Massachusetts Avenue. (BPL) delivered. Blacks voted more heavily than they had previously, and the Italian community gave him a majority of its votes. Even in those Irish wards Hicks carried, White did well. When it was over, Hicks had won half of the city's wards and nearly 90,000 votes. She had lost. White won by about 12,000 votes. In 1971, he won a second term, trouncing Hicks by more than 60,000 votes. Using a similar strategy, White won two more terms, beating City Councilor Joseph Timilty in 1975 and again in 1979.

White's 16 years in city hall may be divided instructively into two parts: the early liberal years during which he focused on the city's neighborhoods, and the second two terms during which he relied more heavily on a political machine and focused most of his attention on developing the downtown. During the early years White also had aspirations for state and national office, and so sought to cultivate an image as a neighborhood-oriented urban activist. He vigorously moved about the city authorizing Little City Halls, community

schools, and new fire and police facilities throughout the neighborhoods. He served as champion of local neighborhood activists in East Boston and Roxbury, creating the image of a dynamic chief executive who was concerned with the ordinary lives of the people.

In all this White was advised by an attractive group of professionals, most of whom came from outside the city. He recruited such people as Robert diGrazia, who modernized and cleaned up the police department; Hale Champion who succeeded Logue at the Boston Redevelopment Authority; personal aides Barney Frank, later a U.S. Congressman; Robert Kiley, subsequently director of New York City's public transit; and Robert Weinberg who became a director of Mass Port. At the same time, White paid close heed to the ethnic and racial aspects of his coalition by appointing significant numbers of blacks and Italians to city hall; he did not neglect the still significant Irish population either. White's style was that of the polished, urbane liberal, so that he was able to court the

After years of neglect and a major fire, most people expected this church to be razed. Instead, architect Graham Gund designed an award-winning residential complex, keeping the tower and street facade of the church and creating an interior courtyard where the sanctuary once stood. Photograph by Peter Vanderwarker.

national press even as he served as champion of the local neighborhood interests.

The development of the downtown area begun during the Collins years became a glittery showplace during White's last two terms. The building boom—one of the most dynamic in the nation—resulted in more than forty new buildings, many of them great towers. With its first "Manhattan-style" skyline and a dizzying array of modern architecture, observers like Fr. Joyce would no longer ask themselves "where is Boston?" A galaxy of new buildings appeared, including the silvery H-shaped Federal Reserve Bank Building on Atlantic Avenue, the "pregnant" Bank of Boston Building on Federal Street, the stark red towers of 60 State Street, the sheer glass Hancock Tower, and the glistening Copley Place in Back Bay.

The building boom was a manifestation of a major change in the city's economy. In the decades since 1960, Boston became a world center of financial and business services. Belden Daniels, a lecturer at MIT, stated that "Boston is the most integrated financial service center in the United States outside New York. There are $300 billion of capital held in downtown Boston." It is estimated that one-third of the assets of the mutual fund industry and half of the American securities held by foreign banks are in Boston banks. The number of lawyers, accountants, and engineers with offices downtown has tripled since 1960.

The downtown retail district, too, thrived. Although some major stores have failed since 1970, Filene's and Jordan Marsh made major investments in their downtown stores. The astonishing success of Fanueil Hall Marketplace—visited by 15 million people a year—proved that there was a bright future for the downtown retail trade.

The old was protected as well. The spectacular if unanticipated success of the Quincy Market restoration provided a national model for such projects and gave encouragement to the historic preserva-

Mayor for a record 16 consecutive years, Kevin H. White's liberal early years were marked by the establishment of Little City Halls and various youth activities. White's last years were controversial, however, when he was criticized for putting downtown business interests ahead of the needs of neighborhood residents. (BPL)

tion movement. From Winthrop Square and Church Green in the Old South End to Lewis Wharf on the waterfront, restoration of the past became a nationally known Boston characteristic.

Showy public events were also an integral part of Mayor White's efforts to transform and enhance the image of Boston. Large, impressive, city-wide events—Summerthing, the Tall Ships, Queen Elizabeth's visit, the Bicentennial, the Pope's visit, and First Night—brought hundreds of thousands of people together to celebrate Boston. Kevin White's career seemed as promising and glamorous as the city.

Still, White could not ascend beyond the orbit of the city. He ran unsuccessfully for governor of Massachusetts in 1970, and his hopes for the vice presidency in 1972 went unfulfilled. Then, in 1972, Federal District Court Judge W. Arthur Garrity heard a suit brought by a group of black parents

Bill Rodgers greets the crowd after running the 1978 Boston Marathon in the record time of 2:09:27. Immediately behind Rodgers is Mayor Kevin White, and to his right, Will Cloney, director of the Boston Athletic Association, and Governor Michael Dukakis. Photograph by Matt Delaney.

who charged that the Boston schools were deliberately segregated. In June 1974, Garrity ordered the School Department to implement a massive, system-wide busing plan to end racial segregation. The School Committee is relatively autonomous in Boston, and White had not been involved in school policy beyond the building of schools. Similarly, he had little input into Garrity's decision, but he supported it and worked publicly and strenuously for its implementation. Inevitably he was caught in the turmoil that surrounded busing in the city, and like the city itself he was tarred.

Education and educational policy in Boston had been a focal point for protest for a decade before the order to achieve desegregation was issued by Judge Garrity. White liberals had attacked the system in books such as *Death At An Early Age* a volatile polemic by Jonathan Kozol, and *Village School Downtown* a more tempered but no less devastating analysis of Boston schools by Peter Schragg, and had tried to reform the schools through the "Citizens for Boston Public Schools." Blacks had more personal complaints about the quality of the education offered to their children, and about the segregation of blacks within the system, whether as a result of housing patterns or deliberately drawn district lines. There were mounting protests by blacks, including student boycott of classes, busing by parents to white schools in the city in "Operation Exodus," and busing of black students to suburban cities under the Metco Program. The protests were given recognition by the passage of the Racial Imbalance Act, initially sponsored by Rep. Royal Bolling in 1965, and by the establishment of a "magnet school." Named for a black activist of an earlier day, the William Monroe Trotter School was built in Roxbury; yet there was little or no change in School Committee policy.

The School Committee did not inspire confidence. Its members had a spotty record for competence and honesty. Worse, the committee had proved impervious to change through electoral reform, and its chairwoman, Louise Day Hicks (and her slogan, "you know where I stand") had become the symbol of intransigent white Bostonians who would resist integrated education at all cost. For others the School Committee became the symbol of all that was wrong with old, divided Boston. A deep hostility that focused on the committee badly divided Bostonians. Its obstinance in the face of black appeals for equal education and its apparent invulnerability to change created a bitterness among liberals. Likewise, the insistent calls for change increased the bitterness of those who resisted that change and sought to control their children's lives within their neighborhoods. All this brought about a brutal, sometimes violent confrontation between blacks and whites.

In its first phase, Garrity's plan called for busing between South Boston and Roxbury, pitting working class Irish against poor blacks. "We cannot permit our city to be polarized by race or paralyzed by fear," Mayor White told Bostonians during a special evening telecast on September 9, 1974, three days before the busing plan was to be implemented. He looked and sounded confident, but he was not. Despite hundreds of meetings with parents, students, the police, and politicians, during which he promised to enforce the law and to protect every single student, White knew that the anti-busing people were determined to cause trouble, perhaps determined enough to turn Boston into another Belfast. South Boston was the center of

resistance. "Southie is having a nervous breakdown, a collective nervous breakdown," White told Bob Kiley, his closest aide.

The battle began on September 12. Police, buses, monitors, and students were assembled at an abandoned shopping mall near South Boston High. A helicopter circled overhead. Additional police encircled South Boston High. Periodically, they sallied out, pushing the demonstrators back, breaking up gangs armed with rocks and bottles. Day after day, week after week, for two years the violent struggle went on. "They were invading our territory," a South Boston youngster replied when asked about racial prejudice, "Southie is my home town, not theirs. Yeah, it was war all right."

In the end, peace was won. In April 1976, tens of thousands of Bostonians staged a march against violence. Speaking to the huge crowd, White did not claim that Boston's problems were ended; he hailed the beginning of the end. "Liberty was born in Boston," he reminded the crowd, "and it will flourish here so long as courageous people of high moral principle are willing to speak what is in their hearts."

Certainly, the busing crisis had shown that there were many courageous people in the city. Still, the halcyon days of the New Boston were over. Boston was seen as a racist city. Eventually, the passions died down and busing became a way of life. In the process the school system changed from 70 percent white and 30 percent minority to the reverse, 70 percent minority and 30 percent white. The system itself shrank in size from 90,000 students to 55,000.

Although he and the city he loved were battered by the school crisis, neither White nor Boston gave up. White's final years were marred by controversy and scandal. Still, his bond with the city was so strong that no one could be certain whether he would run for a fifth term. He chose not to, and retired undefeated. He and the people had created a New Boston.

X
Promise

The campaign to become mayor of Boston in 1983 was historic. It began as usual with a large field, but it was soon evident that only three were realistic possibilities for the run-off: David T. Finnegan, an establishment-backed moderate, who was sometimes talked about as Kevin White's protege; Melvin H. King, a long-time black activist and former state representative from the South End; and Raymond L. Flynn, a populist, and a former state representative from South Boston. Finnegan was the early frontrunner, spending five or six times more money than either Flynn or King. Despite his carefully crafted, lavish campaign, Finnegan was eliminated and King and Flynn finished in a virtual tie (47,432 votes each). For the first time in the history of Boston a black man was in the run-off election for mayor.

Right: In the 1983 city election, Mel King made history as Boston's first black mayoral candidate. Recruiting with a call to join his "Rainbow Coalition," his campaign represented a new era in Boston politics in which a growing minority population has begun to show increased political interest and effectiveness. Photograph by Don West. Courtesy, The Rainbow Coalition

Previous page: Mayor Flynn and these young players enjoyed an afternoon at the ball park during the summer of 1984.

Up to this point, King had not been taken seriously by many voters or by the media. By late September, however, King had not only shown that he could get votes, but he had abandoned his dashiki for a suit and tie and put together a new constituency, a "Rainbow Coalition" consisting of blacks, hispanics, Asians, and a sprinkling of liberal whites along with women, gays, and the elderly. He campaigned in the neighborhoods amongst the have-nots. Black voters were especially excited because the victory of Harold Washington in Chicago made King's campaign to be mayor of Boston seem like the beginning of a new era. Eager volunteers registered nearly 53,000 new voters during the months preceding the election, almost half of whom were blacks and other minorities.

Ray Flynn also portrayed himself as a candidate of the people. An All-American basketball player at Providence College, a graduate of Harvard University Graduate School of Education, a city councilor and a state representative who had opposed busing in 1974, Flynn gradually changed his ideas and his behavior in the nine intervening years. Running on a nearly identical platform as King, Flynn differed in that he insisted that Boston's problems were a result of class, not race. Flynn argued, for example, that *all* poor people in the city's neighborhoods were victims of White's mania for downtown development.

The final campaign was hard fought, but without racial hostility. Both King and Flynn spoke in every neighborhood and usually came away with the respect of those who listened, if not the votes. Outgoing Mayor White summed up the feeling of most Bostonians when he said, "How times have changed. A man or woman being black is not a prohibition on being mayor. . . . I did not believe that 10 years ago."

Still, Flynn easily defeated King by a whopping 66 percent to 44 percent, a split largely along racial lines. Flynn won by huge margins in the white ethnic enclaves of South Boston, Charlestown, East Boston, and West Roxbury. King ran well in the South End, Dorchester, Roxbury, and Mattapan, but his Rainbow Coalition attracted only 20 percent of the city's white votes. Political analysts were quick to point out, however, that the city's white population was declining while its minorities were on the rise.

Ray Flynn spent New Year's Day putting the final touches on his painstakingly prepared inaugural speech. Outside of city hall that same day, Flynn, carrying under his arm a hardbound copy of *Kennedy: A Time Remembered,* bumped into Kevin White and White's press secretary, George Ryan. Like Flynn, Ryan walked book in hand, his an inscribed gift from the outgoing mayor titled *10,000 Jokes, Toasts and Stories.*

Without doubt, Ray Flynn cut a radically different figure from that of his suave, witty, and urbane predecessor. His attitude about his new position, as had been his entire mayoral campaign, was

The Leonard P. Zakim Bunker Hill Bridge adds a striking dimension to the Boston skyline. Courtesy, Central Artery/Tunnel Project

Top left: The first
newspaper in America
was issued in Boston in
1704. The Boston
News-Letter was a
record of local affairs and
ship movements. Later
in the 18th century
newspapers played a
significant role in keeping
colonists informed about
activities and ideas which
culminated in the
Revolution. First National
Bank Blotter Series. (BPL)

Top right: America's
first chocolate mill was
built in Dorchester in
1765, through the
collaboration of Irish
immigrant chocolate-maker
John Hannon, and
Milton physician, Dr.
James Baker. The mill
grew into the Baker
Chocolate Factory which
produced chocolate until
1963. Then, as a division
of General Foods
Corporation, the
company moved to
Delaware. First National
Bank Blotter Series.
(BPL)

Bottom left: The
Committee of Public
Safety was responsible for
stockpiling supplies and
preparing for conflict.
Members included Dr.
Joseph Warren and Paul
Revere. First National
Bank Blotter Series.
(BPL)

Bottom right: In June
1775 Congress
established the
Continental Army,
uniting the militias of
each colony under
federal control. George
Washington took
command of the troops
July 3, 1775.
First National Bank
Blotter Series. (BPL)

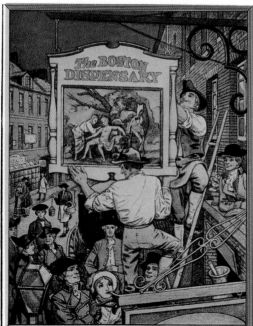

Top left: The new state government of Massachusetts adopted the codfish as its emblem. The codfish replica hung in the Old State House until 1798, when, with great ceremony, it was moved to the New State House. *First National Bank Blotter Series.* (BPL)

Top right: The Massachusetts Charitable Fire Society attempted to minimize the effects of fire in Boston. The society provided monetary relief for fire victims and stimulated research into better fire-fighting techniques. *First National Bank Blotter Series.* (BPL)

Bottom left: Eighteenth-century medical care was primitive. The Boston Dispensary, provided a central clinic for medical advice and treatment. The Good Samaritan became the dispensary symbol. *First National Bank Blotter Series.* (BPL)

Bottom right: The first public high school for girls in Boston was established in 1826 through the support of Mayor Josiah Quincy. Quincy lost political support when he opposed a second girls high school on the unusual grounds that the experiment was so successful it would cost too much money to expand. When the first school closed a short time later, public education beyond elementary school was not available to Boston girls, *First National Bank Blotter Series.* (BPL)

Above left: This two-gabled house on Commonwealth Avenue and Gloucester Street was built for Charles Francis Adams by Boston architects Peabody and Stearns. Its distinctive round turret is topped with a slate roof; its chimney boasts the date of its building in 1886. An 1803 law required buildings over 10 feet to be constructed of brick or stone, with slate or tile roofs. Courtesy, Lisa Rogers

Middle left: Boston's distinctive Victorian-era brownstones line Commonwealth Avenue in the Back Bay. Accented with decorative brick-work and mansard or turreted roofs, the bow-front style was intro-duced to Boston by architect Charles Bulfinch, who borrowed it from England's Robert Adam. Courtesy, Nora Rogers

Above: Dedicated in 1861, the Arlington Street Church's exterior was designed by Boston architect Arthur Gilman after the church of St. Martin in the Fields in London's Trafalgar Square. The church's 16 stained glass windows were created by the Tiffany studios and are believed to constitute the largest collection of Tiffany windows in a single church. Courtesy, Lisa Rogers

Bottom left: Gazing out to sea at the edge of the North End, Christopher Columbus surveys the waterfront park that is named for him. The park is the setting for per-forming arts events and its wisteria-covered trellis is popular for weddings. Courtesy, Nora Rogers

Left: This statue of America's foremost colonial artist, John Singleton Copley, whose subjects included Paul Revere, Mercy Otis Warren, and John Adams, stands across from the original site of the museum where many of his paintings hang. While the Museum of Fine Arts moved to Huntington Avenue in 1909, since 2002 Copley has graced the square that was named for him. Courtesy, Nora Rogers

Below: Bordered by a nearly 700-foot reflecting pool, this fountain enlivens the space between the I.M. Pei designed Christian Science headquarters and the Prudential Center office and retail complex. Courtesy, Nora Rogers

Viewed from the Boston University Bridge, eight-person boats race in the Head of the Charles Regatta. The event has been held each October since 1965, now attracting 7,500 entrants and 300,000 spectators over the three-mile route.
Courtesy, Lisa Rogers

Far left: A vibrant cultural district along Huntington Avenue features Boston University's Huntington Theater; Sympony Hall, seen to the left, famed for its acoustics and the home of the Boston Symphony Orchestra and the Boston Pops; and Jordan Hall, home of the New England Conservatory of Music. Courtesy, Nora Rogers

Left: St. Stephen's Church on Hanover Street, designed by Charles Bulfinch, who also designed the State- house, sits in the midst of the perpetually busy North End neighborhood. The Old North Church is across the street, linked via the tree-lined Paul Revere Mall walkway, which features a statue of the famous patriot. Courtesy, Lisa Rogers

Bottom far left: A bronze statue of the country's 35th president, John F. Kennedy, stands on the west wing plaza of the Massachusetts State House. Dedicated on May 29, 1990, it was designed and sculpted by Isabel McIlvain. Courtesy, Nora Rogers

Bottom left: The Christian Science World Head- quarters features this 5,000-seat church built in 1903. Courtesy, Lisa Rogers

The Massachusetts State House, designed by Charles Bulfinch in 1796, sits atop Beacon Hill. Statues of Daniel Webster, Anne Hutchinson, Mary Dyer, Horace Mann, Civil War General Joseph Hooker, and John F. Kennedy dot the grounds in front of its Federal façade. Copper sheets produced by Paul Revere's mill once sheathed the dome; it later was gilded, except during World War II, when it was painted black. Courtesy, Lisa Rogers

Above: Henry Hobson Richardson's 1872 Romanesque Trinity Church, a National Historic Landmark, is built of granite and red sandstone. The Cathedral of Salamanca in Spain influenced its square tower. Courtesy, Nora Rogers

Left: Massachusetts sculptor Thomas Ball's 1869 statue of George Washington presides over the Back Bay entrance to the Public Garden. Washington's personal library is housed around the corner at 10 1/2 Beacon Street, in the Boston Athenaeum. Courtesy, Lisa Rogers

Above: Commuter boats, luxury boats and harbor cruise ships dock at Rowe's Wharf marina, serving the city's financial district. Courtesy, Lisa Rogers

Right: The graceful multistory arch at the Boston Harbor Hotel at Rowe's Wharf hotel and office complex anticipated the removal of the city's central artery by providing a visual gateway between harbor and city. The hotel's lobby features a collection of nearly 90 maps of Boston Harbor, spanning the 17th to 19th centuries. Courtesy, Lisa Rogers

Founded in 1634, Boston Common, the country's oldest park, is bordered by Beacon Hill and the Public Garden. With room to roam as well as to ice skate, have lunch, or congregate, the Common is a city centerpiece. Courtesy, Nora Rogers

The entrance to the new Prudential Center tower enlivens the Huntington Avenue streetscape, leading to Copley Square's vibrant mix of cultural institutions, shops, and parks. Courtesy, Nora Rogers

Three women key to Boston's and America's life and letters are honored in the Boston Women's Memorial, located on the Commonwealth Avenue Mall between Fairfield and Gloucester streets. The three—Abigail Adams (not shown), known for her keen political acumen and as the wife of John Adams, the second president and mother of the sixth, John Quincy Adams; Lucy Stone, out front in the movements to abolish slavery and for women's right to vote; and Phillis Wheatley, a poet and slave who was the first African to publish a book in America—are featured in this 2003 sculpture by Meredith Bergmann. Courtesy, Nora Rogers

Italian pride is always on display in the friendly and festive North End. Courtesy, Nora Rogers

The Northern Avenue Bridge, closed to vehicular traffic, spans the Fort Point Channel to the vibrant South Boston waterfront, housing the Fort Point Artists' Community, the new Boston Convention and Exhibition Center, Boston Children's Museum, Institute for Contemporary Art and Moakley Courthouse and World Trade Center on Commonwealth Pier. Across the Channel lie South Station and the Federal Reserve Bank of Boston. Courtesy, Lisa Rogers

CowParade Boston, in the summer of 2006, benefited the Dana Farber Cancer Institute's Jimmy Fund. This cow, designed by artist Kathleen E. Hall, is titled Old Cape Cowd. Courtesy, Lisa Rogers

Boston Duck Tours, hosted aboard World War II amphibious landing vehicles, highlight the city's historic sights as well as skyline views seen from the Charles River. Courtesy, Nora Rogers

Numerous widwalk cafes offer opportunities to relax while taking in the beauty of the city. Courtesy, Lisa Rogers

serious, sober, and devoid for the most part of humorous quips and clever phrases. The new mayor carefully planned his inaugural ceremony to reflect his commitment to Boston's neighborhoods and a city government accessible and responsive to Boston's grassroots constituency. Symphony Hall and Fanueil Hall, traditional inaugural sites, were discarded in favor of the spacious Wang Center for the Performing Arts for what would be the largest number of people ever invited to an inauguration in Boston's history. Flynn invited 4,200 guests, many neighborhood residents who had never before attended a mayoral inauguration. Other precedents were dispensed with: dress was semi-formal rather than black tie, and guests were not expected to pay for their tickets. The entire event was paid for by the Committee to Elect Ray Flynn.

The new mayor's schedule of events for inaugural day reflected his ambitious resolve to personally make Bostonians "feel good about themselves and their city." The day began early with the Flynn family arriving in the familiar and by now symbolic 1975 rust-gutted Dodge station wagon Flynn had driven throughout his campaign, for eight o'clock Mass at Don Bosco Technical High School Chapel in downtown Boston where 15 year-old Edward Flynn attended school.

A light snow was falling by the time the inauguration was about to begin. Flynn's 19-minute address, a simple and dignified reaffirmation of his campaign promises, was interrupted 23 times by applause from his ebullient audience, with the retiring Mayor White seated on stage to the right of Flynn one of the most enthusiastic cheerers. By far the most emotional moment of this otherwise low-keyed, straightforward address came when Flynn described his parents, his father, a longshoreman who "left the house each morning on cold winter days just like this, not knowing whether he would find work," and his mother who "worked as a cleaning lady in downtown

Left: A work crew cleans the "99 Steps" in the Wilderness area of Franklin Park. The crew, made up of high school students, was recruited and hired by the Franklin Park Coalition for summer work to help give the park new life after decades of neglect. Courtesy, Franklin Park Coalition

office buildings from 11 at night until seven in the morning." His voice momentarily breaking, Flynn recalled that more than anything else his parents had taught him the importance of dignity and respect for others, "no matter what the cut of coat or color of the skin."

Pledging a city open to all, Flynn made clear his opposition to "Reaganomics" announcing "Our theory of government will be trickle up, not trickle down." In a

Below: The annual Kite Festival at Franklin Park brings together hundreds of people each April for a day of celebration. Courtesy, Franklin Park Coalition

manner reminiscent of another Irish working class mayor, James Curley, Flynn promised: "This will also be an administration that listens. Should you ever feel the need, know that there will be a welcome sign at the office of the mayor, where you will be received with respect." Flynn also called for safeguards for Boston tenants, attention to Boston's neighborhoods, improved educational facilities, and the streamlining of city services. Without doubt the strongest statement made by the new mayor was his commitment to creating racial harmony within the city: "The full weight of city government will be brought down," Flynn declared, "on all those who seek, because of race or color, to deny anyone from any street, any school, any park, any home, any job, in any neighborhood in the city."

Flynn had candidly admitted to reporters prior to the inauguration: "I'm not one of those people who can write those clever phrases," and indeed he had relied on sincerity and plain talk to move his Boston audience. He told reporters that when he sat down to write his first draft of the speech, "two words immediately flashed into my mind: 'You

count.' I wrote them down right away and underlined them and those are the words I want the people of Boston to remember from my speech."

If Flynn's sentiment was not enough, his itinerary for the remaining portion of the day embodied his inaugural pledge to the people of Boston: "You will count during this administration." Following the ceremony, Flynn stopped briefly at city hall to look over his new offices. While he posed for pictures with his daughter on the Queen Anne sofa in the mayor's outer office, Flynn got word that a fire had driven occupants out of the recently completed New Westin hotel in Copley Place. In typical Fiorella La Guardia style, Flynn chased the fire engines to the hotel where he spoke with firemen and guests who had been evacuated. Later in the afternoon the new mayor attended a performance at the D Street housing project in South Boston. Speaking briefly to the audience, which included about 100 persons bused in from public housing projects in Dorchester, Charlestown, and the South End, Flynn reassured them that he would not forget his roots now that he was mayor. "The name is still Ray, and I'm going to come to D Street

Dignitaries gather at the beginning of the annual Walk for Hunger, a project that raises hundreds of dollars for Boston's homeless and hungry residents. Governor Michael Dukakis and his wife, Kitty, join two of Boston's newest leaders: Archbishop Bernard Law, spiritual leader of Boston's two million Catholics; and Ray Flynn, who took office as mayor in January 1984. Courtesy, Photo Service, City Hall

to play basketball." Following the suggestion of mayoral opponent Mel King, Flynn also visited the Franklin Hill Housing project in Dorchester where tenants handed him a list of more than 100 complaints concerning sanitary code violations in the project.

The evening's inaugural festivities, which was headlined by the *Globe,* "FLYNN'S INAUGURAL BALL SHOWS THAT MONEY ISN'T EVERYTHING," likewise emphasized Flynn's sensitivity to economic hardship within the city and his promise to trim city spending and focus attention on the people of Boston. For the over 8,000 supporters who packed the Plaza Hotel, this properly downscale celebration, costing a mere $13,000, epitomized the kind of change they had sought for the city when they chose to back Ray Flynn. Missing was the White penchant for show and lavishness. Flynn held no gala cocktail parties and the ball itself was conducted in the most frugal manner possible. For those participating, this in itself was cause for celebration. Jubilant, although somewhat awed, Flynn arrived at 9:00 p.m. and spoke briefly to the throng of well-wishers: "Tonight is the time for celebration."

Boston's newest immigrants are hispanics from Puerto Rico, Cuba, and Central America, and Asians, especially from Vietnam and Cambodia. These groups are experiencing the same kinds of prejudice, crowded conditions, and difficulties finding work that other groups in Boston's past experienced. Courtesy, East Boston Community News

Ray Flynn was the 46th mayor of Boston. His style was different than his predecessors, but his commitment "to the idea that government is more than merely a broker among narrow, special interests, but is instead the highest expression of common values and goals which we all share," was at once a familiar and noble theme for the people of the city on a hill.

Mayor Flynn, addressing a group of constituents, describes his plans for Boston's elderly residents. Known as a Populist, with concern for the ethnic, age, and class divisions within the city, Flynn's campaign and early months in office raised the hopes of many that their needs will be addressed by a responsive city administration. Courtesy, Photo Service, City Hall

XI
Boston in the 21st Century

Boston Mayor Thomas M. Menino was unhappy with the U.S. Census Bureau statistics showing a decline in the city's population. In 1960 when John F. Kennedy entered the White House, nearly 700,000 people lived in the city on a hill, but only 589,000 called Boston home in the year 2000. However, despite the population dip, Menino was quick to point out glowing data about Boston's vibrant economy, the city's ability to reinvent itself, and its diversity—for the first time in history people labeled as "white" by census takers accounted for less than half of the city's population.

Menino has certainly done a great deal to create a bright new future for Boston. Boston Harbor is now clean and free of sewage and, surprisingly, the Red Sox lifted up the entire city when the team won the World Series in 2004. However, there also have been dark clouds hanging over the metropolitan area during the past several decades.

Boston Mayor Thomas M. Menino. Courtesy, Boston College

Previous page: The Leonard P. Zakim Bunker Hill Bridge adds a striking dimension to the Boston skyline. Courtesy, Central Artery/Tunnel Project

Hundreds of victims of sexual abuse accused Catholic priests of despoiling their childhood and the Boston archdiocese of systematically covering up the crimes. Lawsuits against, and dissent within the church, roiled the community. The "Big Dig" promised to make the lives of Boston commuters easier by restructuring the city's roadways and adding additional tunnels. More than two decades later, the results are still less than perfect.

Although huge public works projects may be the basis for revitalizing Boston, the 1990s saw the disappearance of a number of major businesses long identified with the city. Whether Boston can reinvent itself as it has so many times before remains to be seen.

Isabella Stewart Gardner filled the palazzo she purchased in Venice and then reconstructed in Boston with art works collected throughout Europe. After Gardner's death in 1924, Fenway Court,

as she called her home, opened as a public museum. In the early morning hours of St. Patrick's Day, 1990, guards at the Isabella Stewart Gardner Museum allowed two men they mistakenly assumed to be police officers into the building. Once inside, the "officers" overpowered the guards, handcuffed them, wrapped their heads in duct tape, and tied them to basement posts. After the intruders disabled the museum's surveillance cameras, they moved slowly and selectively through the large upstairs galleries, cutting from their frames two Rembrandt paintings and snatching from an easel Johannes Vermeer's *The Concert* and a landscape by Govaert Flinck. In another gallery, the thieves took five Degas drawings and a bronze eagle perched atop a flag from Napoleon's Imperial Guard. Back on the first floor they grabbed a Manet portrait. None of the objects were insured for theft.

On their way out of the museum, the thieves told the guards: "You'll be hearing from us in about a year." But no one has heard a word from the thieves and to date the case remains unsolved. There have been plenty of false sightings during the 16 years since the robbery. Boston police and the F.B.I. have received tips leading them to art dealers, antique shops, and flea markets throughout the United States and abroad. (One anonymous tipster told the police that James "Whitey" Bulger, Boston's most infamous crime boss, organized the heist to finance his flight from justice and that the paintings were somewhere in Ireland.) Because Isabella Stewart Gardner's will prohibited moving any of the museum's artworks, empty wall spaces remind visitors of the 13 missing paintings.

Three years after the robbery, a little known city councilor provided a new optimistic outlook. During his 10-year tenure on the Boston City Council, "Tommy" Menino preferred to work in the background rather than elbowing his way into the political spotlight. He was known for paying careful attention to his constituents' needs and for brokering compromises among sparring groups. Elected city

The Big Dig project
involved a total rebuilding
of the intersection of two
major highways: the
Massachusetts Turnpike
and Interstate 93.
Courtesy, Central Artery/
Tunnel Project

council president by his fellow councilors in January 1993, Menino became interim mayor in July when Mayor Ray Flynn resigned to become ambassador to the Vatican. Three months later, during his campaign for a full term as mayor, Menino focused exclusively on what he had accomplished as acting mayor. His opponent, six-term state representative James T. Brett, complained that Menino "always refers to the last three months," and not "the last ten years." Brett also grimly insisted the city had plunged into an economic crisis, but Menino spoke glowingly of Boston's designation by *Fortune* magazine as one of the nation's three best cities in which to do business.

Voters overwhelmingly chose Menino's sunny forecast of Boston's future. He won 65 percent of the votes cast—a winning majority that crossed neighborhood, racial, and ideological lines and ended the Irish American stranglehold on the mayor's office. Menino became the first mayor of Italian descent in city history, but his victory was more about multiculturalism than provincial ethnicity. To be sure, he carried the Italian American dominated wards in East Boston and the North End and his own Hyde Park neigh-

borhood, but Menino also won Charlestown and Allston-Brighton and made a strong showing in South Boston. "I'm no fancy talker," he told a cheering crowd, but "I'll be at work tomorrow to sweep the cobwebs out of City Hall."

On November 17, 1993 Menino was sworn in as Boston's 47th mayor. There was no pomp and little ceremony; it was over in five minutes. He promised to be a hands-on mayor and then left for lunch in the North End.

Known as the "urban mechanic" for his careful attention to the city's everyday needs, Menino was enormously popular. Opinion polls gave the mayor 80 percent approval ratings. Among the positive aspects singled out for praise was Menino's effort to bring small businesses and affordable housing to Blue Hill Avenue, a four mile stretch that runs through the heart of the city's African American and Hispanic community from Dudley Square in Roxbury to Mattapan Square. The mayor successfully convinced seven major banks to pledge $35 million in flexible financing to so-called "enterprise zones" located along Blue Hill Avenue and turned over 51 city-owned properties to developers. "We're going to

In April 2004 Boston Archbishop Sean P. O'Malley, O.P., and College President William P. Leahy, S.J.,announced the sale of the cardinal's 19,800-square-foot Brighton mansion and 43 acres of its surrounding land to Boston College. Courtesy, Boston College

bring it back to where it was," Menino said, "a neighborhood that has economic development and hope for the people who live there." Critics noted, however, that nearly all of the shops in the area still had bars on their windows and that the area had one of the highest crime rates in the city. Still, people could see progress and gave Menino credit.

In the fall of 1996 the mayor threw his full support behind a ballot initiative to retain an appointed School Committee. The seven-member appointed committee first took office in 1992 after the Massachusetts legislature approved a home-rule petition abolishing the old 13 member elected body that had become an infamous breeding ground for conflict, corruption, and indecision. Supporters of the elected committee contended that a democratically elected committee was preferable to a committee controlled by the mayor. Menino carried the day, however, winning the vote to retain the appointed School Committee by 40 percentage points. "The message was clear throughout Boston that we should continue the progress we've made in the schools," the mayor said.

Less than a year after this victory Menino launched his reelection campaign. No one stepped forward to challenge the mayor and he coasted to another term. In his 15-minute inaugural address, the

mayor touched on topics such as healthcare, economic development and immigration, but the bulk of his speech dealt with education. He warned school principals "to make changes, or we will make them for you." Referring to a new statewide test that the city's 15,000 high school students were required to pass before graduating, the mayor said, "We have to start preparing our students for that test today," because if it were administered today, "half of our high school students would fail."

Menino also announced the establishment of an after-school program. "Boston, 2-6," was designed to meet the needs of the two-thirds of Boston school parents who worked and could not arrive home by 3 p.m. Finding the money to fund this and other projects would not be easy, the 55-year-old mayor acknowledged, but he said, "I have never been more energized to lead the city I love."

In November 1999 Boston voters again validated Menino's can-do politics. After 28 years on the Boston City Council, the bombastic James Michael Curley-era figure, Albert "Dapper" O'Neil, lost his bid for reelection. A 30-year-old South Boston attorney who reached out to the gay and minority communities defeated O'Neil, who one commentator labeled "a throwback to an era that few of today's politicians or political observers remember."

The City Council's powers pale in comparison to the mayor's and the old ethnic wards are much more diverse. Therefore, no single ethnic or racial group controls either the Council or elects a mayor. When O'Neil's defeat was made known to Menino, he said knowingly and without bitterness, "Write the obituary."

In November 2001 Menino handily won a third term as mayor of Boston. He crushed his opponent, four-term City Councilor Peggy Davis-Mullen, garnering more than 70 percent of the votes cast. Menino's percentage of the votes cast was higher than when he ran unopposed. Only the second woman to run for the mayor's office, Davis-Mullen criticized Menino for lacking a vision for the city's future, but her effort was tarnished by revelations about her unfiled tax returns, unreported rental income, and misstatements on her bar application. On election night Menino told a cheering crowd, "The people understand my vision. They know I am determined to work hard from dawn to dusk because I'm on your side." He concluded by promising, "to make this my best term ever."

Boston prospered during Menino's third term. But the city also convulsed over horrifying revelations that hundreds of Boston Catholics were sexually abused by priests and that they were protected by a hierarchy that included Cardinal Bernard Law, Archbishop of Boston. Guarded optimism had greeted the choice of Bernard Law as archbishop of Boston, the country's most Catholic city. Upon his arrival at Logan Airport in the spring of 1984, the 53 year-old Law, known for his strong will and conservative views, said that his "greatest hope is to be a faithful and good shepherd, a pastor for the archdiocese and for the men and women that constitute the archdiocese and also to be a pastor at the service of the wider community." Mayor Raymond Flynn echoed Law's theme: "The archbishop is reaching out to everybody," the mayor claimed, "bringing together people of diverse backgrounds, and responding to a wide range of concerns: economic justice for the people of the city, particularly attending to the needs of the poor, the elderly, and the destitute."

On March 23, 1984 Law was installed before 2,500 witnesses at Holy Cross Cathedral in the South End, including 130 Catholic bishops and 85 leaders of other faiths. In front of 2,000 members of his clergy during a simple ceremony before the mass, Law asked for their loyalty and spoke about his desire to collaborate with, as well as lead, his clergy. "Ours is not the role of politicians, but ours are appropriately the issues which affect the life and welfare of human persons," Law told the assembled priests. "From the national disgrace of abortion to the scandal of world hunger to the specter of nuclear warfare, I expect you to stand with me in

giving voice to the church's authentic teaching and legitimate concern."

In his first homily, Law spoke out against "the idolatry of self, in the suffocation of consumerism, in the paralysis of materialism, in the excesses of sensuality or in the consequences of sinful decisions, in hunger, poverty, discrimination, war, abortion." The two-and-a-half hour mass was covered live by the city's three major television stations and broadcast on the radio.

Amid praise for Law at his installation, one notable challenge was recognized: the vast difference between directing a small diocese in Missouri to that of Boston—the country's third largest diocese, with 2 million Catholics and 2,000 priests. One priest predicted: "In today's church, priests need affirmation and encouragement, and that will really challenge him, with so many."

Nine months later, Law called on the business community to help bridge the racial divide and give equal opportunities to all. "This is your city," he told 600 business leaders, and we all must join together to improve race relations. Yet even as he challenged the business community and used his fluent Spanish to reach out to Boston's immigrant populations, Law was seen as out of touch. Despite advice from a *Globe* columnist to learn about his new community, take a stand for social justice, and "de-emphasize the pomp of your office by minimizing the use of the regal red, the miter, and the staff," Law insisted on formality, was reluctant to build community relationships, and began to alienate the city's more liberal Catholics with his conservatism.

Law insisted on a strict return to standard church teachings on such issues as abortion, women priests, and the marriage of priests. He raised eyebrows with his outspoken public stances in comparison with his predecessor's quieter style. Soon after his installation, he appeared at a June anti-abortion rally at the State House in support of a constitutional amendment to restrict or ban abortions. "Archbishop Law knows the power of the media and is going to take advantage of the opportunities to exercise his teaching authority on such an issue of deep moral crisis in the nation," Rev. Peter V. Conley, spokesman for the Catholic Archdiocese of Boston, told a *Globe* reporter. At the 1986 Boston College commencement, he told graduates and their startled parents that the Jesuit college was not Catholic enough.

Law's tendency to alienate important segments of the Catholic community, his emotional reserve, and his perceived lack of caring and compassion fueled the anger that erupted in response to the most scarring crisis in the American Catholic Church, one that had ramifications throughout the world.

In 2002 the *Globe* published a series of reports revealing that, for years, the Boston Archdiocese had hidden the fact that priests had been sexually abusing children. What was even more horrifying was that the Church covered up the abuse and allowed abusers to continue to serve in positions where they would have access to children. Cardinal Law was personally involved in some of these decisions, moving priests accused of sexually abusing children from one parish to another without notifying the parishioners of the circumstances surrounding the change, and signing off on psychological evaluations of priests made by non-professionals. When his actions were made public during the course of several lawsuits by alleged victims, a huge public outcry forced Law to resign his post in December 2002.

After an investigation of nearly a year-and-a-half, Attorney General Thomas Reilly reported 789 cases of molestation by 250 priests and church workers over the last 60 years. The attorney general's report said that Cardinal Law "had direct knowledge of the scope, duration, and severity of the crisis experienced by children in the archdiocese." Yet Reilly said that no prosecutions would come about as a result of the investigation, because no laws actually had been broken.

Boston College historian James O'Toole's analysis of the sexual abuse scandal faults Law personally, as well as the appointment system that plucked him from a rural Missouri diocese and placed him in metropolitan Boston. Although Law had attended Harvard University 30 years before his appointment, he arrived in Boston without any local connections or friends. He did not have a single priest at his side during his tenure that he knew from his days at the seminary. There was no one Law could turn to for frank advice. Without these all-important "institutional roots" to assist him, Law responded to the scandal with secrecy and duplicity.

Early in that tumultuous year leading to Law's resignation, a group of parishioners began meeting in one of the affected churches, St. John the Evangelist, which was in Wellesley, a wealthy suburb of Boston. More than 30 children at nearby St. Julia's of Weston had suffered abuse after the transfer of just one priest, and more victims throughout the archdiocese were coming forward.

The lay group "Voice of the Faithful" took as its slogan "Keep the Faith, Change the Church." and set forth to support the victims and the priests who were buffeted by the scandal, while changing the structure of the church. By the summer of 2006 it grew into a national organization with contributions of a half-million dollars.

A year after Law's resignation, he told the Catholic newspaper *The Pilot*: "I felt that we had attempted to address the terrible issue of abuse in an effective way. I thought that what we had in place were things that needed to be in place, but I understood that really the confidence that people had in me as a leader had been eroded on this issue, and it's very important that there be that kind of confidence generally."

Law's successor in July 2003, 59-year-old Archbishop Sean P. O'Malley, O. F. M. not only shunned luxury in favor of simplicity, but he moved quickly to quiet the furor. He agreed to an $85 million settlement with abuse victims, arranged for the sale of the cardinal's Brighton residence and surrounding property to Boston College, and targeted 83 parishes for closure. Recent data shows church attendance and contributions have increased, suggesting that the Boston archdiocese's future may be brighter.

Boston had been battered, but the city's beloved Red Sox gave fans a welcome diversion. As they had since 1918 when they last won the World Series, in 2003 the Red Sox hoped for a championship season—yet ghosts haunted the team. When they were on the field, players told Manager Grady Little they didn't want to make a disastrous mistake; they did not want to be a "Bill Buckner." In the 1986 World Series against the New York Mets, the Red Sox were one out away from victory when first baseman Buckner let a ground ball go through his legs. The Mets scored and went on to win the Series.

In the 2003 American League Championship Series, the Red Sox faced the Yankees in game seven. Boston newspapers headlined the series, "Red Sox Nation vs. The Evil Empire." The starting pitchers were Pedro Martinez for the Sox and future hall of fame and one-time Red Sox pitcher Roger Clemens for the Yankees. Clemens lasted just four innings, giving up six hits and four runs before Manager Joe Torre took the ball. Mike Mussina made the run from the Yankee bullpen to the mound. He had never appeared in relief. Mussina struck out the Red Sox catcher and centerfielder Johnny Damon who hit into a double play retiring the side. The Red Sox led 5-2.

The first Yankee batter to face Martinez in the eighth inning popped out to shortstop, but then Derek Jeter doubled to right and scored on a single to center by Bernie Williams. Red Sox Manager Grady Little walked out to the mound to talk with Martinez; everyone in the Red Sox Nation believed Little was going to take Martinez out. After a short conversation, however, Little patted Martinez on the back and jogged back to the dugout. "Pedro Martinez has been our man all year long, and in situations like that, he's the one we

Fenway Park, the home of the Boston Red Sox opened in 1912, and is the oldest major league baseball stadium in the country. The ballpark's thirty-seven feet high and 240 feet long left-field wall, known as the "Green Monster" was added in 1934. Courtesy, Allison Hutchins

want on the mound over anybody we can bring out of the bullpen," Little later explained.

Hideki Matsui, the Yankee leftfielder, crushed Martinez's pitch for a ground-rule double, sending Williams to third. Next, the Yankee catcher, who Martinez had earlier threatened to hit in the head, hit a blooper to center, scoring Williams and Matsui. The game was tied.

Knuckleball pitcher Tim Wakefield came out to face the Yankees in the bottom of the 11th inning. A well-thrown knuckleball comes at a batter slowly and flutters down in a way that makes it nearly impossible to hit. But the knuckleball Wakefield threw to Aaron Boone stayed high and the Yankee third baseman hit it into the left field seats. The Yankees had beaten the Red Sox—again. The Red Sox front office fired Manager Grady Little.

Boston Globe sportswriter Dan Shaughnessy put his finger on the Red Sox's problem. It was the "curse of the Bambino." Babe Ruth had played for the Red Sox, helping them win World Series titles in 1916 and 1918. But in 1920, Harry Frazee, owner of the Red Sox, sold the "Bambino" to the New York Yankees. According to Red Sox fans, Frazee's act of treachery put a curse on Boston baseball and accounted for the fact that the Red Sox had not won a World Series in all the years since Ruth was sold to New York.

The 2004 American League Championship Series again pitted the Red Sox against the Yankees. The Sox were loose and confident. Curt Schilling started game one for Boston, but despite his record-setting season statistics, he was routed. The Yankees won 10-7. Game two also went to the Yankees; Pedro Martinez gave up a two-run homerun to seal the defeat. Following a rainout, the Sox lost game three at Fenway Park, 19-8. No baseball team in post-season play had come back from a 3-0 deficit. Everyone in Red Sox Nation knew it was over.

A sign on the Red Sox clubhouse door had a different message: "WE CAN CHANGE HISTORY. BELIEVE IT." Derek Lowe pitched well for the Sox,

holding the Yankees to just two runs. When Lowe was replaced in the sixth inning, the Sox led 3-2. But, in the top of the ninth the Yankees had taken the lead 4-3. Kevin Millar led off the bottom of the ninth with a walk. Red Sox Manager Terry Francona sent Dave Roberts to run for Millar. On Yankee closer Mariano Rivera's first fastball, Roberts stole second base. The next batter singled, Roberts raced home, and the Sox tied the game. David Ortiz hit a walk-off homerun in the bottom of the 12th. The Red Sox were alive, but not quite well.

Boston ace Curt Schilling was doubtful. He had a flapping tendon in his right ankle that prevented him from putting pressure on his foot. The team's orthopedic physician stitched skin around the tendon, creating a sheaf that held the tendon in place. The hope was that Schilling would be ready to pitch in game six if the Sox won game five.

Martinez started for the Sox in game five. He was effective, but not overpowering. In the top of the eighth, the Yankees led when Boston reliever Mike Timlin faced Alex Rodriguez with one out and a man on third. "A-Rod" struck out and the score remained 4-2. Ortiz started off the bottom of the eighth by hitting a home run and thanks to Roberts' speed, a single to center and a timely sacrifice fly, the Sox tied the score. With two out in the 14th—game five was the longest postseason game in baseball history—Ortiz came through again. He lined a single into centerfield scoring Johnny Damon from second. The Sox had closed the gap.

Schilling started game six in Yankee stadium. While he warmed up, several of the stitches that held his ankle together broke and blood seeped into his sock. Despite the pain, Schilling pitched brilliantly and in the top of the fourth inning Red Sox second baseman Mark Bellhorn hit a three-run homer. Schilling left the game in the seventh, leading 4-1. The Sox held on and won 4-2.

The Red Sox won game seven easily behind homers by Ortiz, Damon, and Bellhorn. Sportswriters immediately labeled it the greatest comeback in baseball history. The headline in the *Boston Herald* said it all: "BABE, YOU'RE HISTORY!"

Although the Red Sox had lost twice in the past to the National League Champion St. Louis Cardinals, the feeling in Red Sox Nation was that the curse had been broken and the Sox were a team of destiny. The Red Sox swept the Cardinals in four. For the first time in 86 years the Red Sox were world champions. Boston went nuts! On a rainy Saturday morning more than 3 million people jammed the streets of Boston to cheer the Sox.

Legend has it that Boston's streets were laid out in the 17th century to accommodate meandering cows. By 1900 when the population of Boston had ballooned to 560,892 people, hundreds of horse-drawn wagons and trolleys carrying goods and people squeezed through downtown every day trying to reach rail terminals and

wharves and thousands of small business located throughout the city.

A half-century later, automobiles crammed into the same narrow, winding streets. Eventually, as in every other major American city, Boston politicians and planners responded to the gridlock caused by too many cars on too few streets by furiously creating a series of highways and tunnels with the idea of moving cars and people into, out of, and around the city— often without regard to the consequences. The plan to relieve congestion seemed perfect. Storrow Drive was built parallel to the Charles River, in order to move cars east and west around the northern edge of the city; an extension of the Massachusetts Turnpike brought commuters from the western suburbs into the heart of the financial district, rather than dropping them on the western edge of the city; and the Callahan Tunnel (1961) was added to the Sumner Tunnel (1934) to link Boston

One hundred and fifty cranes dotted the Boston skyline during the Big Dig project, the largest in the nation's history. Courtesy, Central Artery/Tunnel Project

with the North Shore.

The Central Artery, an elevated highway, was the most important part of this new road system. It was designed to allow motorists to travel from the South Shore to the North Shore without driving through the city's narrow streets, to provide easy access to downtown Boston, and to create hundreds of parking spaces beneath its huge, green, steel superstructure. In 1950 demolition began in an effort to make room for the Central Artery. More than a thousand homes and businesses were destroyed and nearly 20,000 residents were displaced to make way for the state-of-the art highway. However, serious problems soon emerged after the Central Artery's completion in 1962.

First, the Artery was to have worked in concert with another highway, called the Inner Belt, which would allow through traffic to bypass the city. However, the Inner Belt was never built. So contrary to the plan, the Central Artery served both local *and* regional traffic. Initially, the highway carried only a fraction of its estimated capacity of 75,000 vehicles a day. But by the early 1970s, with Boston's economy on the upswing, more than 200,000 cars and trucks negotiated the Artery each day, causing horrendous

traffic jams through the heart of the city. Second, the Central Artery divided downtown Boston, effectively cutting off the waterfront district and the historic North End from the rest of the city. Third, it was ugly. In some places the road and its access ramps were wider than the length of a football field. The so-called "highway in the sky" cast long dark shadows over local streets and shops—and filled previously quiet neighborhoods with noise and dirt. In other words, by the time the Central Artery was completed it was an obsolete eyesore.

Bostonians began to advocate for a new highway. Residents in the North End complained about their noisy isolation. Meanwhile, Mayor Kevin White spoke on behalf of local business leaders who were fearful of losing their customers, urging the state to do something to address the problem.

Fred Salvucci, Governor Michael Dukakis' transportation secretary, and Thomas "Tip" O'Neill, speaker of the United States House of Representatives, took up the challenge. Because the Central Artery was part of the Interstate Highway System, Massachusetts was eligible for federal funding. After four years of effort, O'Neill persuaded Congress to override President

Ronald Reagan's veto and fund a major transformation of Boston's highways.

Known officially as the Central Artery/ Tunnel project, and to locals as the "Big Dig," the agreed upon plan involved: replacing the six-lane elevated Central Artery with an eight lane tunnel running underneath the city; replacing the bridge over the Charles River with two new bridges; extending the Massachusetts Turnpike into South Boston by building a tunnel under Fort Point Channel; and connecting Logan Airport to South Boston and the Turnpike by adding a third tunnel under Boston Harbor. As envisioned, it was the largest civil engineering construction project in United States history. It was to be completed by 2004 at a total cost of $11 billion.

In the winter of 1991 a huge power shovel mounted on a barge began digging a trench across the harbor from South Boston to East Boston. When completed two years later, the trench was three-quarters of a mile long, 50 feet deep, and 100 feet wide. One by one, 12 double-barreled steel tunnel sections that were

reinforced with steel bars and a concrete foundation, which would be the basis for a four-lane roadway, were floated into the harbor with the help of a lay barge. Both ends of the tunnel sections were sealed with steel plates and carefully lowered into the trench. Each 325 feet long tunnel section interlocked with the next. The tunnel section closest to South Boston was outfitted with a snorkel—a wide air shaft extending above the high water mark—so that workers and equipment could be lowered into the tunnel. Workers cut away the steel plates at each end of the tunnel section, ensured that the gasket placed between the connected sections was watertight, and completed the electrical wiring and roadways. Two huge ventilation systems were constructed to pump in fresh air and suck out automobile exhaust. Named for the famed Red Sox slugger, the Ted Williams Tunnel opened to traffic on December 15, 1995.

The tunnel was then connected to the Massachusetts Turnpike by building concrete tunnel boxes that were positioned *above* an underground subway line and *below* South Station—Boston's busiest railroad station. Because the soil above the Red Line was too weak to support the tunnel boxes, engineers first strengthened the soil by drilling 125 feet down into bedrock and mixing a cement and water

Left: Born in Cambridge, Massachusetts in 1912, O'Neill served in the U. S. House of Representatives for 34 years, including ten years as Speaker of the House from 1977-1987. O'Neill, a liberal Democrat, enjoyed cordial relationships with Presidents Lyndon Johnson and Ronald Reagan, but he was sharply critical of Johnson over the Vietnam war and once said Reagan was a "cheerleader for selfishness." Courtesy, Boston College

During the peak of the Big Dig's construction, about 5,000 construction workers were on the job at any one time. Courtesy, Central Artery/Tunnel Project

The demolition of the elevated portion of I-93 through the city has made an enormous change in the area's visual appeal. Courtesy, Central Artery/ Tunnel Project

The distinctive Leonard P. Zakim Bunker Hill Bridge is a highlight of the new Boston skyline. Its streamlined design draws on Boston's history, with its cables reminiscent of ships' rigging and its towers shaped like the nearby Bunker Hill monument. Courtesy, Central Artery/Tunnel Project

solution into the soil. Workers then constructed an underwater bridge that straddled the subway and held the tunnel boxes in place. To get under South Station, concrete tunnel boxes were built and pushed underneath the railroad tracks by using powerful hydraulic jacks. The entire time the tunnel inched forward—by approximately three feet a day—passenger trains rumbled overhead.

The final challenge was to build a tunnel underneath the Central Artery without tearing it down before the tunnel was complete. To accomplish this, workers built steel reinforced cement walls that extended from the surface to the bedrock, along the length and on either side of the Central Artery. Steel beams were then laid between the walls and men and machines excavated the dirt between the parallel walls. A concrete roof and a steel framework completed the support structure that held up the Central Artery, allowing thousands of cars to pass over the road while the tunnel was being built directly beneath the old "highway in the sky."

A new bridge spanning the Charles River and connecting the appreciatively named O'Neill Tunnel with Interstate 93 remained to be built. The stay-cable suspension bridge was named after Leonard P. Zakim, a longtime civil rights

activist and regional director of the Anti-Defamation League. Its two hollow steel towers, each 270 feet high and shaped like the nearby Bunker Hill Monument, provided anchors for the steel cables which were reminiscent of a ship's rigging. They supported the eight-lane roadway between the towers and two lanes cantilevered on the east side of the bridge. It was, and still is, a breathtakingly beautiful bridge, a distinctive Boston symbol which echoes the city's Revolutionary and maritime past.

To date, the Big Dig has been plagued by trouble. When it was completed in 2003, the project's cost exceeded the original estimate by nearly $5 billion. Several contractors were charged with corruption, and leaks briefly sent water gushing into the I-93 tunnel shortly after it opened. And tragically, in July 2006, a woman was crushed to death by a falling three-ton ceiling tile in the connector tunnel leading to the Ted Williams Tunnel. "It's horrible," a Massachusetts Institute of Technology engineering professor stated, "but the problem may be fixed simply by adopting a more tightly controlled maintenance schedule." However, that assessment proved too optimistic and within a few days following the accident

Governor Mitt Romney stepped into the crisis. By means of a hastily enacted law, the governor took control of overseeing the project. Within days workmen discovered that there was a systemic problem with how the ceiling tiles were suspended and anchored. Romney shut down the connector tunnel and vowed to make it safe.

The harbor is not only visible from many locations in downtown Boston, but it's also clean thanks to a massive effort that began after the city's historic gateway was labeled a "harbor of shame" by George H. W. Bush during the 1988 presidential campaign. No one contested the accuracy of Bush's remark, but Boston Democrats were quick to point out that the harbor's polluted status had been centuries in the making. In fact, the practice of dumping human waste and allowing sewage to leach or flow into Boston Harbor began shortly after settlers arrived in 1630. From time to time over the next century, town government enacted ordinances regulating the disposal of human waste. However, despite a series of laws, most of the city's "nightsoil" still ended up in coastal waters. A 1744 Philadelphia tourist likened the water around Boston's town dock to "a very stinking puddle."

The problem—the aesthetics, the stench, and the fear of epidemic disease—caused the city's first mayor and councilmen to assume responsibility for constructing and maintaining a public sewer system in 1822. But, government's inability to collect the assessments owed to the city by individual users combined with Boston's rapidly increasing population caused the problem to get worse rather than better. Real improvement did not begin until 1877 when the Boston City Council appropriated $3.2 million to build a comprehensive new sewer system. In addition to working in trenches below sea

Boston's red brick Freedom Trail winds down Hanover Street through the North End, connecting the Paul Revere House, Boston's oldest wooden home, and the Old North Church, from whose tower two lanterns gave the signal that the British were traveling by sea to Lexington to rearm themselves. Courtesy, Lisa Rogers

Cobblestones and granite blocks line this section of the HarborWalk, which stretches from Chelsea Creek north of the city to Dorchester, in the south. The walkway highlights the renewed Boston Harbor and links the waterfront to the city's parks. Courtesy, Lisa Rogers

level, the biggest challenge confronting engineers and workers was the construction of a tunnel under Dorchester Bay. It was tough, wet work. Working nearly 150 feet below low water with drills and explosives, workers excavated 25,000 cubic yards of rock and dirt. When the tunnel and sewer system were connected in 1884, Mayor Hugh O'Brien lauded the work. "The water in the bays and docks," the mayor boasted, "has again become pure, as evidenced by its being frequented by fish, which for years have been unable to live in it on account of sewage contamination."

But the promise of clean water and healthy fish was not fulfilled. Engineers had overestimated the tide's ability to remove sewage dumped into the harbor through the Dorchester tunnel. Rather than being pulled out to sea, the discharged sewage tended to float languidly in the

The John Joseph Moakley United States Courthouse provides a striking counterpoint to the Boston skyline. The courthouse is sited on Fan Pier in South Boston, once an important locale for shipping cargo. U.S. Representative Joseph Moakley secured federal resources for the courthouse. The federal government purchased the long-neglected land from restaurateur Anthony Athanas in the late 1980s. Today, sculptures outside the courthouse commemorate the site's shipping history. Nearby, on Pier 4, is the Institute of Contemporary Art. Courtesy, Lisa Rogers

shallow harbor, creating a stinking, greasy film, extending more than mile from the outlet point. By 1939 when the city's population had topped more than 770,000, a study reported that over 250 million gallons of raw sewage per day was discharged into Boston Harbor. In 1952 and 1968 two small sewage treatment plants were added to the system, but neither worked well and the water quality in Boston Harbor did not improve much. By the 1970s Boston's sewage system was near collapse.

To break a political logjam that blocked reform, the city of Quincy, one of the communities tied into the sewer system, sued the Metropolitan District Commission and the Boston Water and Sewer Commission for violating the federal Clean Water Act. In 1982 the suit landed in the federal courts and after two years of negotiation, the way was cleared to begin the project. Over the next 16 years, modern treatment plants were built on Deer Island and connected to a nine-and-a-half mile long outfall tunnel that transported treated sewage into Massachusetts

Bay. The measure of the project's success is a cleaner harbor, as well as the regeneration of plant and animal life. People now flock to the public beaches along the harbor's edge; it is no longer a "harbor of shame."

Reminiscent of the Emerald Necklace, the Boston Harbor Walk links East Boston, via the Rose Kennedy Greenway, to the beautiful John Joseph Moakley Federal Courthouse, which is situated on the Fan Pier at the eastern edge of the harbor and boasts a view of downtown Boston. From the courthouse it's also possible to see Spectacle Island, a 105-acre island park created with 3 million cubic feet of dirt from the Big Dig. Nothing about Spectacle Island's past history—a one-time quarantine station for immigrants, a site for gambling and other illegal activities, and a garbage dump—hinted it would become a family playground, complete with five miles of hiking trails and a hill offering spectacular views of Boston.

In addition to taking down the old Central Artery that divided the city and opened it to the harbor, the Big Dig was supposed to help attract new business to Boston by making it easier to move in and around the city. But, during the decade it took to complete the Central Artery/Tunnel project, the opposite happened. Boston lost a number of its major businesses to a surge in corporate mergers. *The New York Times* purchased the 120-year-old *Boston Globe*, Bank Boston became Fleet, and Fleet was swallowed by Bank of America. Firms outside Massachusetts also acquired Gillette. John Hancock, whose glass tower was the symbol of the "New Boston," remains in name only; a Canadian company bought the insurance company. Boston's claim as an intellectual center also was weakened when *The Atlantic Monthly* left for Washington, D.C. and another division of the publisher Little, Brown moved to New York City. But, the cruelest cut of all, in the eyes of some, came in 2006 when Filene's department store in Downtown Crossing shuttered its doors. As a result of these and other changes, Boston lost 25,000 jobs between 2001 and 2005—and valuable pieces of its historic identity.

Augmented with 4,400 bargeloads of fill from the Big Dig, Spectacle Island's 105 acres are now a family-friendly feature of the Boston Harbor Islands National Park. Courtesy, Central Artery/Tunnel Project

The promenade at the Christian Science center is punctuated by a tower, part of its administrative complex, as well as the Prudential tower and the skyscraper at 111 Huntington, part of the Prudential center. Courtesy, Nora Rogers.

In this new business climate, the *Boston Globe* was the first locally owned company to merge with a larger outside firm. Founded in 1872 by six Boston businessmen, the *Globe* was originally a morning newspaper until Charles H. Taylor, the managing editor and publisher, added an evening edition that ran from 1878–1979. The *Globe* was a private company until 1973 when it went public under the name Affiliated Publications. It continued to be managed by descendants of the Taylor family until it was sold in 1993 to the *New York Times*. William O. Taylor, Affiliated's chairman and president, said the deal "marked the passing of an era in Boston journalism."

BankBoston had been in business for 215 years when its president Charles "Chad" Gifford spoke to Terry Murray, the head of Fleet Financial Group, at a fundraiser for the American Ireland Fund in the fall of 1998. Among the factors that caused Gifford to be receptive to Murray's suggestion that the two talk about a merger were the losses BankBoston had suffered as a result of its investments in Brazil and Argentina. Following some secret one-on-one breakfasts and lunches at Murray's Four Seasons apartment across from the Boston Public Garden, the two men quietly set up a meeting of their key executives. That led to more talks in New York City and all-night sessions with lawyers and merger specialists. Gifford and Murray formally signed an agreement late Sunday night, March 13, 1999.

Community activists and politicians initially were not happy about the merger. BankBoston, they pointed out during a noisy July meeting, had been a leader in making affordable mortgages and small business loans available to people living in Boston's poorer neighborhoods. And, according to critics, Fleet had not been such a good corporate citizen. Fleet executives attending the meeting promised to be more attentive to community needs and U.S. Congressman Barney Frank (D-Newton) noted that banks are required by law to lend to the communities from which they take deposits. These caveats may have helped the bank win approval for the merger from the Federal Reserve and the Justice Department.

Five years later, Bank of America purchased Fleet Bank for $48 billion. CEO Kenneth D. Lewis, an ex-Marine who rewarded high-performing employees with crystal hand grenades and had a 1996 Yankees World Series ring, insisted that his top executives cluster around his office in Charlotte, North Carolina, de-emphasizing the importance of Boston. "Years ago," a software executive recalled, local bankers and business executives came together every two weeks at the Boston Safe Deposit and Trust Company, functioning as behind-the-scenes advisors to Boston's mayor.

The sweeping changes in the city's economic structure, however, put an end to "the Vault," the name given to this group of local, civic-minded, corporate leaders. Although the new companies make charitable contributions, they share little history with, and have less of a stake in, the city.

Merger mania claimed another old Boston company in 2005. The men's razor company that King Gillette began in a tiny factory overlooking a South Boston fish market in 1901 was sold to Procter & Gamble for $54 billion. In addition to job cuts, the company announced that Gillette would be headquartered in Cincinnati, Ohio. Massachusetts' Secretary of State William F. Galvin expressed concern for the economic fallout, noting that the "concluding chapter will continue to play out in the lives of employees and retirees." Boston public relations guru Jack Connors put a positive spin on Gillette's move from Boston. "It's not the first time that Boston has changed," Connors pointed out. "It's one more iteration of a constant, that constant being change."

The intellectual and cultural life of old Boston also changed in the 21st century. AOL Time Warner announced early in 2002 that, for the first time since the publisher Little, Brown was founded in 1837, the Boston office would not make any publishing decisions. The process of moving out of Boston began 14 years earlier when the general fiction and nonfiction divisions of Little, Brown took flight to New York City and then another significant move was made in 1999 when the company sold its landmark headquarters at 34 Beacon Street. AOL Time Warner's nod to nostalgia was that Little, Brown books would still bear the colophon with Charles Bullfinch's Revolutionary War monument on Beacon Hill and also the books' title pages would continue to cite Boston, New York, London. Both gestures did little to satisfy Boston literati.

An intellectual groan also greeted the news that *The Atlantic Monthly* was moving to Washington D.C. after 148 years in Boston. The magazine's devotion to literature, art, science, and politics,

pleaded one-time editor Robert Manning, should not be reduced to "political spam and spin." "That is why," Manning continued, "I am disturbed that the magazine is leaving the city on a hill for the city on the Potomac."

But, perhaps no change symbolized the demise of the old Boston as the sale and closure of Filene's department store. Built in 1912 on the corner of Washington and Sumner streets—and gradually expanding to cover the entire block bounded by Washington, Sumner, Franklin, and Hawley streets—Filene's attracted generations of shoppers from greater Boston to its Beaux Arts-style building. Once a robust center of shopping, by the 1990s Filene's succumbed to new shopping trends, the popularity of suburban malls, and the multiplication of discount outlets. Federated Department Stores, the Cincinnati owner of Macy's, bought the parent company of Filene's in 2005, but failed to breathe new life into the old store and it was closed the following year. In 2006 the Boston Landmarks Commission voted to give Filene's protected status, meaning the façade of the building would be retained. In addition, the legendary Filene's Basement, owned since 1991 by a separate company, remained in the building.

Edward A. Filene pioneered the practice of selling leftover merchandise from his own store, as well as others, at bargain prices; everything automatically discounted week after week until the goods were sold at a price 75 percent below its original price. On any given day, thousands of customers elbowed their way toward the tables on which dresses and shirts and coats were piled high. Often people grabbed a desired item of clothing whether it fit or not, hoping to swap with another customer for the right size or color. Notoriously frugal Governor Mike Dukakis often boasted that much of his wardrobe came from the Basement.

At a June 2006 ceremony commemorating Filene's demise, Mayor Menino unveiled a small green plaque mounted on the side of the building. "Our parents

The Museum of Fine Arts' West Wing entrance, designed by I.M. Pei, features an outdoor sculpture garden. The MFA began in 2006 work on a Foster and Partners master plan that provides a new American art wing, renovated European art galleries, new space for Contemporary Art, a glass-enclosed courtyard and new special exhibit gallery. Courtesy, Nora Rogers

brought us to Filene's to buy our First Communion clothes and our white shoes and we'll always have the memory of coming here with our families," the mayor said. An old street vendor hit on another note: "It's going to be more condos over here," he said. "As far as this being a place to shop, that's all done. That's all done now. You could see it coming, boy."

Boston Mayor Menino and urban economists agree that the old Boston is gone, but they are optimistic that Boston can reinvent itself. Reinvention is nothing new for the city. Over its 375-year history, Boston has been transformed many times. It evolved from a maritime economy to manufacturing, from the production of textiles and leather and shoes to hi-tech and both the life and bio-sciences. "The remarkable thing about Boston as compared to other metropolises like New York City," writes Harvard economics professor Edward Glaeser, "is that it has crisis after crisis and repeatedly figures out a new way to survive and thrive in a changing economy." According to Mayor Menino, a new transformational process is already underway. Greater Boston is a well-

established hub for start-ups and Massachusetts has the third highest rate of patents on new technologies in the country and the second highest rate of turning those discoveries into new companies.

Boston is also solidifying its status as a center for the arts as many of its institutions have either built or made significant additions. In 2005 the Museum of Fine Arts broke ground on a major addition. The same year, its neighbor on the Back Bay Fens, the Isabella Stewart Gardner Museum, rebounded after a disastrous 1990 theft to plan the first major addition to its Italianate palazzo. The Institute for Contemporary Art, a magnificent new structure along the waterfront, opened in September 2006.

If Boston does succeed in reinventing itself, the city's newest residents will be the ones who will do it. Over the past several decades, Boston's neighborhoods have experienced an increase in immigration. The 2000 census showed 50.5 percent of Boston's population as made up of people of color. Immigrants founded Boston and it is clear that immigrants also will shape the city's future.

Copley Square Plaza, bordered to the west by the Boston Public Library (1887, on the National Register of Historic Places) and the New Old South Church (1874, a National Historic Landmark), and anchored by Trinity Church to the east, is a popular gathering spot. Courtesy, Nora Rogers

XII
Chronicles of Leadership

Fortunes have been made in Boston. They have been made in the basic economic function of sea-borne commerce—in the trading of rum, indigo, molasses, codfish, tea, furs, and glass. They have been made in the China trade; in textiles and in leather and in wool; in insurance, investments, and banking; and now they are being made in silicon and wire, in computers and high technology. And each generation of enterprise has left something behind for the welfare and civilization of those who followed. Virtually every institution that is claimed as part of our quality of life, or our culture in Boston, came from benefactors who made their fortunes in business. As they grew, they shared their growth and success with the city. So it grew and succeeded as well.

Business in Boston—right from the settlement of the colony in 1630—has changed and grown as the old city on the hill changed and grew.

Before the hills of the peninsula vanished and the encroachment of land upon water that has marked the history of Boston began, the golden age of the clipper ships saw the spars and rigging of gallant vessels making a crazy network in the harbor; and the waterfront, along what is now Atlantic Avenue, teemed with shipping traffic even as the borsprits of Boston crafts were poking into faraway ports from Liverpool to the Java Straits. Alert Yankee merchants solved the riddle of the China trade, and along the wharves at the bottom of State (then King) Street, men like Thomas Hancock, Peter Faneuil, and Thomas Boylston transacted their business and accumulated their fortunes,

giving proof of the persevering industry of the Massachusetts Bay colonists.

The mercantile capital of John Winthrop and his companies demonstrated its capabilities when, following the War of 1812, as it alternately prospered and suffered, Yankee resources were diverted to the more economically viable business of manufacturing and Boston and its communities fostered a wide assortment of industry. Adding new dimension to commerce through these generations were the colorful cast of immigrants arriving by steamships at the docks of Jeffries Point. They would, in an era of large-scale industrialization, assist in revitalizing the city's economy.

When in the 20th century the textile mills and the leather tanneries faced decline, Boston, pursuing its course along the pathway of prosperity, turned to electronics and experienced new growth. And post-World War II brought a shift to a service- and finance-specialized city in a more diversified economy.

Such change has been the hallmark of Boston. The '50s growth of high-technology, defense-related companies and the explosive boom of the computer industry, combined with the '60s renaissance of Boston's central city, accelerated new commerce, success, and prosperity.

To appreciate its future, we must know of its past. The businesses and organizations whose histories appear on the following pages are each a special part of Boston's past and present. They illustrate the variety of ways individuals, along with businesses and organizations, have contributed to the growth and development of Boston, making it an exceptional place to work and live.

Opposite: These businesses were located on Washington Street, in Roxbury, before the elevated train was built. The site is near the John Shelburne Recreation Complex at Washington Park. Photograph by Henry Hadcock. (SPNEA)

A.W. CHESTERTON COMPANY

In 1865 Thomas Chesterton, then 30 years old, along with his wife Sara and their three small children left Loughborough, Leicestershire, England and traveled to the seaport city of Liverpool. The family had planned to take a ship to Australia, but it was oversold. Thomas then noticed a ship on the next pier, discovered it was bound for the United States and had space. So, he announced to his family, "Well, I guess we'll be Americans," and they set sail.

The Chesterton family arrived at Ellis Island in New York on July 29, 1865. After a period of time, the family moved to the Boston area and settled in the town of Malden. Thomas worked as a huckster/tin peddler, his son Arthur began his career as a book-keeper and a sales agent.

Arthur eventually came to live in Brookline, Massachusetts. He took a great interest in sailing and was, and still is, classified in the permanent Marblehead records as one of the racing greats. Sailing in the largest class of racing boats of the time, the

About 1895 at 49 India Street in Boston, Mr. "A. W." stands in the doorway, second from the right.

Commodore Arthur W. Chesterton, the company's founder.

Massachusetts Bay 25-foot (length overall 40 feet), Arthur was named champion for eight consecutive years, beating every prominent yachtsman of the time. One competitor built eight new boats, one each year, hoping to beat Arthur—and finally did. With that, Arthur Chesterton ended his illustrious racing career. However, he remained an active and enthusiastic yachtsman all his life. He was elected commodore of the Winthrop Yacht Club and later served four years as commodore of the Boston Yacht Club.

Eventually, Arthur went on to become the founder of the A.W. Chesterton Company, which is one of today's oldest and finest, family-owned businesses. Headquartered in Woburn, Massachusetts, the company has been in operation since the 19th century, its roots dating back to 1883. Located at 49 India Street in Boston, the company provided a variety of materials to local industries and to the many ships that used Boston's port.

When the Depression struck, the company was particularly hard hit. Tom

and Dev Chesterton, Arthur's sons, were now involved in the business and each earned $40 a week. However, there wasn't always enough money to pay them. Arthur died during this trying period and Tom and Dev took over the company and began to rebuild it. When World War II began, Dev joined the navy while Tom stayed behind to run the business.

In 1948 Boston wanted to build an overhead expressway, and Chesterton's offices were in the way. So, the business was moved from India Street to Everett, Massachusetts. Later, in the 1950s, the company expanded its product line from its own manufactured pump packing and gaskets to include its own maintenance products, hydraulics, and by the 1960s, mechanical seals.

The third generation, Tom's son James D. Chesterton and Dev's son

Arthur W. Chesterton entered the family business in the 1960s. Arthur focused on production and operations and James on sales and distribution. Up to that point the company had concentrated its effort in North America. However, the time had come for the business to branch out.

Armed with a plane ticket and no money for development, James headed to Europe to hire salespeople and find distributors for the company's products. This gutsy move proved successful and led to Chesterton's expansion into other regions of the world. The A.W. Chesterton Company was transformed into a global enterprise with business in 90 countries.

James also convinced distributors to sell Chesterton products in their territories and, at the same time, he pioneered a new method of bringing products and services to market. The typical distributor had an exclusive geographical area and sold products made by various manufacturers. However, it became essential that at least some of these salespeople receive specialized training and become dedicated to selling only Chesterton

Chesterton receives "E" Award of Excellence in Manufacturing at the White House. Pictured are Dev Chesterton and President Lyndon Johnson.

products. The concept of creating a "specialist" whose expertise was specifying, selling, and applying Chesterton products, offered a competitive advantage and propelled the company to annual growth rates in excess of 25 percent a year for nearly 20 years.

By the 1980s the company's global revenues had grown dramatically and continued to grow substantially year after year. During that time, the business began to manufacture new products that were sold through its distribution system. Through its innovations, the company was able to build an outstanding reputation for providing superior products that were used in many types of equipment and for many different industries. As customers learned the value of lowering overall

operating costs by installing long-lasting, highly-reliable products, they began to request Chesterton sealing device products for use in upgrading plant equipment.

Today, the company has transformed the industry and eliminated the costly practice of plugging leaks. By confining fluids and gases throughout a company's entire plant, Chesterton saves its clients money while keeping chemicals out of the environment and water sewerage systems. The company is able to meet the world's strictest environmental standards and, due to the 30,000 products it manufactures, has become a leader in ecology protection by preventing leaks from valves, pumps, cylinders, and flanges.

Acquired from Commercial Chemical Company in Lawrence, Massachusetts in the late 1960s, today Chesterton's Technical Products division formulates

Early Chesterton factory, Melrose, Massachusetts.

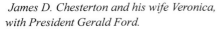

James D. Chesterton and his wife Veronica, with President Gerald Ford.

maintenance chemicals that are used worldwide. Like the rest of Chesterton, it offers superior and unique products while offering cost savings and durability to its customers. A success by all accounts, the Technical Product line represents more than 20 percent of Chesterton's worldwide sales.

Another Chesterton distinction is that it holds a number of high tech patents and boasts a sales and technical staff that can speak a variety of foreign languages. Since its founding, the business has grown by being discriminating in its products, showing customers how to save on their manufacturing and maintenance costs, and building a powerful, customer-supportive distribution and sales team. Over the years, the industry has changed substantially. Today, with Chesterton's help, plants are using more sophisticated equipment, consolidating facilities, and providing improved training for their maintenance crews. Chesterton has secured many "total plant" contracts by providing

A.W. Chesterton receives recognition for industrial contributions to the Commonwealth of Massachusetts from Governor Volpe. Left to right: Jim Chesterton, Governor Volpe, Dev Chesterton, Tom Chesterton and Dick McDermott.

superior value through lower overall cost to the consumer. Over the past two decades, service life has been extended more than 10 times.

Chesterton has always made a name for itself by providing superior customer service. With more than 1,300 product specialists around the world and a team of professional customer service representatives and industry experts, the company offers around-the-clock service focused on exceeding customer expectations. Chesterton specialists are trained to help customers upgrade their plants in industries such as pulp and paper, chemical, electric power generation, water treatment, and automobile manufacturing. Over the years, Chesterton has won many prestigious awards for product excellence. It has been honored with several Vaaler awards from *Chemical Processing* magazine, plus other magazine awards for "Product of the Year." Approximately 50 percent of Chesterton's employees have been with the company for 10 years or more and 25 percent are related to other employees. Chesterton believes that its greatest asset is the dedication and "can do" attitude of its employees.

Corporate leaders Dev Chesterton and Tom Chesterton.

Chesterton's executive team. First row: Andrew Chesterton, executive vice president; Richard Hoyle, CEO; and Brian O'Donnell, vice president and chief operating officer. Second row: Joseph Riley, vice president and general counsel and Thomas O'Rourke, vice president human resources. Third row: Ronald Maxwell, vice president and chief financial officer and Gary Dayton, senior vice president global sales and marketing. Missing: Mary Melia, executive director total quality management.

Throughout its long history, Chesterton has reinvented itself several times to maintain its prowess. As the company continues to move forward through its second century of business, new opportunities offer a bright and prosperous future. Today's markets are changing and Chesterton has embarked upon new strategies to ensure growth in the years ahead. Many of its largest customers are merging and the marketplace is becoming increasingly competitive. Proving the value of products and services while lowering plant costs is even more important today than in the past. These newly consolidated customers are focusing their purchasing power and expect constant improvement in the value of the products they receive. Chesterton is well-positioned to provide best-value solutions through its premium quality products, services, and training.

Andrew W. Chesterton, a fourth generation of the Chesterton family, is currently the executive vice president and responsible for information technology and business excellence, including total quality, environmental, health and safety, alliances and acquisitions, corporate audits, and project support. Additionally, Andrew is responsible for the extensive training of sales people and Chesterton customers so they both can implement practices that promote cost savings and better utilization of Chesterton products.

The company has also developed an array of software tools that are available to its customers on the internet. There, software tools are used to help customers better understand the costs associated with operating facilities and to chart the long-term benefits of upgrading systems with Chesterton products. This also involves developing additional state-of-the-art materials and designs across all product lines, increasing the scope of services provided, acquiring companies that offer complementary products and service capabilities, and forming alliances with other companies.

Chesterton manufacturing plants are ISO 9001:2000 and ISO 14001:2004 certified and the company continues to focus on progress in every area of its business. Improving efficiencies through the use of sophisticated quality tools such as six sigma and lean processes has resulted in reduced costs and accelerated product delivery. Around-the-clock responsiveness has become the hallmark of the company.

By becoming increasingly involved in the progression of its customers' businesses, Chesterton helps its clients become more competitive and prosperous in the industries they serve. With a commitment to its customers and its employees, the A.W. Chesterton Company stands for excellence. Its high standards, long history, and cutting edge approach to business will ensure that Chesterton is around for many, many years to come.

APHIOS CORPORATION

Aphios Corporation, founded by Dr. Trevor Castor, tackles the most challenging problems in healthcare today through safe and natural manufacturing and delivery of biopharmaceuticals. Largely due to Dr. Castor's passion to find treatments for HIV, influenza, certain cancers, and CNS disorders such as Alzheimer's disease, Aphios, which is Greek for "virus-free," aims to improve the quality of life through medicines from natural sources.

Castor's interest in natural healing products and medicinal plants stemmed from his childhood in Trinidad where he observed his maternal grandmother, a Chinese shaman, using herbal medicine and plants to treat Castor's six brothers and one sister. Castor is the middle child and never visited a conventional medical doctor before leaving Trinidad.

As a carefree child living in a poor, working class neighborhood of Port of Spain, Castor paid little attention to his grandmother's techniques or why they worked. But he does recall that she would perform pre-clinical trials of new remedies on wild cats. If the cats

An Aphios microbiologist examines marine microorganisms.

survived (for the most part they did), she would use the remedy on the family. Castor's grandmother passed away when he was 10.

Around this same time, Castor's father told him that he had taught him all that he could. Castor realized his education was on his shoulders. He studied hard and graduated high school at the age of 14 from St. Mary's College in Trinidad, and then started teaching science and mathematics at his alma mater a few years later.

In 1967, with only $20 in his pocket, Castor left Trinidad to attend St. Mary's College in Brooklyn, New York to study business administration. He spent two years there and then moved on to the University of Toronto, Canada, where he received his bachelors of science in chemical engineering. He continued his education and completed a masters of science in chemical engineering and a Ph.D. in mechanical engineering at the University of California, Berkeley. He then worked in the energy industry before making a career change to the biotechnology industry.

When Castor made the transition into the biotechnology world in 1988, he remembered with great curiosity his

grandmother's remedies and resolved to spend about 10 percent of his time researching herbal remedies and natural products and why they work. However, as Castor became more involved in his research, he found evidence to support therapeutic solutions from the natural environment. Aphios now directs 60 to 70 percent of its efforts to natural medicinal research, combing through terrestrial plants, marine organisms, and the human body to mine therapeutic agents.

As Castor began researching the natural products industry, he received little encouragement from pharmaceutical companies. He found that they were not open to discussing their projects and many had abandoned natural product research in favor of producing synthetic compounds.

Pressing on, Castor made a visit to the United States Army at Ft. Detrick, Maryland. There he met with Dr. Daniel Clayman, who was researching new anti-malarial medicines derived from the weed Artemisa annua, or wormwood. Dr. Clayman gave Castor seeds of this plant which he took back to his home in Arlington, Massachusetts to grow. The experiment ended quickly for Castor, who developed severe allergic responses to the plant and suffered from watery eyes, sinus pressure, and a swollen face and glands.

Castor's next visit was to the National Cancer Institute, also in Ft. Detrick, where he spent time with Dr. Gordon Cragg, Dr. Ken Snader, and Dr. Matt Suffness who shared their research on a potential anticancer compound called, Taxol. This compound was isolated from the bark of the Taxus brevifolia tree found in old growth forests in the Pacific Northwest. But there were problems.

The tree was extremely slow growing and extracting the bark would eventually kill the trees. The doctors realized they would need to develop a manufacturing process from a renewable resource from the tree. Castor took

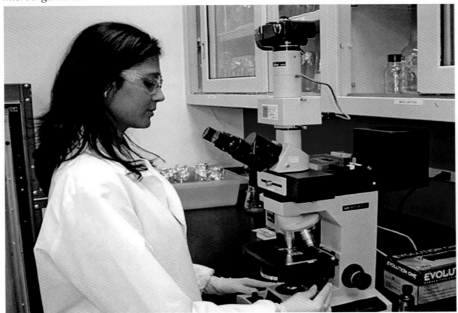

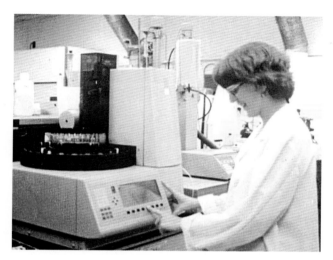

Drug discovery: polarity-guided automated fractionation.

this as his call to action and developed a way to extract and isolate paclitaxel (Bristol-Myers Squibb's brand name Taxol) from the renewable needles of the tree. This process became the basis for other products Castor and his team began to develop and was ultimately one of the early scientific challenges of his emerging biotechnology company.

During this same period, Castor also focused on recombinant therapeutics such as biosynthetic insulin, the first biotechnology product approved by the FDA. He formulated a process that rapidly manufactured this human protein used for insulin replacement. Castor's research caught the attention of Eli Lilly & Company and the National Science Foundation who provided funding for Castor to start Bio-Eng Inc. in 1988, a predecessor company to Aphios.

Over the course of the next five years, Castor ran Bio-Eng from the garage of his home in Arlington, Massachusetts and leased lab space. He worked to establish the basis of his biotechnologies, wrote intellectual property claims to protect his work, and developed a business strategy for future growth of his company. By 1992 Castor was positioned to gather a management team, board of directors,

and small staff of researchers. He incorporated Aphios on September 19, 1993, and set up a lab in Woburn, Massachusetts, where they still operate today.

In the second year of Aphios' history, a tragic hardship hit when one of the Aphios researchers, an intern, was killed in an industrial accident. Castor, who was on shift when the accident occurred, tried to resuscitate the young scientist, who had overlooked operating procedures and placed himself at risk. It was too late.

Castor suffered much anguish over the loss. However, this was not his first experience with emergency situations that left someone teetering between life and death. He had saved more than a dozen lives as a former lifeguard in Trinidad.

The accident raised liability issues. Funders dropped their potential support and insurance companies and corporate attorneys walked away. Castor was forced to find creative ways to make his company work.

Never giving up, Castor brought a multi-disciplinary approach to drug discovery that fostered the use of experts in engineering, biology, chemistry, microbiology, virology, and immunology. He understood that the success of drug discovery would be best served by using the talents and skills of many people. In this way, Aphios develops therapeutics that can make easy and efficient transitions from drug discovery and manufacturing to drug delivery and safety for patients.

Castor's multi-disciplinary approach has been the strength of Aphios and has earned it awards for additional funding, 33 U.S. and international patents, 27 patents pending, and 5 additional patents with collaborators. Aphios has also received grants from the National Institutes of Health, the Advanced Technology Program, the National Institute of Standards and Technology, and the National Science Foundation, and has collaborated with several pharmaceutical and biotechnology companies. Today, Castor continues to lead Aphios in the journey to find safe, natural solutions to fight the health threats of the 21st century.

The research and development staff in 2003.

ArQule INCORPORATED

Dedicated to the research, development and commercialization of next-generation cancer therapeutics, ArQule Incorporated has secured its place as a prominent leader in biotechnology.

With several cancer therapies presently undergoing clinical trials and many of the industry's most significant business partnerships under its belt, ArQule is distinct among its competitors. The company's approach to innovation in drug development began in 1993 and has continued to evolve and strengthen as they have navigated this competitive landscape with agility—nimble in their response to industry-driven changes and steadfast in their mission to develop new medicines that will hold potential for cancer patients worldwide.

"Drop a needle," the great mathematician Euclid suggested, "then wonder as you search for it why you don't see it immediately." The challenge of discovery incumbent upon biotechnology companies is a long and arduous enterprise. Scientists spend years in the laboratory studying tens of thousands of compounds in order to prove just one suitable for the first

phase of clinical trials. Once a small molecule is deemed to be a potential compound for development, it must then be tested extensively on animal and human cells before the first stage of investigational research can even commence—the safety and efficacy of testing being stringently mandated by the FDA. On average, it takes 10 to 15 years and nearly a billion dollars for an effective medicine to go from the laboratory to the pharmacy. With nearly 95 percent of drugs failing in development, most of the work being done never sees the light of day.

Dr. Stephen Hill, president and CEO of ArQule, understands the landscape and has seen the company through the most important years of its growth. With nearly 1,500 biotech companies currently doing business in the United States, firms must be poised with the right balance of science and leadership in order to overcome the many obstacles of this industry. "One of the big challenges of leading an organization," Hill says "is managing the chaos that goes with innovation." Over half of ArQule's team of 100 employees is comprised of world-class, forward-

An annual summer outing in 2002. This shows many former colleagues from the company's Chemical Technology days.

reaching scientists dedicated to understanding the pathways involved in the course that is cancer, and developing novel solutions with which to manipulate those pathways. The rest of the equation is largely dependent on the executive team's ability to manage all the caveats, challenges and risks associated with bringing a new drug to market. Over the last 14 years, ArQule has an impressive track record of making the right choices.

The progenitors of ArQule built the company around the idea of providing chemistry services to pharmaceutical companies (a need the pharmaceutical industry has felt for decades) and in turn, help drug makers discover more effective product candidates in less time. The techniques employed in drug research are generally directed towards understanding the molecular basis of disease. This "biology" knowledge often necessitates decades of research. With the age of technology, new

The ArQule staff in 2007, in the lobby at corporate headquarters.

techniques such as high throughput automated chemistry, can produce a far greater range of desired molecules. Dr. Joseph Hogan, whose background was in chemistry, and Robert Dishman, "a serial entrepreneur," were the two innovative minds behind ArQule's early strategy. Together, they utilized the company's innovative technology in combinatorial chemistry, accelerating the process for pharmaceutical companies in identifying which compounds might prove worthy of development. In the early '90s, ArQule was one of the first companies to leverage their chemistry services with large multi-national companies. This leadership strategy proved to be an archetype for

success. Within a few short years, ArQule had carved out its niche in a highly competitive and growing marketplace by establishing deals with seven leading pharmaceutical firms including Solvay Duphar and Abbott Laboratories, raising over $245 million with an additional $60 million through two public offerings of stock.

Dr. Stephen Hill joined the organization as president and CEO in 1999, shortly after ArQule had established a new state-of-the-art research and development facility in Woburn, Massachusetts. Before joining ArQule, Hill served as director of global drug development at Hoffmann-LaRoche in Basel, Switzerland. Originally from Manchester, Great Britain, Dr. Hill had spent several years as an orthopedic surgeon before lending his business acumen to the corporate arena and

moving his family to northwest Switzerland to direct worldwide regulatory affairs for Roche. Shortly after Dr. Hill joined ArQule, executives John Sorvillo and Jim Kyranos led the company to close a $117 million deal with Pfizer, one of the biggest companies in the world. The two companies entered into a four and-a-half-year agreement that would allow Pfizer to benefit from ArQule's technologies, scientists and facilities, in building additional compound libraries. The accord represented one of the biggest deals ever made in chemistry. ArQule closed a similar agreement with Bayer shortly thereafter worth up to $30 million for the development and delivery of additional compound libraries for the German corporation.

The company grew to over 400 employees and was thriving with a market value of over $30 per share at its peak. Stephen Hill describes this time as being "a double-edged sword." "We were able to broaden our technology platform to enhance what we were able to offer in the area of production, but over time it became clearer and clearer that there weren't more deals of the Pfizer nature," reflects Dr. Hill. Although Pfizer later renewed their program with ArQule, the executive team had already begun changing their strategy to accommodate changes in the global market. During the first few years of the new millennium, more and more businesses began outsourcing jobs overseas to China, India and other places where graduating scientists were in abundance and labor rates were such that workers were earning one-tenth of what a researcher would receive in the U.S. The executive team at ArQule surmised what kind of pressure this would put on them in the long-term. "We deliberately transferred away from that chemistry service business into a more typical biotech research and development company" said Dr. Hill.

Few companies have transitioned from one business model to a very different one without their share of growing pains. Having made the decision to move away from chemistry services and redirect efforts towards their own drug research and development, the executive team sought to acquire a company whose technology complemented their own. In 2001 they found a suitable match but plans for a full integration failed to materialize. This costly setback, coupled with the reality of the Pfizer programs reaching an inevitable end, forced ArQule to lay off more than 300 employees. Under the aegis of Mr. Anthony Messina, vice president of Human Development, and without whom the transition would have been scarcely possible, the company maintained its "people-care approach" championing the notion "that people should be thought of as

assets and not just simple resources like money." "I think it's terrible to lay people off" said Dr. Hill, "and we've had to go through that with significant numbers of people leaving the company's life who have done a great job." As painful as the downsizing was, ArQule's leadership approach was such that the transition was effectuated with grace.

The management team was unrelenting in its search for companies both public and private with resources in biology that complemented their strengths in chemistry. As chance would have it, after searching all of North America and certain companies in Europe, they found Cyclis Pharmaceuticals—a small company located a mere 15 miles from their own headquarters. The team at ArQule was particularly impressed by the work Cyclis had managed with a very limited group of people. Dr. Chiang Li, an MD/PhD graduate of Harvard Medical School and founder of Cyclis, had patented an approach to cancer therapy built around the notion that he could teach cancer cells to recognize their DNA damage and commit cell-suicide, or apoptosis. "The problem with cancer cells is that they don't recognize their own damage, they proliferate and they don't self-destruct like normal cells would" explains Dr. Hill. "Dr. Li's ARQ 501 Activated Checkpoint Therapy is absolutely unique in the approach of activating a checkpoint and switching back the cell's ability to recognize its DNA damage."

The late Dr. Samuel Ackerman, formerly president and CEO of Cyclis, hoped the acquisition would synergize the two companies' expertise and produce "a product that could be advanced through development to reach patients and improve treatments." Dr. Li's discoveries have resulted in ArQule's two primary drug candidates: ARQ 501, currently in Phase II clinical trials with Roche, and ARQ 197. The compound known as

ARQ 197 is one of the first orally-administered drugs designed to inhibit c-Met, an enzyme present in cancer cells. The drug attacks c-Met, thereby selectively preventing abnormal cell growth, sparing normal cells and thus reducing toxicity to patients. By leveraging its unique set of assets, ArQule would soon establish yet another strategic partnership, allowing them to advance their efforts.

As the company made new strides, they augmented the senior executive team by bringing aboard talent that would help see them through their next phase of growth. The new additions included Dr. Tom Chan, senior vice president of Drug Discovery, Dr. Nigel Rulewski, ArQule's new chief medical officer who brings expertise in running clinical trials, and Peter Lawrence who joined the firm as general counsel and chief business officer. In historic fashion, the new executive team led the company in April 2007 into an exclusive agreement with Tokyo-based Kyowa Hakko Kogyo, a deal worth $123 million and one that will allow ARQ 197 to be developed and commercialized in Japan, China, South Korea and Taiwan. This alliance represents one of the biggest deals ever to be made between an Asian pharmaceutical company and a biotech company and provides a strategic partnership that will allow ArQule to continue its research for years to come.

ArQule's current epoch in cancer development is truly a force that has flourished through the company's heritage in chemistry and Cyclis' legacy in biology—this convergence championed by the diverse team of people who have worked at its research facility over the years. It is through the efforts of ArQule's scientific and management team, efforts akin to searching for Euclid's needle in the vast expanse of the unknown, that a new medicine may one day emerge and impact the lives of those suffering from the mysteries of cancer.

BOSTON MEDICAL CENTER

Located in the city's historic South End, Boston Medical Center (BMC) provides pediatric and adult care services, primary and family medicine, and advanced specialty care to the greater Boston community. With more than 30,000 admissions and 1 million patient visits each year, BMC provides comprehensive inpatient, clinical, and diagnostic services in more than 70 medical specialties and subspecialties. It also offers patients cardiac care and surgery; hypertension and neurological care; and orthopedic, geriatric, and women's health services.

Founded in 1996 as a result of a merger between Boston City Hospital (founded in 1855), and Boston University Medical Center Hospital (founded in 1864), as a private and nonprofit facility with nearly 600 licensed beds, BMC is the largest "safety net" hospital in New England. With the biggest 24-hour, level I trauma center in New England, Boston Medical Center's emergency department had nearly 130,000 visits in 2006.

Boston Medical Center proudly opened its centralized cancer and ambulatory care facility in 2006. Named for the late congressman, John Moakley, the facility offers an extraordinary patient experience by bringing together a variety of programs and specialty services in one location. Now able to streamline patient care and provide the latest in technology, the center offers comprehensive cancer treatment, services to address digestive and otolaryngology disorders, a state-of-the-art ambulatory surgery center, and even a breast health center.

When it comes to medical research, BMC is a recognized leader and received close to $90 million in funding in 2006. Researchers conduct clinical and laboratory-based biomedical research and currently oversee more than 400 projects. In the areas

Boston Medical Center's Menino Pavilion.

of Sickle Cell, Parkinson's Disease, cardiology, endocrinology, and infectious diseases, Boston Medical Center researchers are actively working to make new advancements and crucial discoveries.

In yet another accomplishment, Boston Medical Center is proud to be the primary teaching affiliate for the Boston University School of Medicine. It takes to heart its responsibility for training the next generation of healthcare providers and every member of its medical staff holds an academic appointment at the school. To date, BMC operates nearly 50 residency training programs that cater to the needs of more than 600 residents and fellows.

Solid in its commitment to the community, Boston Medical Center has dedicated itself to providing accessible healthcare. In 2006 BMC provided nearly $300 million in free care to the city's uninsured. It also offers numerous outreach programs and services to residents, such as skin cancer, prostate cancer, osteoporosis, and blood pressure screenings; cholesterol tests, flu shots, eye exams, and smoking cessation

counseling. Cancer education and prevention seminars are also offered to the community and the hospital participates in local health fairs.

However, it takes that commitment one step further by finding new ways to embrace the needs of its diverse patient base. Boston Medical Center currently offers an interpreter services program, which is the most extensive in New England. In addition to personal interpreters at the center, accessible 24 hours a day and in more than 30 languages, the hospital also offers video and telephonic interpreting. In 2006 more than 160,000 patients benefited from this valuable service.

With all the charm and warmth of a small town hospital, Boston Medical Center offers state-of-the-art medical care in a world-class environment. A true leader in the city's medical community, Boston Medical Center is working hard to address the needs of tomorrow's patients—today.

ASSOCIATED INDUSTRIES OF MASSACHUSETTS MUTUAL INSURANCE COMPANY (A.I.M. MUTUAL)

At one time in Massachusetts there was a massively dysfunctional workers compensation system of career-ending injuries and careening insurance costs, all mired in litigation. That was then. Now costs are under control, and down by more than half. Massachusetts went from laggard to one of the national standard setters in workers compensation. A.I.M. Mutual has set the benchmark within Massachusetts and, in effect, it is a city on a national hill.

Since its inception in 1988, A.I.M. Mutual has been at the forefront of this transformation—at first getting it started, now making sure it does not retreat. This is A.I.M. Mutual's story—and how it matters to the business executive in the Bay State.

A.I.M. Mutual corporate offices located in Burlington, Massachusetts.

But these improvements can unravel. Some employers in Massachusetts can still be burdened with staggering workers comp costs. Focusing on a safe workplace, Stay at Work/Return to Work programs and medical management keep the inflationary demons at bay. A.I.M. Mutual's commitment to customer service, its mutual company organization structure, its deeply experienced staff, and use of technology, are just part of its continuing business strategy.

From its beginnings in 1988, A.I.M. Mutual has adhered to its founding principles—to provide workers compensation and employers liability insurance coverage at a level of service that sets the industry standard. What seems like a straightforward concept today, was in fact, once a visionary approach to this critical business need.

A.I.M. Mutual introduced workers compensation as a partnership between the employer, the employee and the insurer, and in short order employers welcomed the change and saw the immediate benefits. The company has grown to one of the largest regional workers compensation specialists in all of New England, and has maintained a major share of the Massachusetts market.

Associated Industries of Massachusetts, the largest nonprofit employers association in the Commonwealth, sponsored the founding of the company. It's a relationship that has grown even stronger two decades later.

"Our success is really driven by the service excellence we work very hard to provide," explains John Myers, president and chief executive officer of A.I.M. Mutual. "Our board of directors has been extremely supportive of our

The entire employee group of A.I.M. Mutual during the early years.

technological advances and the innovative programs we've developed. We also have to credit our staff of 200 people. They recognize the importance we place on customer service and never lose sight of it."

As a mutual insurer, its policyholders, not far-away stockholders, own the company. Some of America's historic advances in managing risk are credited to mutual insurers. Why? Because their almost obsessive focus on customer service tends to lead mutual insurers, before other insurers, to creative ways to manage risk. For instance, building safety in America was transformed when mutual fire insurance companies in Massachusetts introduced sprinkler systems among their members. Fire insurance rates ultimately plunged by 90 percent. Mutual companies also look to the long-term rather than focus on quarterly earnings reports to stockholders.

Bringing the idea for A.I.M. Mutual into reality—and keeping the company competitive—was not an easy undertaking, as John Gould, chairman of A.I.M. Mutual's board of directors recalls. Gould, also vice chairman of Associated Industries, was instrumental in guiding the company forward.

"Associated Industries represents almost 7,500 employer members in Massachusetts," Gould says. "We are the employer's voice, and in the 1980s, these employers were facing a workers compensation system in crisis. We needed to take action. We also realized that traditional approaches to workers compensation simply don't work."

With the state's overall economy at the time in a severe downturn, employers had dealt with years of double-digit workers compensation rate increases. In many ways, the workers compensation administrative system was dysfunctional and inefficient. Insurers were increasingly avoiding the Massachusetts market, often making it difficult for employers to find coverage at competitive rates.

Of even greater concern were injured employees who often found themselves caught in a system that was overwhelmingly complex, and that impeded their treatment, dragged out their recovery, and hurt their ability to return to work.

In 1988 A.I.M. Mutual was organized as a reciprocal insurance exchange and licensed to provide workers compensation insurance in Massachusetts. The company issued its first policy on January 1, 1989. Donald Barber spent the next 17 years until retirement as the company's executive vice president and general manager in charge of operations, building strong relationships between employer policyholders and the services A.I.M. Mutual provides its customers.

In those early years, A.I.M. Mutual, with its unique approach, became a haven for many employers seeking effective workers compensation insurance. Meanwhile, the workers compensation system in Massachusetts was far from fixed. Insurance costs continued to surge and the state became one of the three most expensive in the nation in terms of workers compensation costs.

On behalf of the employers it represented, Associated Industries of Massachusetts took an active role in finding a long-term, statewide solution to the problem. It joined with a number of interested parties, including A.I.M. Mutual and other insurers, employers, legislators, medical providers, and attorneys, in a series of proactive sessions.

The result was the landmark Workers Compensation Reform Act of 1991. It simplified a horrendously complex maze for resolving disputes. The Reform Act rejuvenated the workers compensation market in Massachusetts. Insurers gradually returned to the Commonwealth, and employers from out of state began to reconsider Massachusetts as a viable place to do business. Since the early 1990s, workers compensation costs have been reduced by as much as 64 percent largely due to the Reform Act and increased competition.

Massachusetts enjoyed a huge improvement in workers compensation insurance costs relative to other states. It is now the lowest cost state in New England.

To be sure, the situation can worsen. For instance, the number of injuries could jump, or become more severe, the system could become more litigious and workers compensation is not immune to the same forces reponsible for double digit medical cost increases. One guard against this happening is how employers now pay closer attention to workers compensation issues. A.I.M. Mutual, together with Associated Industries, continues to educate employers on important developments in the industry and their potential impact.

Tom Crupi, vice president-loss control, teaching workplace safety issues to policyholders.

This includes educating the employer community about workers compensation issues—for non-policyholders as well as for A.I.M. Mutual policyholders. To that end, the company hosts seminars on a variety of claim-related topics, including "mock" trials involving workers compensation cases, changes in workers compensation law, and effective management strategies based on actual claim situations. Feedback from attendees has been overwhelmingly positive from this annual seminar series.

A typical work injury begins with an accident. Across Massachusetts, accidents happen at upwards of 100,000 times a year.

What does A.I.M. Mutual do about injury prevention? It has one of the largest safety staffs in the state. There are currently thirteen loss control professionals, including five Certified Safety Professionals, three Associate Safety Professionals and a Certified Industrial Hygienist at A.I.M. Mutual who work with policyholders to

identify potential safety hazards in the workplace and educate employees. Knowledgeable in Occupational Safety and Health Administration (OSHA) requirements, they help keep policyholders in compliance with state and federal law by working in partnership with policyholders to complete worksite evaluations, ergonomic studies, noise and air-sample testing and a wide range of on-site training programs.

The injured worker goes to obtain medical treatment. A.I.M. Mutual has always had a medical expertise component in its claim handling, which has been invaluable with healthcare costs on the rise and a system that can be difficult to navigate. A.I.M. Mutual tries to help the injured worker get to the best-qualified doctor. Doing so calls for a lot of planning.

Many workers injured on the job make their living by pushing, pulling and lifting. They may work at machine shops, metal finishers, healthcare, instrument, textile and apparel manufacturers, printers and various branches of the plastics industry. They hurt their shoulders, their necks, and their backs. Many of them don't know where to go to get help, so unless offered skilled assistance, they end up wherever they can get care.

Recently the company introduced a Medical Care Improvement Initiative. This Initiative is designed to provide injured workers with access to quality medical care and patient advocacy through A.I.M. Mutual's affiliation with Best Doctors Occupational Health Institute. The goal is to get injured workers to the right place the first time, on time, in order to receive the best care. They are guided through a medical care delivery process utilizing specially trained nurse advocates and medical directors.

The Medical Care Improvement Initiative is working and is becoming an industry model. Results to date are promising, with significant reductions in time away from work due to disability. A new pharmaceutical program has also helped to better manage the quality and cost of prescription medications for injured employees. The overall results are reduced workers compensation costs for employers, and more importantly, improved medical outcomes for injured workers.

After, or even while recovering, the injured worker returns to work. A.I.M Mutual can't stress enough how important it is to bring an employee back to work as quickly as possible, even in what is called "modified duty." People recover far more quickly with certain injuries if they continue to be involved with their workplace. That keeps costs down, too, but the most pressing goal is to get injured workers the best care possible. If they are able to work while the treatment is ongoing, that's ideal.

In 1996 A.I.M. Mutual changed from a reciprocal exchange to a mutual insurance company. The conversion allowed the company to grow and develop new products. At that time, A.I.M. Mutual was also approved as a servicing carrier for the Massachusetts Assigned Risk Pool,

Michael Kelley, vice president-claims, conducting a session at one of A.I.M. Mutual's annual claim seminars.

where difficult exposure businesses often show up. The company provides the same level of service to these accounts as it does to its own policyholders.

Two subsidiary companies now have joined A.I.M. Mutual Insurance Company. Associated Employers Insurance Company was formed in 2001 and Massachusetts Employers Insurance Company was formed in 2007. A.I.M. Mutual also expanded operations to include New Hampshire in 2001. Finally, A.I.M. Mutual provides Third Party Administration services through an affiliate and also markets employee benefit programs through its agency operation, Employers Associated Insurance Agency, LLC.

A.M. Best Company, the nationally recognized insurance rating organization, rates the company A (Excellent) for its financial strength. A.I.M. Mutual's CFO Greg Shah reported that the Company ended 2006 with consolidated assets of $339.9 million and policyholder surplus at $103.3 million. In its report, A.M. Best noted the company's excellent capitalization, strong operating performance and conservative reserving practices, as well as the inherent benefits derived

from its sponsor, Associated Industries of Massachusetts.

A.M. Best also cited A.I.M. Mutual's product focus and market knowledge as key factors supporting the Company's strong performance in 2006 and further cites "employer involvement, loss control and claims administration practices" in the company's success.

In the company's 19-year history, the board of directors—most who have been on the board for more than a decade—have taken A.I.M. Mutual from modest beginnings to a company with net worth in excess of $100 million that continues to be owned by its policyholders. Ever-present is the company's overriding objective—to extend to policyholders the *Excellence in Service* they have come to expect, and deserve.

A.I.M. Mutual considers this customer-focused strategy its competitive advantage, and the key to continuing the transformation of how Massachusetts employers deal with employee health and welfare business risk.

ATLANTIC POWER, INC.

Atlantic Power's roots in Massachusetts date back to 1904. William J. Connell, Sr. founded the fourth generation company and was also a very industrious entrepreneur. During his career, William Sr. established the first Ford franchise in the New England area, brokered numerous land deals, and founded a variety of businesses that were operated under the W.J. Connell Co. umbrella. Atlantic Power, a value-added distributor in the outdoor power equipment industry, is an offshoot from the original W.J. Connell Co.

In the late 1920s, after three years at the College of William and Mary, William's son, Bill, decided to join his father in downtown Boston to help with the family business, an automotive distribution, service, and repair operation located on Brookline Ave. The two men worked side-by-side for many years until the early 1950s when Bill's daughter caught the eye of a dashing young man named George Stephenson.

W.J. Connell Co. on Columbus Avenue in 1914.

Connell/McCone Co.'s Willys Knight/Overland distributor showroom, circa 1921.

After graduating from Amherst College in 1955, a romance between George and Dorothy started to blossom. They dated for two years while George was doing a stint in the U.S. Army. Within a month after his Army tenure ended, George went to work for Dorothy's father at the W.J. Connell Co., and two months later he and Dorothy were married.

George was eager to learn both the operational details of the company and the wholesale distribution business in general. In his first years with W.J. Connell Co., he worked in the warehouse, pulled orders, and assisted in the purchasing department. It wasn't long before George moved on to become credit manager, assistant treasurer, and then treasurer, all while managing relationships with banking institutions and key manufacturers.

In the early 1970s, the company sold off its automotive and diesel interests in order to focus all of its attention on the outdoor power equipment industry, which had been growing steadily throughout the 1960s. Twenty years earlier, the company had been serendipitously introduced to the power equipment industry when it acquired the William H. Flaherty Company, an automotive distributor that happened to carry the Briggs and Stratton line. By the time the sale of the automotive and diesel division was complete, W.J. Connell Co. represented the three domestic air-cooled engine manufacturers, namely Kohler (the same Kohler that manufactures plumbing supplies), Tecumseh Products Corp., and Briggs and Stratton, which remains Atlantic Power's key line today.

In 1973 William Connell, Jr., who took over as president in 1949, decided to turn over the reins to George, who had been a valuable asset to the company for over a decade and responsible for much of its success. In 1986 the Briggs and Stratton distributorship that George had been overseeing split off from the W.J. Connell Co. The newly formed company was called Atlantic Power, Inc., and with George at the helm, the team set up shop in a 40,000-square-foot facility in Foxboro and a 50,000-square facility in Somerset, New Jersey.

William J. Connell, Jr. and William J. Connell, Sr. at the company's groundbreaking ceremony for their offices at 210 Needham Street in Newton Upper Falls in 1951.

W.J. Connell Co. on Brookline Avenue, circa 1938.

Just two years later in 1988, George and Dorothy's son, John, graduated from Haverford College. Eager to see the world, John traveled for a year throughout Central America, Mexico, Australia, New Zealand, and Papua New Guinea. Upon his return, he worked as a commercial lender in Philadelphia. After a few years, however, John realized his calling was back in Foxboro. In 1992 John joined his father at Atlantic Power.

There was a lot for John to learn about the company as the value-added distributor continued to grow more complex. However, much like his father, John absorbed every aspect of the business. He was a quick study and was eager to make Atlantic Power all that it could be.

By 1998 John had assumed the day-to-day responsibilities of the business and a short two years later, he took over as president and CEO. In 2000 he named Gary Bucciantini—a long-time, multi-talented Atlantic Power employee—as executive vice president and COO. During their tenure, John and Gary have put together a talented

management team that includes vice president and sales manager Darold Dunham and operations manager Gregg DeMontigny.

"Gary, Darold, and Gregg have been huge contributors to our success and have really helped me form a terrific team at Atlantic Power," says John. "All of these men have tremendous industry skill and experience, and they are terrific leaders. It has become cliché, but we really do believe it's a top priority to invest in and nurture our human capital."

George remains as the company's chairman and comes to work each day, but has been careful to respect John's role within the company. "My dad was willing to step back and let me take over," says John. "Many family-owned companies don't survive because of a multitude of intergenerational issues. My transition into the leadership role was smooth, mostly because my dad turned over the reins fully. Full responsibility, full accountability."

George's role as an advisor, according to John,

has allowed him to provide perspective, guidance, and wisdom. "When I came to work for the company," George says, "my father-in-law welcomed my input and gave me a lot of responsibility. I used that same approach with John as he was coming up within Atlantic Power. Today he's an outstanding leader and has been able to keep the business thriving." Indeed, John has done just that.

Once he assumed responsibility for running the company, John used the business' cash reserves to make strategic acquisitions both within and outside the outdoor power equipment industry. These acquisitions helped Atlantic Power to grow while continuing to thrive in an increasingly competitive industry.

And, although the corporate offices remain in Massachusetts, John and COO Gary Bucciantini, combined the company's Foxboro and Somerset, New Jersey facilities and moved them to a newly constructed, state-of-the-art, 80,000-square-foot complex in Castleton, New York in the spring of 2001. There, the company houses its educational center where it offers in-depth training to thousands of technicians on the business' various product lines.

Equipped with the latest technology, the center is complete with a demon-

W.J. Connell Co.'s auto service area on Brookline Avenue, circa 1938.

stration room, a "tear-down" room, a computer training center, focus rooms, and a climate-controlled air-exchange engine-running room. An intensive 36-hour course that focuses on the company's key product line, Briggs & Stratton, is also a vital part of each technician's training.

"Our customers sell and service outdoor power equipment, which helps people and communities maintain their 'green spaces' and other outdoor areas" says John. "They are fully certified to work on chainsaws, lawnmowers, snow blowers, riding tractors, generators, pressure washers, outboard motors, and all other power equipment that is in need of repair."

John and Gary also streamlined the company's warehouses to increase productivity and shave costs. "When I started in 1992, the company shipped out 40 packages a day," says John. "Now, with Gary's warehouse architecture design and on-going operational 'best practice' initiative, we are capable of shipping up to 1,500 packages daily to customers in New England, New York, New Jersey, Pennsylvania, and Delaware."

Starting with $7 million in revenue and 25 employees back in 1986, the business has grown into a $35 million company with 75 employees. Thanks to the strength of the Connell and

Atlantic Power in 2006.

Top: John Stephenson, Gary Bucciantini, and George Stephenson.

Above: The "tear down" room at Atlantic Power's facility in 2006.

Stephenson families, Atlantic Power is a thriving business—and ready to tackle whatever comes its way.

"For over 100 years my family, and dedicated, key employees like Gary, Darold, and Gregg, have run value-added distribution companies—with the 'value-added' being the skills that we employ beyond physical distribution," says John. "Currently, that includes sales and marketing, education and training, and technical service in support of the products we sell. Today, the world and our global economy are changing at an incredible pace. All companies and organizations have to determine how they are going to evolve to create value for the next generation of customers, employees and stakeholders. Taking the next entrepreneurial steps…this will be our challenge for the next decade."

HARVARD UNIVERSITY

One cannot think of Boston without immediately thinking of Harvard. Rapidly approaching its 400th anniversary, it is the oldest institution of higher learning in the entire country. With a history that dates back to just 16 years after the arrival of the Pilgrims at Plymouth Rock, the university has produced more than 40 Nobel laureates. In an equally impressive achievement, seven U.S. presidents have graduated from Harvard, including John Adams, John Quincy Adams, Theodore Roosevelt, Franklin Delano Roosevelt, Rutherford B. Hayes, John Fitzgerald Kennedy, and George W. Bush.

With just nine students and a single headmaster in its early years, the school's enrollment now boasts 18,000. An additional 13,000 students are enrolled in one or more courses in the Harvard Extension School. More than 14,000 people work at today's Harvard, including 2,000-plus faculty members—a far cry from its start .

Its humble beginnings dates back to 1636. Then called Harvard College, the school was established by vote of the Great and General Court of the Massachusetts Bay Colony. It was named for its first benefactor, John Harvard of Charlestown. Upon his death in 1638, Harvard, a young minister, left his library and half his estate to the new institution.

During its formative years, the college offered a traditional academic course load based on the English university model. However, it was consistent with the prevailing Puritan philosophy of the first colonists. Although many of the school's first graduates became ministers, the college was never affiliated with any religion.

In the 18th and 19th centuries, Harvard expanded its curriculum, especially in the sciences. As its reputation grew, the college was able to attract a number of famous scholars, including the elder

Harvard Hall on the left is just past Johnston Gate, and a dormitory, Hollis Hall, is on the right. Courtesy, Thomas H. Caldwell

Oliver Wendell Holmes, Henry Wadsworth Longfellow, and Gertrude Stein. However, it was Charles W. Eliot, the institute's president from 1869 to 1909, who turned the relatively intimate, local college into a modern-day university.

Under Eliot's guidance, Harvard's medical and law schools were revitalized and today are ranked number one and two respectively by *U S News & World Report*. Graduate schools for business, dental medicine, and arts and sciences were also established. Enrollment tripled and the faculty increased by nearly 500 percent. The school's endowment also jumped from $2 million to more than $22 million.

Walking through today's campus is a lesson in both history and classic American architecture. The longest standing building at Harvard is Massachusetts Hall. Built in 1720 during the Revolutionary War, it sheltered soldiers from the Continental Army. Today it houses offices for the university's president and vice presidents, and provides living spaces for freshmen students.

Another historic landmark is Wadsworth House, built in 1726. Although it currently houses a variety of offices, it served as the temporary headquarters for General George Washington in 1775. The cathedral-like Memorial Hall, erected in 1878, is yet another significant historical structure. It commemorates the many Harvard men who died in the Civil War, while fighting for the Union. Today, the building's theater is a popular meeting place and offers lectures, concerts, and a variety of performances.

In recent years, Harvard has made progressive efforts to sustain its legacy throughout this century—and beyond. It continues to find new ways to "internationalize" the Harvard experience and grow its science program. Even more significantly, Harvard takes great strides to ensure that it attracts the strongest students out there— regardless of their financial status.

Although Boston is home to many fine educational institutions, none are as highly regarded throughout the world as Harvard University.

THE BEAL COMPANIES

The Beal Companies is a closely held firm actively pursuing investment opportunities in all segments of the real estate industry. The more than a century old firm offers professional services for select clients while also developing and managing real estate for its own portfolio. Since 1888 the Beal family has built a full service real estate business with an enviable reputation. Headed by partners, Robert L. Beal and Bruce A. Beal, chairman and president, respectively, the firm is also anchored by an executive team of Michael A. Manzo, Peter B. Nichols, Stephen N. Faber, and John H. Schwarz. The companies' specific activities include the acquisition and development of commercial, historic, and residential properties; asset management for the Beal firm and others; brokerage and consulting; appraisal and tax assessment; as well as financing and construction management services.

Since the firm's beginnings, its services have evolved and judiciously adapted to the changing and emerging real estate market of greater Boston. The company began at a time when transformation and opportunity went hand and hand. In 1888 Boston was the

Seaport Center, located at 70 Fargo Street in South Boston.

The 128,000-square-foot life science building in Kendall Square, Cambridge.

center of a complex metropolitan area and in an era of building when Abraham B. Beal seized the opportunity to build both retail and multi-family properties in the Fenway area. Abraham Beal's company grew steadily and he began developing and managing a variety of properties, ranging from residential to industrial, in Boston, Brookline, Allston/Brighton, and Cambridge. He was joined in the early 1900s by his sons Julius and Benjamin Beal.

At the turn of the century, the city burst with new institutions. Fort Hill had disappeared and, with it, the last trace of the colonial waterfront. The tidal salt marsh, known as the Back Bay, was filled and as a result, the area reigned supreme as a residential district. Transportation using electricity was beyond imagination and horse-drawn vehicles caused unending traffic problems. It was a transitional period for the first crude application of electricity, which marked the era for unprecedented social and industrial progress. The Beal family became a significant part of this progress as it purchased and managed real estate throughout the metropolitan area. One of the first firms to do appraisal and consulting work, the Beals became experts in the field of eminent domain.

In 1931 Alexander S. Beal, son of Julius, joined Beal & Company, Inc., specializing in real estate appraisal and tax valuation analysis of commercial, industrial, farm, waterfront, and residential real estate throughout the eastern and southern United States. In the 1960s, Bruce A. Beal played an instrumental part in introducing the concept of the condominium in Boston, converting the first major luxury apartment building in Cambridge to condominiums. The firm also purchased 230 units at Walden Park in Cambridge in 1975. In 1976 Robert L. Beal joined his father and brother and the name of the firm was officially changed to The Beal Companies that same year.

The Grain Exchange Building at 177 Milk Street, one of Boston's most striking historic buildings in the downtown area, was purchased by the firm in 1978. This historic renovation received an award from BOMA in 1993 as the Historic Office Building of the Year. The firm acquired 79 Milk Street in 1979, the first structural steel building ever constructed in Boston, which was built in 1902. The firm also purchased Cambridge East Office Park that same year, which consisted of 22 buildings containing 200,000 square feet. Beal was one of the first firms to develop and lease space to companies looking for what was referred to at the time as "wet laboratory space," long before "biotech" became a well-known term. Later, the name of the property was changed to Life Science Square and in August of 2006, Beal sold the entire complex for a record high per square foot price for the area.

In the mid 1980s, The Beal Companies proposed to the city of Boston that it acquire from the federal government the Custom House, which in the 1940s, was one the tallest buildings in the city. The city successfully purchased the building in 1987. In 1996 Beal refurbished the Custom House and, in a joint venture with the Marriott Hotel Corporation, converted one of Boston's oldest skyscrapers into historic time-share units. The Marriott Custom House officially reopened for business in 1997 and has become one of the most beloved historic buildings in Boston.

Cognizant of the emerging biotech companies' growing need for space, The

Ledgemont Center in Lexington, in the midst of fall foliage.

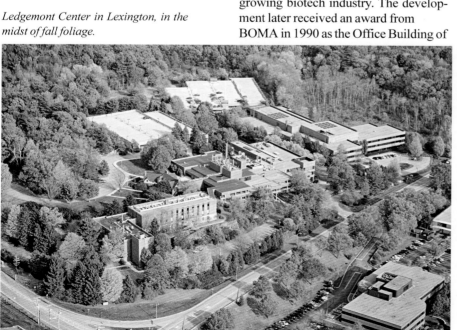

The Grain Exchange at 177 Milk Street in downtown Boston serves as Beal's headquarters.

Beal Companies acquired Ledgemont Center in Lexington, Massachusetts, then the headquarters of Kennecott Copper. Beal expanded the property in the 1980s to 400,000 square feet with a focus on leasing to companies in the growing biotech industry. The development later received an award from BOMA in 1990 as the Office Building of

the Year. Beal also acquired 89 Broad Street in 1983 and restored The Batterymarch Building to its original art-deco facade. The building was built in the 1920s and at the time was the second largest office building in Boston.

Over the past few years, The Beal Companies have found success in the development of multiple properties in the Boston area. The Waltham Corporate Center, which was developed by Beal, is a class A office facility located on America's technology highway, Route 128. Some of the current tenants include Keyspan's New England HQ, and Mass General West. Three Hundred Third Street in East Cambridge was another successful Beal development. It was originally leased to Palm Inc. on a long-term net lease. Due to a change in its business plan, Palm never occupied the building and the property was subsequently converted to bio-tech and lab use. The property was then re-leased to biotech firms and sold to a leading biotech REIT. During the mid 1980s, The Beal Companies purchased the former American Mutual Insurance Company's corporate headquarters along with additional land for development on Wakefield's picturesque Lake Quannapowitt. The property, which had been deemed surplus by American Mutual was extensively renovated and refurbished and successfully repositioned as a multi tenant office development. After a successful lease up to a variety of high tech and corporate office users, The Beal Companies completed the master planning , permitting, and construction of an additional 130,000 square feet of class A office space and adjacent, three story structured parking garage. In 2004 the company sold the fully leased office buildings, but has maintained its ownership interest in additional land for future development.

In early 2006 The Beal Companies purchased One Kendall Square, a 676,440-square-foot office and lab complex home to tenants including Genzyme Corporation. Beal bought the property in partnership with Greenwich, Connecticut-based Rockwood Capital Corporation for $210.5 million. The nine-building complex at One Kendall Square remains very active in the market with significant recent residential and retail leasing.

In early 2006 the company acquired the Seaport Center (formerly known as The Fargo Building) in Boston's emerging seaport district. Beal, along with its capital partner, Rockpoint, teamed up to purchase this property. Another Beal development originated in 2006 was The Clarendon Building, a 32-story structure located at the corner of Clarendon and Stuart Street in Boston's Back Bay District, containing 285 residential apartment units (107 condominium-ownership units and 178 market-rental units). In addition to its residential units, the 531,494 square foot building will have three other major components for residents' convenience: a new USPS Back Bay Post Office, retail shops and restaurants, and valet parking on three levels. Another noteworthy aspect of the Clarendon is it represents a fifth

Arsenal on the Charles in Watertown.

generation of the Beal family actively involved in Boston real estate development. Bruce A Beal, Jr. is a partner at the Related Companies, LLP of New York City. The Related Companies and Beal are teaming up on this venture and Bruce Jr. is playing a significant role in the project.

In addition to the expertise of Robert L. Beal and Bruce A. Beal, the continued success of the firm relies heavily on the strong reputation of the Beal name, the

immensely successful history of real estate ventures, and the company's executive team. Michael A. Manzo, a partner of The Beal Companies and a senior vice president of Beal and Company, Inc. negotiates major leases, project and deal structuring, and secures equity and debt financing for clients of The Beal Companies as well as the company's own projects. Peter B. Nichols, a partner in The Beal Companies and a senior vice president of Beal and Company, Inc. focuses primarily on commercial property acquisitions and development projects for the firm and its clients. Stephen N. Faber, vice president of asset management of Beal and Company, Inc. is responsible for the asset and property management of Beal owned and managed real estate, including management of individual assets and portfolio management for a variety of property types including office, retail, multi-family, and planned unit developments. John H. Schwarz serves as chief financial officer of Beal Companies.

More information about the company can be viewed at www.bealco.com.

Artist's rendering of One Kendall Square in Cambridge.

MASSACHUSETTS GENERAL HOSPITAL

Massachusetts General Hospital (MGH) is an American institution, helping people live healthy lives and forwarding the advancement of medical science for nearly two centuries. MGH, founded in 1811, is the oldest hospital in all of New England, and the third oldest general hospital in the entire nation. It was designed by famed architect Charles Bulfinch, designer of many of New England's finest historical buildings, including Harvard's University Hall and the Maine State House. MGH has an illustrious history of providing the highest quality care and advancing medicine through rigorous, cutting edge research. This is a fitting position for the original and continuing teaching hospital of Harvard University.

The hospital's mission has always been two-fold: to provide top-notch patient services and to to further medicine through research and scholarship. Since its founding, MGH has been at the forefront of developing medical procedures and technology. In fact, many of the hospital's achievements through the years reflect its significant contribution to medical science. In 1846, the use of ether to sedate surgical patients was demonstrated at MGH, offering pain-free surgery for the first time in history. In 1880 a MGH physician discovered the underlying nature of appendicitis, giving rise to the proper diagnosis and treatment of the life threatening condition. MGH was also the first hospital in the nation to use a then-revolutionary technique, the X-ray, just 30 days after its discovery of the technique by the German, Wilhelm Conrad Rontgen in 1896.

The hospital's accomplishments in the 20th century were no less momentous, reflecting its status as the

Massachusetts General Hospital.

largest hospital-based research program in the United States. The hospital's annual research budget is nearly $463 million, supporting its extensive and comprehensive studies into every aspect of medical science and practice. In 1925 MGH established the very first clinic dedicated to studying cancerous tumors. In 1945 a researcher at MGH's gynecological service provider, Vincent Memorial Hospital, refined the use of the standard Pap smear test, still utilized with regularity today, to detect cervical cancer. Hospital surgeons accomplished an amazing feat for the first time in history: the successful reattachment of a person's severed limb In 1962. In cooperation with MIT and Shriners Burn Center, MGH researchers created the first artificial skin made from real human skin cells in 1981. The hospital has also been on the forefront of mapping the human genome, discovering the genes associated with early onset Alzheimer's (1987), as well as Lou Gehrig's disease, Huntington's disease and

neurofibromastosis (1993), and Batten disease (1995). The hospital's most recent accomplishments lie in the diagnosis and specialized treatment of myriad medical problems, from specific cancers to endocrine disorders to preserving reproductive health.

MGH is indispensible to its surrounding communities. The hospital admits over 45,000 patients and sees over 1 million outpatients per year. Over 34,000 operations are performed yearly, and over 3,500 new Massachusetts residents are welcomed to the state annually by MGH's obstetrics staff. The hospital is also the largest non-government employer in the state of Massachusetts, employing over 10,000 people.

Given its stature and contributions, it is no wonder that Massachusetts General Hospital consistently receives top marks from *U.S. News and World Reports* as one of the nation's finest medical institutions.

BOSTON GREEN GOODS, INC.

Mercia Tapping is an innovative, entrepreneurial woman who spent much of her life ahead of the times. Now, the times are finally beginning to catch up with her vision for a healthy planet with healthy people.

Tapping understands both success and failure. In 1974, the British native founded an energy efficiency consulting company. The premature concept folded as the United States' energy crisis came and went, but Tapping's entrepreneurial spirit didn't give up—nor did it give in. She maintained a successful technology consulting company and learned plenty along the way.

Today, Mercia Tapping heads up Boston Green Goods, Inc. which consists of several successful e-commerce websites she has founded including AllergyBuyersClub.com, SleepBuyersClub.com, and GreenandMore.com, as well as a print catalog and wholesaling division for its own proprietary branded goods operating under its own name. The company is officially one of the top 500 Internet retailers in the United States and grew by nearly 27 percent to reach $14.7 million in sales in 2006.

Mercia Tapping, CEO and president, Boston Green Goods, Inc.

Company executives expect the firm to grow by 20 to 25 percent this year to over $18 million in sales.

The pioneering entrepreneur launched AllergyBuyersClub.com in 1998 just before the peak of the early dot-com heydays that saw the likes of Amazon.com and Yahoo! rise to stardom. Again, she was ahead of her time. Three years later the Internet bubble burst and many online venues went bankrupt. This time around, though, Tapping won out. AllergyBuyersClub.com, an e-commerce website that sells healthy home products, kept its virtual doors open while most its competitors shut the lights off and went back to the bricks and mortar business world.

Tapping used her own bank account to finance her vision with a classic start in the basement of her home. The Internet entrepreneur tried several times to turn the heads of the investment and banking industries with no success. She was repeatedly rejected as the suds from the busted Internet bubble continued flowing down the drain, leaving a bad taste in the mouths of venture capitalists who lost millions in hyped up dot-coms that crashed.

Tapping, though, was determined that her dream would not go down the drain. AllergyBuyersClub.com survived the e-commerce debacle despite seemingly endless obstacles, in essence, simply because she refused to give up on helping others get relief from allergies. It is now the leading e-commerce site in its niche. Today, she is preparing to repeat the process with green products on GreenandMore.com using the same business model that has won the loyalty of thousands of customers to date.

Because there is no lack of online home product stores in the Internet shopping world, Tapping needed more than a niche—she needed a creative hook. AllergyBuyersClub.com differentiates itself, Tapping says, with its business model. The company's website focuses as much on educating people on how to lead a healthy lifestyle than it does on selling products. But, of course, product sales are the lifeblood of the company.

AllergyBuyersClub.com sells appliances like air cleaners, dehumidifiers, steam cleaners and water filters. It also sells home goods such as blankets, sheets, pillows, dust mite covers and comforters. The website allows customers to shop by category, such as brand, allergy type—cats, dust, mold or pollen—and sleep problems. It also offers advice on all of its products so customers can easily choose the right one for their individual needs.

Here's how it works: The company's research team rates and reviews products sold, providing customers with honest reviews, including pluses and minuses of each product. It is still innovative for a retailer to critique its own product offerings, Tapping insists. "Our customers and vendors are always astonished at the depth of knowledge we offer about our products," she says. "We find that being truthful about the products we sell, and caring for customers is good business and brings our customers back to us."

Boston Green Goods offers a full selection of air purifiers on its websites.

Although national in scope, the Boston-based company does about 15 percent of its business locally through its portfolio of websites. Two years ago, Boston Green Goods expanded its horizons offline, launching a print catalog for AllergyBuyersClub.com that was mailed out to 2 million people in 2007. Tapping says the catalog is profitable, but does not disclose what percentage of the company's revenues come from this channel.

A determined woman in a male-dominated industry, Tapping has received numerous industry accolades. In 2004 she won the Stevie Award for Women Entrepreneurs. The company was also approached by the hit ABC television series, *Extreme Makeover: Home Edition*, to recommend healthy home products for two of its episodes. And in 2006 the company was named one of the top 20 small businesses in the *Boston Business Journal's* annual "Best Places to Work" listing. The paper cited out-of-the-box ways the company motivates its employees and garners loyalty.

Although the Internet is itself innovative, Boston Green Goods relies on

Gary McEldowney, marketing director, works with Mercia Tapping to manage the company's online marketing and consumer catalog programs.

loyal employees to run the show. It doesn't take outsiders very long to figure out that Boston Green Goods is unique, Tapping says. "Our employees keep telling us they have never worked in a place they enjoy so much," she says. "Our goal is for people to work hard, but enjoy it, and feel appreciated."

In 2006 nearly 20 percent of the company was turned over to employees. It was one of the many ways that Tapping shows her appreciation for their help in growing the company from ground zero to a profitable and expanding the Internet venture. Diversity is also part of the corporate culture at Boston Green Goods. Half of the company's 32 employees are women, with many nationalities and ethnic backgrounds well represented, Tapping says.

Like many Fortune 500 companies, Boston Green Goods believes in the concept of continuous learning. Junior staffers are invited to meetings for the sole purpose of witnessing how senior staff conducts business with each other and outside vendors. Senior and mid-level staff attend conferences across the nation to advance their own learning and stimulate their thinking. And sales and customer service staff receive 20 days of training and development each year.

When it comes to recruiting, Tapping depends on her employees to help the cause. Half of Boston Green Goods new employees come through existing employee referrals. "People rarely leave here because the culture is so positive, pay is competitive and the benefits are simply the best around," Tapping declares. "We quite routinely have staff take 'sabbatical leave' from their regular job if we think they are getting stale or business is slower in certain parts of the company at certain parts of the year."

Tapping maintains employee loyalty by putting herself in their shoes. She understands that unless she takes care of her employees first, she can't take care of her customers. "I want people to be smiling as they come through our front doors in the morning," she says. "Outside consultants and visitors constantly remark on how different the 'feeling' is in our offices since people are smiling and getting along with each other."

Boston Green Goods offers several initiatives to keep employees smiling. Despite increased financial pressures, for instance, the company still pays for 100 percent of individual employee healthcare. Tapping does this because she believes in the importance of everybody enjoying access to affordable healthcare. Boston Green Goods also has a subsidized Weight Watchers program on-site. The company offers two $750 prizes to the "biggest losers" at the end of the session. Boston Green Goods provides a 3 percent contribution that vests immediately—with no employee matching required—into a 401(k) plan. At the end of the year, the company has in the past put a percentage of its profits into the fund.

The company also rewards longevity. Vacation time increases at all levels according to how long an employee has been with the company. Staff can earn up to three weeks of annual vacation. Of course, Tapping also realizes that

The company sells vapor steam cleaners for chemical-free home cleaning.

sometimes certain individuals deserve special recognition. In those cases, bonuses are designed for the hard working employees, such as an all-expense paid, weeklong vacation for the family at a top tier resort.

Tapping insists that the physical environment improves people's mood, so the company's offices are airy and all employees have access to natural light. She also believes in making it as easy as possible for staff to get the job done, no matter what life throws at them. Remote access capabilities through a virtual private network, for example, allows employees who are sick or who have ill family members to work from home without losing a day's pay. "We are very liberal in letting employees flex their time in order to attend family and school events, or attend to family problems," Tapping says. "This continues to be one of the attractive features of our culture to employees with young children."

As the self-proclaimed "keeper of the culture" at Boston Green Goods, Tapping puts a premium on fun. She believes it's therapeutic, and she demonstrates her belief in a weekly departmental meeting that is known for its noisy laughter wafting down the hallways. There are also on-site events designed to spark giggles, like the Halloween costume contest where the creativity of employees continues to reach new heights each year. Tapping even takes employees off site for special events to demonstrate her appreciation. Last year she took the entire company and their families to Cirque de Soleil.

A smaller, but also appreciated perk lets customer service representatives rack up points for high customer satisfaction scores. They can trade in those points for a free shopping spree of returned goods in the product warehouse. Another much-anticipated treat is the annual "truckload raffle," Tapping explains. The company trucks

In 2004 the company moved to its current 10,000 square-foot executive office space located in Waltham, Massachusetts.

in hundreds of boxes of demo and dented goods from its warehouse and raffles them off. Employees can win thousands of dollars of free goods, including vacuum cleaners, luxury bedding, air cleaners and portable air conditioners.

The employees show their affection back to the British native, too. "I was touched this last year when employees threw a surprise party for me after I became an American citizen," Tapping recalls. "Our offices were festooned in red, white and blue as were all our employees. Employees all brought in an American dish to share and presented me with a specially put together CD of American music. They told me I gave so much to them that it was time to give back."

The success of the company is allowing Tapping to pursue one of her old dreams: going green. Tapping lived with solar panels on her home in the United Kingdom some 45 years ago, and in 1974 founded an energy efficiency consulting company, which folded. But she never lost sight of her commitment to the environment. In September 2007 the company launched GreenandMore.com which

offers authentic eco-friendly products and information to inspire people to live a greener life. The mission of the website is to support the needs of the rising environmentally conscious community and give customers the opportunity to give to the environmental organization of their choice.

Tapping will face admitted challenges to see her passion succeed, though. Having leaped over the hurdle of reinventing its infrastructure in 2006, the company is now staring down a different obstacle: getting enough manpower organized to implement all of Tapping's new ideas.

"Our research team intends to both educate the public on going green, while helping them sort through the myriad of product choices now quickly becoming available," Tapping says. "Our future and my legacy will be to apply our existing, very successful e-commerce model, where we compare and review products, to the green products industry as a whole."

MASSACHUSETTS INSTITUTE OF TECHNOLOGY (MIT)

Known around the world, Massachusetts Institute of Technology (MIT) is a university like no other. With a mission to educate students in science and technology in a way that will best serve the nation and the world, MIT takes the phrase "higher learning" to a new level.

The institute is committed to knowledge—generating, disseminating, and preserving it. Its foundation is based on using that knowledge to address and ease the world's many challenges. By combining rigorous academic study, a sense of appreciation for new discoveries, and an intellectual and supportive school community, students learn to focus their efforts to better humanity.

MIT welcomed its first students in 1865, just a few years after its founding charter was approved. The school's opening marked the culmination of William Barton Rogers' efforts to establish an independent educational institution that addressed the issues facing an America that was becoming more and more industrialized. As a distinguished natural scientist, Rogers believed that the combination of teaching and research—which focus on real-world problems—provided students with the best possible education.

Today, MIT remains committed to that same guiding principle. As a world-class educational institution, MIT's five schools and one college offer students the opportunity to learn, grow, and make the world a better place. Its programs cut across the traditional departmental boundaries, and empower students to think freely and act responsibly.

With more than 4,000 undergraduates and 6,000-plus graduate students in 2006, only 13 percent of MIT's first-year applicants were offered admission to the institute. As further evidence of the high caliber of its students and faculty, MIT has been home to 63 Nobel Prize winners over the years, seven of whom are currently on the faculty.

With its School of Engineering; Sloan School of Management; School of Science; the Whitaker College of Health Sciences and Technology; and the MIT-WHOI Joint Program in Oceanography and Applied Ocean Science and Engineering, students are able to pursue a variety of scientific endeavors. Aside from a bachelor of science degree, masters degrees are available in business administration, city planning, engineering, and science. Doctorate degrees are obtainable in both philosophy and science.

Although MIT is mostly known for its technical and scientific curriculum, study of the arts is also an integral part of its curriculum. More than half of the undergraduate student body enrolls in art related courses each year and 75 percent of the institute's incoming freshman have experience, or an interest, in the arts.

With MIT's School of Architecture and Planning and School of Humanities, Arts, and Social Sciences, students are able to pursue majors and minors in music, theater, writing, architecture, and art. The school's Dramashop, MIT Symphony Orchestra, and four dozen other music, dance, and theater groups offer students the ability to pursue their artistic interests, while benefiting from the guidance of the school's distinguished arts faculty. From chamber music to Shakespeare to modern dance, students are able to immerse themselves in MIT's rich, artistic offerings.

More than anything, however, MIT's creative, collaborative, and strategic approach to education is what has made it a world leader. With an emphasis on shared knowledge for the greater good, MIT graduates are helping to create a more relevant and hopeful tomorrow.

The Great Court at MIT, the foremost technological institute in the world, located on the banks of the Charles River.

BOURNEWOOD HOSPITAL

Bournewood Hospital stands today in Brookline, just outside Boston, in the same setting in which the psychiatric hospital has existed since 1895. The four Victorian buildings that comprise the hospital were designed more than a century ago by Boston architect William Ralph Emerson, who was known for his shingle-style houses and inns. But where a century ago patients played billiards, tennis, croquet, and relaxed in the small library, there are now facilities for programs and services, including inpatient psychiatric treatment for adults and children/adolescents, a chemical dependency/dual diagnosis program, an acute residential treatment program and intensive outpatient service facilities for adults, adolescents and children. Where patients sometimes stayed for months, even years, they now stay for days. Where care tended to be provided for only the wealthy, it is now provided for people from all walks of life.

Despite the changes that have come about over the years at Bournewood Hospital, one thing has remained the same: the hospital's commitment to providing outstanding personalized patient care. These days this accomplishment is in large part due to the commitment of Nasir A. Khan, MD,

A map of Brookline from 1919.

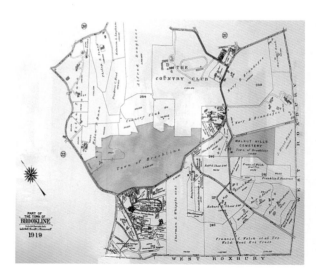

An aerial view of Bournewood Hospital as it looks today.

who for more than a quarter of a century has served as chairman and CEO of the hospital's operating organization called Bournewood Health Systems. Khan and his clinical staff work hard on a daily basis to overcome the challenges inherent in running a hospital in today's competitive marketplace in order to effectively carry on a tradition of excellence that began in 1884, when Henry Rust Stedman, MD, built the facility on its original location on the Minot Estates in Forest Hills, Boston.

Stedman, who took pride in tailoring the treatment provided to meet each of his patient's individual needs, later relocated Bournewood to its current home on the former Dodge Farm Estates. In those early days, each patient had a private room and his or her own "companion" or mental health counselor. It is interesting to note that

one of these companions was Amelia Earhart, who worked at Bournewood for a summer two years before her historic flight. It is also important to point out that there were no psychiatric medications available back then to help patients recover, so the presence of the companion was an important part of the treatment plan.

Stedman ran the hospital until 1917, when he passed on the reigns to George H. Torney, MD. Then in 1945, Solomon Gagnon, MD, took over the ownership, and stayed in this role for more than 30 years. Under Gagnon's reign, things begin to go downhill for the facility, which had until then been known as a "high-class" institution. But by the late 1970s, things had worsened for Bournewood to the point that it was facing severe financial difficulty and had even lost its hospital accreditation, putting its future in jeopardy.

In 1979, Khan, a local psychiatrist who practiced at Bournewood, was asked to step in to help turn things around. Khan had been born in London to Indian parents and had come to the United States in 1965, when he began his residency at the Harvard Department of Psychiatry at Boston City Hospital. Prior to coming to Bournewood, he had served as the superintendent of Danvers State Hospital.

As the fourth psychiatrist to run the hospital, Khan called on his past experience overseeing hospital administrative affairs to make significant changes to improve conditions, such as recruiting key staff and developing new clinical programs. These changes, and others Khan implemented, had a beneficial effect on the patients, as well as on the employees. By 1982 the hospital had regained its accreditation, and was even among the first hospitals in the country to be accredited under new standards of the Joint Commission on the Accreditation of Hospitals.

Today Khan continues to lead Bournewood. The facility, which began

Nasir A. Khan, MD, the CEO and Chairman of Bournewood Health Systems.

with a total of 16 beds in Stedman's day, is now licensed by the state for 90 beds and treats approximately 3,600 patients each year with a comprehensive continuum of care that is tailored to meet a range of needs and situations. "We offer a variety of intensive inpatient and outpatient options and have physicians on site 24 hours a day, 7 days a week," Khan says. "This enables us to treat patients at whatever point they enter our system, and then they can step down into less restrictive programs as they move along the recovery process, or step up if they need more intensive care, so no matter what their situation, they will have the support they need to be successful."

Bournewood is also now a major teaching institution that trains medical students, psychiatric residents and fellows, psychologists, social workers, nursing students and active therapy students from a number of top universities, colleges and training centers in the Boston area. These relationships provide valuable learning opportunities for students, and also offer important stimulation for patients and staff.

In addition to his role at Bournewood, Khan stays active in the medical field at large. He is an assistant clinical professor of psychiatry at Tufts University School of Medicine and an adjunct assistant professor of psychiatry at Boston University School of Medicine. Over the years, he has also been an active member of many organizations, and has been elected president of the Association of General Psychiatrists, the Massachusetts Association of Behavioral Health Systems and the Charles River District Medical Society and elected a trustee of the National Association of Psychiatric Health Systems.

Were Stedman alive today, he would no doubt be pleased to discover that, thanks to the vision and perseverance Khan brings to the facility, Bournewood continues to provide a nurturing setting where mentally and emotionally disturbed people can work on renewing their health. But now, in addition to receiving the same personalized care that has always been available at Bournewood, patients also have the benefits of modern medicine to help make their recovery process more effective than ever before.

The Dodge Building on Bournewood's campus in the early days.

BRIGHAM AND WOMEN'S HOSPITAL

With its rich history dating back to 1832, Brigham and Women's Hospital (BWH) is renowned around the world for its excellence in patient care, stunning innovations in research and physician training, and deep commitment to the community. BWH was formed in 1980 after an unprecedented merger between three of Boston's oldest and most respected hospitals: the Peter Bent Brigham Hospital, the Robert Breck Brigham Hospital, and Boston Hospital for Women. As trailblazers in medicine, BWH has no peer.

With nearly 800 beds, Brigham and Women's Hospital is situated in the heart of Boston's Longwood Medical area. As a teaching affiliate of Harvard Medical School, it offers extensive inpatient and outpatient services, state-of-the-art diagnostics, and high quality primary and specialty care at its clinics and health centers. Since its inception, BWH has built on a solid reputation for cutting edge care and research and encouraging investigation, collaboration, and discovery among its caregivers and scientists to bring the best healthcare options to patients.

The hospital is able to boast many significant "firsts." Today, BWH is recognized as one of the world's

Boston Lying-in Hospital.

The Free Hospital for Women.

leaders in transplantation. In 1954 a Brigham team led by Dr. Joseph Murray performed the first successful human organ donor transplant, a kidney, from one brother to another. In recognition of this achievement, Dr. Murray received the Nobel Prize for medicine in 1990. In 2006 BWH performed for the first time in its history 100 kidney transplants in one year. The first heart transplant in New England was performed at BWH in 1984; two decades later, the 500th transplant was successfully performed at the hospital. At BWH, the first heart-lung transplant in Massachusetts was performed in 1992; the first triple organ transplant in the country was performed in 1995; and the first in the nation quintuple lung transplant was performed at BWH in 2004.

Other medical milestones include developing the iron lung to save polio victims, inventing the blood bag, administering anesthesia for the first time in an American maternity hospital, developing non-invasive fetal heart monitoring, pioneering the CA-125 blood test to monitor ovarian cancer patients, and becoming an international leader in medical error prevention with computerized order entry. In 1926 physicians Williams Murphy, George Whipple, and George Minot discovered liver extract as the cure for pernicious anemia, leading to a Nobel Prize for all three men in 1934.

In the research arena, Brigham and Women's Hospital is a biomedical powerhouse. A top recipient of grants from the National Institutes of Health, BWH researchers have set new standards for research excellence, such as supporting transformative research whose promise can be realized within five years, and facilitating the transfer of research from the lab to the patient's bedside. Every day researchers strive to bring deeper scientific understanding

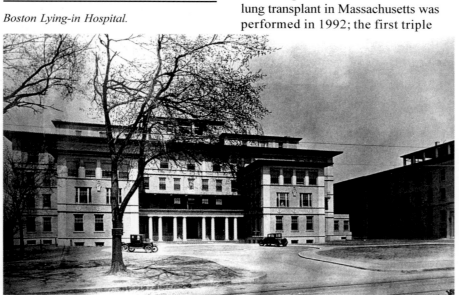

Robert Breck Brigham Hospital.

to medicine to achieve improved outcomes. Cardiac care, for example, has been revolutionized due to groundbreaking research at BWH. The TIMI Study group, which stands for Thrombolysis in Myocardial Infarction, began in 1984 as a single clinical trial of a new clot-busting drug for heart attack patients, and now such drugs are commonplace when treating patients with heart attacks. BWH researchers are the driving force behind using C-reactive protein levels as an indicator of heart disease and preventive measures such as lowering "bad cholesterol" levels, or so-called LDLs.

In the neurosciences, in addition to leading the way in research for treatments for multiple sclerosis and Alzheimer's disease, BWH has pioneered research in the "amyloid hypothesis" giving clinicians an understanding of how this protein accumulates in the brain and leads to dementia. Much the same way, BWH researchers are uncovering the biomarkers for MS.

National landmark epidemiological studies conducted at BWH, such as the Brigham and Women's Nurses' Health Study, the largest prospective study ever conducted into the the risk factors for major chronic diseases in women, has changed the way care is delivered. Among some of its important results, the NHS has found that aspirin has been shown to reduce women's risk of developing stroke; being overweight reduces the risk of breast cancer in premenopausal women and increases the risk after; weight and exercise are important predictors of longevity; and

physical activity, moderate alcohol intake, and high vegetable consumption help maintain memory.

The hospital's Physicians' Health Study was the first to prove that daily low-dose aspirin significantly decreased the risk of a first heart attack. BWH is also the only Massachusetts hospital participating in the Women's Health Initiative (WHI), a long-term national research study that has focused on strategies for preventing heart disease, breast and colorectal cancer, and osteoporotic fractures in postmenopausal women. Among its many significant findings are that adverse effects outweigh and outnumber the benefits from HRT (hormone replacement therapy). There were more cases of breast cancer and cardiovascular disease in women taking estrogen and progestin, while the main benefits were fewer hip fractures and cases of colorectal cancer.

With nearly 13,000 professionals on staff and more than 3,000 doctors, some of the country's most respected physicians call BWH home. Brigham and Women's has been ranked on *US News and World Report's* Honor Roll of America's best hospitals for 14 consecutive years. It is also one of only two hospitals in the country to be named to Solucient's list of Top 100 Hospitals 11 times since the inception of the quality performance award. In a special quality and safety benchmarking study, BWH was also recognized by the University HealthSystem Consortium (UHC) as one of five top performing academic medical centers in the country

two years in a row. Each year BWH serves more inpatients than any other hospital in Massachusetts. In 2006 inpatient admissions totaled more than 45,000, ambulatory visits reached 900,000, and more than 56,000 patients were treated in the emergency department.

Brigham and Women's Hospital is proud to highlight its five "centers of excellence," hubs for treatment and research, to address the most pressing of healthcare challenges in the areas of cardiovascular, cancer care, women's health, neurosciences, and orthopedics and arthritis.

Heart disease is the number one killer of men and women in the United States, and BWH's predecessor institution, the Peter Bent Brigham Hospital, led the fight against this deadly condition for decades. Today, BWH's Cardiovascular Center is one of the largest and most renowned programs of its kind in the world. With a comprehensive, integrated team of cardiologists, cardiac surgeons, vascular surgeons, cardiac anesthesiologists, cardiovascular radiologists, and cardiovascular nurses, BWH provides the most advanced care possible. In addition to pioneering minimally invasive heart surgeries, cardiovascular investigators are searching for effective treatments for inherited heart disorders, and clinical trials of new devices and drug therapies will continue to revolutionize how cardiovascular disease is treated.

BWH has never been content with the status quo. The construction of the Carl J. and Ruth Shapiro Cardiovascular Center—which opens in 2008—is just one example of the important steps that BWH is taking to advance treatment and discovery in the clinical and research fronts as part of the fight against heart disease. The 10-story, 350,000-square-foot facility will house five floors for inpatient care and two floors each for clinical and diagnostic testing, surgery, and radiology, making the center a full-service complex.

The new Shapiro Cardiovascular Center will offer patients a true integration among related disciplines and revolutionize the delivery of cardiovascular care. Patients will consult with a team of specialists, all under one roof, encouraging communications and promoting comprehensive care. Inpatient rooms have been designed to offer comfort and privacy for patients and their families, while treatment areas of the new facility boast an unprecedented flexibility, such as a "hybrid" operating room so angioplasties and bypass surgeries could take place in the same location, reducing the need for seriously ill patients to be moved. BWH is also setting aside space for future advance-

---

In February 1984 BWH became the first New England Hospital to perform a heart transplant. The first patient was 43-year-old Gerald Boucher, at left, and eight days later, 16-year-old Matthew Shelales became the second.

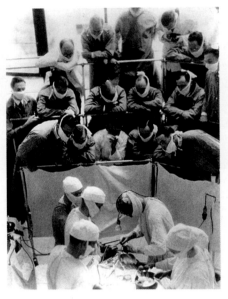

Dr. Harvey Cushing, the father of modern neurosurgery, performs his 2,000th brain surgery while serving as chief of surgery at the Peter Bent Brigham Hospital from 1912 to 1932.

---

ments, such as procedures that will use robots and real-time body scans.

And, if the most advanced medical facilities weren't enough, BWH has gone above and beyond by ensuring that the Shapiro Cardiovascular Center has minimal environmental impact. The center will be a "green" building, meeting the Leadership in Energy and Environmental Design (LEED) guidelines, the nationally accepted benchmark for the design, construction, and operation of high performance green buildings.

Brigham and Women's, through its close collaboration with Dana-Farber Cancer Institute, has become one of the world's premier cancer centers. The Dana-Farber/ Brigham and Women's Cancer Center offers patient-centered care to adult patients in specialized cancer centers, each devoted to helping patients fight a different type of cancer. Dedicated, experienced pathologists use advanced tools and techniques to diagnose and stage

cancers and provide critical information for treatment planning. A multi-disciplinary team of specialists collaborate to deliver innovative, multi-modality treatment techniques designed to improve patient outcomes and quality of life.

BWH's Gastrointestinal Cancer Treatment Center, for example, manages one of the largest volumes of patients with gastrointestinal malignancies in the country. Clinicians and researchers with the Thoracic Oncology Program perform basic, clinical, and epidemiological collaborative projects designed to translate findings into improved therapies for thoracic malignancies. Currently, the program is examining gender-dependent markers in lung cancer in an effort to bring together clinical data and epidemiological tools to better diagnose and treat lung cancer in women. Nationally recognized breast surgeons at the Breast Oncology Center are offering new techniques to improve results and minimize side effects of surgery, while radiation oncologists in the center are employing novel techniques for highly precise, effective, and safe delivery of treatment that protects surrounding tissues and organs. The center also offers medical therapies and clinical trials that target distinct and major categories of breast cancer.

In 2006 BWH conducted its first radioembolization of the liver, a process that delivers radiation to liver tumors and spares healthy tissue. Many types of liver tumors that have been unresponsive to chemotherapy have responded to this treatment. In yet another surgical advancement, BWH in 2005 began using the da Vinci robot in its gynecologic laparoscopic cancer surgeries, helping to decrease patient hospital stays. What used to require open surgery and a three-to-five day stay now allows patients to return home the next day.

BWH's history of excellence in women's health dates back to 1832 when one of its predecessor hospitals, the Boston Lying-In opened as one of the country's first maternity hospitals. Today, women's health at BWH is coordinated through the Mary Horrigan Connors Center for Women's Health and Gender Biology and the Department of Obstetrics and Gynecology and encompasses two distinct but intertwined areas of clinical focus and research: reproductive health and gender biology. Each woman receives care informed by an understanding of how sex and gender differences affect disease development and treatment, and it is provided through a system built around her needs and is effective at improving health and quality of life.

BWH's Center for Women and Newborns in the Connors Center has the largest birthing center in the region, offering state-of-the-art birthing suites. Its Newborn Intensive Care Unit cares for more than 1,300 infants annually; and it features overnight rooms for parents, as well as private, post-partum, and ante-partum rooms that promote family-focused care. Caregivers provide a full range of routine care and screenings, infertility, evaluation, and procedural and technological interventions. Fetal medicine and prenatal

BWH continues to innovate using the da Vinci Robot in gynecologic cancer and bariatric surgeries.

Cardiologists Eugene Braunwald, Christopher Cannon, and Stephen Wiviott are part of the Thrombolysis in Myocardial Infarction (TIMI) trials, a series of studies that have changed the way physicians treat heart disease.

specialists focus on the comprehensive assessment and therapy of fetal disease through collaboration with its multidisciplinary staff. BWH also houses one of the first and most comprehensive centers for women with cardiovascular disease and women with bone and joint disease in the U.S. Gynecologic cancer patients are also cared for in the Connors Center, where women with gynecologic cancer—and those who are at high risk—can receive the latest and most advanced diagnostic tests and treatments available.

When it comes to patients who suffer from diseases of the nervous system, Brigham and Women's Hospital's

Neurosciences Institute offers world-class care. With one of the largest and most comprehensive teams of neuro-surgeons, neurologists, psychiatrists, and radiologists available, specialists have the most advanced tools and facilities at their disposal, including interventional radiology suites, image-guided neurosurgery rooms, and one of the largest neuroscience intensive care units in the world. The dedication by its physicians and scientists to advanced therapies and treatments provides patients with the finest of care, and the center's basic and translational research enterprise informs everything they do. A recent milestone included neurosurgeons performing the hospital's 1,000th intraoperative MR-guided brain tumor craniotomy. By utilizing an open MRI scanner to produce high resolution and real time images of the patient's brain, surgeons were able to more effectively remove tumors of the brain. BWH, through the Stroke and Cerebrovascular Center, was

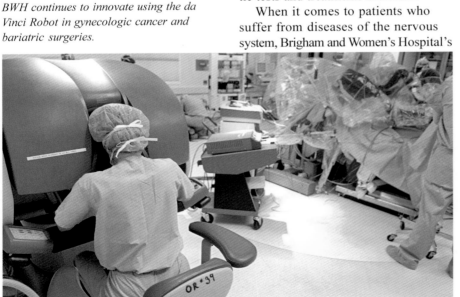

also recently designated as a primary stroke service hospital.

The Orthopedic and Arthritis Center at Brigham and Women's Hospital has built on the outstanding achievements that the hospital's predecessor, Robert Breck Brigham Hospital, began decades ago. BWH has one of the largest clinical and research teams devoted to advancing the understanding and treatment of bone and joint diseases in the world. Specialists offer advanced cartilage repair techniques to preserve joints and maximize function. The center is dedicated to the care of patients in their late teens to early 50s with early arthritic disease and cartilage damage due to degenerative and traumatic conditions of the knee, shoulder, hip, and ankle. The nation's first autologous repair of cartilage was performed at BWH in 1995, and in June 2006, the 400th was performed—the highest volume of autologous repair in the U.S. The center has pioneered a variety of advancements that include the discovery of new medications for rheumatoid arthritis and minimally invasive procedures for joint replacement.

BWH is recognized as a national leader in patient safety and quality improvement. The hospital has pioneered the use of computers and technology in medication ordering and

BWH's landmark use of eMAR and barcoding technology has pharmacists like Tola Dawodu scanning bar codes as they fill prescriptions.

Dr. Joseph Loscalzo, chairman of the Department of Medicine, reviews laboratory research with investigator Laura Coleman.

delivery, storage of medical records, and radiology. The Computerized Physician Order Entry system allows physicians to access patients' medical records and histories, order tests and medications, and analyze test results. BWH's electronic Medication Administration Record, or eMAR, uses barcoding technology with prescription drugs, ensuring patients are receiving the correct drugs in the correct doses. This system has had far reaching success in eliminating medication errors.

Brigham and Women's Hospital is able to combine the values of a nurturing environment focused on patient-centered care with the most advanced technology and pioneering research. In 2006 in conjunction with the National Institutes of Health and Amgen, BWH launched the first women's genome health study. Through this initiative, researchers hope to find the genetic causes for heart disease, cancer, stroke, and other common health problems. That same year, the National Committee for

Quality Health Care presented Brigham and Women's Hospital with the National Quality Health Care Award based on the hospital's ability to implement new and emerging technologies, maintain its financial stability, and include its staff in the decision-making process.

In addition to offering the highest quality healthcare, Brigham and Women's Hospital has made a reputation as a trusted and respected part of the community. In 2005 Dr. Gary Gottlieb, president of BWH, co-chaired and served on Boston Mayor Thomas Menino's task force on health disparities. According to a study released by Mayor Menino, African American men in Boston die five years sooner (on average) than white men. Blacks are also twice as likely to die from diabetes and four times more likely to contract HIV. Under Gottlieb's leadership, Brigham and Women's Hospital is taking an active role in combating these inequalities. An initiative at BWH is helping the hospital track the care that patients receive and follow their progress. By collecting and analyzing this data, Gottlieb hopes that they can begin to understand the disparities and turn them around.

Gottlieb also takes an active role in establishing BWH as a responsible

corporate citizen, and Brigham and Women's Hospital is constantly evaluating how it can better serve the community. To that end, the hospital is an active participant in the city's SkillWorks program. Organized by The Boston Foundation, this collaborative effort offers those in the low wage sector the chance to improve their job skills and embark upon new career opportunities. Gottlieb has vowed to increase the number of internal promotions so more people have the opportunity to train and move up into nursing and technical positions at the hospital. Minority

Dr. Lawrence Cohn, senior cardiac surgeon, has performed more than 10,000 cardiac surgeries during his career.

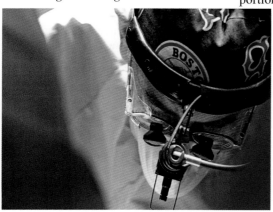

The main campus of Brigham and Women's Hospital is on Francis Street in Boston's Longwood Medical Area.

employees are also able to pair up with mentors to help them manage their careers at BWH. Some employees even receive additional training at local colleges, paid in full by Brigham and Women's Hospital.

In an effort to recruit a workforce that mirrors the community that BWH serves, the hospital also actively participates in outreach programs at local high schools. Students are advised about the career opportunities available in healthcare and are encouraged to enter summer work programs at the hospital. According to Gottlieb, BWH wants to secure a substantial portion of its labor base from the surrounding communities.

By understanding the importance of empowering and training its staff, by embracing its role as a community leader, and by pursuing the latest healthcare technologies, research, and treatments, Brigham and Women's Hospital is able to provide its patients with revolutionary care in the most compassionate fashion. "For the Brigham and

Women's Hospital community, our steadfast belief in our mission provides the compassionate compass that guides us," said Gottlieb. "We allow our hearts and minds to lead us in directions that can expand our vision and challenge us to be the very best healthcare clinicians, scientists, teachers, and neighbors. Our focus is to care for those who depend on us and to offer all who step inside our doors the breadth and depth of our collective wisdom and compassion."

Dr. Gary Gottlieb.

CBT ARCHITECTS

Look across the Boston skyline, take a walk through the city's historic districts, or visit a local college campus, and you're certain to come across the work of CBT Architects. Whether it's a contemporary high-rise tower, an elegant hotel, a renovated college classroom, or an historic courthouse, CBT Architects has been leaving its imprint on the Boston area and beyond since 1967. That's the year that three young architects—Maurice Childs, Richard J. Bertman, and Charles N. Tseckares—officially joined forces to incorporate their own firm.

Considering that architecture firms have one of the highest failure rates of all new businesses, the move was risky. But, it paid off. After 40 years in business, CBT Architects has earned a place as one of the premiere architectural firms in the region. With Tseckares

200 Newbury Street. Photo by Edward Jacoby

The tower at the intersection of Clarendon and Columbus. Photo by Neoscape

and Bertman still on board, the firm's leadership team has expanded to include partners Robert A. Brown, Margaret Deutsch, David Hancock, David Nagahiro, Christopher Hill, Lois Goodell, James McBain, and Alfred Wojciechowski.

How did CBT defy the odds? In large part, it's because the founders understood that succeeding in the field required more than just excellence in design. Strong project management, a commitment to business development, and an ability to service clients were equally important. The founders each had complementary strengths in these areas and had the foresight to hire employees who possessed the qualities they lacked.

Also part of their blueprint for success was the development of a corporate culture that ran contrary to

what was found in most other architectural firms at the time. The founders vowed to create a working environment that encouraged teamwork and groomed employees for advancement within the company. With this philosophy as CBT's foundation, the firm grew quickly—expanding the size and scope of its projects, branching out into new areas, and adding to its staff.

The firm first gained recognition for its work in historic preservation. In the 1970s a growing public awareness of historic architecture sparked a movement to renovate and adapt historic buildings for new uses. The innovators at CBT capitalized on this trend by identifying historic buildings that could be renovated and then searching for clients to purchase the buildings and hire them as the architects. The tactic boosted cash flow and led to preservation projects for colleges and corporate clients. In 1974 CBT earned the Special

Award for Historical Preservation from the National Trust for Historic Preservation, which helped put CBT on the architectural map. Based on this prestigious achievement, CBT was tapped for a speaking tour about historic preservation and earned a reputation as an expert in the burgeoning field.

Today, with 210 employees, CBT's architectural endeavors reach far beyond preservation and include academic, commercial, mixed-use, civic, hospitality, residential, and international projects. In addition to architecture, the firm also provides services in urban design, interior design, and graphic design.

The award-winning firm's client list reads like an edition of Who's Who, including dozens of elite colleges, major corporations, and civic municipalities. Academic projects include master planning, classrooms, housing, learning centers, athletics facilities, and arts centers for institutions, such as Harvard University, Wellesley College, Babson College, and Penn State. Corporate clients include the Ritz-Carlton and the Boston Stock Exchange. Public libraries, courthouses, museums, and performing arts centers are counted among their many civic projects. Their work in preservation also involves a wide spectrum of clients.

No matter what type of project the professionals at CBT are tackling, they take a holistic approach that considers the entire scope of the task. They envision every design project in relation to its surrounding environment, its intended use, and their clients. The design outcomes are master plans, buildings, and interior spaces that resonate with the spirit of those they serve—from 21st century cities to historic college campuses to individual residences.

To ensure that their projects are welcomed by local communities, CBT has fine-tuned its communication skills.

In the 1980s communities developed concerns about architectural projects and the impact they would have on their neighborhoods. People began going to court in an attempt to halt projects they felt didn't fit the scale of their neighborhoods. To avoid this kind of problem, the CBT team became experts at representing their clients and their design vision to the community. With an ability to gain the trust of the local community, they were able to avoid challenges that might have permanently stalled projects.

Case in point is a project for a high-rise in the Back Bay that languished amid community protest. CBT's designs addressed the concerns of neighbors and helped obtain the necessary permits from authorities so the project was able to get back on track. This marked CBT's first foray into the high-rise arena and opened up the doors to a host of other high-rise projects.

The team at CBT continually strives to be at the forefront of architectural and design trends. Perhaps nowhere is that more apparent than with the firm's commitment to sustainability. A buzzword that's popping up everywhere today, sustainability involves design that balances economic efficiency, environmental harmony, and social benefit. Although the concept, which includes using energy conservation techniques and renewable materials, has only recently reached mass appeal, it's been a part of the practice at CBT since 1970.

In that year the firm completed the first project that met the standards set by the Vermont Act 250, the first sustainable legislation introduced in the United States. The new code dictated

Restored copper and slate tower at Harvard Memorial Hall. Photo by Peter Vanderwarker

elements, such as insulation thickness and the types of trees that could be used to surround the structure. Based on their successful completion of this project, CBT was able to secure more work in this emerging field.

Today many of CBT's projects involve sustainability. These projects allow CBT to introduce clients to the financial and operational benefits of green buildings, lower energy, reduced waste and water use, lower environmental and emissions costs, improved operations and maintenance and, most importantly, increased productivity from a healthier workspace. Currently, CBT has more than 30 LEED-certified (Leadership in Environmental and Energy Design) professionals on staff and affiliations with the U.S. Green Building Council and the Massachusetts Green Roundtable.

As CBT's reputation has grown over the decades, so has the size of its projects. CBT is currently involved in large-scale urban design projects that span several million square feet and include retail, office, and residential space. One such project is NorthPoint, a new mixed-use, transit-oriented neighborhood on 52 acres of former railway yards. CBT is providing master planning services in collaboration with Ken Greenberg for the creation of NorthPoint, which will be built on abandoned rail yards between the municipalities of Charlestown, Somerville, and East Cambridge. The 52-acre site will comprise 5.2 million square feet of residential, office, and retail space; a hotel; and a central park of more than six acres. This project has

View of NorthPoint toward Charlestown.

earned the firm the Urban Design Award from the American Institute of Architects, and it has also been selected for inclusion in the American Institute of Architects *150 Years* book.

One of the firm's most far-reaching projects to date has been the redevel-

opment of Boston's Prudential Center. One of the largest development projects in the city, it includes 1.8 million square feet of office, residential, and retail space. Expansions to the complex, which was originally built in the 1960s, include the Belvedere Condominiums, the Winter Garden, Shaw's Supermarket, two office buildings, 111 Huntington Avenue, 888 Boylston Street, and the Mandarin Hotel and Residences. Each of these new architectural pieces possess a unique identity that gives them presence on the skyline and establishes a strong image of forms joining the Prudential Tower. The redevelopment project proved so successful that CBT and the properties owner, Boston Properties, were honored with the Urban Land Institute Global Award for the Prudential Center.

Another large-scale, mixed-use development project that helped define CBT as one of the premier architectural firms in the area is Columbus Center,

SquashBusters' park-facing exterior.
Photo by Robert Benson

located at the junction of Columbus Avenue and Clarendon Street. This 1.4 million-square-foot urban development spans the Massachusetts Turnpike and includes a signature 34-floor tower that houses a luxury hotel, condominiums, and retail space.

The CBT team has been involved in several other high-profile projects in the Boston area, including Niketown at 200 Newbury Street. The Niketown building proved significant as one of the first new commercial structures erected on the distinguished retail corridor. Although the building is nestled amid masonry row houses that have been converted to retail use, CBT opted not to imitate the style of those surrounding structures. Instead, the new building possesses a dynamic image that's appropriate for a national retailer, yet still compatible within the Back Bay National Historic District.

In addition to these commercial endeavors, CBT has earned accolades for its design, preservation, and renovation work at colleges and universities throughout the region. Among CBT's most remarkable projects is the restoration of the 70-foot spire on Harvard University's Memorial Hall. The spire, which was destroyed in 1956, had been modified twice since it was originally built in 1874. That meant the university and CBT had to choose one of three designs to use as a model for the restoration. CBT conducted extensive research to help the university choose the version that best captured the building's architectural style and sense of history. The complex restoration project received preservation awards from the Massachusetts Historical Commission, Cambridge Historical Commission, and the Victorian Society in America.

However, not all of CBT's academic projects focus on restoration or preservation. Many have involved designing new multi-use facilities, such as the distinctive Badger & Rosen SquashBusters Center at Northeastern

View of 111 Huntington from the Charles River. Photo by Jonathan Hillyer

University. This structure includes separate university and SquashBusters locker rooms, the SquashBusters' administrative offices, a conference room, and tutoring classrooms. Fraught with numerous design challenges, this project highlighted CBT's ability to implement creative solutions to produce a dynamic facility that combines aesthetics and functionality.

There's no denying that CBT has had a dramatic impact on the skyline and streets of Boston and surrounding cities. But, the founders and partners of the firm have also contributed to the region in other ways, as well. Three partners have served as president of the Boston Society of Architecture, and they have served on the design review committee for the Back Bay and

Boston's Landmark Commission, and been active in the Boston Preservation Alliance, and school construction in Winchester, Massachusetts. This community involvement cements their contribution to Boston and the surrounding areas.

Although CBT has earned a strong reputation for its work in the Boston area, it's now recognized for projects that reach far beyond New England. CBT's project list has grown to include an array of large-scale international projects. But, even its work in far-off countries relies on lessons learned in the dense urban centers and ex-urban campuses of the Northeast. By adapting what they've learned from those projects, they've been able to meet the demands of newly emerging commercial districts and historic universities from the Caribbean to the Middle East. International projects include the Puerto Rico Convention Center District, the Waterfront at Pitts Bay Road in Bermuda, the American University in Beirut, and the Docklands in Melbourne, Australia.

Even though the award-winning firm has expanded dramatically in the past four decades, it has held fast to the basic business philosophies and corporate culture the founders instilled back in the 1960s. That explains why some of the firm's first clients are still on the client roster decades later and why so many of CBT's cadre of highly skilled employees have stayed with the firm for years. By focusing on teamwork within the office and taking innovative approaches to the needs of their clients, CBT has distinguished itself in an increasingly competitive field.

EASTERN NAZARENE COLLEGE

Eastern Nazarene College is located immediately south of Boston in historic Quincy, Massachusetts, the birthplace of Presidents John Adams and John Quincy Adams. The college prepares a diverse student body to serve an ever-changing world by combining the best in education and Christian faith. It also combines the advantages of an attractive, park-like suburban campus with the unparalleled opportunities of one of the world's leading academic and cultural centers. ENC, while sponsored by the Church of the Nazarene, serves students from many Christian denominations. Its unique academic and religious atmosphere draws students from all over the United States and several foreign countries.

The forerunner of Eastern Nazarene College, the Pentecostal Collegiate Institute, was established in 1900 in Saratoga Springs, New York. In 1902 the school moved to North Scituate, Rhode Island and operated an elementary school, secondary school, and a Bible training program. In 1918 Eastern Nazarene College was chartered by

Main entrance to Eastern Nazarene College.

the State of Rhode Island, and the following year it moved to Quincy, Massachusetts.

Today's campus is situated on the site of the former Quincy family estate, the same place where Boston Mayor Josiah Quincy erected his summer home in 1846. The Quincy Mansion, later the location of Quincy Mansion

School for Girls, still stood on the property when the college purchased the campus in 1919.

Eastern Nazarene College was rechartered by the Commonwealth of Massachusetts in 1920. The early emphasis of the college was on the training of ministers and Christian workers within a liberal arts context. During the 1930s, however, the curriculum was expanded to include music and teacher training, programs that have been exceptionally strong over the years. Because of a solid liberal arts core curriculum, ENC has trained teachers that have been in great demand not only in Boston area public schools, but also in school districts across the nation. Teacher training remains an important part of ENC's curriculum to this day, and the college offers a variety of undergraduate and graduate programs in education.

The academic character and reputation of the college were forged by an exceptional scholar, Bertha Munro, who served as academic dean from the 1920s through the 1950s. In 1939

Approach to the campus in Quincy, Massachusetts, circa 1920.

her longtime friend and internationally recognized chemist, Dr. James Houston Shrader, joined the faculty. Shrader introduced strong programs in the natural sciences, enabling graduates to gain admission to medical schools and graduate programs. With these new programs, the college was able to offer expanded degree offerings and secure accreditations.

Following World War II, the college experienced a burst of growth. Under the leadership of Edward S. Mann, who served as president for more than two decades, the original buildings were all replaced, a new curriculum was instituted, and a new and credentialed faculty was recruited. The Wollaston Church of the Nazarene was erected on a corner of the campus, which provided chapel facilities for the college. The college also constructed a new classroom building, dormitories for men and women, a student center, an apartment building for students, and a physical education facility.

Prior to World War II, few ENC faculty members had doctorates. Following the war, many veterans

Students gather on the ENC campus in the 1960s.

The administration building, designed by two students, still stands as the campus keystone building.

chose college teaching careers. After earning master's degrees, many more began teaching as instructors while pursuing doctoral studies under the GI Bill. ENC had a substantial number of faculty members who followed this path, and the number of doctorates on the teaching staff increased rapidly during the 1950s and 1960s. Among them was Timothy Smith, who taught at ENC from 1949 to 1954 while he completed his doctorate in history at Harvard. Smith went on to become one of the leading American social and religious historians of his time.

With expanded opportunities in higher education, many ENC graduates embraced the chance to pursue careers in medicine, dentistry, law, and social work. Special campus programs were sponsored by the National Science Foundation in an effort to train public school teachers in science and mathematics. Members of the science faculty conducted significant research and new faculty members were active in professional organizations. Noteworthy in this regard was John S. Ridgen, an ENC graduate who received his Ph.D. in physical chemistry from

Johns Hopkins University and did postdoctoral work in physics at Harvard. From 1961 to 1967 he chaired ENC's Physics Department. Rigden went on to become editor of the *American Journal of Physics*, director of development of the National Science Standards Project at the National Academy of Sciences, and chairman of the History of Physics Forum of the American Physical Society.

Although the college's emphasis was on scholastics, intercollegiate athletics were introduced to the student body in the 1950s. In addition to sports, students also came to enjoy a variety of other pursuits. The drama program became a popular and steadfast fixture at the school, with thousands of people attending the fall and spring student productions. An intercollegiate debate program was established and flourished at the school. From this initial program came the school's first students who went on to attend law school, including Richard Schubert, who went to Yale Law

School and became a top executive for Bethlehem Steel Corp. Schubert has served as U.S. undersecretary of labor, president of the American Red Cross, founding president of the Thousand Points of Light Foundation, chair of the Peter F. Drucker Foundation, and vice chair of the Josephson Institute for the Advancement of Ethics.

Under the leadership of President Cecil Paul, an adult education program was instituted in business administration in 1990. Located initially in an office building several miles from the main campus, the program quickly expanded to offer courses at several sites in Eastern Massachusetts. Eventually, the college secured its own facilities for adult studies about one half mile from the main campus at the site of the former Howard Johnson candy factory. The school renovated the building into a modern educational facility, complete with a day-care center. Once the new facility opened, the adult education program expanded to include graduate programs and additional degrees. With the new site up and running, ENC boasted two

Eastern Nazarene College's A Cappella choir travels widely, and gives a concert at Jordan Hall in Boston annually.

The Cecil R. Paul Center for Business is the home of ENC's Adult and Graduate Studies Division.

campuses. This changed the character of the school in many significant ways. Several departments moved to the new campus, regular day classes were offered in the new facilities, and a shuttle bus service was established to run between the two locations.

An equally significant change came when the undergraduate business program was greatly expanded. What was originally one of the smallest programs is now one of the largest in the college. Other majors adapted successfully to the changing times, such as Communication Arts, which expanded to offer specialization in

Public Relations, Marketing, and Advertising in 2005. Other new majors included Criminal Justice and Contemporary Music and Recording.

As a fully accredited traditional liberal arts college, today Eastern Nazarene College has about 1,200 students enrolled in its residential undergraduate, adult studies, and graduate programs. ENC students enjoy an amazing acceptance rate at top graduate and medical schools and a 100 percent admittance rate into law schools. ENC is known for its wealth of educational, cultural, and service opportunities. Several of ENC's faculty members have established international reputations in their fields, continuing the rich tradition of Timothy Smith and John Rigden. But at ENC the faculty emphasis remains on teaching and mentoring students in a spiritually informed and academically supportive environment. With a solid reputation for cultivating redemptive people who seek to live lives of leadership and service, ENC is poised to embrace its next century of growth and achievement as an important part of greater Boston's educational landscape.

NEWTON-WELLESLEY HOSPITAL

Newton-Wellesley Hospital is located just west of Boston in the City of Newton. The hospital prides itself on its dual nature—an intimate community care center and a cutting edge medical facility. For five out of the past six years, the hospital has been named by Solucient, a nationwide, independent ranking company, as one of the country's 100 Top Hospitals: Benchmarks for Success. Newton-Wellesley sets itself apart by bringing the most advanced medical care to its communities and the surrounding regions, while providing an uncompromising level of service to patients.

Newton-Wellesley Hospital began in 1881 as the vision of Newton's Mayor, Royal Pulsifer, and a local clergyman, the Reverend George Shinn. According to the legend, the men were sitting up late at night, in the home of a dying woman. Weary, they began roaming the town, seeking someone who would keep vigil with the woman and give her comfort. They awakened a neighbor, an Irish woman, and explained the dying woman's plight. Without hesitation, she came to sit with the woman and help her through her final hours.

At this moment, the men realized the need for a hospital in the growing community of Newton. They enlisted local physicians and community leaders, and in January 1881, formed a corporation to create a cottage hospital for Newton. The hospital would be a

Newton Hospital Training School for Nurses: Class of 1896.

The vegetable gardens of the Newton Hospital, pictured with the Haskell-Emerson-Bray-Eldredge surgical wards, at center. The Pratt-Converse Nurses Home is on the hill and the original, 1886, Cottage Hospital to the right. 1898.
Inset: Newton Cottage Hospital: Ward and Administration Building. 1886

small, personal facility where residents would feel comfortable and would provide medical care and comfort to its patients. By 1885 enough support and money was raised from the community to purchase nine acres of land and break ground for the hospital. On June 5, 1886 Newton Cottage Hospital opened its doors. The very first patient was admitted on June 12, 1886. At the time, the Hospital consisted of a clinical ward, an administration building and three employees—a matron, who served as administrator and nurse, a cook/housekeeper and a handyman.

From the beginning, the hospital received support from the city and citizens of Newton. Facilities expanded quickly with the help of major benefactors such as Leeson, Pratt, Converse, Bray, Coburn, Eldredge, Emerson, Haskell, Dennison and other community notables. And the gentlemen weren't the only ones interested in the success of the Hospital. In July 1885 the Ladies Aid Association of Newton Cottage Hospital was founded. Thirty-three women assembled in the parlors of the Eliot Church in Newton. Their immediate goal was to furnish the new hospital. Within a

month, the ladies had raised enough money to pay for half of the beds. Today, this group, now called the Newton-Wellesley Hospital Auxiliary, continues to provide for the hospital, raising funds through projects such as the Thrift Shop, the Hospital Gift Shop, Flower Shop, Mother/Baby Boutique and Coffee Shop.

In 1890 the Cottage Hospital officially became Newton Hospital. Other landmark events for the hospital that year included: its first birth, first ambulance—a horse-drawn carriage—and the graduation of its first nurses from the Newton Hospital Training School for Nurses, which was officially established in 1888. Before it closed in 1986, the Training School would graduate 98 classes and grow into one of the most prestigious nursing institutions in New England. The hospital has long relied on its nursing staff to provide the highest level of medical and personal care to its patients. The Training School provided 3,349 of these high-caliber nurses to the community, country, and profession.

There have been a number of interesting events that have occurred throughout the hospital's history. Academy Award-winning actor Jack Lemmon was born in the south wing elevator in 1925. Eventually, his timing improved considerably, as he starred in numerous comedies. The blizzard of 1978 was a storm-of-the-century, and allowed Newton-Wellesley's true colors to shine. Even in the midst of a disaster, the hospital staff remained calm and collected to take care of their patients, as well as a large number of stranded motorists rescued from nearby Route 128. Despite being stranded in the snowstorm, the staff was able to feed and care for everyone needing assistance over the course of three days.

The hospital, located on mile 17 of the Boston Marathon route, serves as an official medical provider for the historic, national event. The hospital is perfectly positioned to come to the aid of any runner that is experiencing physical difficulty during the race. Newton-Wellesley also offers its assistance before and after the race. Approximately 20 medical professionals work at the hospital tent at the Athlete's Village to take care of runners before the race begins. This includes everything from providing Band-Aids and water as well as more race-specific help, such as instructing

Michael S. Jellinek, M.D., president, Newton-Wellesley Hospital

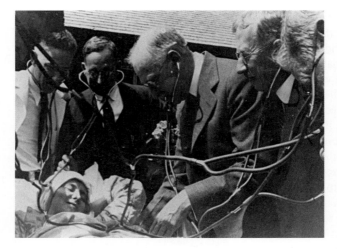

Newton Hospital medical staff, using an Octopus Stethescope, examine a patient. As many as eight physicians could participate at the same time, making this stethescope indispensible for teaching and collaboration. circa 1930.

runners on proper stretching techniques and noting the pre-race weight of runners in case of the potentially life-threatening hyponatremia, or water intoxication. In the days following the Marathon, a team of Newton-Wellesley sports medicine specialists, in conjunction with the Boston Athletic Association, host a Post Marathon Athlete's Injury Clinic to help runners who may have injuries that develop in the days after the race. The Clinic gives athletes immediate access to specialty care for potentially serious problems that may arise during the race, such as stress fractures, so they don't have to wait weeks to see a specialist.

After the 2003 closure of neighboring Waltham Hospital, Newton-Wellesley Hospital saw a considerable increase in the demand for its services. In 2007, to accommodate this increase, the Hospital opened the new Maxwell Blum Emergency Pavilion with twice the number of state-of-the-art adult and pediatric treatment rooms to significantly improve patient wait times. Waiting areas were also expanded to help accommodate family members and keep them closer to patients

receiving treatment. The added space allowed for the addition of diagnostic capabilities within the Emergency Department including CT, X-ray and ultrasound equipment. This reduces the amount of back and forth travel patients must deal with during an emergency situation, reducing treatment time and patient discomfort.

The old Emergency Department space, which originally opened in 1929, will eventually be transformed into a state-of-the-art cancer center, combining Newton-Wellesley's existing Breast Center, which screens for and treats breast cancer, and adding therapeutic treatment for lung, prostate and lymphatic cancer, complete with radiation treatment options. The treatment options offered at the new cancer center will be the best available; the Breast Center already offers the most advanced screening options including digital mammography and computer-assisted diagnostics that help identify and track women that may have an increased genetic disposition to breast cancer.

The hospital keeps up with the changes in technology and uses the latest advancements available. Physicians at Newton-Wellesley prescribe medication through computerized physician order entry (CPOE), which is currently used in only 5 percent of the nation's hospitals. This system ensures proper prescription fulfillment and also automatically checks for improper dosages, possible allergy concerns and drug interactions with other medications that particular patient may be taking. The Hospital is also one of the few in the country to use smart pumps. These devices, which are programmed to check for adverse interactions, are attached to IV pumps to automatically control the dosage given to patients. These technologies help reduce human error and assist the staff with delivering the safest, most effective care possible. Newton-Wellesley is currently planning to implement a bar-coding system to further minimize any chance of human error. With this system, patients' wristbands, nurses, medications and medication pumps will all have a specific barcode. When a physician prescribes medication, all four will be matched in order to quadruple check that the correct patient is getting the correct medication in the correct dose.

In Massachusetts, community healthcare is a collaborative effort. In 1999 Newton-Wellesley Hospital became part of Partners HealthCare System. Brigham and Women's Hospital and Massachusetts General Hospital, both located in Boston, and both part of Partners, work together to bring the very best care and latest technology to their respective patients.

The hospital takes a measured approach to healthcare that includes

The 35,000 square foot Maxwell Blum Emergency Pavilion was opened in January, 2007. With 36 state-of-the-art treatment rooms, it is expected to provide emergency care to 55,000 adult, pediatric and trauma patients each year.

Newton-Wellesley Hospital's campus, 1945. Opened in 1929, the 129-bed South Wing was the first of the Hospital's centralized buildings, and was the last of the Hospital's expansion buildings to be constructed without necessitating demolition of the original cottage wards.

not only top-notch treatment, but also wellness, education and support groups. The Wellness Center at Newton-Wellesley offers exercise and fitness classes that are open to the public such as yoga, Pilates, Tai Chi and many other strength training options. There are also education classes for expectant and new parents and even a sibling preparation class to help children adjust to their growing families. A wide variety

of support groups are available to help people cope with various diseases, disorders and changing life stages. These include groups for diabetics, those suffering from Parkinson's, those dealing with food or substance addiction, those who have lost a loved one as well as myriad other specialized groups.

As Newton-Wellesley grows, its management takes special care to maintain the balance and personalized approach that has long defined the hospital. Members of the management team and other hospital employees take shifts greeting at the front door of the hospital. This gives every member of the staff the opportunity to interact with patients firsthand and offer the highest level of customer care.

Newton-Wellesley Hospital has recently passed an impressive mark—its quasquicentennial, or 125th, founding anniversary. For those past 125 years, Newton-Wellesley has grown and matured along with the changing medical landscape. The hospital has been witness to deadly epidemics and world wars and has seen the rise of antibiotics and rapidly developing medical techniques, from X-rays to MRIs. Through the years, the hospital has continued to meet the community's growing medical needs by offering advanced, comprehensive services while always remaining true to its local roots and values.

EMERSON COLLEGE

Boston is renowned as the center of the academic universe. Colleges and universities abound within city limits, encompassing some of the most revered and respected learning institutions in the United States. Included in this elite group is Emerson College, a unique school that has focused on educating students for professions in communication and the arts since it was founded in 1880.

The school's founder, Charles Wesley Emerson, taught courses in voice, the reading of prose and poetry, Bible and hymn reading, and English literature, among other subjects, at the newly formed Boston Conservatory of Elocution, Oratory, and Dramatic Art. Ten students enrolled in the school's inaugural class, attending their lessons at 13 Pemberton Square.

By 1890 Professor Emerson's now-eponymous school was well on its way to becoming a pioneering institution. Though Emerson has continually challenged the academic status quo and blazed trails in the fields of communica-

View of the Little Building Residence Hall from Boston Common.

The 14-story Ansin Building is the academic and administrative hub of Emerson College and houses its award-winning radio station, WERS-FM.

tions and the arts over the years, its mission has remained intact: to provide educational programs that prepare men and women to assume positions of responsibility and leadership in communications and the arts and to pursue scholarship and creative work that brings innovation and diversity to these disciplines.

Vice President of Public Affairs David Rosen recently elucidated Emerson's approach to academics: "Emerson's curriculum is informed by a set of core values—freedom of expression, diversity of perspective, cultural awareness, integrity, civility, and the responsibilities of ethical choices—and stresses rigorous inquiry and learning based on experience. Emerson College strives to instill in its students a true love of learning, a sense of perspective, and a professional work ethic."

Over the years, Emerson's enrollment has increased to 4,000. The student

body is comprised of 3,100 undergraduate and 900 graduate students who come from nearly every state in the union, as well as 33 foreign countries.

The college is composed of two schools: the School of Communication and the School of the Arts. Both provide top-notch pre-professional instruction in a broad liberal arts context. The curricula of both schools combine theory and practice. Students acquire technical and practical skills while receiving a solid, well-rounded education.

The School of Communication encompasses a wide range of communication forms, with courses of study in marketing communication; organizational and political communication; journalism; and communication sciences and disorders, which includes the fields of speech pathology and audiology. In fact, Emerson has the distinction of being one of the very first colleges in the nation to offer specialized training in these fields, with this program debuting in 1935.

The School of the Arts offers comprehensive and highly regarded programs in visual and media arts (including film), performing arts and writing, literature and publishing.

Above and beyond academic rigor, Emerson and its students have always risen to the challenge of pushing the boundaries of their fields of study, often with historic results. A brief list of some of Emerson's milestones provides insight into American academic history. Emerson was the first college or university in the nation to begin a children's theater program in 1931. The college was also given the first non-commercial FM broadcast license in New England by the FCC in 1941, resulting in radio station WERS. Today, the student-run station is consistently rated one of the top college radio stations in the country by *The Princeton Review* and other organizations. Emerson College was also the first college in the country to offer a graduate program in professional writing and publishing, now a common and valued offering at the most prestigious graduate institutions in the nation.

Personal and professional accomplishments are not the only aims of Emerson students. Community service and outreach figures prominently into campus life, with keen attention focused on helping others. From AIDS and breast cancer awareness campaigns, to tutoring in public schools and winter clothing drives, Emerson students reach out to help others in unique ways. In fact, all of the Greek organizations on campus have only a service or professional focus, indicating the true priorities of the student body.

Campus life also offers a myriad of extra-curricular activities, from traditional collegiate endeavors such as debate club and student government, to uniquely Emersonian activities such as the annual televised "EVVY Award" competition and show that acknowledges student accomplishments, student magazines, Shakespeare society, a recording organization, and a screenwriting club. The college is also an NCAA Division III school, with sports teams for soccer, lacrosse, basketball, baseball, softball, volleyball, crosscountry, and tennis.

Emerson College also has strong comedy training, another distinct

Student disc jockey hosts music program at Emerson College's award winning radio station, WERS (88.9FM).

The landmark Cutler Majestic Theatre at Emerson College was fully restored to its original glory in 2003.

feature of its curriculum. The school has specialized classes in comedy writing and stand-up comedy, and a small group of students can be seen regularly frequenting the comedy clubs in Boston and New York City.

The school is also developing the American Comedy Archives, the first and only collection of comedy materials housed at an academic institution for the purpose of helping students, faculty, and alumni explore the history, meaning, and application of comedy as an art form. The growing collection currently includes film, videotapes, and memorabilia as well as approximately 60 original oral history interviews with some of the most influential American comic voices. These comedians are captured on film, explaining points of interest such as how they got into comedy or the mechanics of what makes something funny. Emerson counts comic luminaries Jay Leno, Denis

Leary, Anthony Clark, Laura Kightlinger, Steven Wright, Henry Winkler, and Doug Herzog (the president and CEO of Comedy Central) among its alums. In 2006 Leary, Clark, Wright and other comic alumni performed at Emerson to celebrate the 30th anniversary of Emerson's student comedy club (the Emerson Comedy Workshop) and to raise money for the college's scholarship fund.

These Emerson alumni are joined by a host of other graduates who have made a name for themselves in their respective fields. Emerson College served as the early training ground for television notables such as Norman Lear, who created groundbreaking shows like *All in the Family*; Kevin Bright, co-creator and executive producer of the show *Friends*; Max Mutchnick, co-creator and executive producer of *Will & Grace*; and Vin Di Bona, creator and executive producer of *America's Funniest Home Videos*.

The Emerson network spans both coasts. At least 2,200 alumni live in the Los Angeles area. Sometimes referred to as the "Emerson Mafia," the West Coast alumni group helps recent graduates find entertainment industry jobs across all levels of production, from behind-the-scenes work and writing, to on-camera jobs and post-production.

Los Angeles is also the site of Emerson's extended campus, a locale where students can take night classes and learn about the entertainment industry through daytime internships. Each semester, approximately 90 students, mostly seniors, travel to L.A. to learn about the industry firsthand. According to David Rosen, most go with the goal of never returning to the East Coast. He notes that they often succeed, having found the connections and opportunities they need to begin their entertainment careers.

Students also have an opportunity to take a semester abroad at Kasteel Well, an authentic 12th century castle in the Netherlands that serves as Emerson's European campus. The castle comes complete with beautiful gardens and moats and sits close to the German border near Dusseldorf. Each semester, about 100 students venture across the Atlantic to explore European history, culture, language, and art. Students take one major learning excursion during the semester to a historic European locale.

The women's basketball team practices in the college's new gymnasium.

Students celebrate winning an award at the annual EVVY competition, modeled after the Emmy Awards.

Emerson College continues to evolve in many ways. The college's curriculum is adapting to the changing modes of communication and the arts. David Rosen indicates that the rise of the internet has had an enormous impact on Emerson. "We now have programs called new media," he says. "This encompasses areas such as Web development, video game development, software programs and applications such as Second Life, and the online 3D virtual world."

"More broadly," he continues, "digital technology has had a very positive effect at the school." It is now a cornerstone of Emerson College's film program, transforming the art form and opening up new ways to teach the subject.

"Emerson has really capitalized on technology to stay at the forefront," Rosen says. "We built three new TV studios, all of which utilize new digital equipment." The DiBona production studio in the Tufte Performance and Production Center is comparable to any national broadcasting set-up. In fact, Rosen recounts an anecdote about a professional cameraman on a tour of the school's facilities. The gentleman, who worked for the news division of one of the big three networks, was blown away by the facilities and

equipment and said, "Geez, we've got to get something like this (at our network)!"

The cutting edge facilities are not merely on hand to impress, however. Rosen notes that the benefits students gain are twofold. Not only do they have the opportunity to learn on the highest-quality equipment and facilities, but they are also ahead of the learning curve when seeking jobs in their respective fields.

Since the early 1990s, the Emerson campus has seen a Renaissance as it has relocated all of its facilities from the staid Back Bay neighborhood of Boston to the city's bustling Theatre District. A decade before the relocation began in earnest, the college acquired the historic Majestic Theatre at 219 Tremont Street. The theater, built in 1903, has received a full face-lift and restoration. This effort has yielded much acclaim, including an impressive award from the National Trust for Historic Preservation. The theater reopened in 1989 and was later renamed the Cutler Majestic Theatre at Emerson College. It serves as a learning center and performance space for both

The new Piano Row Residence Hall and Max Mutchnick Campus Center houses 560 students and provides space for a variety of student activities and organizations.

Emerson students and professional performing artists.

From 1992 to 2006 Emerson purchased and renovated four additional buildings in the Theatre District and built two new structures—the 14-story Piano Row Residence Hall and Max Mutchnick Campus Center and the

Emerson students relax on the grounds of historic Boston Common, which serves as an extension of the Emerson campus.

10-story Tufte Performance and Production Center. The state-of-of-the art facilities inside these buildings were designed with Emerson's distinctive curriculum and student body in mind. Today, for the first time ever, Emerson has a fully contiguous campus. It overlooks historic Boston Common and is a stone's throw from the fabled Boston Public Gardens.

In 2007 Emerson College began the final component of its expansion plan. The Paramount Center on lower Washington Street will include a fully renovated Paramount Theatre, a new black box theater, multiple rehearsal rooms, a film screening room, and a student residence hall. Plans also include yet another residence hall, which will open in the Colonial Building on Boylston Street.

The growth is a tacit acknowledgement of the school's increasing national visibility and reputation. Enrollment at Emerson has increased substantially in recent years, bolstered by the growing market in communications fields, world-class facilities, outstanding faculty, and a practical approach to education. The college has recently incorporated more business-minded classes into its regular curriculum to give students

even more practical knowledge to support their career aspirations.

However, the positive impact of Emerson's growth is not only a boon to the school community. Emerson's success translates into success for the city of Boston, as Emerson's campus, students, and activities cross over into the city's cultural scene. The revamping of the city's Theatre District owes a lot to the efforts of Emerson College.

The next step for Emerson, according to David Rosen, is to take time to

An Emerson student works the controls during a production in the Di Bona Television Studio.

incorporate change. "Over the next decade, the rate of growth and expansion will slow," Rosen explains. "The college will consolidate its gains and build on its historical and new strengths."

Yet beyond the success of the school, its expansion, and forays into new media, the true testament to the success of Emerson College has always been its students and alumni. "Our kids are not daunted by anything," Rosen says. "They aren't afraid of failing or falling, and sometimes they do," he continues. "But more often than not, they succeed because they have an uncanny ability to just go out there and do it." This ability is clearly fostered by Emerson College.

EMMANUEL COLLEGE

Emmanuel College is a coed, residential Catholic liberal arts and sciences college surrounded by the excitement, resources and culture of Boston. Founded by the Sisters of Notre Dame de Namur in 1919, Emmanuel's 17-acre campus is in the heart of the Longwood Medical and Academic Area, and is neighbored by world-class medical institutions, two major art museums and historic Fenway Park.

The Sisters of Notre Dame de Namur were founded in 1804 by St. Julie Billiart with the mission of the education of youth, especially the poor. It was Sister Helen Madeleine Ingraham, SND who continued that mission more than 100 years later in Boston, where she helped to found Emmanuel College. Emmanuel was the first Catholic women's college in

New England, opened at a time when women were yet to have the constitutional right to vote and young, working-class women did not often attend liberal arts colleges. The result was a new group of educated women who would be in leadership roles in many professions.

Sister Janet Eisner, SND, the president of the college, is an Emmanuel graduate, and has led the college for more than 25 years. Sister Janet first attended Saint Mary's High School in Lynn, Massachusetts, became a novice with the Sisters of Notre Dame, and then received her bachelor of arts from Emmanuel. She also holds a master of arts from Boston College and a Ph.D. in English from the University of Michigan. Sister Janet came back to Emmanuel first as the director of admissions and later as a member of

the English department faculty. She became president of the college in 1979.

Emmanuel has gone through many changes during Sister Janet's time as a student, faculty member and administrator, but the educational mission of the college has remained its foundation. As president, Sister Janet has led the college through challenging times, including declining enrollment. To address these challenges Sister Janet evaluated ways in which the college could improve its position, including the development of graduate and professional programs, a strategy to use real estate to its advantage, and

The Jean Yawkey Center at Emmanuel College with Merck Research-Laboratories Boston in the background.

eventually, a plan to become a coeducational institution in 2001.

"Even when—especially when—trends were working against us, we made decisions that would enable this college to thrive in the long term," says Sister Janet. "It required patience and taking the long view." The tremendously successful results of their long-term strategy become clearer every year.

In 1996 another key initiative launched which helped further the college's plan to increase enrollment and thrive in the 21st century—the Colleges of the Fenway (COF) consortium. It was Sister Janet's vision to bring together a group of six neighboring colleges in an effort to enhance the educational experience of students and to slow down the escalating costs of higher education. Her mission was to enable Emmanuel students to utilize the resources of the

Emmanuel's historic Administration Building on The Fenway.

Boston educational community to their advantage, an area in which she used her incredible skills of bringing talents together to serve the greater student good.

Equally important, the consortium offered a solution to the dramatically increasing financial costs associated with higher education, which would have otherwise curtailed the educational programs any single school could offer students. By joining together, the six schools make it possible for an Emmanuel student, for example, to attend classes at any of the other five institutions for full credit. It also made available the facilities of each school, including libraries, athletic facilities, and art studios to a total student enrollment of more than 10,000. Today, the six colleges offer their students 2,500 courses at no additional cost, and boast 800 full-time faculty. In addition to Emmanuel, the other colleges include the Massachusetts College of Art, the Massachusetts College of Pharmacy and Health Sciences, Wentworth Institute of Technology, Wheelock College, and Simmons College.

The Jean Yawkey Center is the "living room" of the college's campus.

Emmanuel College students prepare for a day of service in the city of Boston.

In order to support its educational mission, Emmanuel also looked for ways to better use its resources, particularly real estate. One phase of this plan was to identify a section of the college's property which could become an "endowment campus"—land that could be leased to an outside concern and afford the college additional resources.

In this area, Sister Janet possesses what seems to be an almost innate, intuitive sense about education, finances, and real estate, which could easily make her a formidable force in the lay business world. A testament to her tremendous entrepreneurial skills and vision for Emmanuel's strategy was evident in her work to bring pharmaceutical giant Merck Research Laboratories to the Emmanuel campus. In October of 2001 Merck broke ground on the Emmanuel campus, constructing its largest state-of-the art research facility to date.

This partnership has provided unprecedented educational opportunities for Emmanuel students. Merck scientists regularly lecture at Emmanuel and have created a paid summer internship program solely for Emmanuel science students. And with the laboratories' goals of developing treatments for all diseases that currently lack effective cures, including cancer and AIDS, students are exposed to some of the most cutting edge developments in scientific research.

The college's transition to coeducation has had extremely positive results. This move drove enrollment to its highest levels ever, which in turn more than doubled the college's faculty. Currently, Emmanuel, with an endowment of $80 million, has a total of 1,600 traditional undergraduate and 750 graduate and professional students enrolled, representing 24 countries and 32 states.

In 2002 Emmanuel inaugurated the Carolyn A. Lynch Institute, a collaborative initiative of the college and the Lynch Foundation to develop and retain teachers in the urban school setting and to train teachers in math and the sciences.

"With the resources of the Carolyn A. Lynch Institute, Emmanuel has developed a model program demonstrating how a college in partnership with local public and parochial schools can contribute to the quality of urban education and in the process improve the lives of students," stated Sister Janet.

In 2004 Emmanuel opened the new Jean Yawkey Center, which houses the Maureen Murphy Wilkens Atrium, named in honor of one of Emmanuel's graduates and donors; student meeting rooms; dining facilities; classrooms; a fitness center; as well as an NCAA regulation-sized gym with a seating capacity of 1,400. A generous gift from the Yawkey Foundation, in part, made the new Center a reality, and it was named in honor of the late philanthropist Jean Yawkey.

The Center also houses the Jean Yawkey Center for Community Leadership, which in Sister Janet's words, "enables Emmanuel College to build upon a strong foundation of service and further its volunteer efforts. The Jean Yawkey Center is the 'living room' of the College, providing a place where the community can gather for many activities and it is the focal point for community outreach."

Emmanuel is also in the planning stages for a new Academic Science Center, which will hold 12 laboratories, including 10 teaching and two research labs, and five class-rooms. The new Science Center brings with it the added benefit of an expanded science faculty, as well as creating a research facility whose results could potentially benefit the health of people around the world. The College is also restoring and renovating its large Administrative Building, adding new classrooms and facitlies.

More than just a college, Emmanuel is a community that provides educational opportunities and spiritual support in a complex and ever-changing society. At its core is the Emmanuel College Chapel. From the moment students first attended Emmanuel College many years ago the Chapel has been a place of celebration and reflection. Students once celebrated graduation in the Chapel, alumni have married, and together students and faculty continue to worship there.

The mission of Emmanuel's Campus Ministry is deeply rooted in the teachings of the Catholic Church. Through core religious values such as prayer and sacraments, exceptional educational programs and a vast array of community service opportunities, Emmanuel's goals are to enrich the spiritual lives of its students and help them to build a stronger relationship with God and the world in which they live.

Community service is strongly emphasized in the lives of Emmanuel students and provides a powerful learning experience through myriad opportunities.

As soon as they arrive on the campus, all incoming Emmanuel students learn about service opportunities in Boston during "Welcome Week." On Orientation Service Day, these students serve at various Boston nonprofit organiza-

Sister Janet Eisner, SND, Emmanuel College president.

tions including The Greater Boston Food Bank, Charles River Conservancy, St. Francis House, Project Hope, and the Franklin Park Zoo. Students are also given many opportunities throughout the year to participate in a number of charitable events including the Boston Breast Cancer Walk, Walk for Hunger, MS Walk for Life and Charles River Clean-Up on Earth Day. An astounding 85 percent of Emmanuel's students participate in community service programs.

One of the more popular community service programs at Emmanuel is Alternative School Break, a weeklong service project for which students live in a communal setting helping them to bond with each other and with the culture in which they are serving. In 2007, 49 students and staff members dedicated a week to volunteer service in Phoenix, Arizona and New Orleans, Louisiana.

In Emmanuel's traditional undergraduate division, students can earn bachelor of arts, bachelor of fine arts,

and bachelor of science degrees. As part of its graduate & professional programs, Emmanuel offers a bachelor of science in nursing, and the bachelor of science in business administration degree. Graduate degrees awarded include the master of arts in teaching, master of education in school administration, master of science in management, and master of science in human resource management. Emmanuel also offers a certificate program, the graduate certificate in human resource management.

Emmanuel continues its mission to educate anyone who seeks to improve their life, no matter their financial status. More than 75 percent of Emmanuel students receive need-based financial aid.

Studying at Emmanuel is about much more than attending classes and taking tests to attain a degree. "We challenge our students to act, to lead, and to give generously to others," comments Sister Janet. "We believe education is inclusive and that the world of ideas demands diversity. And we most definitely believe in the transformative power of real-world experience, through internships, through the sophisticated resources available in Boston's learning community and in service learning and opportunities abroad."

The mission of Emmanuel College has always been at the core of every major decision and development at the college. Throughout its history there has been a deep commitment to enhancing and improving the Emmanuel experience and to transforming the lives of its students.

"We have always been much more than our buildings," states Sister Janet. "What makes Emmanuel great, what has always made us great, is our people and the relationship among us, our dedication to enriching the educational and spiritual lives of our students and our commitment and service to the community beyond."

LOWELL GENERAL HOSPITAL

For more than a century, Lowell General Hospital has built a strong tradition of medical innovation and compassionate caring to meet the healthcare needs of the Merrimack Valley. Built for the people and by the people of Lowell, the history of the hospital is intricately woven with the history of the city and its residents.

Throughout the 1800s the city of Lowell's industrial textile mills attracted immigrants from across the globe. However, by 1890, the same mills that had garnered prosperity for Lowell earlier, had severely degenerated. Mill owners exploited immigrants as a source of cheap labor and were responsible for crowded working and living conditions that offered a breeding ground for transmission of disease.

Although two hospitals existed in Lowell, one had deep religious affiliations, while Lowell Corporation Hospital, a private facility, treated only industrial and mill workers. After being reprimanded by Lowell Corporation Hospital for treating a non-employee, physician and surgeon Lorenzo S. Fox decided it was time to create a new hospital that would serve the entire community.

Fox joined forces with Larkin Thorndyke Trull, a prominent Lowell attorney, and 50 local doctors and philanthropic-minded citizens to form the Lowell Free Hospital Association, which ultimately became Lowell General Hospital Corporation. On July 16, 1891, Lowell businessman James K. Fellows was inspired to purchase the 12.5-acre estate of the Samuel Fay family in the Pawtucketville section of Lowell for the sum of $30,000. This parcel of land was donated to the Lowell General Hospital Corporation and is the location of the hospital's main campus to the present day.

On July 20, 1893, Lowell General Hospital opened its doors to patients. The Lowell General Hospital Training School for Nurses opened that same year, with its first nursing class comprised

Graduates of the Lowell General Hospital Training School for Nurses made integral contributions to the development of the hospital. Photo, circa 1970.

of eight students. After more than 90 years of producing the best and brightest nurses in the area, the Lowell General Hospital Training School for Nurses closed its doors in the 1980s. Graduates from the School for Nurses have played a pivotal role in the development of healthcare throughout the region and many continue to serve as valued employees at LGH.

Throughout the years, Lowell General Hospital has continued to grow and change to meet the needs of the community, transforming from a modest community hospital into a regional medical center of excellence.

Today, the hospital has expanded to 10 buildings on the original site, including the Hanchett Building, donated in 1937 by Frank Hanchett, and the Mansfield Pavilion, completed in 1974. The LGH campus spreads far beyond Lowell, however, with satellite locations in Chelmsford and Westford. As the hospital develops its facilities, it continually expands programs and services to meet the specialized needs of all ages, from prenatal care to end-of-life care.

Lowell General is committed to

leading the way in introducing new services and opportunities to the 250,000 residents of Greater Lowell, serving as a model of excellence for other community hospitals. Over the past 20 years, in particular, LGH has aggressively sought to bring much-needed services to the region, from a 24-hour Trauma Center to a Pain Management Center to a Sleep Lab and Neurodiagnostic Center.

LGH took a major step in cardiac care in 1991 with the opening of the area's first cardiac catheterization laboratory. New hope was brought to area cardiac patients in 2003 with the implementation of enhanced external counterpulsation (EECP) therapy, providing non-surgical treatment for relief of angina and circulatory conditions. In 2004 Lowell General Hospital became the first hospital in the community approved to provide primary angioplasty, a life-saving emergency procedure to open blocked arteries with a balloon-tipped catheter and metal mesh stent. Two years later LGH became the first community hospital in Massachusetts (under the MASS COMM clinical trial) to successfully perform non-emergency angioplasty, a lifesaving procedure that can stop a heart attack before it happens.

Today, the hospital is bringing cardiac care in the region to a new level with a multi-million dollar expansion of The Heart Center at Lowell General Hospital. With multiple new state-of-the-art cardiac catheterization suites, and a 64-slice cardiac CT scan, The Heart Center will provide some of the most advanced cardiac testing and treatment procedures north of Boston.

Since 1893 LGH has been the Merrimack Valley's most trusted birthing center, bringing more healthy babies into the world than any other hospital in the region. What was once a simple maternity ward has expanded into The Regional Center for Maternal and Pediatric Care at Lowell General Hospital in partnership with Tufts-New

England Medical Center and Floating Hospital for Children. Bringing Boston-level care directly to the residents of the Merrimack Valley and southern New Hampshire, The Birthplace at Lowell General delivers nearly 2,000 babies each year and offers parents the advantage of the community's only Level II Special Care Nursery and a direct link to Tufts-NEMC/Floating Hospital. The Birthplace and The Children's Place, a family-centered inpatient unit for children and adolescents, are staffed by Tufts-NEMC/Floating specialists 24 hours-a-day, seven days-a-week.

In 1998 the Greater Lowell community welcomed The Cancer Center at Lowell General Hospital, a cutting-edge treatment facility that has brought advanced outpatient care, hope, and support to area patients living with cancer. In 2002 The Cancer Center introduced positron emission tomography (PET), bringing the premier technology for diagnosing cancer to the people of Greater Lowell. With the implementation of intensity modulated radiation therapy (IMRT) in 2006, patients at The Cancer Center

Past and present coexist in Lowell General Hospital's eclectic architectural design and long-standing commitment to community service.

now have access to state-of-the-art radiation treatment that offers a stronger, more individualized defense against hard-to-reach cancer.

In 2007 The Cancer Center expanded its facility to accommodate additional patient treatment areas, and to provide an array of services under one roof. With participation in clinical trials and the addition of multidisciplinary clinics providing patients with more encompassing care, The Cancer Center provides the most comprehensive cancer care in the Greater Lowell area.

The area's newest state-of-the-art Endoscopy Center opened at Lowell General Hospital in 2003. Using endoscopy, physicians can make a visual examination of areas inside the body, without invasive surgery. Among other vital uses, endoscopy can help detect and screen for colon cancer and diagnose and treat stomach and gastrointestinal problems.

The expansion of space and services continued into 2007 with the creation of Lowell General Hospital at Chelmsford. Conveniently located minutes from Routes 3 and 495, the campus includes medical facilities at 10 Research Place, containing The Surgery Center— the only day-surgery center in the area— The Center for Wound Healing, a Patient Service Center for testing and x-rays, and physician offices. The newest addition to the LGH at Chelmsford campus is 20 Research Place, which houses a variety of physician offices, as well as The Center for Weight Management and Bariatric Surgery, and outpatient clinics for The Regional Center for Maternal and Pediatric Care. Also in Chelmsford, The Women's Imaging Center provides a convenient and peaceful environment where women can have annual mammograms, bone density testing and other diagnostics specific to women.

With each new day LGH seeks new opportunities to bring state-of-the-art healthcare to its patients. Today,

Lowell General at Chelmsford, which is in close proximity to The Women's Imaging Center, includes The Surgery Center and The Patient Service Center.

surgeons at Lowell General use computer-aided, image-guided navigational surgery that works like the global positioning system (GPS) in a car, telling surgeons exactly where they are in a patient's anatomy and giving them the ability to "see" on a computer where they need to go and navigate instruments exactly to the site of disease or problem.

Radiologists can attack a cancer tumor from inside the body without medicating or affecting other parts of the body, using embolization and radiofrequency heat to cut off the blood supply and "kill" the tumor.

These advancements of today are paving the way for the innovations of tomorrow at Lowell General Hospital. During the more than 100 years that Lowell General Hospital has served the Merrimack Valley, technology and capabilities have constantly changed. However, the commitment to provide quality, comprehensive, compassionate medical care to all the people of the community remains the constant factor in the continuing legacy of Lowell General Hospital.

Then, as now, the core mission of Lowell General Hospital stands strong and unwavering for the community it serves.

McCARTER & ENGLISH, LLP

The Boston office of McCarter & English, LLP is a tale of two cities, two law firms, and a shared vision. The firm was established in 1844 in New Jersey and moved to Newark to meet the needs of the burgeoning industrial economy that existed after the Civil War. In 2006 the Boston law firm Gadsby Hannah LLP joined forces with McCarter. With a reputation for "hitting above its weight," Gadsby brought to McCarter the heritage of its founders: Paul Hannah, chief of staff for General MacArthur while in Japan from 1945 to 1946, and Edward Gadsby, chairman of the Securities and Exchange Commission from 1957 to 1961. These distinguished legacies have enhanced and strengthened a culture of exceptional advocacy, unparalleled client service, and commitment to community and country. Today, McCarter has over 400 lawyers in eight East Coast offices, including Boston, Hartford, Stamford, New York City, Newark, Philadelphia,

The McCarter & English, LLP Boston office overlooks the Rose Fitzgerald Kennedy Greenway and Boston Harbor.

Wilmington, and Baltimore. The firm serves people and companies facing complex, global issues and day-to-day business disputes and transactions, offering pragmatic advice, negotiating successful transactions, and defending them with passion.

From its earliest roots, the firm has represented an array of interesting and diverse clients. Around the turn of the century, Annie Oakley, the famous

McCarter partners are joined by City of Boston Mayor Thomas M. Menino. From left to right: Andrew Berry, Leonard Lewin, Mayor Thomas Menino, Lois Van Deusen, and McCarter special counsel, Paul Cellucci, who is a former Ambassador to Canada and Governor of Massachusetts.

sharpshooter of Buffalo Bill Cody's Wild West Show, turned to McCarter for help. When a local newspaper reprinted a story from Chicago accusing her of some scandalous conduct, she sued the paper for libel. One of the founders of the firm, Conover English, took the case to trial opposite William Edwards, an es-teemed veteran trial lawyer. As Conover told the story to his son, Nicholas English, Oakley testified as the plaintiff and "made a monkey out of old Billy Edwards when he tried to cross-examine her because she was too smart." Oakley won the case, an apology, and a $3,000 damages award.

Another prized client, Thomas Edison, was considered by Conover English to be one of the best witnesses he ever put on the stand. At the time he became a regular client of the firm, Edison was already hugely successful and headed a multimilllion-dollar business empire. On the witness stand,

The Boston Convention and Exposition Center, a state-of-the art facility constructed by McCarter client, the Massachusetts Convention Center Authority.

Edison could turn his partial deafness to his own advantage: "If he didn't want to answer a question," Conover would recall, "he could always say he didn't hear it." While the question was repeated, "he would think up a superb answer which would demolish the opposition."

Combining its own storied accomplishments with entrepreneurial energy, Gadsby Hannah brought an equally impressive legacy to McCarter in Boston. Clients include major universities, public authorities, financial institutions, major retail chains, and a wide array of businesses and executives in energy, hightech, healthcare, and other industries. The firm maintains a nationally recognized construction practice and regularly staffs trial and transactional teams with lawyers who have engineering degrees and a deep knowledge of construction and engineering projects. As an example, in July 2006, on the eve of deliberations before a Boston jury, engineering and design firms agreed to pay the Massachusetts Convention Center Authority (MCCA), a McCarter client, a combined sum of $24,000,000 for deficient work involved in the design of the massive new Boston Convention and Exhibition Center in South Boston. The case centered on claims that deficient work and design errors increased the cost of the project. "We are obviously very pleased with the settlement in this case and feel strongly that McCarter's formidable construction and engineering experience put us in an advantageous position both before and during the trial," said Jim Rooney, executive director of the MCCA. "In my 30 years of service with public authorities, I cannot recall a more favorable settlement."

Many of McCarter's lawyers in Boston are "home grown" from all corners of the city and its neighborhoods. The firm's lawyers devote their efforts to a wide variety of charitable and civic endeavors to give something back to the community. Many donate their time or serve on the boards of local organizations. A small sample includes: Friends of the Shattuck Shelter, for Boston's homeless; the Woman's Lunch Place, a daytime refuge for women and children in the Back Bay; the Sofia Snow Place, for Boston area seniors; and the North Bennett Street School, devoted to teaching and preserving traditional crafts. In addition, McCarter has a nationally recognized pro bono program and recently received the Beacon of Justice Award from the National Legal Aid & Defender Association for its pro bono work on behalf of Guantanamo detainees.

Looking to the future, in its offices overlooking Boston Harbor, McCarter & English embodies the rich tradition and history of the city with the creative exuberance of its huge student population and thriving entrepreneurial markets. Traditional practice areas such as Business and commercial litigation, insurance coverage, intellectual property, mergers and acquisitions and real estate are combined with cutting edge initiatives in climate change and renewable resources and public strategies. Whether harnessing cleaner fuel for the future, perfecting new construction techniques, facilitating trade around the globe, or discovering the latest technological advances, McCarter's clients are changing the way we live. McCarter & English lawyers take special pride in helping their great clients do great things.

SUFFOLK UNIVERSITY

Suffolk University is as vibrant and forward-looking an institution today as it was when it was founded in 1906 with the then-novel idea of giving non-privileged people a chance to improve their lives through education. From its earliest incarnation, Suffolk University was seen as offering a beacon of hope to immigrants and working people seeking higher education.

University founder Gleason Archer hailed from rural Maine and worked his way through college and law school. In 1906, shortly after passing the bar, Archer began teaching law to working men in his home in the evenings. His mission was unusual for the time—to provide access to professional higher education to those with limited time and financial resources.

From the start, Suffolk was a school that embraced a diverse student population. Immigrants, people of African and Asian descent, Native Americans, and women found a place at the university at a time when they were not welcome at long-established schools. As the university continues into its second century, it remains true to its original

As a young attorney who had pursued his education with the help of a benefactor, Gleason Archer wanted to help others in turn. He practiced law by day and turned his home into a classroom for working people by night.

mission of offering access to excellence for all deserving students.

Three academic units now make up Suffolk University, which serves more than 8,700 students. The university's College of Arts and Sciences, Sawyer Business School, and Suffolk Law School offer rich and varied curricula. Collaboration among these schools adds depth and resonance to the efforts of each department and faculty member.

The College of Arts and Sciences was founded as an evening school in 1934. Today, it offers more than 70 programs of study at the undergraduate and graduate levels

through 17 academic departments. The college's 38 post-graduate courses of study include two doctoral programs.

In 1996 the New England School of Art & Design became part of the college. The school offers students a high-quality art and design program supported by the extensive resources of a major urban university.

The college curriculum allows students to develop specialized knowledge and skills, while giving them time to explore minor programs that reflect their personal interests and talents. Through internships, service learning, and a broad range of extra-curricular activities, students can combine their academic interests with hands-on experience. And, innovative programming such as the Distinguished Visiting Scholars Program brings some of the most formidable minds in the world today into the university community.

In 1937 the College of Business Administration welcomed its first students, offering a curriculum that combined academic theory with practical skills. Now, as the Sawyer Business School, it has broadened its focus to encompass both global business and public service. The school's outstand-

The Suffolk Law School building on Beacon Hill was topped with an enormous electric sign in the 1920s. Legend has it that the sign caused some consternation among Harvard University partisans associated with the nearby Massachusetts State House.

The Suffolk University Student Council of 1939-1940 included representatives of the Suffolk Law School, the College of Liberal Arts, and the School of Business Administration.

ing international faculty brings un-precedented experience and research to the classroom, and students are offered many opportunities for international study or internships.

The business school offers innovative programs in business and in public administration. Nine undergraduate majors are offered, and graduate programs lead to more than a dozen advanced degrees, including joint degree programs with the law school.

Within 20 years of its founding, Suffolk Law School was the largest evening law school in the United States. Today, the university's law school graduates make up nearly 2 percent of all lawyers in America—and every day they make positive contributions to their profession and to the nation.

The law school offers Juris Doctor and Master of Laws degrees. Its expansive curriculum combines a strong academic foundation with expertise in an array of specialty areas. Nationally known faculty and a range of practical experiences provide superior preparation for law practices in the 21st century.

President David J. Sargent has led Suffolk during a period of dynamic growth, during which it has been transformed from a commuter school to a major global university.

Suffolk Madrid students gather at the Cathedral of Salamanca, Spain during a regional tour.

The law school also brings legal education to the wider world through a pioneering partnership with the Massachusetts Supreme Judicial Court, which broadcasts its oral arguments live through the school's website.

Under the leadership of President David J. Sargent, the university has strengthened and expanded its

academic programs. Suffolk stays on the vanguard of technology by providing state-of-the-art campus facilities and a faculty that makes the most of high-tech tools in the classroom and online. The university also has solidified its longstanding commitment to superior instruction with the founding of the Center for Teaching Excellence.

The Suffolk faculty is recognized for strong scholarship, innovative teaching techniques, and the ability to bring out the very best in each student. Faculty and administrators take pride in creating a personal, student-centered academic environment where students are known by name. They take the time to recognize each student's promise, raise his or her expectations, and build important mentoring relationships. A general emphasis on small classes and personal attention demonstrates the institutional commitment to ensuring that all students maximize their educational experiences.

Generations of remarkable students have found a purpose at Suffolk University. They have gone on to leadership roles in law, business, public service, science, and the arts, achieving success while remaining committed to the greater good.

The global institution of today is led by a man who, like the university's founder, hails from a small New England town and has used his intellectual gift to better the lives of others. President David J. Sargent has enjoyed a lengthy history with Suffolk University that began during his student days at the law school. He holds the rare distinction of serving his alma mater as professor, scholar, law school dean, and president.

Sargent studied pre-law courses at the University of New Hampshire and was the first in his family to attend college. He went on to Suffolk Law School, where he was president of his class, graduated magna cum laude in 1954, and ranked number one.

Sargent soon gained a reputation as an accomplished trial lawyer, specializing in litigation and labor law. He returned to Suffolk Law School as an adjunct professor in 1956 and soon was promoted through the ranks to professor of law. Sargent was a popular and engaging teacher, specializing in wills, trusts, and torts.

Suffolk University's campus is in the heart of Boston, offering easy access to the city's cultural, government, business, and legal institutions.

Commencement at Suffolk Dakar is a colorful affair in the tropics of West Africa. Students graduating after two years of study may transfer their credits to an American university. Many Dakar graduates have completed their educations and emerged as top students at Suffolk's Boston campus.

The nation called upon Sargent's scholarship during the 1960s and 1970s as it engaged in an intense debate on tort reform. He traveled across the country to lecture on this subject, testifying before legislative committees in 30 states as well as before the United States Congressional Committee. Sargent also served as chairman of the Massachusetts Chief Justice Commission on Court Reform.

From 1972 to 1989, Sargent directed Suffolk Law School as dean and significantly strengthened its curricula and national reputation during this dynamic period in the school's history. Sargent assumed the university presidency in 1989 and has presided over a time of tremendous growth.

While Suffolk's downtown Boston location initially served as a convenient spot for commuters and workers, the university's reputation for excellence spread, and students from across the nation and around the world were attracted to its urban setting. Under Sargent's tenure, Suffolk University has been transformed from a commuter-based institution to a major urban university with a full complement of resident life services for a diverse student population.

The university now offers students the opportunity to live in affordable, safe, on-campus housing. Suffolk University opened the doors of its first residence hall on Tremont Street in 1996. The 11-story residence hall overlooks Boston Common and features incredible views of the Boston skyline. It allows students to immerse themselves in the fuller and richer educational experience offered by a residential campus. A second residence hall opened in August 2003, offering views from a Beacon Hill skyscraper over the State House's Golden Dome to the Charles River and Boston Common.

Under Sargent's leadership, a spectacular law school building was constructed, and a grateful university community named it for him. Most recently, the university acquired the Rosalie K. Stahl Center at 73 Tremont Street and built a stunning new library on three levels of the building.

Innovation and change have been the hallmarks of Sargent's tenure, yet he has stayed true to the university's original mission. Today Suffolk has a diverse student body with students from around the world and of all economic and cultural backgrounds. The school that 100 years ago brought new possibilities to Boston-area working people now provides world-wide access to an excellent education.

While the university was focused on Boston for many years, today it embraces a global vision. Suffolk is engaged in the globalization of student learning and experience and offers higher education opportunity beyond our nation's borders. Course offerings and teaching reflect the emphasis on international education, and students may take advantage of partnerships with institutions around the world. Moreover, Suffolk campuses in Dakar, Senegal and Madrid, Spain open the doors to learning for many overseas students.

In 1995 Suffolk established a campus in Madrid and began a partnership with the people of Spain that has been productive for both American and European students. The Suffolk Madrid campus attracts students from Europe,

The university's theatre department has won many national accolades for both its student actors and productions. It presents the highest quality professional and student productions in dance, theatre, and music.

The law school library is one of three on Suffolk's Boston campus.

Asia, Africa, and the Americas. Its programs encourage the sharing of ideas, the exchange of unique perspectives, and full participation in the international experience.

The Madrid Campus stands in a quiet residential section of the university quarter. As a complement to Suffolk's outstanding academic program in Madrid, students may take advantage of additional educational, social, and cultural opportunities through Suffolk Madrid's relationship with nearby Universidad San Pablo-CEU—one of Europe's most prestigious universities.

In Africa, Suffolk worked with the government of Senegal to establish a campus in its capital, Dakar, in 1999. This move opened the door to American-style higher education for the West African region. Each year about 100 degree-seeking students from 30 countries around Africa enroll in Suffolk-Dakar's business and liberal arts programs. Many of these students have gone on

to graduate school. In addition, about 500 students enroll yearly in the English-language study program at Suffolk Dakar.

The university has been a trailblazer in democratizing education in Africa. The Senegalese government sees Suffolk Dakar as a valuable asset in helping West Africans attain the education that is so important for the development and future of their continent.

Study abroad provides opportunities to learn about other cultures, and Suffolk has many global partnerships. Among them is the law school's relationship with the University of Lund in Sweden. The school's summer program provides U.S. law students with an opportunity to participate in comparative and international public and private law courses while living in a charming, medieval city. The close interaction of law students and law faculty from the University of Lund and other international law faculties distinguishes Suffolk's program from most other foreign summer law programs and offers students an excellent opportunity to learn about different legal cultures.

Gleason Archer was motivated to offer classes to working people through a commitment to public service, and his legacy lives on. The university serves the public good through education and services such as legal clinics and community outreach. It also cultivates an ethos of service in its students, staff, and faculty, both through example and encouragement. Many Suffolk University alumni have made careers in public service, and others have served the public good in the course of their careers and their private lives.

Suffolk's Organization for Uplifting Lives through Service (S.O.U.L.S.) is a major resource for service opportunities for members of the Suffolk University community. It offers opportunities for involvement in a range of activities, from mentoring at-risk preschool children or serving distressed communities through Alternative Spring Break, to efforts on behalf of the homeless. S.O.U.L.S. also works to encourage the development of curriculum-based service learning opportunities and to promote social change through service initiatives.

Through the law school's clinical programs, the university has made a long-standing commitment to serving diverse populations within the Boston area. Students admitted to these civil and criminal clinical programs represent clients under the direct supervision of experienced attorneys and law school faculty. Among the clinical programs are the Voluntary Defenders Program, the Battered Women's Advocacy Program, the Family Advocacy Clinic, the Housing and Consumer Advocacy Clinic, Evening Landlord-Tenant Clinic, and the Disability Advocacy Clinic.

Suffolk University fields teams in 12 varsity sports and competes in NCAA Division III.

Jaime Joseph and Shalini Sookar, interior design students from the New England School of Art & Design at Suffolk University, began to find success even before graduation when their work was featured on the weekly home makeover series Designer Finals *on HGTV, the Home and Garden Television channel.*

One alumnus who was the personification of the Suffolk University tradition of public service was the late Congressman John Joseph "Joe" Moakley of South Boston, who represented the Massachusetts Ninth Congressional District from 1973 until his death in 2001. He dedicated his career to making life better for untold numbers of people—not only his constituents, but also people across the state and around the world.

The John Joseph Moakley Archive and Institute at Suffolk University was established in 2001 upon Congressman Moakley's gift of his papers. It is dedicated to the preservation, study, interpretation, and celebration of Moakley's legacy, and its programs encourage service and public policy leadership.

A university exists in the context of the world around it, and Suffolk has collaborated with other institutions, the courts, government, and business to offer internships and other educational opportunities to its students. Creative partnerships with institutions here and abroad serve both to ease the entry into the university community and expand academic horizons. They also provide benefits to people and institutions far outside the sphere of the classroom, and new ideas and affiliations are being explored continuously.

One particularly fruitful partnership began in 1971 when Edward Clark, then a professor of English in the college, established the Collection of African American Literature. In teaching courses in African American literature, Clark had been forced to rely on mimeographed handouts because of the limited choice of writings in print. He knew there had to be a treasure trove of literature from more than three centuries of African American life in America, so he forged a union between Suffolk University and the nearby Museum of African American History to begin collecting the works of African American writers from the 18th century to the present.

That collection, which is housed in the Mildred F. Sawyer Library of Suffolk University, now has more than 5,200 volumes, including the works of some 1,200 African American authors. The holdings range from oral histories and personal essays to poetry, drama, and fiction. The National Park Service joined the collaborative effort in 1980. History Professor Robert A. Bellinger, the current director, has added media such as music, movement, and quilts to the collection.

Boston's historic Beacon Hill neighborhood offers students easy access to cultural resources such as the Museum of African American History, as well as to the centers of business, government, law, finance, and commerce. While the setting is decidedly urban, one of the university's residence halls overlooks the Boston Common that anchors Boston's "Emerald Necklace," and students are only steps away from the Boston Public Garden, the Charles River, Faneuil Hall, and the Freedom Trail.

Its location and culture have led to Suffolk's being called "the school with a heart in the heart of the city." The university's munificent reputation

These Suffolk Law School alumni were sworn before the Bar of the U. S. Supreme Court in May 2004, sponsored by Dean Robert Smith.

stems from the many people who have devoted their careers to the school and its students. Former Bursar Dorothy McNamara—known to generations of students as Dotty Mac—was one such person. When confronted with a student who couldn't afford tuition, Dotty Mac would say, "Don't worry hon; pay when you can."

The Dotty Mac approach may not be considered sound fiscal policy, but it built tremendous loyalty among students and alumni—and the vast majority did eventually pay. As part of its mission of opportunity and access, the university continues to do all it can to support each student's quest for learning.

Part of that effort entails making classes accessible to both full-time students and those who are pursuing careers. Part-time and evening programs are available, and the business school offers an online MBA program and other flexible programming that allows students to continue their careers while honing their skills. The university also offers programs at three satellite locations in Massachusetts.

The culture of caring at Suffolk also extends to its 53,000 active alumni, who are part of a worldwide university community. They support the school

and its students in many ways, serving as mentors, offering internships, and providing networking opportunities.

The handful of students who gathered in Gleason Archer's living room in 1906 changed their own destinies, but they, and thousands of Suffolk University graduates since then, also have made great contributions to society. Through professional accomplishment, community involvement, and family responsibility, Suffolk University alumni make the world a better place every day.

As it continues into its second century, the university remains grounded in its mission of access and opportunity for all deserving students, regardless of race, religion, ethnicity, gender, or sexual orientation. Gleason Archer believed in what he called "the gospel of self-help and hard work," and generations of students have shown that those who have the desire to learn and the ambition to use their education will succeed at Suffolk and beyond.

TELEPHONE WORKERS' CREDIT UNION

The founding of Telephone Workers' Credit Union dates back to the early 1900s. What began as a modest institution with 2 employees, 147 members, and total assets of $941.31 in 1917, today boasts nearly 30,000 members and is one of the oldest and most established credit unions in New England.

When the credit union originally opened its doors on Milk Street in downtown Boston, Charles F. Donahoe, the institution's first manager, set the tone for the future. Tasked with bringing a greater measure of security to all telephone workers (in those days they were all employees of New England Telephone), the credit union's goal was to promote thrift and financial assistance to its members. Donahoe's leadership in those early years, first as manager, then director, and finally president, served as a solid foundation for today's institution.

In order to better serve its existing members and support the credit union movement of cooperative, not-for-profit financial institutions, TWCU distributed approximately 25 percent of its assets in 1922 to initiate additional

TWCU's board of directors, circa 1967.

telephone credit unions throughout the state. In August of that year, TWCU transferred more than $30,000 of its money to the Western Mass Telephone Workers Credit Union so it could begin to serve members in that part of the state. Later, in November, $25,897, $21,916, and $32,025 were

transferred to Northern, Central, and Southern Mass credit unions, respectively, so they could begin their operations. Today, all four of those credit unions continue to serve members in their communities.

The Telephone Workers' Credit Union has served its members and communities-at-large in good times and bad. A prime example of this would be October 29, 1929, otherwise known as "Black Tuesday," the day when share prices on the New York Stock Exchange collapsed. From October 1 of that year until November 30, the credit union experienced loan growth of nearly 10 percent and asset growth of more than 7 percent. The stock market and the economy recovered by early the next year, only to crash again in late 1930.

During the Great Depression, the credit union continued to service its clientele. Throughout 1934 its assets grew by more than 43 percent and the institution continued to provide a safe

TWCU's current board of directors.

financial environment for its members' savings. TWCU continues to strive for that same level of performance and, today, has incorporated that commitment into its mission statement.

In 1993 TWCU moved its main branch to 100 High Street in Boston, where it remains today. In the summer of 1994 the credit union expanded into the South Shore and opened its Braintree branch on Granite Street. Several years later, in early 1999, TWCU expanded into the North Shore and opened its Stoneham branch on Main Street.

There have been numerous changes in the financial services industry over the years; however Telephone Workers' Credit Union's dedication and commitment to its members remains its top priority. When the institution opened in 1917, TWCU was just one of a handful of credit unions that had been chartered in the U.S. With a philosophy of maintaining a member-owned and controlled financial service cooperative, TWCU has delivered quality services at fair prices for nearly a century.

Thanks to TWCU, members have been able to purchase their first home, first car, and been able to send their children to school. No matter what the need of a member's growing family, Telephone Workers' Credit Union has offered countless personal loans and services to help enhance the lives and lessen the burdens of its membership.

Through its unique credit union model, members' savings provide the funds for loans that other members need. "We're proud of the decades of tradition, dedication, and hard work that have made Telephone Workers' Credit Union what it is today," says Kenneth Dyer, TWCU's current president. "We appreciate the loyalty and support of our members—past, present, and future."

The recent consolidation of several financial services companies in New England has made it possible for

Miriam Hines has been an employee of Telephone Workers' Credit Union for more than half a century.

TWCU to offer its services to an even larger group of members. On December 1, 2005 its membership voted to expand its field of membership to allow all those that live, work, or attend school in the greater Boston area to join the Telephone Workers' Credit Union. This charter change has allowed TWCU to directly serve its surrounding communities and remain a member owned, Boston-based, financial institution.

Dyer attributes the institution's success to its members and volunteer board of directors, which oversees the development of new products and

services. "It's the members, who start with a savings account and continue to use our loan and investment products throughout their lives as they work toward and into retirement, that make us successful. The credit union would not have grown into one of the largest credit unions in Massachusetts without them" he says.

However, it's also the contributions of the employees that have made the credit union what it is today. Many staff members have been with TWCU for more than 25 years, and most have served the agency for over a decade. However, none come close to Miriam Hines who recently celebrated her 53-year anniversary as a TWCU employee.

"Our philosophy is still old New England," says Dyer. "Provide value, treat people with respect, and remain worthy of the trust they have placed in you." Indeed, TWCU's investment in customer service, technology, and the communities in which they serve has been a winning combination. "It's our mission, it's our responsibility, and it's our passion," says Dyer.

TWCU staff pose for a photo while volunteering at a local soup kitchen in 1993.

THOM CHILD & FAMILY SERVICES

Founded in 1921 by Dr. Douglas Thom (1887–1951), the Habit Clinic (Thom Child & Family Services) was located in the South End of Boston, where it operated for the next 30 years. Dr. Thom established the "Habit Clinic" based on the Baby Hygiene Movement of the early 20th century. The goal of the clinic was to help parents cope with the behavioral and developmental difficulties which some children coming to the "new world" faced, including sleeping issues and eating irritability. Dr. Thom believed that preventing infant mortality and morbidity was primary, but that there was also a key psychological component to the development of a healthy and whole child that needed to be addressed.

Having acquired a wealth of knowledge on the latest theories of human personality development, and the crucial role that development played in early childhood, Dr. Thom was enlisted as a consultant by the Boston Baby Hygiene Association in 1921. He

Dr. Douglas A. Thom.

authored a series of federally supported publications on child rearing practices and children's social and emotional development (preceding Spock and Brazelton), which quickly brought him national recognition as an expert in the field.

In 1949 the Habit Clinic was renamed in honor of its founder, The Douglas A. Thom Clinic, Inc. Its focus changed from a child guidance clinic serving inner city families to an outpatient children's mental health facility. The clinic also served as an important training ground for future mental health professionals in the areas of psychology, psychiatry, and social work well through the 1970s.

In the 1980s the clinic became Thom Child & Family Services when its focus changed once again as it began work in the Early Intervention (EI) area, dealing with children from birth to three years old. The clinic maintained its mental health facility until 1993, when it was forced to close due to lack of stable funding. Thom Child did undergo a period of expansion as the Massachusetts Early Intervention system matured. Where other EI programs and facilities faltered due to financial pressure and other challenges, Thom Child specialized in taking on "work-out" situations. This would become an area where Thom Child would realize tremendous growth in the future.

According to executive director Peter Woodbury, in the 21st century Thom Child has gone through a full cycle, where today's services are much more like those offered when the center first was established by Dr. Thom. Part of that "full cycle" that Woodbury speaks of is evident in the areas that Thom Child focuses on with children. Today's children deal with many of the same problems that children were dealing with in 1921, including vision or hearing problems, coordination and motor skills, speech development, or behavioral or attention deficit issues.

Thom Headquarters at 315 Dartmouth Street, 1951–1993.

Massachusetts' Early Intervention system is one of the most successful public/private ventures in the country. EI is in part the result of and partially funded by IDEA, Individuals with Disability Education Act, a federal law enacted in 1975 and amended again in 1997. Private health insurance, Medicaid and the Massachusetts Department of Public Health also provide funding for EI. EI in Massachusetts is a statewide, family-centered, developmental service. Thom Child & Family Services programs offer the earliest possible intervention and support for children from birth to three years old with developmental difficulties. Currently, Thom's staff of allied health professionals (physical, occupational and speech therapists, nurses, developmental educators, mental health professionals and others) work with families of children for whom there are developmental concerns due to identified disabilities, or whose typical development is at-risk due to certain birth or environmental circumstances. EI provides comprehensive, integrated services, utilizing a family-centered

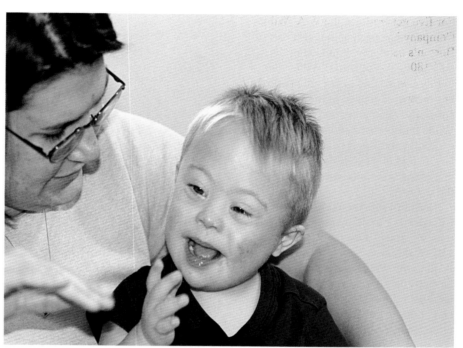

Thom's Work with At-Risk Children.

Thom's Work with at-risk children.

approach to facilitate the developmental progress of each child.

Thanks to the efforts of agencies like Thom Child & Family Services, Massachusetts has one of the strongest and most advanced EI systems in the United States. Thom Child currently has sites in nine areas of the state, from Boston to the western communities of Massachusetts. One of the successful aspects of the program is teaching parents and children how to overcome disability challenges that in the past would have sent these children to hospitals or rehabilitation facilities for care. The staff works in partnership with those individuals in the child's natural environment, which may include settings other than the child's home. The success of this program has saved millions of dollars in rehabilitative care and special education services over the years.

Thom Child has also developed a specialized medical billing service. Its practice management system, Thom Biller, is a comprehensive billing and accounts receivable software program for agencies that provide human services. Thom Biller has a proven track record of meeting nonprofit billing requirements in Massachusetts. This state-of-the–art software is designed to maximize collections while providing comprehensive accounting reports for a wide range of Early Intervention, mental health, and other human services.

Peter Woodbury envisions continued growth for Thom Child & Family Services and attributes this to what he calls an "economy of scale." Through their understanding of how to get federal and state agencies, health insurers, parents, and EI providers to work in tandem, Thom Child & Family Services has created a public/private venture that is a winning exercise for all involved, most importantly the at-risk children it is meant to serve.

THE W.A. WILDE COMPANY

For five generations, the W.A. Wilde Company has been an integral part of Boston's economy. Founded in the mid-1800s by William A. Wilde, this family owned and operated business has prospered—even in the face of adversity. The pioneering spirit of the Wilde family inspired an ongoing evolution and has produced one of the largest and most well-respected direct marketing solutions companies in the country.

Back in 1868, the W.A. Wilde Company's mission was much different than it is today. Originally located at 117 Washington Street in Boston, William A. Wilde opened a publishing business that specialized in non-denominational religious books, biographies, and children's literature. An experienced book agent and energetic entrepreneur, William catered to the country's insatiable appetite for knowledge in a post Civil War climate.

From its founding to the present day, Wilde has relocated many times to accommodate its growth and business development needs. This photo shows the company offices at 120 Boylston Street in Boston at the turn of the 19th century.

Company founder William A. Wilde served as president from 1868–1904 and became a noted public benefactor when he constructed and donated the Acton Memorial Library to the town of Acton in 1890.

He established a network of wholesalers and retail bookstore outlets to sell his publications throughout the country. Wilde became most widely-known for *Peloubet's Select Notes*, a weekly commentary on the International Sunday School Lessons that would be published by W. A. Wilde Company for over a century.

Over the next few decades, and into the 20th century, business grew and William moved the operation to several larger facilities. With success came responsibility and, as a community-minded entrepreneur, he constructed a library in his hometown of Acton, Massachusetts and donated it to the town in memory of the Acton citizens who fought in the Civil War. Shortly afterwards, William's sons William Eugene and Allan joined the business. Together, the brothers worked side-by-side with their father until William Sr. passed away in 1902.

In 1904 William Eugene took over the prosperous business. However, it wasn't long before the W.A. Wilde Company was faced with increased competition and steadily rising printing and paper costs. In 1919 an announcement was mailed to all of its customers indicating that the price of Wilde's Bible Pictures would rise to one and a half cents each. Due to a price increase of nearly 100 percent for its printing and paper costs, Eugene had no choice but to raise his retail prices.

With advances in the printing process and more readers hungry for new titles, Allan Wilde took over the business from his brother in 1928. Over the years, the W. A. Wilde Company had collected more than 200,000 names, recorded and stored on 3 x 5 index cards. Distribution of books and prints became easier and more economical as this early mailing list was used to mail publications catalogs directly to established customers. Allan's 1935 mail order catalog listed 164 major titles. The 320-page *Piloting the U.S. Air Mail* by

Lewis E. Theiss retailed at a cost of $1.75.

By 1937 Allan's son took over the reins at the W.A. Wilde Company. Alfred's tenure at the company coincided with major changes in the publishing industry. He started to sell books directly to public libraries and also began to market titles for other major publishers like Random House, Harper Brothers, and Grosset & Dunlap. However, the war, combined with severe paper shortages, created a tight market. Major New York publishers were the only ones able to compete, and smaller independent publishers were forced to find new paths to profitability.

By the late 1950s, the U.S. postal system was proving to be a viable, economical means of marketing titles directly to consumers, and direct mail was an emerging industry. Alfred's son Thomas had recently graduated with honors from Babson College, an internationally-renowned business school in Wellesley known for its emphasis on entrepreneurial leadership. Although he had thoughts early on of becoming a farmer, Thomas was eager to preserve his family's heritage by joining the business.

In addition to his primary responsibilities, Thomas started marketing services that helped secure subscribers for financial newsletters. He even produced his own weekly newsletter, Pulpit Workshop, designed to help Protestant ministers develop their sermons. All the while, Thomas was honing his skills and finding new ways to market services and find customers. This expanding focus required additional production space, and the company relocated to Natick in 1959.

Throughout the 1960s, Alfred and Thomas resolutely explored new avenues for growing the family business in an increasingly competitive industry. With Alfred's encouragement and support, Thomas embraced the possibilities offered by new technol-

Thomas A. Wilde is the sixth Wilde family president to accept the challenge of leading a company whose evolution keeps pace with advances in technology.

Thomas H. Wilde has devoted over 50 years to keeping Wilde on the cutting edge of technology and is an industry-recognized leader in direct marketing.

ogy. They purchased a Pitney Bowes mailing machine to collate materials to be inserted into envelopes, and gradually the company began to change direction as the publishing backbone gave way to automated mailing services and hand assembly for the book binding and game manufacturing industries.

When Thomas took over the company in 1971, the W.A. Wilde Company was still negotiating between its traditional publishing past while striving to establish itself as a direct mail presence. With more and more advertisers seeking to reach more and more consumers, Thomas made it his mission to keep on the forefront of technology. In 1973 the company purchased its very first computer, many years before most people had ever even seen one. Each year, Thomas added more advanced services to help companies reach consumers in a more sophisticated way.

It wasn't long before Thomas' son, Tom A. Wilde, was brought into the fold. While in high school, "Tom Jr." joined the W.A. Wilde staff. He delivered mail, answered phones, mowed the lawn, and maintained the grounds. After he graduated in 1984 from Babson College, his father's alma mater, with a degree in business administration, Tom took a full-time position at the W.A. Wilde Company as a customer service representative. He then moved up to client service director, then vice president of sales and marketing, and finally vice president and general manager of the company's database and response fulfillment services division.

For the next 14 years, the father-son team worked side-by-side to keep the company on the cutting edge. In the early 1980s they perfected their ability to offer match mail packages, which allowed clients to place each customer's name and address on the envelope in addition to the supplemental materials inside the package. They were also the first company in New England to offer polybagging services, which placed each client's mailing materials into clear plastic envelopes. "This was an important step in direct mail because instead of hiding the client's materials in a standard, paper envelope, you could show off the design elements or the enclosed materials in a see-through plastic cover," Thomas Sr. says. Business was good and in 1983 the Wilde family designed and constructed new offices in Holliston, where they remain today.

In 1986 the company acquired Great Northern Envelope so they could offer additional printing services. And, in 1991 they introduced advanced barcode technology to their clients. "Essentially, the new barcode advancement allowed us to sort mailing materials in a different way," says Thomas Sr. "This created less work for the post office and passed a savings onto our clients."

In 1996, to accommodate the growth the company was experiencing in its database and fulfillment services, the Wildes built a new 91,000-square-foot facility. Three years later, they acquired L.W. Robbins Associates, a full service direct marketing agency specializing exclusively in nonprofit agencies. Through this new subsidiary, the company was able to utilize a variety of direct response fundraising strategies and technologies that allowed clients to maximize the value of their donor outreach efforts.

By the time 1998 came around, Thomas Sr. transferred the presidential reins to his son, while retaining the title and role of chairman of the board. Eager to continue the upward momentum, father and son joined forces to find new ways to expand services and increase production. In 2002, in yet another effort to increase the company's capacity, a second production house was purchased. This enabled the business to boost its output, ultimately creating 600 million pieces of direct mail

In the late 19th and early 20th century, Wilde published Bible Pictures "for use in the church, school, and home." Over 800 religious subjects were available, priced at two cents each.

a year. In another successful business move, the company launched a new division. Wilde Direct was created to offer clients a new level of marketing and creative services. In addition to traditional direct mail programs, Wilde Direct put clients on the forefront of technology with a variety of programs that embraced the information age. From websites to wireless devices, clients could tailor their marketing efforts to meet the needs of today's changing marketplace.

Although as a child, Tom's career goal was to play Major League Baseball or to attend clown college (he had already learned to ride a unicycle and juggle), he had never anticipated

joining the family business. "I know there are probably people who would look at me now and think it was a foregone conclusion that I would succeed my father in leading the company, but it wasn't that way at all," Tom says. "I was never groomed to be the heir apparent when I was growing up. I have to give my father a lot of credit for never forcing the business on me. He let me find my own way there."

Under Tom's guidance, the W.A. Wilde Company continues to be a leader in its field. Over the last several years, the business has earned countless awards from the New England Direct Marketing Association (NEDMA), the Mailing & Fulfillment Services Association (MFSA), and the National Postal Forum. As the person primarily responsible for the business' successful transition into direct mail and as a well-respected and nationally-recognized leader within the industry, Thomas Sr. remains actively involved with the company.

Thanks to the family's pioneering spirit, the W.A. Wilde Company has succeeded where many businesses have failed. Now a fifth-generation, family-owned enterprise, Tom and his father are always one step ahead of the game. "To be truly competitive, a good company has to evolve over time to continue to meet the needs of its clients," Tom says. "We were able to thrive in those early days because we were innovative and we weren't afraid to change focus," adds Thomas. "We've always prided ourselves on thinking outside of the box." With that can-do attitude and nearly a century-and-a-half of success under its belt, the W.A. Wilde Company plans to continue its multigenerational legacy as a vital part of Boston's economy.

WHEELOCK COLLEGE

Founded in 1888, Wheelock College is a four-year, coeducational, private college with a public mission—to improve the lives of children, families, and society in general. The college accomplishes this through educating students with a passion to change the world. The school's programs in the arts and sciences and the professional areas of child life, education, juvenile justice and youth advocacy, and social work are known nationally and internationally.

The college is named for founder Lucy Wheelock. She was convinced that early childhood education was the solution to many of society's problems, and educated her students about the lives of poor immigrant families in Boston's Portuguese, Filipino, and Italian neighborhoods. This philosophy became part of the early foundation of the school and represented Wheelock's continuing involvement with multicultural education and neighboring communities. That philosophy is reflected in today's Wheelock College as a place for students to share a passion for improving society, understanding the importance of a balanced education,

Wheelock is located along the Riverway in Boston, across from Longwood Park.

Purchased in 1999 and completely renovated, the Brookline campus opened in 2003.

and in building a meaningful personal and professional life.

The academic experience at Wheelock integrates rigorous study, a diverse co-curricular life, and meaningful field experience where students learn to turn their passion into rewarding professional careers. Wheelock students are encouraged to combine arts and sciences coursework, majors,

and professional concentrations to create a program of study that interests, challenges, and prepares them for success in their chosen careers.

Every undergraduate at Wheelock takes a required full-year course called human growth and development (HGD). In this class, students work individually and collaboratively to understand the essentials of psychology and sociology and how these subjects support their understanding of children, families, and cultures across the life cycle.

Field experiences are a staple of the education at Wheelock. Students are immersed in professional environments, gaining hands-on experiences in different settings. They are encouraged to engage in field experiences beginning with their first semester on campus. Working in diverse, urban, multilingual communities helps Wheelock students to grow personally. They are able to build on their professional capacity to work with children and families across socioeconomic, racial, ethnic, and religious backgrounds.

Throughout Wheelock's long history, the school has built productive relationships with many Greater Boston schools and community organizations at which students are placed for their field experiences. Settings vary from after-school programs to adolescent services, Head Start programs, hospitals, healthcare centers, museums, public schools, social service agencies, and childcare programs. Numerous Boston public schools and renowned medical facilities in the Longwood Medical Area work with Wheelock alumni and faculty to provide opportunities for students to experiment with different techniques, ideas, and environments. Many Wheelock graduates enter the working world with four, five, or six professional experiences on their resumés and graduates are highly sought-after in the professional world.

The Wheelock faculty includes renowned scholars, leaders, and advocates—nearly 90 percent of whom hold the most advanced degrees offered in their fields of expertise. They are distinguished authors, engaging speakers, and leaders in their industries. Many Wheelock faculty members are held in the highest regard for their seminal work in education, child life, social work, and most every profession that seeks to improve the lives of children and families.

In addition, other faculty members are outstanding scientists and mathematicians, artists and musicians,

Students work individually and collaboratively to understand children, families, and cultures across the life cycle.

human development specialists, and published scholars in English, political science, history, and other important subjects in the arts and sciences. One of the most respected values of the school's faculty is their ability to integrate classroom theory and scholarship with research and real world practice. Outside the classroom, faculty members serve as academic advisers, fieldwork supervisors, and, often, as advisers for student organizations.

Wheelock's student-to-faculty ratio of 10:1 is low, by design. Small classes mean that students enjoy thought-provoking dialogue with distinguished scholars and practitioners. It also allows the benefit of a close relationship between students and faculty who get to know each other as individuals. Because of this low student-to-faculty ratio, Wheelock faculty knows their students' names, abilities, and goals.

The school's undergraduate curriculum integrates the liberal arts with several professional disciplines. Students can choose to major in one of their arts and sciences disciplines or social work. They then have the option

The library offers comfortable spaces for individual study and group work.

of adding a concentration to their major —similar to a double major.

Outside of the classroom, Wheelock students enjoy a variety of campus activities. They are active in more than 20 student clubs and organizations and have a strong connection to the surrounding community through service projects and involvement in outreach programs. Wheelock also competes in NCAA Division III athletics, including five sports for women: basketball, field hockey, soccer, softball, and swimming and diving. Varsity men's sports in tennis and baseball will begin competition in the fall of 2007.

The Wheelock community has access to the William J. Holmes Sports and Fitness Center at Simmons College, a 60,000-square-foot facility located just steps from the campus. The facility houses state-of-the-art cardiovascular and weight training equipment, basketball, racquetball and squash courts, an indoor track, swimming pool, and dance studio.

Wheelock is also part of The Colleges of the Fenway consortium, a collaboration between Emmanuel College, Massachusetts College of Art, Massachusetts College of Pharmacy and Health Sciences, Simmons College, Wentworth Institute of Technology, and Wheelock College. The consortium allows Wheelock students to be an integral part of a small college community, while having the advantage of a virtual university that boasts over 9,800 full-time undergraduate students and 3,100 different courses.

Wheelock students can take advantage of the courses, services, and social activities found at all these schools. Students can also participate in social activities such as the Colleges of the Fenway Chorus and Orchestra and intramural sports.

In 1999 Wheelock College received a donation from an anonymous donor that allowed the school to address its longtime lack of space through the purchase of the land and buildings at 43 Hawes Street in Brookline. The renovation, which was unveiled in 2003, resulted in a single, accessible, unified structure that retained the splendor of the original building.

Since 2004 the leadership of Jackie Jenkins-Scott, the 13th president of the college and one of a handful of female African Americans presidents, has guided Wheelock College. Jenkins-Scott received a bachelor's degree from

Many classes involve small group discussions between students and professors.

Wheelock offers state-of-the-art technology in computer labs and wireless internet connections across campus.

Eastern Michigan University, a master's in social work from Boston University's School of Social Work, and completed a post graduate research fellowship at Radcliffe College. She was awarded an honorary doctorate degree in education from Wheelock College in 2003, when she served as the commencement speaker. She also holds honorary doctorate degrees from Northeastern University, Bentley College, and Mount Ida College.

Jenkins-Scott currently serves as a board member of the Kennedy Library Foundation and Museum, the Beth Israel Deaconess Medical Center, and the Tufts Health Plan. She has received numerous awards and citations including the 2004 Pinnacle Lifetime Achievement Award from the Greater Boston Chamber of Commerce and the 2004 alumni award from Boston University. President Jenkins-Scott also serves as co-chair on Governor Patrick's Higher Education Working Group.

With its Boston location, Wheelock students have unlimited opportunities to enjoy time outside of the classroom. The campus is just a short walk

from a number of highly regarded museums, such as the Museum of Fine Arts, and Fenway Park, home of the Boston Red Sox, is nearby. Students also spend their time volunteering in homeless shelters, cleaning parks around campus, fundraising, and working with different non-profit organizations.

Currently, Wheelock educates 700 undergraduate students, 70 percent of whom live on campus. Nearly 20 percent of Wheelock students are African American, Latino, Asian, Native American, or have a multiracial background. Students attend Wheelock from all six New England states, New York, New Jersey, Pennsylvania, and beyond. Some 85 percent of students receive financial aid in the form of merit scholarships, grants, work-study, and/or loans.

Wheelock prides itself on providing a place for students who want to become leaders, advocates, and professionals whose work improves the lives of children and families. Its admission policy is based on the whole person, not just the student's scores submitted with the application. The school seeks interesting people from diverse backgrounds who see themselves as agents of change. Wheelock also looks at the scholastic achievements, strong academic evaluations, and dedicated involvement in co-curricular and community activities of each of its student applicants.

"The life and prosperity of a community is generally dictated by the degree of education it obtains," says President Jenkins-Scott. "While we continue providing our students with invaluable educational experiences in the classroom and in practicum placements, we encourage them to live the words of our founder: 'not only to know, but to do, and to feel the joy of service to humanity.'"

A TIMELINE OF BOSTON HISTORY

1630 English Puritans, with John Winthrop as their governor, sailed in April from Southampton, England and chose the Shawmut Peninsula for their settlement because it had good spring water. They named it Boston.
1636 Anne Hutchinson was tried for heresy and banned from the colony, then excommunicated from the Boston church.
1636 Harvard College founded.
1675 Three Wampanoag Indians were found guilty of the murder of John Sassamon, who had warned of an attack on the Boston settlement, igniting "King Philip's War."
1676 Metacomet, the Wampanoag leader whom the Puritans called "King Philip," was killed in a surprise attack and his head was displayed in Boston. His death spelled the end for the war, in which several thousand Native Americans and Englishmen were killed
1692 Twenty men and women were put to death as witches in Salem.

In 1770 Paul Revere purchased this house, now Boston's oldest, at 19 North Square and lived there with his large family. In 1908 the home became one of the first historic house museums in the country and is run by the Paul Revere Memorial Association. Courtesy, Lisa Rogers

In 1742 Peter Faneuil, a wealthy merchant, gave Boston "a large brick building...for the use of a market." Courtesy, Nora Rogers

1740 English preacher George Whitefield embarked on an evangelical tour of the colonies, and preached to a crowd of 30,000 on Boston Common.
1742 Peter Faneuil, a wealthy merchant, gave Boston "a large brick building...for the use of a market."
1747 Four British naval officers are taken hostage and held in the Old State House as public outcry builds against forced impressments of colonists into the navy.
1760 Governor Francis Bernard named Thomas Hutchinson to the Superior Court.
1765 Samuel Adams, son of a Boston brewer and educated at Harvard, was elected to the Massachusetts assembly. Enraged Bostonians rebelled against the Stamp Act, which taxed newspapers, attorney's licenses, and land deeds to help underwrite the expenses of the British empire.
1766 The British Parliament repealed the Stamp Act.
1767 Phillis Wheatley, a young Boston slave, published her first poem.
1768 John Adams opened a law office in Boston.
  Bostonians resisted the new Townshend taxes on such goods as paper, glass and tea, organizing an embargo on English imports.
1769 To restore order, two regiments of British regulars were quartered in Boston. Guards stopped everyone going to and from the town and a show of might was evident.
1770 Taunted by a crowd, sentries outside the Boston customhouse fired on the group, killing five in the "Boston Massacre." Crispus Attucks, a black man, was among the dead.
1772 Samuel Adams was chosen to lead a committee charged with recording and publicizing infringements by the Crown on the rights of the colonists.
1773 Parliament gave the East India Company the exclusive rights to sell tea in the American colonies. Three ships arrived laden with tea and Thomas Hutchinson, now lieutenant

governor, refused Adams' entreaties to send them back. Disguised as Indians, 60 men dumped 342 chests of tea into Boston Harbor. In response, Parliament forced the closure of the harbor until the tea was paid for. General Thomas Gage, commander of the British army in America, was made governor of Massachusetts.

1774 John Adams, John Hancock, and Samuel Adams were chosen as delegates to the Continental Congress.

1775 In "The Shot Heard Round the World," Gen. Gage's troops, sent from Boston, met at Concord's Old North Bridge militiamen who were warned by Paul Revere and William Dawes. Ninety-three Americans and 272 Redcoats were killed; the militiamen trapped the British army inside Boston. The Battle of Bunker Hill, actually fought on Breed's Hill in Charlestown, resulted in enormous losses for the British. British continued to occupy the town, creating food shortages for Bostonians.

1776 Gen. George Washington liberated Boston from the British occupation on March 17, known as Evacuation Day.

On July 18, the Declaration of Independence was read from the balcony of the Old State House.

1781 Elizabeth Freeman was the first African slave emancipated after the passage of the Massachusetts Bill of Rights.

1783 The Massachusetts courts declared slavery unconstitutional.

1786 The Charles River Bridge, connecting Boston and Cambridge, was opened on the 11th anniversary of the Battle of Bunker Hill.

1787 Charles Bulfinch submitted plans for a new State House, to be built on Beacon Hill.

1788 Paul Revere, patriot and silversmith, built his own foundry for casting stoves and anvils.

1789 Thousands of Bostonians cheered President George Washington as he paraded through Boston.

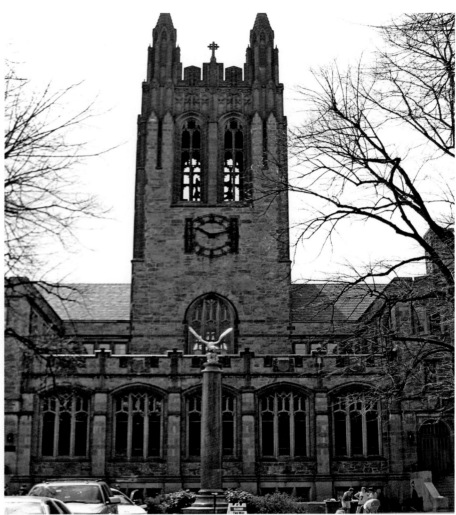

In 1863 Boston College was incorporated when the Massachusetts legislature approved its charter. Courtesy, Nora Rogers

1792 Paul Revere cast his first bell, for the Second Church of Boston.

1800 Revere built a mill for rolling copper into sheets, producing material to sheath the new State House dome on Beacon Hill and to copper-bottom the *U.S.S. Constitution.*

1806 The African Meeting House, formally known as the First African Baptist Church, was built on Beacon Hill. William Lloyd Garrison's New England Anti-Slavery Society held its first meeting there. African native Cato Gardner raised more than $1,500 of the $7,700 building cost.

1822 Governor John Brooks approved the incorporation of the City of Boston after a Federalist-led campaign to change the government from a town to a city, to be governed by a mayor and an elected council. The new city's motto, placed on its seal, was *"Sit Deus nobiscus sicut fuit cum patribus nostris"* ("May God be with us as he was with our fathers").

1825 Boston's second mayor, Josiah Quincy, led an effort to build a new market complex near Fanueil Hall. The centerpiece of the project completed in 1826, was a 500-foot long, domed classical building called "Quincy Market."

1834 Bronson Alcott, educator and Transcendentalist, opens with Elizabeth Peabody the experimental Temple School for boys and girls.

1837 Horace Mann became the first secretary to the Massachusetts Board of Education.

1838 The temperance movement was successful in outlawing the sale of distilled spirits in Massachusetts.

1841 The Transcendentalist community Brook Farm was established in West Roxbury.

1847 Fleeing famine in Ireland, 35,000 Irish immigrants settled in Boston, crowding into already overpopulated sections of the city.

1862 Architect Gridley Bryant was selected to design Boston's new city hall. Built of granite and topped with a dome, statues of Benjamin Franklin and Josiah Quincy graced the building's plaza.

1863 Boston College was incorporated when the Massachusetts legislature approved its charter.

1869 Boston University received its charter.

1872 Boston's warehouse district in the oldest part of the city was destroyed by a devastating two-day fire.

Massachusetts Institute of Technology was established.

1876 The first permanent home of the Museum of Fine Arts, designed by Sturgis and Brigham, was built in Copley Square.

1877 Trinity Church, designed by H.H. Richardson and the centerpiece of Copley Square, was consecrated. Frederick Law Olmsted's grand plan of a green belt of parks around the city, the Emerald Necklace, was accepted.

1881 The Boston Symphony Orchestra was founded by Colonel Henry Lee Higginson. The orchestra gave its first concert under the direction of Georg Henschel.

1893 Boston's subway, the nation's first, opened.

1895 The Boston Public Library opened in Copley Square across from Trinity Church.

1900 Through filling in bogs and

In 1847, fleeing famine in Ireland, 35,000 Irish immigrants settled in Boston, crowding into already overpopulated sections of the city.

marshes and annexing nearby towns, Boston had grown to 24,000 acres from its pre-Civil War size of 780 acres.

1903 On New Year's Eve, Isabella Stewart Gardner opened her stunning, art-filled Italian palace on the Fenway to society, with a concert by the Boston Symphony Orchestra.

1910 The Boston census counted 30,000 Italians living in the North End and 40,000 Jews residing in the West End as Boston's foreign-born population skyrocketed to more than three-quarters of its residents.

1914 James Michael Curley won the

Boston mayoral election. The brash former Congressman was loved for using his power to help the poor but reviled for his spending.

1915 Black activist William Monroe Trotter led 2,000 black Bostonians to the State House to protest the showing of the film *Birth of a Nation.*

Women's activist Maud Wood Park of the Massachusetts Women Suffrage

Association led an effort to pass a referendum favoring voting by women.

1918 With Babe Ruth on their team, the Boston Red Sox won the World Series.

1919 An epidemic of influenza swept the city, killing 6,000 people and infecting more than 85,000.

Boston police overwhelmingly voted to strike; two-thirds of them lost their jobs.

1920 Babe Ruth was sold to the New York Yankees.

1921 Nicolo Sacco and Bartolomeo Vanzetti were found guilty of armed robbery and murder.

1929 James Michael Curley was elected to a third term as Boston's mayor.

1940 The Hatch Memorial Shell, an outdoor concert stage, was constructed on the east bank of the Charles River and became the venue for the Boston Pops' July 4th concert.

1942 A fire at the Cocoanut Grove nightclub results in 492 deaths.

1946 Ted Williams' hitting led the Red Sox to the American League pennant.

1950 Construction of the Central Artery began along the city's waterfront.

1951 Superhighway Rte. 128 opened, forming a ring around Boston.

1969 Designed by Kallman, McKinnell and Knowles, Boston's modernistic city hall was officially occupied by Mayor Kevin White.

1974 Federal District Court Judge W. Arthur Garrity ordered the Boston School Department to end racial segregation by implementing a system-wide busing plan.

1984 Bernard Law was appointed Archbishop of Boston.

1986 The Red Sox won the American League pennant, but lost to the New York Mets in the World Series.

1987 Federal funding was approved for the nation's largest public works project, the Central Artery/Tunnel Project, known as the "Big Dig."

1990 The Isabella Stewart Gardner

Designed by Kallman, McKinnell and Knowles, Boston's modernistic City Hall was officially occupied by Mayor Kevin White in 1969. Courtesy, Nora Rogers

Museum was robbed of several masterpieces, including those by Johannes Vermeer and Rembrandt von Rijn.

1993 Thomas Menino was elected Boston's 47th mayor.

The *Boston Globe* was bought by the *New York Times*.

1997 Thomas Menino was reelected as mayor.

2001 Thomas Menino elected to a third term as Boston's mayor.

2002 The *Boston Globe* published articles exposing a history of sexual abuse of children by Boston priests.

2004 The Red Sox defeated the New York Yankees to win the American

League Championship and swept the St. Louis Cardinals to win the World Series for the first time in 86 years, breaking the legendary "Curse of the Bambino."

The "Big Dig" was completed.

2005 Thomas Menino was elected to a fourth term as Boston's mayor.

2006 The Institute for Contemporary Art opened on the waterfront.

BIBLIOGRAPHY

Ainley, Leslie G., *Boston Mahatma* (Boston: Bruce Humphries, 1949).

Amory, Cleveland, *The Proper Bostonians* (New York: Dutton, 1947).

Antin, Mary, *The Promised Land* (Boston: Houghton-Mifflin, 1912).

Bailyn, Bernard, *The New England Merchants in the Seventeenth Century* (Cambridge: Harvard University Press, 1955).

Banner, James, *To the Hartford Convention* (New York: Knopf, 1970).

Bartlett, Irving, *Wendell Philips: Brahmin Radical* (Boston: Beacon Press, 1961).

Beatty, Jack, Rascal King: *The Life and Times of James Michael Curley, 1874–1958* (Reading, Mass., 1992).

Blodgett, Geoffrey, *The Gentle Reformers: Massachusetts Democrats in the Cleveland Era* (Cambridge: Harvard University Press, 1966).

Brooks, Van Wyck, *The Flowering of New England* (New York: Dutton, 1936).

Brown, Richard D., *Revolutionary Politics in Massachusetts* (Cambridge: Harvard University Press, 1970).

Brown, Thomas N., *Irish-American Nationalism* (Philadelphia: Lippincott, 1966).

Commanger, Henry Steele, *Theodore Parker: Yankee Crusader* (Boston: Little, Brown, 1936).

Conroy, David W., *In Public Houses: Drink and the Revolution of Authority in Colonial Massachusetts* (Chapel Hill, N.C., 1995).

Curley, James Michael, *I'd Do It Again –A Record of All My Uproarious Years,* (Englewood Cliffs, New Jersey: Prentice-Hall, 1957).

Cutler, John Henry, *"Honey Fitz," Three Steps to the White House: The Life and Time of John F. "Honey Fitz" Fitzgerald* (New York: W. W. Norton, 1949).

De Marco, William, *Ethnics and Enclaves: Boston's Italian North End* (Ann Arbor: UMI Research Press, 1981).

Dever, Joseph, *Cushing of Boston: A Candid Biography* (Boston: Humphries, 1965).

Dinneen, Joseph F., *The Purple Shamrock: The Hon. James Michael Curley of Boston* (New York: W. W. Norton, 1949).

———, *Ward Eight* (New York: Harper & Brothers, 1936).

Firey, Walter, *Land Use in Central Boston* (Cambridge: Arno Press, 1947).

Fisher, David H., *Paul Revere's Ride* (New York, 1994).

Forbes, Esther, *Paul Revere and the World He Lived In* (Boston: Houghton Mifflin, 1943).

Formisano, Ronald P., *Boston Against Busing: Race, Class, Ethnicity in the 1960s and 1970s* (Chapel Hill, N.C., 1991).

Fowler, William *The Baron of Beacon Hill: A Biography of John Hancock* (Boston, 1980).

———, *Samuel Adams: Radical Puritan* (New York, 1997).

Fox, Stephen R., *The Guardian of Boston: William Monroe Trotter* (New York, Atheneum, 1950).

Gamm, Gerald H., *Urban Exodus: Why the Jews Left Boston and the Catholics Stayed* (Cambridge, Mass., 1999).

Gans, Herbert, *The Urban Villagers* (New York: Free Press, 1962).

Green, Martin, *The Problem of Boston: Some Readings in Cultural History* (New York: W. W. Norton, 1966).

Handlin, Oscar, *Boston's Immigrants* (Cambridge: Atheneum, 1941, 1968).

Horton, James O. and Lois E., *Black Bostonians: Family Life and Community Struggle in the Intebellum North* (New York: Holmes and Meier Publishers, Inc., 1979) .

King, Mel, *Autobiography* (Boston: South End Press, ?).

Kirker, Harold, *Bullfinch's Boston, 1787–1817* (New York: Oxford, 1964).

Knights, Peter, *The Plain People of Boston, 1830–1860* (New York: Oxford, 1971).

Kozol, Jonathan, *Death at an Early Age* (Boston: Houghton Mifflin, 1967).

Labaree, Benjamin, *The Boston Tea Party* (New York: Oxford, 1964).

Lane, Roger, *Policing the City: Boston 1822–1885* (Cambridge: Atheneum, 1967).

Lepore, Jill, *The Name of War: King Philip's War and the Origins of American Identity* (New York, 1998).

Lord, Robert H., et.al., *History of the Archdiocese of Boston,* 3 volumes (Boston: Pilot Publishing Co., 1945).

Lukas, Anthony J., *Common Ground* (New York, 1985).

Lupo, Alan, *Liberty's Chosen Home: The Politics of Violence in Boston* (Boston, 1988). (Boston: Little, Brown, 1975).

Mann, Arthur, *Yankee Reformers in the Urban Age* (Cambridge: University of Chicago Press, 1954).

McCaughey, Robert, *Josiah Quincy: The Last Federalist* (Cambridge: Harvard University Press, 1974).

Merwick, Donna, *Boston's Priests, 1848–1910: A Study of Intellectual and Social Change* (Cambridge: Harvard University Press, 1973).

Middlekauf, Robert, *The Mathers* (New York: Oxford, 1971).

Morgan, Edmund, *The Puritan Dilemma: The Story of John Winthrop* (Boston: Little, Brown, 1958).

Morison, Samuel Eliot, *Builders of the Bay Colony* (Boston: Houghton Mifflin, 1930) .

———, *Harrison Gray Otis: Urbane Federalist* (Boston: Houghton Mifflin, 1969).

———, *Maritime History of*

Massachusetts (Boston: Houghton Mifflin, 1921).

———,*The Maritime History of Massachusetts, 1783–1860* (Boston: Houghton Mifflin, 1961).

———, *One Boy's Boston, 1887–1901* (Boston: Houghton Mifflin, 1962).

O'Connor, Edwin, *The Last Hurrah* (Boston: Little, Brown, 1956).

O'Connor, Thomas, H., *Boston A to Z* (Cambridge, Mass., 2000).

———, *Bibles, Brahmins and Bosses* (Boston: Boston Public Library, 1976).

———, *The Boston Irish: A Political History* (Boston, 1995).

———, *Civil War Boston: Home Front and Battlefield* (Boston, 1997).

O'Toole, James M., *Militant and Triumphant: William Henry O'Connell and the Catholic Church in Boston, 1859–1944* (Notre Dame, 1992).

Pleck, Elizabeth Hafkin, *Hunting for a City: Black Migration and Poverty in Boston, 1865–1900* (New York: Academic Press, 1979).

———, *Black Migration and Poverty: Boston, 1865–1900* (New York, 1979).

Rogers, Alan, *The Boston Strangler,* (Beverly, Mass., 2006).

Russell, Francis, *A City in Terror: The 1919-The Boston Police Strike* (New York: Viking, 1975).

———, *Tragedy in Dedham: The Story of the Sacco-Vanzetti Case* (New York, 1971).

Ruttman, Darrett B., *Winthrop's Boston: Portrait of a Puritan Town* (Chapel Hill, North Carolina: University of North Carolina Press, 1965).

Schneider, Mark, R., *Boston Confronts Jim Crow, 1890–1920* (Boston, 1997).

Schragg, Peter, *Village School Downtown* (Boston: Beacon Press, 1967).

Shannon, William V., *The American Irish* (New York: Macmillan, 1966).

Solomon, Barbara Miller, *Ancestors and Immigrants: A Changing New England Tradition* (Cam-

bridge: McGraw-Hill, 1956).

Story, Ronald, *The Forging of an Aristocracy: Harvard and the Boston Upper Class, 1800–1870* (Middletown, Conn., 1980).

Tharp, Louise Hall, *Mrs. Jack: A Biography of Isabella Stewart Gardner* (Boston: Little, Brown, 1965).

Thernstrom, Stephen, *The Other Bostonians: Poverty and Progress in the American Metropolis, 1880–1970* (Cambridge: Harvard University Press, 1973).

Thomas, John L., *The Liberator: William Lloyd Garrison* (Boston: Little, Brown, 1963).

Trout, Charles H., *Boston, The Great Depression and the New Deal* (New York: Oxford University Press, 1977).

Von Frank, Albert J., *The Trials of Anthony Burns: Freedom and Slavery in Emerson's Boston* (Cambridge, Mass., 1998).

Warden, Gerald B., *Boston, 1689–1776* (Boston: Little, Brown, 1970).

Warner Jr., Sam Bass, *Streetcar Suburbs: The Process of Growth in Boston, 1870–1900* (Cambridge, Mass., 1962).

Wayman, Dorothy G., *Cardinal O'Connell of Boston* (New York: Farrar, Straus and Young, 1955).

Whitehill, Walter Muir, *Boston: A Topographical History* (Cambridge: Belknap Press, 1959, 1968).

———, *Boston in the Age of John F. Kennedy* (Norman, OK: University of Oklahoma Press, 1966).

Whyte, William Foot, *Street Corner Society: The Social Structure of an Italian Slum* (Chicago: University of Chicago Press, 1943).

Winship, Michael P., *The Times and Trials of Anne Hutchinson* (Lawrence, Kan., 2005).

Winsor, Justin, ed., *The Memorial History of Boston...,* 4 volumes (Boston: Ticknor and Co., 1880).

Woods, Robert A., *Americans In Process* (Boston: Arno Press, 1903).

———, *The City Wilderness, A Settlement House Study by Residents and Associates of the South End House* (Boston: Arno Press, 1898).

Woods, Robert A. and Kennedy, A. J., *The Zone of Emergence: Observations of Lower Middle and Upper Working Class Communities in Boston, 1905–1914,* preface by Sam Bass Warner, Jr. (Cambridge: MIT Press, 1962).

Zobel, Hiller, *The Boston Massacre* (New York: W. W. Norton, 1970).

This mural of nine notable Boston women, commissioned by Workingmen's Co-operative Bank, depicts: Anne Hutchinson, who challenged the Puritan power structure; Phillis Wheatley, poet; Sister Ann Alexis, founder of the Nazareth Home; Lucy Stone, suffragist; Mary Baker Eddy, founder of the Christian Science Church; Ellen Richards, first woman to graduate from MIT; Mary Morton Kehew, leader in the Women's Educational and Industrial Union; Anne Sullivan, Helen Keller's teacher; and Melnea Cass, NAACP president in the '60s. Courtesy, Workingmen's Co-operative Bank

INDEX

General Index

Italicized numbers indicate illustrations.